THE CRIMINAL JUSTICE SYSTEM
A Social-Psychological Analysis

A SERIES OF BOOKS IN PSYCHOLOGY

Editors: *Richard C. Atkinson*
Gardner Lindzey
Jonathan Freedman
Richard F. Thompson

THE CRIMINAL JUSTICE SYSTEM
A Social-Psychological Analysis

EDITED BY

Vladimir J. Konečni and Ebbe B. Ebbesen

UNIVERSITY OF CALIFORNIA, SAN DIEGO

W. H. FREEMAN AND COMPANY
San Francisco

Project Editor: Pearl C. Vapnek
Designer: Robert Ishi
Production Coordinator: Bill Murdock
Illustration Coordinator: Cheryl Nufer
Compositor: Graphic Typesetting Service
Printer and Binder: The Maple-Vail Book Manufacturing Group

Library of Congress Cataloging in Publication Data

Main entry under title:

The Criminal justice system.

(A series of books in psychology)
Includes bibliographies and indexes.
1. Criminal justice, Administration of—United
States—Addresses, essays, lectures. 2. Criminal
psychology. 3. Judicial process—United States—
Psychological aspects. I. Konečni, Vladimir J.,
1944–   . II. Ebbesen, Ebbe B. III. Series.
HV6791.C753   364′.973   81-14355
ISBN 0-7167-1312-8   AACR2
ISBN 0-7167-1313-6 (pbk.)

Printed in the United States of America

1 2 3 4 5 6 7 8 9   MP   0 8 9 8 7 6 5 4 3 2

To Egon Brunswik, Kurt Lewin,
       and our psychology/law students

CONTENTS

PREFACE

During the past decade, a discipline that is primarily concerned with the role of psychological factors in the legal process and the application of psychological principles to legal matters has developed rapidly. The growth of the discipline—legal psychology—can be easily documented and has been reflected in a relatively large number of edited volumes, symposia at psychological conventions, and the founding of a specialized journal (*Law and Human Behavior*). Although the practitioners of legal psychology have rather diverse backgrounds, social psychologists probably represent a majority and seem to have played a particularly prominent role.

The discipline has experienced acute growing pains. In our opinion, at least four broad classes of difficulties can be readily identified. First, instead of attempts to develop systematic and coherent theoretical positions that are specially suited to the new field, there has been a haphazard introduction of various theoretical approaches developed in other disciplines within psychology, especially in social psychology. Second, the range of research methods has been quite limited, and the methods used have often been poorly suited to a comprehensive analysis of legal issues. Third, the choice of research problems and settings has been very narrow in scope. Finally, many studies have reflected considerable naiveté concerning the actual operation of the legal system, not to mention the fine points of the law. In summary, much of the discipline seems to capture the worst of both worlds, in the sense that neither is the analysis of legal issues profiting from the psychological perspective, nor are the disciplines within psychology from which the theories and methodologies were being rashly imported being systematically advanced through the introduction of legal contexts. In many instances, investigators have seemed to continue their ongoing research programs, merely including in their experiments some legal aspects, either because of convenience, or to give studies an air of "applied importance," or simply because legal psychology was becoming a "hot area." Needless to say, many of these efforts were regarded with considerable skepticism by people in the legal profession.

The present book is a reflection of the contributors' and our own concerns about the nature of the development of legal psychology. It is our belief that one of the most important objectives of legal psychology is to enhance the understanding of the operation of the legal system by using psychological research methods. Social psychology, because of its traditional concern with the development of new research methods, with external validity, and with applied issues, should play a special role in this undertaking. However, we think it reasonable to argue that the emphasis should be on the understanding of the legal process, instead of the research efforts being limited to using the legal system merely as a place to test perhaps fascinating, but nevertheless highly idiosyncratic, features of the social-psychological theories currently in vogue. This entire volume therefore addresses a single issue, and one that is meaningful from the *legal* point of view: How does the criminal justice system operate, and how can its operation be elucidated by using psychological approaches and methods of inquiry?

The criminal justice system can be approached and studied from many points of view. The emphasis in this book is on an empirical and quantitative analysis of the decisions made by the various participants in the criminal justice system (the offender, the victim, the eyewitness, the police officer, the bail-setting judge, the district attorney, the juror, the sentencing judge, the probation officer, the parole board, etc.) at various key points in the processing of a criminal case. After the two introductory chapters on theory and methods, a number of chapters reporting research results follow. These have been written by various contributors. Each chapter deals with a key decision point in the processing of a criminal case. The ordering of the chapters follows the procedurally determined temporal sequence of events in a typical case. Thus, the chapters trace the history of the offender from the decision to commit a crime to the decision of the parole board whether or not to grant parole. Between these two decision points, the various chapters are concerned with the victim's decision whether or not to report the crime, with the police officer's decision whether or not to make an arrest, with the judge's decision concerning the amount of bail to set, with the district attorney's decision which charges (if any) to file, with the decisions that various participants in a trial have to make, with the judge's sentencing decision,

and so on. In a polemical final chapter, we have ventured some recommendations for changes in the criminal justice system.

Most of the chapters in the research part of the book report data.
One exception to this is a chapter on the police feedback cycle, which
makes concrete proposals for improved functioning of the police in
the community (by taking into account the internal structure of a
police department, the external demands on the police, and the information available to the individual officer when making decisions in
the field), and thus complements the chapter that directly analyzes
the decision to make an arrest. In addition, the chapter on the gathering of evidence is a review, rather than a data, chapter; we felt that
readers would benefit more from a comprehensive review of this one
area in which a great deal of research has been done since the beginning of the century, than from being informed of a relatively small
set of new data. In addition to the fact that most of the research
chapters present new findings, in most cases the data were collected
in real-world settings, such as the courtroom, or else the chapters
deal with archival information from actual legal cases, such as the
filed charges or sentencing decisions. The only exceptions to this are
the chapters that deal with the offender's decision to commit a crime
and the victim's decision to report the crime, both of which are
decisions that would have been difficult, if not impossible, to study
as they occur naturally. In fact, even in one of these chapters (concerned with reporting the crime), every effort was made to make the
experimental situation as naturalistic as possible.

We feel that we owe the readers a few words of explanation concerning the term "social-psychological" in the title of the book. Several of the chapters in the book are indeed concerned with certain
traditional social-psychological problems, at least in part. However,
many of the chapters, including our own, have little, if any, social-
psychological emphasis in the sense of dealing with the concepts
and theories one finds, for example, in textbooks on social psychology.
Some of these chapters are highly quantitative and take a strong
systems-analysis orientation to the decision-making issues in the
criminal justice system. Nevertheless, for several reasons, we feel that
even these chapters, and thus the book as a whole, have a distinct
social-psychological flavor, if not of the traditional variety. First, the
book is concerned with the analysis of an intact *social* system of
decision-makers. Second, the decisions made by some participants
in the system become information to which other participants in a
system are exposed and that they presumably take into account when
reaching their own decisions. In this sense and some others (for
example, in actual persuasion attempts that occur in the courtroom
and elsewhere in the system), the relationships between participants

in the criminal justice system are as good examples as any of *social influence*. Both of the above arguments rest on the premise that phenomena, rather than concepts and theories currently in vogue, define the domain of social psychology. Third, we feel that the concern expressed in many chapters with the use of complementary research methods, with multiple dependent measures, with careful attention to the issues of experimenter demand and bias, with external validity and generalizability, and with an applied orientation in the Lewinian tradition of "action research" are all characteristic of social psychology to a greater degree than perhaps any other discipline in psychology. Finally, there is the not entirely irrelevant fact that the majority of the contributors to the book consider themselves primarily social psychologists.

The decision-making approach to the legal system, and the sequential analysis of the key points in the processing of a case, are not unique to our book; for these general features we are indebted to the pioneering efforts of Leslie T. Wilkins and the related contributions that he generally inspired (for example, the work of A. K. Bottomley, W. R. LaFave, F. W. Miller, and others). In addition, our own and our contributors' emphasis on studying the legal system *in situ* has undoubtedly been in part inspired by the important early work of Hans Zeisel. Nevertheless, it would seem that the present book goes well beyond the previous efforts in that the authors whose work is brought together here present a variety of new approaches, statistical techniques, methodological procedures, theoretical insights, and data—all within a unified framework. For this reason, although the overall approach of the book is essentially a social-psychological one, we hope that students and practitioners from several disciplines, such as law, sociology, criminology, public administration, as well as various branches of psychology, may find the work reported here useful and relevant to their concerns.

Because the editors contributed equally to this volume, the order of our names on the title page was determined randomly.

October 1981   *Vladimir J. Konečni*
La Jolla   *Ebbe B. Ebbesen*

CONTRIBUTORS

John S. Carroll, Ph.D.
Associate Professor
Department of Psychology
Loyola University of Chicago
Chicago, IL 60626

Ebbe B. Ebbesen, Ph.D.
Professor
Department of Psychology
University of California, San Diego
La Jolla, CA 92093

Robert M. Garber, M.A.
Chairperson
Counseling Department
Pierce College
Woodland Hills, CA 91371

Arthur M. Gelman, J.D., Ph.D.
Senior Research Associate
INSLAW, Inc.
Washington, DC 20005

J. Douglas Grant, M.A.
President
Social Action Research Center
San Rafael, CA 94903

Joan Grant, Ph.D.
Project Director
Social Action Research Center
San Rafael, CA 94903

Martin S. Greenberg, Ph.D.
Associate Professor
Department of Psychology
University of Pittsburgh
Pittsburgh, PA 15260

Norbert L. Kerr, Ph.D.
Assistant Professor
Department of Psychology
Michigan State University
East Lansing, MI 48824

Vladimir J. Konečni, Ph.D.
Associate Professor
Department of Psychology
University of California, San Diego
La Jolla, CA 92093

Felice J. Levine, Ph.D.
Program Director
Law and Social Sciences
National Science Foundation
Washington, DC 20550

Christina Maslach, Ph.D.
Associate Professor
Department of Psychology
University of California
Berkeley, CA 94720

Michael K. Mills, Ph.D.
Assistant Professor
Department of Marketing
University of Southern California
Los Angeles, CA 90230

Ezra Stotland, Ph.D.
Professor of Psychology
Director, Society and Justice Program
University of Washington
Seattle, WA 98195

June Louin Tapp, Ph.D.
Professor of Child Psychology
Adjunct Professor of Law
University of Minnesota
Minneapolis, MN 55455

Hans H. Toch, Ph.D.
Professor of Psychology
School of Criminal Justice
State University of New York
Albany, NY 12222

Leslie T. Wilkins, F.S.S.
Research Professor
School of Criminal Justice
State University of New York
Albany, NY 12222

Chauncey E. Wilson, B.S.
Engineering Psychologist
U.S. Army Human
    Engineering Laboratory
Aberdeen, MD 21001

THEORETICAL ISSUES

Social Psychology and the Law: A Decision-Making Approach to the Criminal Justice System

Ebbe B. Ebbesen and Vladimir J. Konečni

This chapter describes the theoretical approach that has guided much of our own research on the criminal justice system. In developing this theoretical approach, we have focused on the *behavior* of the participants in the system rather than on the letter of the law. Furthermore, we do not describe how participants in the criminal justice system *ought* to behave; instead we attempt to provide a theoretical approach useful in understanding how they actually do behave. Because the extent to which rules of law and discretion mix in determining the behavior of participants in the criminal justice system is largely unknown, much of our knowledge about the behavior of participants can come only from empirical investigations. For this reason, we believe an adequate theoretical treatment of the criminal justice system must be closely linked to the empirical determination of factors that control the behavior of the participants, whether or not these factors are legally sanctioned.

THE RULE OF LAW VERSUS DISCRETION

The traditional view of the criminal justice system, as presented in most legal textbooks, portrays the behavior of the participants in the system as determined largely by the rule of law, due process, and administrative guidelines. Each action by a participant is seemingly constrained by a set of rules, precedents, statutory limitations, constitutional interpretations, and so on, all designed to minimize the chances of convicting the innocent, to prevent personal abuses of legally sanctioned power, to insure due process, and to create an atmosphere of impartial and fair treatment. These rules are expected to prevent participants from taking some actions (such as a judge telling a jury how to vote or a police officer coercing a suspect to supply a confession) and require them to perform other actions (such as a police officer reading *Miranda* rights to an arrestee or a judge informing defendants of the charges against them). In fact, the traditional view assumes that few actions can be taken without being fully scrutinized for adherence to established rules and guidelines. Failures to conform to existing rules are believed to result in mistrials, dismissals, and appeals to higher courts. Although it is admitted in this traditional view that there may be some areas in the system where small degrees of discretion do exist, by far the majority of actions are assumed to be highly constrained.

A consequence of this traditional view of the criminal justice system is the belief that a complete understanding of the operation of the system can be acquired merely by studying the full complexity of the procedural requirements described in various constitutional, common, and statutory laws, administrative policies, and procedural guidelines. If the actions of the participants in the system are highly restricted by various rules, then one need only know the rules in order to understand how participants in the system behave.

More recently, another view of the criminal justice system has been proposed (Bottomley, 1973; Chambliss, 1968; Cicourel, 1968; Davis, 1969; Frank, 1949; Green, 1961; Hogarth, 1971; Nagel and Neef, 1977; Shaver, Gilbert, and Williams, 1975; Wilkins, 1962, 1964). This view asserts that most of the rules and policies provide very broad, rather than specific, guidelines for action—so broad, in fact, that in many instances the participants are virtually free to behave as they wish. For example, the sentencing of convicted adult felons in most states in the United States and in England is determined by a judicial decision (Carter and Wilkins, 1967; Dawson, 1969; Hood, 1962; Thomas, 1970). The options available to the judge and many of the steps that must be taken prior to reaching a decision are constrained by both law and administrative policy. However, because the range of sentencing options typically available to the judge is so broad, and because the rules do not specify, in detail, how the judge is to take account of such factors as prior record, social history, remorse, education, occupation, potential for rehabilitation, and so on, people convicted of the identical crime can, and often do, receive very different treatments, even from the same judge (Hogarth, 1971; O'Donnell, Churgin, and Curtis, 1977).

Similar situations in which participants have more or less complete discretion over a wide range of decision alternatives exist throughout the criminal justice system. Police officers have discretion in deciding when and whom to arrest and, within wide limits, what crimes the arrestee is to be charged with (Kadish, 1962; LaFave, 1965; Piliavin and Briar, 1964; Reiss, 1971; Toch, 1969). Subsequently, assistant district attorneys can decide to drop, reduce, or add charges (Miller, 1970). In preliminary hearings, the presiding judge can often dismiss all or some of the charges and reduce others (Miller, 1970). District attorneys can plea bargain to whatever extent they deem appropriate and thereby again alter the nature of the charges, as well as affect the final sentence (Newman, 1966; Rosett and Cressey, 1976). Similar opportunities to determine in a discretionary manner how a case is handled exist throughout the system.

In summary, according to the more recent view, the operation of the criminal justice system cannot be understood by examining laws, policies, and procedural guidelines, mainly because the actual operation of the system consists of the various behaviors of the participants, and in most cases these behaviors are highly *discretionary* and thus only *loosely* constrained by the rule of law.

THEORETICAL APPROACHES
TO THE CRIMINAL JUSTICE SYSTEM

A number of theoretical perspectives have been taken in an attempt to explain the discretionary actions of participants in the criminal justice system. One that is common among social psychologists is to use quasi-legal settings, procedures, and materials as a testing ground for concepts currently of interest in a field of inquiry other than the law (Davis et al., 1975; Kaplan and Kemmerick, 1974; Landy and Aronson, 1969; Lerner, 1970; Mitchell and Byrne, 1973; Pepitone, 1975; Pepitone and DiNubile, 1976; Shaver, Gilbert, and Williams, 1975; Sigall and Ostrove, 1975; Vidmar, 1972). Concepts are borrowed from social-psychological theories and then empirically tested under conditions that attempt to simulate a few isolated, impoverished aspects of the legal system. Often, the role that the decision under study plays in the system is completely ignored so as to make it appear that the theoretical concepts are important and apply to "relevant" and "meaningful" settings. Equity principles, attributional biases, perceived similarity of attitudes, attraction, polarization effects in group decisions, and impression management are but a few examples of social-psychological concepts that have been or could easily be used to "explain" the behavior of participants in artificial simulations of the legal system.

Several features of this kind of approach should be noted. First, it implicitly assumes that a small set of mediational constructs will be sufficient to account for the behavior of most of the participants in the legal system. Everyone is assumed to be affected by, say, attributional biases. Different mediators might be proposed to explain the behavior of district attorneys than to explain jury decisions but, nevertheless, only a few concepts should be required to understand the behavior of each type of participant. Second, many potentially important causal factors of concern to participants in the criminal justice system may be of little importance in a theoretical analysis based on concepts borrowed from social psychology. For example, when trying to predict a judge's sentencing decision, the sentence recommendation of a probation officer may appear—to social psychologists—to be of less importance than, for example, the attitude similarity between the defendant and the judge, primarily because the latter is a popular theoretical concept and the former is not. Thus, the real interest in this kind of general approach is not in accounting, *as completely as possible*, for the behavior of participants in the criminal justice system, but rather to determine whether a variable derived from social-psychological theories accounts for some variance in a subject's quasi-legal behavior, even if it explains only a meager (but statistically significant) portion of that variance. Third, as we discuss in the next chapter, simulation methodology may not prove adequate to the task it has been given. Fourth, the emphasis on testing ideas borrowed from theories developed elsewhere (e.g., small-group dynamics and attribution theory) tends to direct attention almost exclusively toward certain participants (e.g., juries) and away from the larger picture, i.e., the description of the actual operation of the *entire* criminal justice system that would be invaluable from a predictive point of view. Methods and procedures for studying the variables that affect the behavior of participants in the system are chosen, not because they provide externally valid representations of processes in the criminal justice system, but because they may result in internally valid tests of hypotheses (see Chapter 2 for further discussion of this point).

A somewhat different theoretical approach from that described above—but one that also attempts to explain the discretionary actions of participants—postulates the existence of global individual-difference factors (Gaudet, Harris, and St. John, 1933; Green, 1961; Hamilton, 1976; Hogarth, 1971; McFatter, 1978; Nagel, 1962, 1963). Attitudes toward law and order, philosophies of sentencing, liberalism/conservatism, political party affiliation, personality characteristics, economic background, financial interests, sex, age, race, and legal training are examples of some of the global individual-difference factors that have been examined in recent years. In general, individual-difference factors have been able to account for a significant portion of the variation in judicial decisions, but usually only a small percentage of the total variation is explained by such global factors. Furthermore, even if individual-difference factors were capable of explaining a larger portion of the variation, the causal influence of situational factors (e.g., the size of one's case load, the number of cases that are backlogged, who one's superior is, and the current political climate), role-related variables (e.g., the fact that assistant district attorneys are more likely to be promoted for obtaining convictions, and police officers are more likely to be rewarded for making arrests), and case factors (e.g., race, prior record, educational background, and severity of crime) are generally ignored in this theoretical approach (but see Bottomley, 1973, for an exception). If case factors, for example, do account for variation in the decisions made by key participants, then a theoretical approach that focuses exclusively on global individual-difference factors will necessarily leave unexplained some potentially explainable variation in each participant's behavior. In short, causal factors, other than those used to explain differences between participants, will almost certainly be required if a complete account of the day-to-day operation of the criminal justice system is the goal.

THE PRESENT APPROACH: AN INTERCONNECTED NETWORK OF DECISION-MAKERS

Our own theoretical approach to the criminal justice system is quite different from the two outlined above, but shares much with that described by Wilkins (1964) and pursued by the American Bar Foundation (especially Dawson, LaFave, Miller, and Newman) and the President's Commission on Law Enforcement and the Administration of Justice (1967a, 1967b). Rather than view the system merely as an interesting domain in which to test theoretical concepts borrowed from other fields, our goal is to understand how the criminal justice system actually operates. What circumstances determine which of the many decision options typically available to participants in the system are actually chosen? What causal factors account for the most variation in these decisions, both within a single participant (e.g., a particular sentencing judge) and within a class of particular participants (e.g., judges of a county superior court)? What are the causal relationships between actions taken by participants at different points in the system (e.g., the effect that a judge's decision to release a defendant on his own recognizance has on the sentencing recommendation that a probation officer provides to a different judge several months later)?

What the rule of law constrains

We view the laws, policies, and guidelines relevant to the operation of the criminal justice system as providing only a broad framework that primarily constrains:

1. The range of decision options typically available to different participants.

2. The temporal order in which decisions about a case (defendant) will be made.

3. The class of participants (e.g., district attorneys, judges, defendants, probation officers) that will make the decisions.

4. Gross aspects of the way in which case-relevant information is gathered, selected, and exchanged (e.g., the point at which a probation officer conducts interviews, the fact that a police officer often describes aspects of cases to an assistant district attorney, who then files a complaint, and so on).

The laws, policies, and guidelines generally:

1. Do not specify the exact types of information that the participants must take into account (e.g., Should the fact that the defendant had two prior felony convictions be taken into account?) or the ordering of the different levels within each type (e.g., Is a threat with an unloaded handgun worse than one with a kitchen knife?).

2. Do not precisely instruct the participants about the relative importance that should be given to the different types of information (e.g., How much more or less important is prior record than severity of offense?).

3. Do not provide the rules that should be used to combine different types of information (e.g., Should different factors be configurally combined, or would a simple additive rule suffice?).

4. Do not outline the role, if any, that social-influence channels should play in a given participant's decision (e.g., How much weight should a probation officer's sentencing recommendation be given?).

Decision nodes, or classes of participants

The fact that decisional freedoms exist in a context in which the temporal flow of decisions is largely constrained suggests a conceptualization of the criminal justice system as a temporally ordered and interconnected network of decision "nodes." A given node would consist of a class of decision-makers, each of whom is required by procedure or law to reach a specified decision. The members of a particular class of participants have in common the fact that they chose from the same set of decision alternatives at the same point in the temporal flow of events. For example, a group of judges, each of whom determines the sentences for convicted felons, would constitute a particular node in our conceptualization. Only those decisions that affect the progress of cases through system, i.e., are related to the method of disposition of cases, are defined as nodes. For example, a judge's decision about *when* to schedule a preliminary hearing would not, in general, be included as a decision node in our approach. On the other hand, it is important to note that not all of the important nodes need be included in legal guidelines. Some nodes might refer to decisions that are largely available for public inspection (e.g., the charges listed in an indictment), while other nodes might refer to decisions made away from the public eye and not specifically included in guidelines (e.g., various stages in the plea-bargaining process).

It is important to emphasize that even though we claim that the decision strategy for each node is far from specified by legal or administrative guidelines, we assume that the decisions of the participants can, nevertheless, be described by an *empirically* derived rule. That is, the behavior of the participants is assumed to be orderly rather than random. Furthermore, even though every case might be different in one respect or another (as many participants in the system are quick to point out), there are enough similarities among cases that rules capable of predicting decisions can be discovered.

On the other hand, our approach in no way requires that identical decisions be reached by decision-makers in different nodes even when participants in the different nodes are exposed to *identical* patterns of case characteristics. Any number of factors might lead participants in different nodes to use different decision strategies. For example, the incentive structure for police officers is quite different from that for assistant district attorneys. The arresting officer may have a supervisor who values felony over misdemeanor arrests, or the officer's promotions may depend, in part, on the *number of arrests*; whereas an assistant district attorney may be more concerned about *conviction rate*. For this reason, even though the decision-makers in both nodes may be exposed to the same information pool, e.g., in deciding on which charges to book the defendant (the police officer's decision) and which charges to include in the complaint (the assistant district attorney's decision), they may well use entirely different decision strategies.

As the above discussion suggests, it would be possible to focus research attention on factors (e.g., incentive structure) that lead different decision nodes to use different strategies. This seems an admirable aim. However, we currently know very little about the nature of the decision strategies that are actually being used by the different classes of participants. For example, it is possible for decision-makers to agree frequently in the selection of decision options, yet use quite different strategies in reaching those decisions (Einhorn, 1974). Furthermore, decision strategies can differ in a number of ways (selection and classification of information, subjective evaluation, weighting, combination, and so on), and until the exact nature of differences in decisions is known, searching for more abstract explanations for the differences seems futile.

Connections among nodes

The connections among nodes are seen as causal pathways, many of which involve social influence. More specifically, a connection between two nodes is assumed to exist if events in one node control the decisions reached in the other node. The causal influence from one node to another may be direct (as when a district attorney attempts to influence a judge's bail decision by argument) or indirect (as when a pretrial decision by a judge not to release defendants on their own recognizance adversely affects the severity of the sentences given by another judge much later in the processing of the cases), and unidirectional or bidirectional (in the latter case, as when a defense attorney and a district attorney attempt to influence each other's decisions during plea bargaining).

PREDICTING THE OPERATION OF THE CRIMINAL JUSTICE SYSTEM

To provide a complete and predictively useful account of the operation of the criminal justice system from our theoretical perspective requires that we:

1. Define classes of participants (decision-makers) according to the type of decision that is made.

2. Specify the range of decision options available to each class.

3. Identify the exact types of information available to each class of participants prior to a decision.

4. Obtain estimates for the subjective values and weights of these various types of information.

5. Select models of the combination strategies used at each point.

6. Trace the causal influence channels connecting the different classes of participants.

If all of these components have been correctly defined and estimated, the result is a predictively accurate *theory* of the particular criminal justice system being studied. If any of these steps is missing, or if the empirically derived solutions at a given step are in error (e.g., an important influence channel has been overlooked, or a particular type of information has been greatly underweighted at a given node), the theory will generally provide unsatisfactory predictions of the behavior of participants in the system.

The temporal flow of cases

The first step in constructing a predictive theory of the criminal justice system based on our approach is to define the set of decisions and classes of participants making those decisions and to place these decision nodes in an appropriate temporal order. Figure 1.1 shows one model (from President's Commission, 1967a) with relevant base-rate data from the Index Crimes for the United States in 1965.

This model provides a useful starting point, although several important decision nodes are conspicuously absent. The temporal flow of cases through several major decision events (whether to commit a crime, whether to arrest, whether to charge with a felony, whether to dismiss the charges, whether to plea bargain, what sentence to give, and whether to release from prison) can be seen clearly, however. Of equal interest are some surprising statistical facts about the progress of cases through this social structure. For example, a rather dramatic difference seems to exist among the nodes in determining what charges, if any, should be brought against defendants. In approximately 40% of the cases, the district attorney reduced or dropped completely the charges that the arresting agency felt were appropriate. Judges decided to dismiss approximately 5% of the cases in which adults had been formally accused of a crime by the district attorney. Note also that most guilty determinations (73%) were

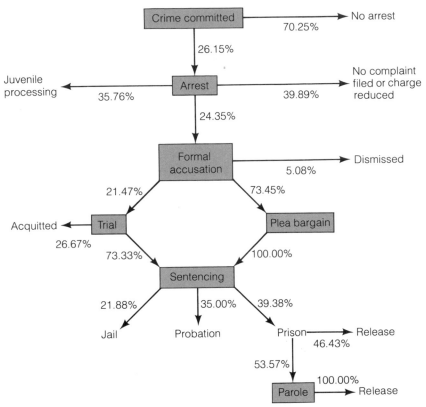

Figure 1.1
A model of the major decision nodes in the criminal justice system and of the temporal flow of cases through those decision nodes. Each box represents a decision that determines the eventual disposition of the case. Arrows represent the flow of cases from one decision to the next. The percentages indicate the proportion of cases reaching a particular decision node that were disposed of in the labeled manner. (From President's Commission on Law Enforcement and the Administration of Justice, 1967a.)

obtained because the defendant had pleaded guilty. Contrary to common opinion, as exemplified by the broad news coverage typically given to jury trials, such trials played only a minor role in determining the disposition of cases.

The relatively infrequent use of jury trials is of interest because it highlights a difference between the present approach and most others. A major portion of the research in social psychology that deals with legal issues has been concerned with jury decision making (Tapp, 1976). However, as the previous data suggest, one could literally treat jury decisions as *noise* in the system and lose very little predictive ability. If the goal is to understand how the system actually operates, researchers would do much better to concentrate on the defense attorney's and assistant district attorney's decision not to go to trial, and the defendant's decision to admit guilt of some offense in exchange for other charges being dropped (Gregory, Mowen, and Linder, 1978), than to study jury decisions in great detail.

Several important nodes are left out of the model in Figure 1.1. Following the decision by a potential defendant to engage in an action that might be defined as a crime, an important node to include prior to arrest is the victim's (when there is one) decision to report the crime. These first two nodes, along with the decision to arrest, determine, in part, the nature of the information that is used in the remaining steps of the system. Whether a given action is to be classified as a criminal one largely depends on decisions made at these three points. For example, whether a sexual encounter is considered rape or lawful intercourse, whether an aggressive interchange is defined as an assault or an argument, or whether the removal of property is called theft or borrowing depends on the label that the "victim" decides to use to describe the event. Unless victims consider themselves to be such, it is unlikely that particular interpersonal encounters will formally enter the criminal justice system. In addition, while most police manuals instruct officers to enforce all laws against all people without exception (Goldstein, 1960), it is clear that they also provide officers with considerable discretion in terms of when, how, and whether to arrest, as well as what charges to file. Besides, many laws are so vague that officers are forced to make discretionary decisions about the intent of the legislature in passing the law.

Not shown in the model in Figure 1.1 is the fact that a very large proportion of police arrests are for criminal actions that have not been reported by victims. Instead, officers, as part of their patrol, make a decision to investigate a situation that appears suspect; as a consequence, an arrest is made. Because many arrests are of this nature, most police departments also include some arrest review procedure prior to booking the accused. This review is another important node left out of the model in Figure 1.1.

Soon after the district attorney has filed a complaint and decided on a specific set of charges, an arraignment and a bail hearing are held. The presiding judge's decision about the amount of bail to set, if any, forms another node of considerable significance for later events. For example, the kind of information about the defendant that will be available to participants at later decision nodes depends on whether the defendant is in jail or not. Defendants' contacts with their attorneys and the presentence investigation by probation officers might be limited or altered if they take place in a county jail rather than in a private office.

Several preliminary hearings in which a judge (and/or a grand jury) decides whether a felony (as opposed to a lesser crime) has been committed and whether "reasonable grounds" exist as to the defendant's guilt are important decision nodes that occur after a complaint has been filed but before the final determination of guilt is made. Concurrent with these events, plea bargaining is usually taking place. Various official and unofficial encounters between the defense and district attorneys, often involving the judge, usually occur during plea bargaining. Following the guilty plea, and after gathering considerable background information about the defendant, a probation officer usually makes a specific recommendation regarding the suitability of the defendant for probation, sets limitations on the defendant's behavior that are included as conditions of probation (e.g., not to associate with known drug users, to attend evening school), and in many jurisdictions also makes recommendations about the specifics of the sentence (e.g., the amount of the fine, the number of days in the local county jail, etc.) if straight probation is not considered appropriate. These decision nodes are also missing from the model in Figure 1.1.

Figure 1.2 presents a more complete and representative model of the temporal flow of major decisions in the criminal justice system of most states. It also provides a structure for linking together most of the empirical-research chapters of the book. These chapters were written by individuals especially familiar with the decision node that forms the subject of their chapters. Unfortunately, some decision nodes presented in Figure 1.2 are particularly difficult to study, either because obtaining relevant data is extremely time-consuming or because the participants refuse to expose the process to thorough observation. Chapters on these nodes are therefore conspicuously missing from this book. On the other hand, by asking the various contributors to concentrate on the decision-making process of the relevant node, we attempted to provide a view of the remaining parts of the system that is more or less consistent with the theoretical approach that is described in this chapter.

Figure 1.2
A more detailed model of the major decision nodes in the criminal justice system. This model provides a method of organizing most of the chapters in this volume. The case-processing data presented in this figure are from the more than 145,500 felony arrests made in the state of California in 1977. Percentages were computed on a node-by-node basis. The data were obtained from the California Bureau of Criminal Statistics.

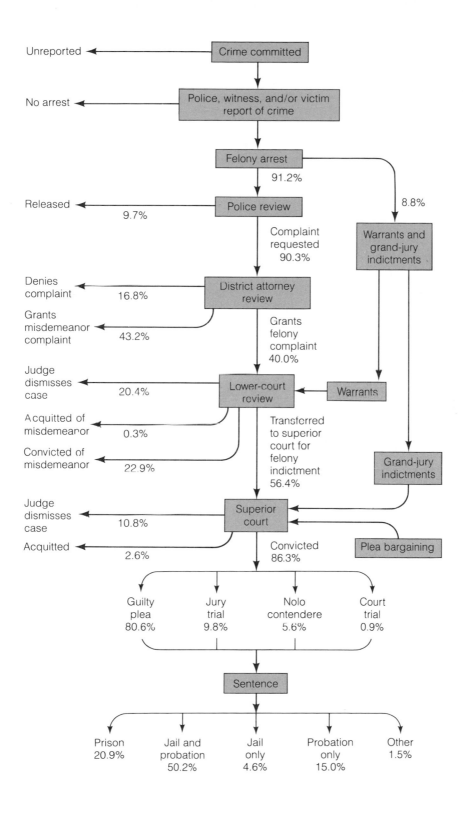

Unreported ← Crime committed

No arrest ← Police, witness, and/or victim report of crime

Felony arrest 91.2%

Released 9.7% ← Police review — Complaint requested 90.3%

8.8% — Warrants and grand-jury indictments

Denies complaint 16.8% ← District attorney review

Grants misdemeanor complaint 43.2% ←

Grants felony complaint 40.0%

Warrants

Judge dismisses case 20.4% ← Lower-court review ← Warrants

Acquitted of misdemeanor 0.3% ←

Convicted of misdemeanor 22.9% ←

Transferred to superior court for felony indictment 56.4%

Grand-jury indictments

Judge dismisses case 10.8% ← Superior court

Acquitted 2.6% ←

Convicted 86.3%

Plea bargaining

Guilty plea 80.6% Jury trial 9.8% Nolo contendere 5.6% Court trial 0.9%

Sentence

Prison 20.9% Jail and probation 50.2% Jail only 4.6% Probation only 15.0% Other 1.5%

The unit of analysis

Once a set of decision nodes has been defined and the nodes have been placed in a particular temporal order, the next step in developing a predictive model is to select the unit of analysis that is to be used in constructing empirically derived decision rules for the various nodes. Our approach differs from some others in that the *case* (a particular person who has committed or has been charged with a crime) constitutes the basic unit of analysis rather than such things as type of crime, court, county, state, and so on. That is, we do not advocate developing models of decision strategies by comparing decision rates across several states, counties within a state, or the same state at different points in time. If the goal is to predict the decisions a given case will elicit as it moves through the system, then confining empirical analyses to the level of cases seems most appropriate.

The categories of case-relevant information used as potential predictors of decisions and the rules used to classify decision options are defined, in our approach, in terms compatible with the language of the criminal justice system rather than with theoretical concepts borrowed from other areas. For example, crimes are coded in terms of established penal-code categories and not in terms of some independent metric of severity. Similarly, categories of information defined as different by the legal system (e.g., the defendant was under the influence of alcohol versus drugs when the crime was committed) are not collapsed merely because an attribution theorist could claim that a judge or jurors will make similar attributions about the causes of the defendant's actions in both instances.

A consequence of using categories that are derived from the legal system is that we tend to ignore mediational explanations for the decision rules that are discovered. An assistant district attorney's use of the arresting officer's violation of search-and-seizure laws in deciding whether to prosecute a given case is not explained in terms of perceptions of equity, attributional bias, interpersonal attraction, or any other mediational concept typically cited by social psychologists to"explain" behavior. Instead, we focus on the percent of variance that can be statistically explained by variables that are commonly known and well understood by participants in the criminal justice system. In the above example, we would be content to note that violations of search and seizure accounted for a particular percentage of the attorney's refusals to file charges. It is not that we deny the possibility of constructing models that emphasize mediational accounts of the behavior of participants; we merely question the ability of such account to add anything useful to the descriptive accounts that are more easily communicated to legal professionals.

Decision strategies

The empirical derivation of models of the decision strategies used in each node is the last step in the process. The goal of this stage of the analysis is to select from the many possible factors (i.e., categories of information and sources of influence) those that account for the largest percent of variance (unexplainable by other already known factors or combination of factors) in the decision being studied. Causal pathways from other decision nodes are also examined by including events in prior nodes as possible predictors of the current decision. The particular modeling procedures and quantitative techniques used depend on the node being analyzed; however, multiple-regression analysis and log-linear analysis constitute two of the more common techniques.

It is important to note that these empirically derived decision strategies need not bear any resemblance to the strategies that the participants *claim* they use in reaching their decisions. Our concern is with discovering those factors that account for variation in the decisions and the best way to put them together to predict the most variance in future decisions. Participants may report that one or more factors have an influence on their decisions, and these reports may indeed reflect the amount of time the participants spend thinking about these factors. Yet, these same factors need not account for variation in the decisions. People may spend time thinking about things that in fact rarely affect the final decision and/or rarely think about things that do. We do not contend that people do not accurately report their own phenomenology or any other mediating events; we simply contend that such events need not offer the most useful causal model of the frequent decisions that the participants must make. The purpose of our decision models is not to simulate the phenomenology of the decision-maker, but rather to provide a procedure for combining and weighting different types of information so that accurate case-by-case predictions of the behavior of the participants can be made.

Disparity: individual differences within a node

An important feature of our approach is that it can provide an account of differences in the behavior of participants within a node that is compatible with, and utilizes the same concepts as, the explanation of the behavior of the node treated as a single unit. For example, the same decision-making concepts (e.g., the kinds of information available, their subjective values, their relative weights, the rules used to combine them) can be used to understand the way in which judges set bail in bail review hearings (Ebbesen and Konečni, 1975) and the individual differences among the various judges within this node. Furthermore, by studying a particular node in the context of other decision nodes rather than in isolation (as is often done by others), our approach offers the opportunity to distinguish real from spurious individual differences in decision-making strategies among the participants within a particular node (see Ebbesen and Konečni, 1981).

More specifically, differences among participants in the frequency with which various decision alternatives are selected (e.g., a greater likelihood of plea bargaining by one assistant district attorney than another) may reflect either systematic differences in the distribution of features of cases assigned to different participants within a node or more basic differences in their decision strategies. Various features of cases may well be used as criteria by participants at other nodes in the system to decide which individual within a different node will handle a given case. For example, defense attorneys may believe that certain judges will be more or less favorable to a particular kind of case and attempt to arrange the situation so that a preferred individual makes the required decision.

It is of interest to note that such modes of behavior can serve to maintain *false* beliefs about the existence of individual differences and also provide an alternative explanation for some findings from other individual-difference studies. A particular judge might have a reputation for lenient decisions with regard to rape cases and because of it be exposed to a higher—compared to other judges—percentage of cases that involve rape-related charges. As a consequence, this judge's frequency of selecting certain sentencing options might well be different from other judges' (e.g., more probation decisions). Such differences in sentencing behavior might serve to maintain the image of the judge as relatively lenient. Furthermore, if the reputation were derived not from the actual decisions but rather from the judge's general demeanor or attitudes expressed in court or elsewhere, then a "discovered" relationship between those attitudes and the decisions made by the judge could be an artifact of various defense attorneys' decisions to seek that judge out when handling cases with particular attributes. In short, the fact that individual differences in decisions can be predicted by personality or attitude factors establishes neither that individual difference variables are causes of judicial decisions nor that the *reported* individual differences are real. Individual differences within a node must be seen in light of the operation of social-influence channels among nodes before the real nature of individual differences can be known (see Nagel and Neef, 1977, for a similar point).

Our theoretical approach allows for several different types of "true" individual differences. For example, when deciding whether to arrest an individual, police officers may differ in their perceptions of the seriousness of particular criminal actions or of particular mitigating circumstances. Alternatively, the relative weight given to knowledge of the person's past criminal activity, the circumstances of the current investigation, the number of arrests made that month, and other relevant factors might vary from one officer to the next. Officers might also differ in the strategies they use to combine the various factors to reach a final decision. Thus, individual differences might emerge in scaling, weighting, and combination strategies. As can be seen, the same decision-making concepts are used to describe individual differences within a node as to describe the aggregated action of that node when treated as a part of the entire system.

JUSTICE AND OTHER IDEALS

In using our theoretical approach, we do not attempt to impose particular social or political values or to suggest how the criminal justice system *ought* to operate. The book does not contain advice on how to eliminate injustice, nor does it take sides on issues such as whether sentencing should fit the crime or the individual, whether the bail system should be eliminated, and whether plea bargaining or parole procedures are unjust. Instead, the aim is to develop a predictively useful *description* of the system, which can then be compared to a large variety of standards obtained from any number of sources. Unless one knows how the system actually operates, many attacks on the current system for not conforming to a particular standard may be unjustified, and other attacks may be warranted. For example, some might argue that race should not be a factor in determining the sentence that a defendant receives. Attacks on the system from this perspective because blacks or chicanos are more likely than whites to receive certain sentences might be shown to be misdirected once a complete description of the system is known. Differential prison rates, for example, across race might prove to be due to any number of other factors correlated with race. Members of one racial group may be more likely to commit the types of crimes that more frequently result in prison sentences. Violence may be more acceptable to some subcultures than to others, and those subcultures may be correlated with race. For example, street gangs that condone and even approve of violent crimes may be more likely to occur in densely populated urban areas, and these areas may also contain disproportionate numbers of youths from one or another race. Changing social conditions (e.g., unemployment rates across races, social acceptance of drug use) are also likely to affect the relative number of individuals from different racial groups that are arrested for different types of crimes. If a condition of probation is that an individual be steadily employed, and unemployment is associated with race, the likelihood of receiving straight probation as a sentence could appear to be affected by race. In short, defendant characteristics, such as race, age, and sex, that seem to affect the decisions of participants in the system may be correlated with other features of the case that are the actual factors controlling the decision. Once the decision strategies are discovered, it may turn out that the issue is not how to prevent a defendant's race (sex, age, or whatever) from being considered, but whether, say, the specific nature of the crime should play the role that it does.

The present approach also allows us to evaluate claims that certain factors have not been taken into account by key participants to the extent that they should. For example, it might appear that severity of the crime is not sufficiently affecting the nature of the sentence convicted felons receive. Evidence might emerge as a result of studying the causal pathways among nodes that severity is strongly influencing an earlier decision, such as the district attorney's decision to reduce or drop charges, and that the weak effect of severity later on in the process is due to its having been taken into account at an earlier decision node.

An empirically derived theory of the operation of the system can also be compared to the participants' own standards of how the system should be and is operating. Discrepancies can provide useful information not only about how to alter the system but also about the quality of the participants' own data gathering and conclusion drawing. Much of the information that one participant has about the behavior of other participants may be obtained by hearsay or be based on features of behavior that are actually irrelevant to the day-to-day operation of the system. For example, defense and district attorneys might develop beliefs about how judges make decisions on the basis of what judges claim, in court, are the important aspects of a case. These claims may have little to do with the factors that actually predict the judges' decisions, however, either because the judges are mentioning factors that they believe the public would like to have considered or because they are describing features of their thought processes that are not associated with the ability of specific factors to predict decisions over many cases.

One commonly agreed upon standard within the criminal justice system requires that different decision-makers within a given node should reach identical decisions when given the identical pool of information about a case. Many critics of the criminal justice system delight in describing what appear to be major violations of this standard. The validity of such criticisms depends on the claim that different participants within a node are exposed to identical information pools or at least that the information sets are identical in all *relevant* respects (President's Commission, 1967b). Therefore, unless the pool of information that is to be used in a decision is clearly specified, the presence of disparity can always be justified by a claim that cases differ along one or more unknown dimensions that are assumed to be taken into account by all of the participants in a similar manner. Thus, decision disparity can be discussed only in the context of a specified information pool. Because there is little agreement about which factors should and should not be taken into account at various points in the system, the question of disparity within a node is of secondary interest in this book.

References

Bottomley, A. K. *Decisions in the penal process.* South Hackensack, NJ: F. B. Rothman, 1973.

Carter, R. M., & Wilkins, L. T. Some factors in sentencing policy. *Journal of Criminal Law, Criminology, and Police Science*, 1967, 58, 503–514.

Chambliss, W. J. (Ed.). *Crime and the legal process.* New York: McGraw-Hill, 1968.

Cicourel, A. V. *The social organization of juvenile justice.* New York: Wiley, 1968.

Davis, J., Kerr, N., Atkin, R., Holt, R., & Meek, D. The decision processes of 6- and 12-person mock juries assigned unanimous and two-thirds majority rules. *Journal of Personality and Social Psychology*, 1975, 32, 1–14.

Davis, K. C. *Discretion in justice: A preliminary inquiry.* Baton Rouge: Louisiana State University Press, 1969.

Dawson, R. O. *Sentencing: The decision as to type, length and conditions of sentence.* Boston: Little, Brown, 1969.

Ebbesen, E. B., & Konečni, V. J. Decision making and information integration in the courts: The setting of bail. *Journal of Personality and Social Psychology*, 1975, 32, 805–821.

Ebbesen, E. B., & Konečni, V. J. The process of sentencing adult felons: A causal analysis of judicial decisions. In B. D. Sales (Ed.), *Perspectives in law and psychology. Vol. 2: The jury, judicial, and trial process.* New York: Plenum, 1981.

Einhorn, H. J. Expert judgment: Some necessary conditions and an example. *Journal of Applied Psychology*, 1974, 59, 562–571.

Frank, J. *Courts on trial: Myth and reality in American justice.* Princeton, NJ: Princeton University Press, 1949.

Gaudet, F. J., Harris, G. S., & St. John, C. W. Individual differences in the sentencing tendencies of judges. *Journal of Criminal Law, Criminology, and Police Science*, 1933, 23, 811–816.

Goldstein, J. Police discretion not to evoke the criminal process: Low-visibility decisions in the administration of justice. *Yale Law Journal*, 1960, 69, 543–557.

Green, E. *Judicial attitudes in sentencing.* London: Macmillan, 1961.

Gregory, W. L., Mowen, J. C., & Linder, D. E. Social psychology and plea bargaining: Applications, methodology, and theory. *Journal of Personality and Social Psychology*, 1978, *36*, 1521–1530.

Hamilton, V. L. Individual differences in ascriptions of responsibility, guilt, and appropriate punishment. In G. Bermant, C. Nemeth, & N. Vidmar (Eds.), *Psychology and the law*. Lexington, MA: Heath, 1976.

Hogarth, J. *Sentencing as a human process*. Toronto: University of Toronto Press, 1971.

Hood, R. G. *Sentencing in magistrates' courts*. London: Stevens, 1962.

Kadish, S. H. Legal norm and discretion in the police and sentencing processes. *Harvard Law Review*, 1962, *75*, 904–931.

Kaplan, M., & Kemmerick, G. Juror judgment as information integration: Combining evidential and nonevidential information. *Journal of Personality and Social Psychology*, 1974, *30*, 493–499.

LaFave, W. R. *Arrest: The decision to take a suspect into custody*. Boston: Little, Brown, 1965.

Landy, D., & Aronson, E. The influence of the character of the criminal and his victim on the decisions of simulated jurors. *Journal of Experimental Social Psychology*, 1969, *5*, 141–152.

Lerner, M. The desires for justice and reactions to victims. In J. Macaulay & L. Berkowitz (Eds.), *Altruism and helping behavior*. New York: Academic Press, 1970.

McFatter, R. M. Sentencing strategies and justice: Effects of punishment philosophy on sentencing decisions. *Journal of Personality and Social Psychology*, 1978, *36*, 1490–1500.

Miller, F. W. *Prosecution: The decision to charge a suspect with a crime*. Boston: Little, Brown, 1970.

Mitchell, H. E., & Byrne, D. The defendant's dilemma: Effects of jurors' attitudes and authoritarianism of judicial decisions. *Journal of Personality and Social Psychology*, 1973, *25*, 123–129.

Nagel, S. S. Judicial backgrounds and criminal cases. *Journal of Criminal Law, Criminology, and Police Science*, 1962, *53*, 333–339.

Nagel, S. S. Off the bench judicial attitudes. In G. Schubert (Ed.), *Judicial decision making*. London: Collier-Macmillan, 1963.

Nagel, S. S., & Neef, M. *The legal process: Modeling the system*. Beverly Hills, CA: Sage, 1977.

Newman, D. J. *Conviction: The determination of guilt or innocence without trial*. Boston: Little, Brown, 1966.

O'Donnell, P., Churgin, M. J., & Curtis, D. E. *Toward a just and effective sentencing system: Agenda for legislative reform*. New York: Praeger, 1977.

Pepitone, A. Social psychological perspectives on crime and punishment. *Journal of Social Issues*, 1975, *31*, 197–216.

Pepitone, A., & DiNubile, M. Contrast effects in judgments of crime severity and the punishment of criminal violators. *Journal of Personality and Social Psychology*, 1976, *33*, 448–459.

Piliavin, I., & Briar, S. Police encounters with juveniles. *American Journal of Sociology*, 1964, *70*, 206–214.

President's Commission on Law Enforcement and the Administration of Justice. *The challenge of crime in a free society*. Washington, DC: U.S. Government Printing Office, 1967. (a)

President's Commission on Law Enforcement and the Administration of Justice. *Task force report: The courts*. Washington, DC: U.S. Government Printing Office, 1967. (b)

Reiss, A. J., Jr. *The police and the public*. New Haven, CT: Yale University Press, 1971.

Rosett, A., & Cressey, D. R. *Justice by consent: Plea bargains in the American courthouse.* Philadelphia: Lippincott, 1976.

Shaver, K. G., Gilbert, M. A., & Williams, M. C. Social psychology, criminal justice, and the principle of discretion: A selective review. *Personality and Social Psychology Bulletin,* 1975, *1,* 471–484.

Sigall, H., & Ostrove, N. Beautiful but dangerous: Effects of offender attractiveness and nature of the crime on juridic judgment. *Journal of Personality and Social Psychology,* 1975, *31,* 410–414.

Tapp, J. L. Psychology and the law: An overture. *Annual Review of Psychology,* 1976, *27,* 359–404.

Thomas, D. A. *Principles of sentencing.* London: Heinemann, 1970.

Toch, H. *Violent men: An inquiry into the psychology of violence.* Chicago: Aldine, 1969.

Vidmar, N. Effects of decision alternatives on the verdicts and social perceptions of simulated jurors. *Journal of Personality and Social Psychology,* 1972, *22,* 211–218.

Wilkins, L. T. Criminology: An operational research approach. In A. T. Welford, N. Argyle, D. V. Glass, & J. N. Morris (Eds.), *Society: Problems and methods of study.* London: Routledge & Kegan Paul, 1962.

Wilkins, L. T. *Social deviance.* London: Tavistock, 1964.

METHODOLOGICAL ISSUES

Social Psychology and the Law: The Choice of Research Problems, Settings, and Methodology

Vladimir J. Konečni and Ebbe B. Ebbesen

The purpose of this chapter is to examine three related issues:

1. The relative values of laboratory simulations and *in situ* research on legal decision-making.

2. The relative values of various data-collection methods, given that the *in situ* research strategy has been adopted.

3. The implications of 1 and 2 for the choice of research problems in social-psychological approaches to legal issues.

These three topics will, admittedly, be examined from the standpoint of a basic premise about the interface of psychology and the law that has motivated this entire volume; namely, that the task of using psychological methods to gain a comprehensive understanding of the operation of the legal system should take precedence—especially in the early stages of the development of legal psychology—over the testing and application of the currently popular psychological theories in legal or quasi-legal contexts.

LABORATORY SIMULATIONS VERSUS *IN SITU* RESEARCH

A close examination of the literature in legal psychology shows that a large proportion of all research studies falls into the categories of jury decision-making (Efran, 1974; Kalven and Zeisel, 1966; Kerr et al., 1976; Landy and Aronson, 1969; Mitchell and Byrne, 1973; Nemeth and Sosis, 1973; Sigall and Ostrove, 1975; Vidmar, 1972a), eyewitness identification (Buckhout, 1974; Buckhout et al., 1974; Doob and Kirshenbaum, 1973; Egan, Pittner, and Goldstein, 1977; Levine and Tapp, 1973; Loftus, 1975; Loftus, Altman, and Geballe, 1975), and procedural justice (Doob, 1976; Farmer et al., 1976; Lawson, 1970; Thibaut and Walker, 1975; Walker et al., 1974). Of these, jury decision-making research has been by far the most voluminous and visible (Davis, Bray, and Holt, 1977; Tapp, 1976). Perhaps more than 90% of the research studies in all of these areas, especially in jury decision-making, has been conducted in the laboratory (Bermant et al., 1974; Davis, Bray, and Holt, 1977; Konečni, Mulcahy, and Ebbesen, 1980; Tapp, 1976). In view of this state of affairs, the relative utility of laboratory simulations and naturalistic research for the success of efforts to reach a sound understanding of the criminal justice system and process should be closely examined.

Many of the reasons that laboratory studies can cause serious problems with regard to the generalizability of findings are well known and need be only briefly mentioned here. For example, the researchers' implicit claim that college students can successfully mimic the responses of the participants in the real-world legal system has been frequently criticized (Miller et al., 1977), as has the fact that laboratory subjects' behavior and decisions have no real consequences (Ebbesen and Konečni, 1980; Wilson and Donnerstein, 1977), unlike decisions made in the real world. Another frequent criticism has been that the materials presented to the subjects in the laboratory vastly oversimplify the kind and amount of information to which the participants in the real-world criminal justice system are exposed, and that the stimuli and stimulus dimensions are typically presented in decomposed rather than more wholistic form, which is typical of the real world (Ebbesen and Konečni, 1980; Gerbasi, Zuckerman, and Reis, 1977). Another frequent and obvious criticism, directed particularly at jury-simulation studies, has to do with the fact that laboratory subjects' decisions are often made in the absence of key procedural features that characterize decision-making in the criminal justice system, such as, for example, the absence of the discussion and deliberation stage in which actual juries engage, the absence of a foreman, etc. (Izzett and Leginski, 1974; Myers and Kaplan, 1976; Vidmar, 1972b). A related criticism has to do with the nature of the dependent measures that are often used in laboratory tasks (Ebbesen and Konečni, 1976; Konečni, Mulcahy, and Ebbesen, 1980). For example, laboratory juries frequently judge the extent of guilt of the defendant on a scale, whereas their real-world counterparts have to make a dichotomous decision. Similarly, laboratory jurors are frequently asked to determine the fictitious defendant's sentence, even though in many states the judge, and not the jury, does this (see

Table 5 in Bray, 1976). Moreover, laboratory jurors are forced to set prison terms for types of crimes that in the real world almost never result in a prison sentence (Ebbesen and Konečni, 1976).

If one considers the possible motivations of the researchers who do laboratory experiments in which some or all of the features criticized above are present, one is inevitably led to the conclusion that either they are not truly interested in understanding how the criminal justice system operates or they believe that a correct understanding of the functioning of the system and the behavior of the participants in it can be obtained regardless of the subjects, the consequences of the decisions, the materials and information presented to the subjects, the decision alternatives at the subjects' disposal, etc. A considerable amount of evidence suggests that the latter view is naive and untenable because subjects' decisions are generally quite *task-specific*. Since this appears to be true not just in experiments concerned with legal issues and decisions, but in many different kinds of experimental tasks, the discussion that follows is concerned with the problem of task specificity in decision-making research in general (Ebbesen and Konečni, 1980).

It is instructive to consider first the conclusions that are currently being drawn from the laboratory simulations of various types of decision-making. Humans emerge as intellectual cripples, biased by cognitive processes that interfere with rational decision-making (Dawes, 1976; Slovic, Fischhoff, and Lichtenstein, 1976). They are oversensitive to variables not included in normative models (Kahneman and Tversky, 1972) and undersensitive to variables that are (Kahneman and Tversky, 1973). They become more variable when given more information (Einhorn, 1971; Hayes, 1964) and increase their confidence in the accuracy of their judgments when they should not (Kahneman and Tversky, 1973; Slovic and Lichtenstein, 1971).

If one eliminates the derogatory tone of these conclusions, a simple statement remains suggesting that decision-makers often seem to be responsive to task characteristics that are incidental to, and not specified by, prior theoretical conceptions (Olson, 1976) and, more importantly, researchers do not know when such oversensitivities will occur. In some tasks certain variables have smaller effects than expected; in other tasks the effects are larger than expected. Put differently, there are no theories that can tell us when people will be Bayesian, when they will average, when they will add, when they will be sufficiently sensitive to characteristics of data samples, etc. It is quite unclear which features of tasks control when and which of these many different processes will have causal effects on decisions.

Given the state of affairs described above, it seems to make more sense to assume that subjects *create* decision rules and processes specific to each particular decision task than to try to develop ever more elaborate theoretical models that take into account the broad range of task-specific behaviors. If the former view is adopted, one would not be surprised to find that the substantively irrelevant aspects of a task or of a measurement procedure would have an effect on the results and that the factors, such as the features of the material presented to the subject, the consequences (or lack of them) of the decisions, the order in which the information is presented, whether or not the stimuli are presented in decomposed form, whether or not a subject knows that the material comes from a fictitious legal case, the number of times a decision is made, the response scales used, the presence versus absence of a deliberation stage, the amount of time available for making a decision, and so on, might well substantially affect subjects' decisions.

If subjects indeed create decision strategies to fit various elements of a task, how can one place any confidence in the information allegedly obtained about the legal system from the ubiquitous laboratory simulations? For example, it is not unreasonable to expect that a student jury given two or three bits of information about a case on a piece of paper may well react to these bits in quite a different way than a real jury does to information about similar issues in a trial. Trivial features, such as the number of words required to describe, say, the defendant's credibility (or levels thereof) and family history, respectively, may determine which of these will be given greater weight by the student jurors. In a real trial, information is presented over much longer periods of time, by different participants, and impressions presumably jell gradually. The presentation of some types of information (e.g., family history) may take far less time in a trial than that of others (e.g., the defendant's credibility), but the latter bit of information might be presented less explicitly than the former. Note also that presenting information in decomposed form to subjects automatically eliminates a major decision-making task that real-world jurors have to face—that of *extracting* information from the ritualistic and often incomprehensible goings-on that a typical trial involves, and of deciding how to evaluate the various bits of information.

Similarly, finding oneself in a 2 × 3 × 4 within-subjects simulated-jury experiment and making the guilty/not guilty decision 24 times in a row within 10 minutes on a 100-mm scale are clearly somewhat different from being on a jury once in a lifetime, watching a 7-day trial, and deliberating for 2 days behind closed doors with eleven complete strangers. A picture of the "defendant" appended to the sheet that gives other information about the "case" (which is how the variable of the defendant's "attractiveness" is typically manipulated in psychology/law experiments) may place too much or too little (Who knows?) emphasis on the defendant's appearance (in comparison to a real trial), but it would seem more than plausible that the subjects exposed to the information in this way would respond to it *differently* than would real jurors to a live defendant. Note that we are not arguing that the real-trial procedures are better, more rational, or more conducive to the advancement of justice than are the laboratory procedures. It is simply that the laboratory experiments are presumably attempting to simulate the real-world legal process and decisions, and not the other way around.

A few of the above criticisms lose some of their force if one believes that the real world is "additive," i.e., that factors occurring in it have only main effects and do not interact with each other. However, a more plausible view of the world is that it is highly "interactive" (Cronbach, 1975). The high frequency of findings of interactions in psychological, especially social-psychological, experiments supports this view. Sometimes the interactions are between the major factors under investigation, but as often as not they fall in the category of "context effects"—an umbrella term that subsumes the interactions between the major factors under investigation and certain aspects of the research setting, the experimental task, the particular confederate used, the time of day, and a myriad of others. Thus, it would seem that the inference that because a particular factor has a particular main effect in a laboratory experiment it would have a similar effect on the real-world decision in an entirely different setting, with different participants, is probably quite suspect. Moreover, quite apart from the "interactive-world" idea, the above criticisms are nevertheless valid from the standpoint of the "percent-of-variance-accounted" argument discussed in Chapter 1 and later in this chapter.

One could also argue that some simulations are better than others and that many of the problems mentioned can be avoided by conducting "good" simulations. However, to the extent that a simulation is trying to discover something about the operation of the real-world legal system—a goal that we heartily endorse—how can one know whether a simulation is "bad" and which of several simulations is the "best," without actually collecting the data in naturalistic settings, that is, in the real-world legal system? If one accepts the view that on logical grounds only a real-world study can validate the results of the simulation, it only makes sense to begin the research program by doing real-world studies (especially in a young and largely unmapped discipline), and that in situations where there are limited funds, time, and manpower—frequently encountered in the social sciences—the choice as to which type of study to do is obvious.

What should one do in situations where real-world research cannot be carried out? For example, many aspects of the legal system are confidential. It is impossible for researchers to be present during jury deliberations, and it is extremely difficult to obtain access to files containing information that leads to certain decisions (e.g., the prosecutor's files). Many would probably think that simulation research in these cases is fully justified even if all of our criticisms are correct. A more cautious point of view, and one that we favor, is that erroneous information obtained by scientific methods (and therefore having an aura of truth) is more harmful than no information at all, especially when issues as sensitive as legal ones are being dealt with and when people's futures are quite literally at stake.

An important argument against the point of view espoused here should be considered next. Much of the evidence against the use of laboratory simulations comes from real-world studies based largely on *correlational* data. Therefore, it could be argued that the discrepancies between laboratory and real-world studies are due to the inability to tease apart real from spurious causal relationships in the real-world data (Phelps and Shanteau, 1978). However, it could be reasonably maintained that *all* decision models, whether based on data from simulations or on observations of real-world events are, in fact, only *paramorphic representations* (Hoffman, 1960) of the *actual* decision processes of the subject (whether the subject is a judge or a sophomore in an experimental situation). Models merely *simulate,* i.e., are correlated with, the input–output relationships that are observed (Payne, Braunstein, and Carroll, 1978).

In addition, experiments do not eliminate the possibility that causal relationships other than those proposed as explanations may be producing the results. The fact that randomization generally breaks the correlation between one variable and all prior variables has no implications for the correlations between that one variable and all *following* variables. A manipulation might create many mediating variables and processes each of which, individually or in combination with others, might play a causal role in a final decision (Costner, 1971). Because these mediating processes might be correlated with each other, one winds up in a similar position to the researcher dealing with real-world correlational data. The best one can hope is that the models one develops will describe and predict patterns in the data.

Finally, it should be pointed out that various statistical techniques for estimating causality from correlational data—such as path analysis and other types of causal analysis—are being continuously refined and made increasingly sophisticated (Blalock, 1971; Heise, 1975; Mayer and Arney, 1974).

We realize that some of our remarks may lead to the accusation that we are preaching scientific nihilism. After all, if laboratory tasks create specific decision processes rather than tap some basic ones, then why not assume that real-world tasks also create just as task-specific decision strategies? We agree with the latter point, but disagree that nihilism is the consequence. It seems to us that in the area of legal decision-making, as well as in many other types of decision-making, the really important truths are to be found in the real world rather than in laboratory simulations, no matter how high the *face* validity of the latter might be. We would prefer to base our conjectures about how people make various types of decisions on observations of actual people making actual decisions. Moreover, even if real-world judges' decision strategies do change when certain features of their real-world legal task change—for example, because of administrative or legal modifications—such changes merely reflect the reality of decision-making in actual courts. Quite another matter are changes in decision strategies that are brought about by scientists' often arbitrary decisions to change this or that feature of the laboratory task. Such changes typically have no substantive, let alone practical, importance or relevance, and their effects on subjects' decision strategies are therefore of minimal interest.

In addition, we are not arguing that laboratory simulations should be abandoned altogether. There are conditions in which they might serve as useful tools in teasing apart further questions about the real-world process. However, rather than assume that the simulations are good, one ought to collect sufficient evidence to test whether the constructed tasks have captured the necessary detail of the real world to be *real* simulations.

Because of the various considerations described above, we have, in our own work, always collected data from actual cases and from the real-world participants in the criminal justice system. In many projects, we have also conducted simulations, and it was in part the discrepancies between simulation and *in situ* studies (which will be discussed in detail in our chapters on bail setting and sentencing) that led to our skepticism about the utility of laboratory simulations for studying the legal system and to our decision, in editing this book, to give precedence to researchers who have obtained data in real-world legal settings.

THE CHOICE OF METHODOLOGY
IN NATURALISTIC SETTINGS

The decision to collect data from the participants and/or in settings within the criminal justice system by no means resolves all problems regarding generalizability and external validity. For example, the decision to go to judges' chambers and conduct interviews about the factors that affect their sentencing decisions may lead to conclusions about the causes of sentencing that are quite incorrect. The judges may deliberately try to mislead the interviewer for self-presentation or political reasons, or may be quite unaware of the factors that they are actually taking into account in sentencing. Similarly, sitting at the probation/sentencing hearing and meticulously coding the goings-on, as well as the sentence that is imposed, may lead to similarly erroneous conclusions, because the information that best predicts judges' behavior may be contained elsewhere (such as in the probation report) and never surface in the hearing itself. Thus, neither the decision to deal with the actual participants in the legal system nor the decision to collect data in the actual settings guarantees to any extent that the findings will lead to the discovery of the real causes of a participant's behavior and therefore have external validity.

In attempting to cope with these problems in our own research, we have been guided by several considerations. One of the steps we took in almost all of our projects in both the criminal and the civil areas of legal decision-making (e.g., on bail setting, sentencing, police decision-making, prosecutorial decisions, personal-jury and child-support decisions), many of which are not reported in this book, was to use more than one research method, thus generally following the Campbellian tradition (Campbell and Stanley, 1966; Webb et al., 1966). When using a multimethod approach, one's confidence in a conclusion to which all of the various methods lead is, of course, much greater than if only one method had been used. Unfortunately, in our work, the results from the multiple methods have seldom led to a single, common conclusion. When this happens in other areas of research, there is a deadlock that cannot typically be resolved by applying a priori and logical criteria. However, we believe that when one studies an intact, functioning social network—such as the criminal justice system—there are certain logical and practical criteria that would lead one to trust the conclusions reached by one method over those reached by another on a priori grounds, with the important proviso that the researcher is interested in how the system actually operates, rather than in the phenomenology of the participants.

Let us suppose that a particular legal decision has been examined in a variety of ways including:

1. An elaborate interview with the participant making the decision.

2. A lengthy questionnaire that the participant fills out.

3. The observation and coding of the public hearing (using the customary time-sampling observational techniques that code the behavior, appearance, and other characteristics of all the

participants present; the order in which, and to whom, they speak; the issues that are brought up in the hearing, and by whom; etc.) at which (and, ostensibly, as a function of which) the relevant decision has been made.

4. An archival analysis, i.e., coding of at least two kinds of written materials (to the extent that they exist): the transcript of the hearing and the file containing a variety of documents pertaining to the case that is available to the key decision-maker.

In this situation, if the various methods were to lead one to different conclusions, we would be inclined to trust the archival analysis of the documents available to the decision-maker more than any other method, provided that this analysis had most of the following characteristics:

1. The coding categories used are similar to those used by the participants in the real-world system, rather than derived from the currently popular social-psychological theories. This typically means that the coding categories will be concrete and low-level, as opposed to abstract and high-level. An example would be the coding of a category "prior record" in terms of the actual number of prior felony convictions, rather than coding "consistency of prior criminal behavior" (a more abstract concept derived from attribution theory) on a 5-point scale. Such a procedure makes the coding more reliable and also facilitates the communication of the research findings to the participants in the legal system—if one's goal includes producing change in the system. Moreover, having done the initial coding in terms of very concrete, low-level categories, one can always subsequently collapse across these categories (or levels within a category) to achieve a more abstract classification.

2. Coding is as exhaustive as possible, covering as much information in the written materials in the file as possible, so that initially a very large number of predictors (i.e., coding categories) is isolated. This step, of course, minimizes the likelihood that an important predictor will be omitted from the analysis.

3. The statistical analyses examine the effects on the criterion decision of various combinations of predictors, with a relatively large number of predictors in each "predictive set," so that both main effects and interactions can be captured.

4. Prior to archival analyses, a sufficient amount of background research had been done by the investigators concerning the actual, routine, day-to-day operation of the system so as to leave

no doubt that the file being coded is, in fact, at the disposal of the decision-maker prior to the time when the decision is being made. Note that whereas it is important to demonstrate that the decision-makers *could* have seen a particular bit of information in the file, it is not necessary to demonstrate that they have actually done so, especially for every case. It may well be that the bits of information that are being coded are correlated with other bits of information at either the same or a higher level of abstractness and that the decision-makers are actually attending to these other bits of information as they examine the file. This, however, in no way precludes that the *coded* categories are treated as "true predictors." (In fact, one could argue that even if the decision-makers do not see a file, a predictor isolated from the file that accounts for a very large percent of the variance in the decisions could be considered a "true cause.")

Given that such precautions have been taken, we would trust the conclusions based on the archival methodology more than those based on other methods for a number of related reasons. First, the use of both the interview and the questionnaire for studying decision-making in the legal system is highly suspect because the participants in the system (especially judges, assistant district attorneys, police officers, parole officers, and probation officers) may well subjectively believe—in line with their deeply ingrained view that "every case is complex and unique"—that they are responding to various multifaceted and complex aspects of the case and combining these many bits of information in a complex, configural manner (amply aided by their judicial training, experience, skill, and wisdom), when in fact they may be responding to very few bits of information, combined in a simple manner. Thus, whereas the content of the decision-maker's minds as they are pondering the decisions—at least as revealed by interviews and questionnaires—may be highly complex, very few mundane and simple predictors may account for a large percent of the variance in the output decisions. In fact, because of what may be called "judicial evaluation apprehension," the interview and the questionnaire may be poor methods *even* when one is interested in the phenomenology of these decision-makers (rather than in factors that actually predict their decisions). To take a hypothetical and extreme example, racist judges may well *want* to systematically give harsher sentences to defendants of a certain race, and also be *under the impression* that race is one of the major factors in their sentencing decisions; yet they would be very unlikely to admit this in an interview or a questionnaire. The final twist would come when one found out, upon examining 300 cases in which a racist judge had passed sentence, that other factors, say, prior record and severity of the crime, accounted for 96% of the variance, whereas race accounted for less than 1% (even if the direction were "predicted" by the judge). In other words, the questionnaire and interview responses may not reflect what judges think or intend; moreover, even if they do, neither the judges' private responses (intentions and thoughts) nor the public ones (questionnaire and interview responses) may affect what they actually do!

Second, coding archival materials has an advantage over observing and coding hearings in that:

1. More predictors are typically available in written materials.

2. The nature of the two research situations is such that greater coding reliability can be obtained in the archival case (because of time and other pressures in observational research).

3. Archival research is less obtrusive (although this does not necessarily always have to be the case).

4. When one examines the system as a whole, it is clear that written materials accompany a defendant through the system; therefore, the predictor of a particular decision that is discovered in the written materials is also more likely to be the predictor of many subsequent decisions by other participants in the system, by virtue of the same piece of paper (such as the "rap sheet," the prior record of the defendant) being a part of the case at almost every node in the system.

Third, perhaps the greatest value of the archival approach is that when archival materials are a routine part of the procedure, they are typically very detailed and contain a large number of bits of information. For example, a probation report contains many types of information about the defendant's history that will never emerge in any kind of hearing or trial, in addition to most of the information that is available from hearings (e.g., the defendant's sex, age, and other demographic characteristics).

Finally, a potentially considerable benefit of archival materials is that certain predictors that can be isolated from the files temporally precede the location of other predictors in the causal chain. Occasionally, this means that the best predictor of a particular legal decision may be a factor available in the files (and thus one that can be discovered by both researchers and participants in the system) even before the offense—about which the various decisions in question are subsequently made—is even committed! For example, in a study of the processing of mentally disordered sex offenders (MDSOs) in California (Konečni, Mulcahy, and Ebbesen, 1980), we found that the convicted offender's prior sex-related criminal record almost inevitably led the court-appointed psychiatrists to diagnose and classify the offender as "sexually deviant" and an MDSO, respectively, which, in turn, resulted almost automatically in the judge's verdict that the defendant be sent to a mental hospital (rather than be remanded to the trial court for sentencing). In other words, the offender's prior sex-related criminal record is an excellent predictor of both the final and the intermediate decisions, and this information is known even before the offense under consideration has been committed. The psychiatric diagnosis and classification, and the judge's verdict, may be correlated with many other predictors, but the simplicity and temporal primacy of the prior sex-related criminal record forces other predictors into the role of epiphenomena. For example, differences in the content of probationary reports and psychiatrists' letters can be considered as merely serving to justify an already formed conclusion based on the prior sex-related criminal record, in order to give the appearance of complexity to the processing of MDSOs and to smooth out the rough edges of the causal sequence.

Although this particular example may be somewhat extreme, the fact remains that the archival method has several apparent advantages over other methods, not the least of which is that the meticulous coding of the defendant's file may yield factors capable of predicting the outcome of a case very early in the process.

THE CHOICE OF RESEARCH PROBLEMS

The choice of research problems clearly depends on many considerations, among the most important of which are theoretical and methodological concerns. The message we tried to convey in the previous chapter on theoretical issues and in the present one on methodological issues can be summarized as follows:

1. In a young and largely unmapped discipline, such as legal psychology, it makes sense first to pay attention to understanding, at least in general terms, the operation of the system that is the bread and butter of the discipline, namely, the legal system, rather than worry in these initial stages about issues and problems imported from other disciplines.

2. In situ research, especially of the archival variety, seems to be superior to other approaches when the primary goal is to un-

derstand the operation of an intact, functioning social system that one cannot experiment with at will.

3. Given limited resources and time, the potential pressures from the impatient public and legislatures, and a need for well-documented, data-based change, the particular decisions made by participants in the criminal justice system that should be especially attractive for research seem to be those that account for the *greatest percent of variance in the processing of cases through the system as a whole.*

In fact, one could argue that the first two points reduce to the third and that percent of variance accounted for is the key factor in our analysis of the sort of research problems one might choose. After all, the decision to try to understand the functioning legal system (as opposed to, for example, the development of norms and moral judgment in preschool children) clearly has a bearing on the amount of variance in the output of the legal system that one is going to understand. Similarly, certain methods and approaches may be better than others in *correctly* identifying the predictors of certain decisions and thus contributing to the percent of variance explained.

The percent-of-variance argument (also discussed in Chapter 1) and its relationship to the choice of research problems can perhaps best be illustrated by reference to some data concerning real-world legal decisions. Figure 2.1 presents the data for the processing of criminal cases in San Diego County, California, for the years 1976 and 1977. Several things should be noted about this figure. First, the general pattern of the data for San Diego County is quite similar to the federal data presented in Figure 1.1 and the California state data in Figure 1.2. Second, the figure shows that for a full 63% of all felony arrests, a felony complaint is not filed. Third, of the 19% convicted of a felony, 78% were convicted because of a guilty plea, whereas only 6% had a jury trial. Finally, of all the felony arrests in San Diego County in 1976–1977, only 1.2% had a jury trial.

Many other statistics could be extracted from Figure 2.1 that challenge both the popular view of the operation of the criminal justice system (myths perpetuated both by the entertainment industry, through the Perry Mason types, and by the news media, through their selective coverage that focuses on sensationalist or unusual cases) and the wisdom of the overall research effort in legal psychology, where a very high percentage of studies is devoted to decisions (such as jury verdicts) that occur extremely rarely and thus account for a very small proportion of the total variance in the processing of criminal cases.

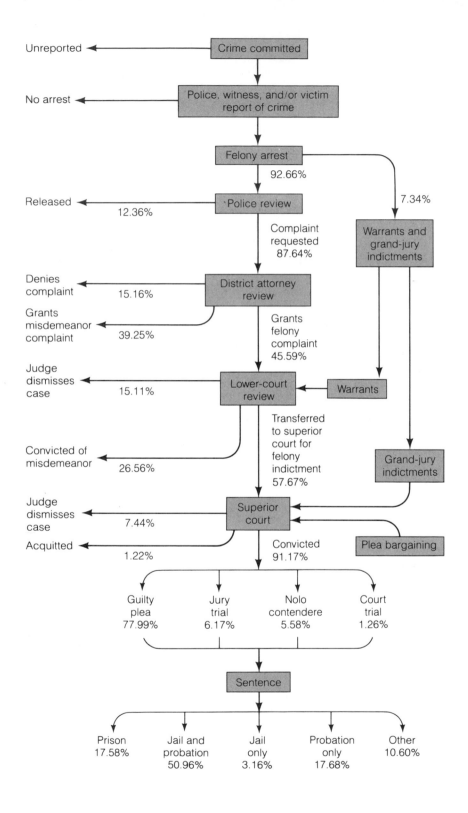

Figure 2.1
Case-processing data for 1976 and 1977 in San Diego County, California. Approximately 24,000 adult felony arrests were made during this two-year interval. The percentages show how these cases were disposed of at each decision node.

In a sense, Figure 2.1 essentially maps out both the system and the problems to be studied in that it identifies the key decision points. These could be viewed as the major "bifurcation points" regarding whether or not a case remains in the system or drops out. A simple rule of thumb would be that the closer a node is to a 50/50 split (that is, 50% of cases being passed on to the next node in the felony-processing system, and 50% exiting the system either altogether or with charges reduced to a misdemeanor). the more important that decision is and the more intensely it should be studied—if one's goal is to understand the operation of the system.

On the basis of these considerations, it would seem to us that there is a real need to spread research efforts more evenly throughout the system and away from certain heavily "overpopulated" nodes (such as jury research); this is simultaneously one of the major purposes of this book.

References

Bermant, G., McGuire, M., McKinley, W., & Salo, C. The logic of simulation in jury research. *Criminal Justice and Behavior*, 1974, *1*, 224–233.

Blalock, H. M., Jr. (Ed.). *Causal models in the social sciences*. Chicago: Aldine-Atherton, 1971.

Bray, R. M. The mock trial: Problems and prospects for jury research. Paper presented at 84th Annual Convention of American Psychological Association, Washington, DC, 1976.

Buckhout, R. Eyewitness testimony. *Scientific American*, 1974, *231* (6), 23–31.

Buckhout, R., Alper, A., Chern, S., Silverberg, G., & Slomovits, M. Determinants of eyewitness performance on a lineup. *Bulletin of the Psychonomic Society*, 1974, *4*, 191–192.

Campbell, D. T., & Stanley, J. C. *Experimental and quasi-experimental designs for research*. Chicago: Rand McNally, 1966.

Costner, H. L. Utilizing causal models to discover flaws in experiments. *Sociometry*, 1971, *34*, 398–410.

Cronbach, L. J. Beyond the two disciplines of scientific psychology. *American Psychologist*, 1975, *30*, 116–127.

Davis, J. H., Bray, R. M., & Holt, R. W. The empirical study of decision processes in juries: A critical review. In J. L. Tapp & S. J. Levine (Eds.), *Law, justice, and the individual in society: Psychological and legal issues.* New York: Holt, Rinehart and Winston, 1977.

Dawes, R. M. Shallow psychology. In J. S. Carroll & J. W. Payne (Eds.), *Cognition and social behavior.* Hillsdale, NJ: Lawrence Erlbaum, 1976.

Doob, A. N. Evidence, procedure, and psychological research. In G. Bermant, C. Nemeth, & N. Vidmar (Eds.), *Psychology and the law.* Lexington, MA: Heath, 1976.

Doob, A. N., & Kirshenbaum, H. M. Bias in police lineups—Partial remembering. *Journal of Police Science and Administration,* 1973, *1,* 287–293.

Ebbesen, E. B., & Konečni, V. J. Fairness in sentencing: Severity of crime and judicial decision making. Paper presented at 84th Annual Convention of American Psychological Association, Washington, DC, 1976.

Ebbesen, E. B., & Konečni, V. J. On the external validity of decision-making research: What do we know about decisions in the real world? In T. S. Wallsten (Ed.), *Cognitive processes in choice and decision behavior.* Hillsdale, N.J.: Lawrence Erlbaum, 1980.

Efran, M. G. The effect of physical appearance on the judgment of guilt, interpersonal attraction, and severity of recommended punishment in a simulated jury task. *Journal of Research in Personality,* 1974, *8,* 45–54.

Egan, D., Pittner, M., & Goldstein, A. B. Eyewitness identification: Photographs versus live models. *Law and Human Behavior,* 1977, *1,* 199–206.

Einhorn, H. J. The use of nonlinear, noncompensatory models as a function of task and amount of information. *Organizational Behavior and Human Performance,* 1971, *6,* 1–27.

Farmer, L. C., Williams, G. R., Lee, R. E., Cundick, B. P., Howell, R. J., & Rooker, C. K. Juror perceptions of trial testimony as a function of the method of presentation. In G. Bermant, C. Nemeth, & N. Vidmar (Eds.), *Psychology and the law.* Lexington, MA: Heath, 1976.

Gerbasi, K. C., Zuckerman, M., & Reis, H. T. Justice needs a new blindfold: A review of mock jury research. *Psychological Bulletin,* 1977, *84,* 323–345.

Hayes, J. R. Human data processing limits in decision-making. In E. Bennett (Ed.), *Information systems, science and engineering. Proceedings of the First International Congress on the Information Systems Sciences.* New York: McGraw-Hill, 1964.

Heise, D. R. *Causal analysis.* New York: Wiley, 1975.

Hoffman, P. J. The paramorphic representation of clinical judgment. *Psychological Bulletin,* 1960, *57,* 116–131.

Izzett, R., & Leginski, W. Group discussion and the influence of defendant characteristics in a simulated jury setting. *Journal of Social Psychology,* 1974, *93,* 271–279.

Kahneman, D., & Tversky, A. Subjective probability: A judgment of representativeness. *Cognitive Psychology,* 1972, *3,* 430–454.

Kahneman, D., & Tversky, A. On the psychology of prediction. *Psychological Review,* 1973, *80,* 237–251.

Kalven, H., Jr., & Zeisel, H. *The American jury.* Boston: Little, Brown, 1966.

Kerr, N. L., Atkin, R., Stasser, G., Meek, D., Holt, R., & Davis, J. H. Guilt beyond a reasonable doubt: Effects of concept definition and assigned decision rule on the judgments of mock jurors. *Journal of Personality and Social Psychology,* 1976, *34,* 282–294.

Konečni, V. J., Mulcahy, E. M., & Ebbesen, E. B. Prison or mental hospital: Factors affecting the processing of persons suspected of being "mentally disordered sex offenders." In P. D. Lipsitt & B. D. Sales (Eds.), New directions in psycholegal research. New York: Van Nostrand Reinhold, 1980.

Landy, D., & Aronson, E. The influence of the character of the criminal and his victim on the decisions of simulated jurors. *Journal of Experimental Social Psychology*, 1969, *5*, 141–152.

Lawson, R. G. Experimental research on the organization of persuasive arguments: An application to courtroom communications. *Law and the Social Order*, 1970, 597–608.

Levine, F. J., & Tapp, J. L. The psychology of criminal identification: The gap from Wade to Kirby. *University of Pennsylvania Law Review*, 1973, *121*, 1079–1131.

Loftus, E. F. Leading questions and the eyewitness report. *Cognitive Psychology*, 1975, *7*, 560–572.

Loftus, E. F., Altman, D., and Geballe, R. Effects of questioning upon a witness's later recollection. *Journal of Police Science and Administration*, 1975, *3*, 162–165.

Mayer, T. F., & Arney, W. R. Spectral analysis and the study of social change. In H. L. Costner (Ed.), *Sociological methodology: 1973–1974*. San Francisco: Jossey-Bass, 1974.

Miller, G. R., Fontes, N. E., Boster, F., & Sunnafrank, M. Methodological issues in jury research: What can a simulation tell us? Paper presented at 85th Annual Convention of American Psychological Association, San Francisco, 1977.

Mitchell, H. E., & Byrne, D. The defendant's dilemma: Effects of jurors' attitudes and authoritarianism on judicial decisions. *Journal of Personality and Social Psychology*, 1973, *25*, 123–129.

Myers, D. G., & Kaplan, M. F. Group-induced polarization in simulated juries. *Personality and Social Psychology Bulletin*, 1976, *2*, 63–66.

Nemeth, C., & Sosis, R. H. A simulated jury study: Characteristics of the defendant and the jurors. *Journal of Social Psychology*, 1973, *90*, 221–229.

Olson, C. L. Some apparent violations of the representativeness heuristic in human judgment. *Journal of Experimental Psychology: Human Perception and Performance*, 1976, *2*, 599–608.

Payne, J. W., Braunstein, M. L., & Carroll, J. S. Exploring predecisional behavior: An alternative approach to decision research. *Organizational Behavior and Human Performance*, 1978, *22*, 17–44.

Phelps, R. H., & Shanteau, J. Livestock judges: How much information can an expert use? *Organizational Behavior and Human Performance*, 1978, *21*, 209–219.

Sigall, H., & Ostrove, N. Beautiful but dangerous: Effects of offender attractiveness and nature of the crime on juridic judgment. *Journal of Personality and Social Psychology*, 1975, *31*, 410–414.

Slovic, P., Fischhoff, B., & Lichtenstein, S. Cognitive processes and societal risk taking. In J. S. Carroll & J. W. Payne (Eds.), *Cognition and social behavior*. Hillsdale, NJ: Lawrence Erlbaum, 1976.

Slovic, P., & Lichtenstein, S. Comparison of Bayesian and regression approaches to the study of information processing in judgment. *Organizational Behavior and Human Performance*, 1971, *6*, 649–744.

Tapp, J. L. Psychology and the law: An overture. *Annual Review of Psychology*, 1976, *27*, 359–404.

Thibaut, J., & Walker, L. *Procedural justice: A psychological analysis*. Hillsdale, NJ: Lawrence Erlbaum, 1975.

Vidmar, N. Effects of decision alternatives on the verdicts and social perceptions of simulated jurors. *Journal of Personality and Social Psychology*, 1972, *22*, 211–218. (a)

Vidmar, N. Group-induced shifts in simulated jury decisions. Unpublished manuscript, University of Western Ontario, 1972. (b)

Walker, L., LaTour, S., Lind, E. A., & Thibaut, J. Reactions of participants and observers to modes of adjudication. *Journal of Applied Social Psychology*, 1974, *4*, 295–310.

Webb, E. J., Campbell, D. T., Schwartz, R. D., & Sechrest, L. *Unobtrusive measures: Nonreacting research in the social sciences.* Chicago: Rand McNally, 1966.

Wilson, D. W., & Donnerstein, E. Guilty or not guilty? A look at the simulated jury paradigm. *Journal of Applied Social Psychology*, 1977, *7*, 175–190.

THE DECISION TO COMMIT
THE CRIME

Editors' Introduction

Social norms and definitions of criminal activity have differed vastly from one historical period to another, and from one locale or culture to another. Regardless of the particular set of norms governing human behavior in a particular culture at a particular time, and the specific definitions of what deviations from the norms are to be considered criminal or at least require socially controlled sanctions, there have apparently always been individuals willing to violate the norms and engage in criminal behavior. The criminal justice system, as we know it, is the current version of the institutionalized efforts to control such behavior. Thus, it is only fitting that the next chapter examine the factors that might influence the offender's decision of whether or not to commit a crime. Not only is it important to understand this decision because it controls the entry of individuals into the rest of the system, but much of the effort of the remainder of the participants in the criminal justice system (ranging from police officers to juries to sentencing judges to scholars whose study of concepts like deterrence influence the sentencing process) can be conceptualized as a more or less concerted effort to make the potential offender's decision a negative one.

This chapter begins by reviewing views of the distinction between criminal and noncriminal behavior and the views formulated in several disciplines (including psychology and economics) about the causes of criminal behavior, the concept of deterrence, and related issues. The chapter then provides a useful critique of the use of aggregate statistics on which have been based the majority of the more empirical efforts to understand criminal behavior and investigate the deterrence hypothesis. Individual-statistics approaches are reviewed next, and much of the remainder of the chapter is devoted to Carroll's own work, using the individual-statistics approach, to investigate people's evaluation of crime opportunities.

Carroll's research involved an experimental simulation using both juvenile and adult research participants, some of whom were prior offenders. Carroll fully recognizes the problems of simulation research (many of which are discussed in detail throughout this volume), and it is easy to agree with his assessment that the preferable on-the-spot research of decisions concerning the commission or noncommission of actual crimes is extremely difficult for ethical, legal, and practical reasons (although Carroll's most recent research efforts have attempted to overcome these obstacles by studying shoplifting in naturalistic settings). In addition to using both offenders and nonoffenders as subjects, Carroll makes a serious effort to improve the accuracy of the interpretations of the results of his simulation by comparing the levels of the factors used in the simulation to the prevailing levels of the same factors in the real world (although the factors that Carroll studies are, of course, only a small set of the many that the would-be and would-not-be criminals probably evaluate when considering various crime opportunities). Reservations about simulation research aside, Carroll's work provides interesting information about the factors that may affect the evaluation of crime opportunities. In addition, Carroll's findings that people often respond to only one factor in making such evaluations and that different people appear to respond to different single factors (if borne out by real-world data) suggest that law-enforcement and other measures aimed at increasing deterrence are likely to be ineffective for large segments of the population at risk simply because most measures involve changes in only one factor, e.g., increasing the length of the prison sentence or increasing the likelihood of obtaining a prison sentence.

3

Committing a Crime:
The Offender's Decision

John S. Carroll

A car, door unlocked, keys in the ignition; a 15-year-old thinking it over. A woman carrying a big handbag; a counter full of goods at a busy department store. A junkie, desperately searching for something to turn into cash, and then into a fix. Friday evening, and the cash register in the liquor store must have twice what it had on Thursday. A college professor wondering how much to tell the IRS she spent on professional books last year. An automotive executive looking over a report showing that there is a potentially hazardous design problem in the 1981 model; a recall would really hurt financially.

These are the moments when a person decides whether or not to commit a crime, or selects a target, a moment, and a method. This is the first behavior of direct relevance to the functioning of the criminal justice system: the decision to commit a crime. Victims, police, prosecutors, judges, juries, and parole boards may later deliberate about the offender, but it is the offender's decision that propels this sequence of events. The purpose of this chapter is to examine the offender's decision.

CRIMINAL AND NONCRIMINAL BEHAVIOR

We generally think of any act that breaks a law as a crime. Yet the crime itself is often one episode in a sequence of behaviors that may include "casing" or examining potential crime opportunities, purchasing equipment that will be used in the crime, disposing of gains, eliminating evidence, and so forth. Many of these behaviors are not in themselves crimes (e.g., buying a screwdriver), but they are part of a structured set of acts that we can call criminal behavior.

Criminal behavior sometimes includes considerable preparation; at other times crime may be an opportunistic act. This chapter most directly addresses criminal behavior that at some point includes an awareness of some potential consequences of the crime and a conceptualization of crime as a goal. In short, offenders have some control over their acts. By contrast, crimes are sometimes spontaneous acts of the moment (crimes of passion or pathological acts) in which the offenders did not conceptualize the crime as a goal and could not really control their behavior. Only a small amount of criminal behavior falls into this latter category. Ramsey Clark (1971) conjectures that "seven out of eight known serious crimes involve property . . . their main purpose is to obtain money or property" (p. 39).

This chapter will examine aspects of criminal behavior involved in how crimes are conceptualized, how goals are established and realized, and how choices are made. I will not present a theory of what causes criminal behavior; such a task would be little different from constructing a general theory of behavior. It should be noted that virtually every theory of behavior has been applied as a theory of criminal behavior: psychoanalytic, learning, biological, personality, sociological, economic, and so forth (Megargee, 1975; Schrag, 1971).

Criminals and noncriminals

It is very tempting and historically common in criminology to make the *category error* of attributing criminal behavior to criminal people (Shaver, 1975). In short, crimes are acts criminals do; noncriminals do not commit crimes. In this manner the study of criminal behavior becomes the study of criminals. This is indeed the response of most middle-class people to crime: crime is outside, identified with criminal types who must be punished, isolated, or corrected. For this reason, the upstanding citizen who commits a crime is an ambiguous and dissonant event—this person is *not* a criminal and yet *did* a crime. Reactions to white-collar crime demonstrate the public's reluctance to associate a crime with a person who is not a "criminal" (Sutherland, 1949).

Research has shown that most people have exhibited criminal behavior sometime during their lives. The vast majority of us do violate the law. The President's Commission on Law Enforcement and the Administration of Justice (1967) reported that more than 90% of a sample of 1,690 adults *admitted* committing one or more acts for which they might have received a jail or prison sentence. Theft by employees, tax fraud, shoplifting, vandalism, smuggling small items, personal alcohol and drug use represent millions of criminal acts and billions of dollars in social costs. Many of these crimes are undetected, and/or considered normal business or personal conduct. However, the fact remains that criminal behavior is a feature of "good citizens" as well as of "criminals." We could each be arrested and convicted were our conduct fully known. Labeling theory is based on the premise that the powerful (rich, high status, politically influential) get away with crime while the powerless are prosecuted and stigmatized (Becker, 1963).

Types of criminal behaviors

Because criminal behavior is not a unitary phenomenon, it is often useful to think of different kinds of criminal behavior, and different kinds of criminals. For example, Clinard and Quinney (1973) postulated nine criminal behavior systems:

1. Violent criminal behavior involving persons, including murder, assault, and rape. These crimes are typically committed for personal reasons.

2. Occasional criminal behavior involving property. These offenders share the values of society despite occasional property violations.

3. Conventional criminal behavior. Offenders often have early careers in crime and exposure to groups whose norms support theft for gain. There is at least a partial commitment to criminal behavior as a way of life.

4. Professional criminal behavior. Highly specialized offenses requiring technical skills and often accomplices. Motivated by economic gain, offenders associate mainly with other professional criminals and have high status among criminals.

5. Public-order criminal behavior. Mostly victimless crimes in which offenders do not consider themselves as criminals and are often part of a deviant subculture.

6. Political criminal behavior. Crimes against and by the government. Offenders do not think of themselves as criminal and are often strongly supported by others.

7. Occupational criminal behavior. Consumer fraud, embezzlement, professional malpractice, and other crimes often considered normal business practice.

8. Corporate criminal behavior. Violations of laws regarding mergers, safe products, advertising, and so forth. Offenders are often high-status individuals and regard the offenses as necessary for business, a view supported by others in business.

9. Organized criminal behavior. Organized groups of people committed to crime as a means of acquiring money, usually in rackets like gambling, prostitution, and drugs.

It should be clear from this typology that criminal behavior can be the result of many different processes. Typological theories attempt to classify offenders by which process is generally regnant (Megargee, 1975, reviews several typologies). Other theories of criminal behavior seem to focus on single aspects such as the offender's personality, the social history of the offender, the society, or the criminal justice system. Theories can themselves be placed in typologies (Carroll and Payne, 1977; Schrag, 1971).

Rather than attempt to devise a new theory of criminal behavior or to integrate all the traditional theories, this chapter will focus on one issue that encompasses both a response of the criminal justice system to criminal behavior *and* a response of potential criminals to the acts of the criminal justice system: deterrence. In this manner we will focus on a smaller domain of criminal behavior and relate our ideas more closely to current policy debate.

DETERRENCE AND THE EVALUATION OF CRIME OPPORTUNITIES

The deterrence hypothesis proposes that an increase in the certainty or severity of punishment for crime reduces the incidence of crime. This hypothesis has a great deal of intuitive support. After all, we slow down on the highway when police are evident. Everyone tries to avoid punishment, don't they? Yet, efforts to demonstrate a deterrent effect on crime have not yielded strong support. Perhaps the most thorough examination of the literature on deterrence concluded:

> We cannot yet assert that the evidence warrants an affirmative conclusion regarding deterrence. We believe scientific caution must be exercised in interpreting the limited validity of the available evidence and the number of competing explanations for the results. Our reluctance to draw stronger conclusions does not imply support for a position that deterrence does not exist, since the evidence certainly favors a proposition supporting deterrence more than it favors one asserting that

deterrence is absent. The major challenge for future research is to estimate the magnitude of the effects of different sanctions on various
crime types, an issue on which none of the evidence available thus
far provides very useful guidance. (Blumstein, Cohen, and Nagin,
1978, p. 7)

A selected review of the deterrence literature follows, organized in
a manner that foreshadows our theoretical and methodological
approach.

Aggregate data

Most research investigating the deterrence hypothesis has relied on
statistics that aggregate across large numbers of offenders and offenses. Certainty of punishment has been operationalized as clearance
rate (the proportion of offenses of a given type known to the police
that led to an arrest) or more simply as arrest or conviction rates (the
number of arrests or convictions for a given offense type divided by
the known number of offenses of that type). Severity of punishment
has been operationalized as the mean time served for a given offense
type, or the mean sentence, or the maximum penalty established in
the criminal codes. Frequency of crime usually has been operationalized as the number of crimes of a given type known to the police.

These aggregate data are used to examine the relationships of certainty and severity of punishment to crime rate across time and/or
jurisdiction. Both economists and sociologists have used these data,
yet have drawn different conclusions. As stated by Palmer:

Although there is a danger of oversimplification, it is probably safe to
say that many economists have concluded that an increase in the expected punishment does reduce crime, while many sociologists have
concluded such an increase does not deter crime or has too small an
effect to be considered a useful instrument of social policy. Therefore,
to some extent the debate about the deterrence hypothesis is a debate
between disciplines. (Palmer, 1977, p. 9)

Economics   Economists concerned with deterrence have generally
conceptualized criminal behavior as a rational choice aimed at receiving maximum pleasure for minimum pain. In short, a criminal
can get more from criminal than noncriminal pursuits, and therefore
crime is a rational choice (i.e., crime pays). More formally, economists have assumed that people evaluate the expected utility *(EU)* of
criminal and noncriminal opportunities, and select the alternative
with the highest utility (Becker, 1968). Expected utility is defined as

expected gains less expected losses. Expected gains are computed by multiplying the value of a desired outcome by its probability of occurrence, and expected losses are computed similarly. In simplified form, the *EU* of a particular crime opportunity might be considered as

$$EU = p(S) \times G - p(F) \times L$$

where $p(S)$ is the probability of succeeding at the crime, G is the gain to be achieved (e.g., money), $p(F)$ is the probability of failing at the crime, and L is the loss if failure occurs (e.g., a prison sentence).

Sociology   Sociologists have generally been concerned with the root causes of crime in the prior socioeconomic history of offenders and their environment (e.g., Cloward and Ohlin, 1960; Reckless, 1961). Sociologists have also been advocates of rehabilitative and social-action approaches to the crime problem, rather than deterrence. Sociological research employing aggregate data has used simpler analytic models and generally found an effect for certainty of punishment but not for severity of punishment (Zimring and Hawkins, 1973). An interesting variant on this result is the work of Tittle and Rowe (1974), which suggests that probability of capture may have a deterrent effect only above a "critical level for a tipping effect," which they estimate as 30% chance of arrest.

Problems with aggregate data   The validity of aggregate data can be challenged on several grounds. First, the assumption that sanctions affect crime rates but that crime rates do not affect sanctions is questionable (Blumstein, Cohen, and Nagin, 1978). Increasing crime rates could produce harsher penalties and more police to combat crime. Increasing crowding in prisons as a result of higher crime rates could lead judges to reduce sentences. Some unmeasured cause could produce both higher crime rates and lesser penalties, such as high proportions of juveniles in the population. Or, jurisdictions may differ in the availability of criminal and noncriminal opportunities in a way that is confounded with crime rates and sanctions.

Second, crime rates are a very poor estimate of crimes committed. Victimization studies have shown that only about half of crime is reported, with underreporting varying greatly by crime and locale (Hindelang, et al., 1977, p. 358; see also Chapter 4, this volume). Crime waves can be created or eliminated by changes in the public's willingness to report crime or by changes in the way the police record crime. This error can introduce a spurious relationship between crime and risk of punishment. Those jurisdictions that underreport crimes will have lower crime rates *and* higher punishment risks (number of arrests or convictions/crime rate), inducing an apparent deterrent effect (Blumstein, Cohen, and Nagin, 1978). Additionally, official labels of crime type are misleading because difficulty in obtaining evidence and the plea-bargaining process cause large numbers of offenses to be recorded as lesser offenses at various points in the system (Rosett and Cressey, 1976).

Third, apparent deterrent effects actually can be due to incapacitation. Greater sanctions in the form of prison sentences remove offenders from crime opportunities and thus lower crime rates, but not because of deterrence (Blumstein, Cohen, and Nagin, 1978).

Finally, the deterrence hypothesis assumes that offenders are aware of the objective sanctions. As stated by Henshel and Carey:

> Deterrence, when and if it exists, is a state of mind. If the mind in question holds no cognition relative to the punitive sanction (i.e., it has not been heard of, believed in, or felt applicable), then the *objective existence* of sanctions with specified levels of severity, certainty, and swiftness is of no consequence. (Henshel and Carey, 1975, p. 57; emphasis in original)

Individual data

Several different approaches have been used to address the deterrence issue from the perspective of the individual who is considering criminal opportunities. None of these has amassed substantial empirical bases as yet, but a direction for future research has been set.

Economics   Manski (1978) has made the only theoretical statement regarding the collection of data on individual criminal behavior and its use in an individual utility approach to modeling the behavior. He suggests that self-report surveys of criminals, official records of individual criminal histories together with plea- and sentence-bargaining decisions, and victimization surveys could provide information leading to a model of individual criminal behavior. Manski is appropriately cautious in expressing the difficulties of acquiring and analyzing such data.

Sociology   Several researchers have examined the extent to which people actually know the legal penalty for crimes. Henshel and Carey (1975) summarize several studies documenting the ignorance of the public in regard to the severity of criminal sanctions. For example, a California study found that more than one-quarter of respondents would not even guess the maximum legal sentence for a given crime

(California Assembly Committee on Criminal Procedure, 1968). Further, delinquents and institutionalized youthful offenders were as uninformed as the general public; only adult offenders in prison knew more of the law, a knowledge probably acquired after the criminal behavior. Waldo and Chiricos (1972) found that self-reported marijuana use and theft were unrelated to perceptions of the severity of punishment for these crimes.

In regard to the perceived certainty of punishment, Claster (1967) found that delinquents and nondelinquents evaluated arrest and conviction rates similarly. However, delinquents perceived themselves as less likely to be arrested if they committed a hypothetical crime than did nondelinquents. Jensen (1969) and Waldo and Chiricos (1972) found that a belief in the certainty of punishment was negatively related to self-reported offenses, and Jensen found that belief in the certainty of punishment declined markedly with age.

A separate sociological approach to crime has treated crime as an occupation. This analysis, which is particularly relevant to professional criminals, treats crime as a way of life, with shared conceptions of norms, status, and skills. Whereas amateur criminals, whose lives are conducted primarily in the "straight" society, wish to avoid detection, experienced criminals wish to avoid conviction (Letkemann, 1973, p. 30). Extensive interviews with criminals have documented their technical and interpersonal skills, and the nature of criminal society. These interviews indicate that certainty and severity of punishment are not static properties of the crime, but are under partial control of the criminal. The perception of risk is more complex than what aggregate statistics reveal. The thief perceives risk as avoiding the victim; the robber perceives risk as managing the victim. The safecracker perceives risk in the actual safeblowing (the cash is "safe"); the burglar faces risk during entry and exit and when disposing of the goods (Letkemann, 1973, p. 152). The criminal's skill in leaving no evidence that will stand up in court, in manipulating the legal system through bargains and bribes, in setting up and carrying out crimes and disposing of the gains is indicative that an experienced criminal faces different opportunities and sanctions than does an amateur criminal (Inciardi, 1975; Letkemann, 1973). Thus, within the same jurisdiction (and hence the same aggregate sanctions), individual differences in the perception of sanctions emerge both from differential knowledge of sanctions and from differential skill in avoiding or minimizing sanctions.

Clinical psychology   Clinical psychologists who have interviewed criminals in diagnostic or therapeutic settings have often interpreted criminal behavior as a symptomatic product of intrapsychic process-es. Thus, "when a person commits a crime, he does not think of the consequences. The offender commits a crime because criminality is his particular outlet, just as the seriously mentally ill person's outlet is his psychosis" (Abrahamsen, 1960, p. 274). One psychiatrist ac-counted for the fact that pickpockets liked to "work" the crowds at public hangings of criminals because by watching the execution the pickpockets had "vicariously paid for past sins . . . then proceeded to pick pockets [as] revenge for their vicarious execution" (Zilboorg, 1954, pp. 65–66).

This approach would suggest that criminals do not conceptualize the possible sanctions they face and therefore cannot be easily de-terred from crime. Similarly, the view that criminals want to be caught to expiate their guilt stands in opposition to the assumptions of the deterrence hypothesis. Supporters of the deterrence hypothesis would surely argue that little criminal behavior is actually produced in this manner.

Experimental psychology   Psychologists have attempted to experi-mentally manipulate the perceived rewards and costs associated with the immediate crime situation. Rettig and Rawson (1963) provided hypothetical crime situations in which certainty of gain, amount of gain, certainty of punishment, and severity of punishment were all present at either high or low levels. Subjects rated each situation on their willingness to carry out the offense. Amount of punishment had the strongest effect on decisions, although the others had significant effects. Rettig (1964) gave a situation involving bank fraud to pris-oners and again found severity of punishment to be the strongest influence. Stefanowicz and Hannum (1971), in contrast, found that female prisoners responded only to the amount of gain. Krauss et al., (1972) found that psychopathic prisoners were sensitive to probabil-ity of gain and that both psychopathic and nonpsychopathic pris-oners were sensitive to severity of punishment. Feldman (1966, de-scribed in Feldman, 1977) found that delinquent and nondelinquent boys considered the penalties more when rewards were high rather than low. Amount of gain was more important than certainty of gain, and level of punishment was more important than certainty of detec-tion, although presence of a police officer was more important than level of punishment.

The above studies, all using variations of the Rettig and Rawson (1963) procedure, suffer from the use of ambiguous or limited ma-nipulations. For example, Feldman (1966) manipulated probability of money being present as "definitely" or "possibly" and probability of being caught as "high" or "low." The likelihood of widespread individual differences in the interpretations of these terms makes the results questionable. Similarly, amount of money was $25 or 50¢, and severity of punishment was probation or correctional institution. Clearly, the generality of these manipulations leaves much to be desired.

A STUDY OF THE EVALUATION
OF CRIME OPPORTUNITIES

Carroll (1978) conceptualized criminal behavior as including a decision process loosely organized in two stages: (1) the evaluation of a crime opportunity on four dimensions, and (2) the combination of these four dimensions into a judgment of the desirability of the crime opportunity. The four dimensions, suggested for their heuristic and illustrative value rather than as a formal theory of the criminal decision, were certainty of gain, amount of gain, certainty of punishment, and severity of punishment.

Carroll represented each crime opportunity in the form of a three-outcome gamble (Payne, 1975). Each gamble consisted of a pie diagram divided into three parts. One part represented a monetary gain, the second a punishment, and the final part a neutral outcome (no money, no capture). The use of the neutral outcome enabled the sizes of the pie segments for gain and punishment to be independently varied. The size of the segment represented the certainty of that outcome: probability of gain was either 10%, 30%, or 80%; and probability of punishment was either 5%, 15%, or 40%. Amount of money to gain was either $100, $1,000, or $10,000; and severity of punishment was either probation, 6 months in prison, or 2 years in prison.

Individual interviews were conducted with 23 adult male offenders from a state prison, 13 adult male nonoffenders from a community-college night class, 23 juvenile male offenders from a juvenile detention and diagnostic center, and 20 juvenile male nonoffenders from a high school. Each subject evaluated each of 72 different crime opportunities on a response scale consisting of a large line marked off from 10 to 90, anchored on the low end by the worst crime opportunity in the study and at the high end by the best crime opportunity. An example of one crime opportunity and the response scale is shown in Figure 3.1. Following this, 18 crime opportunities randomly chosen from the set of 72 were rated again as a measure of within-subject consistency.

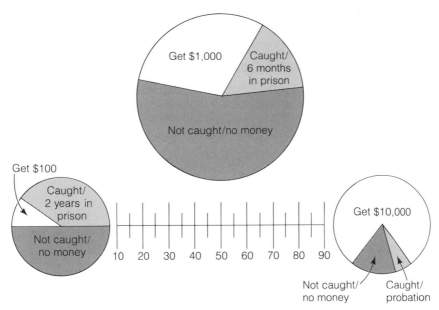

Figure 3.1
Sample crime opportunity with response scale. (From J. S. Carroll, A psychological approach to deterrence: The evaluation of crime opportunities. *Journal of Personality and Social Psychology*, 1978, *36*, 1512–1520. Copyright 1978 by the American Psychological Association. Reprinted by permission.)

Results of the study

Analyses carried out individually on each subject's responses and on the complete data showed that the desirability of crime opportunities was affected principally by the four dimensions of certainty of gain, amount of gain, certainty of punishment, and severity of punishment. These four effects totaled 53% of the variance, whereas the interactions among these dimensions were quite small. The two interactions predicted by the expected-utility model (see the equation on p. 54)— certainty of gain with amount of gain, and certainty of punishment with severity of punishment—together accounted for about 2% of the variance. Amount of gain was the most important dimension, followed by severity of punishment, certainty of gain, and certainty of punishment.

The second interesting result was that more than 70% of the subjects focused principally on only *one* dimension, evidenced by that dimension accounting for at least twice as much variance as any other dimension. Classifying subjects by which dimension they most used, 51% of the subjects focused on amount to gain, 24% on severity of punishment, 18% on certainty of gain, and 8% on certainty of punishment.

The third result was that the offender/nonoffender and juvenile/ adult groups of subjects did not differ substantially in their use of information. Adults used probabilities less and money slightly more than did juveniles, but these effects were not pronounced. Offenders rated crime opportunities as generally more desirable than did nonoffenders.

Decision strategies   Carroll (1978) interpreted his results as demonstrating that, given a simplification of the complex situation of a crime opportunity, evaluations of the simplified stimuli will be even further simplified. In agreement with studies of decision-making (Ebbesen, Parker, and Konečni, 1977; Payne, 1975; Slovic and Lichtenstein, 1968), people adopted simple, additive, and even unidimensional strategies. Ebbesen and co-workers suggest that in real-world decisions, as opposed to laboratory settings, simple strategies may be even more prevalent. Thus, some people are drawn by money, some avoid certain types of risk, and so forth.

Subjects were also asked whether the judgments they made on the crime opportunities were something like what potential offenders think about: 59% said they were, and most of those who disagreed argued that there is *less* rationality—people act on need or impulse, do not think, do not know the consequences, or consider only money.

Deterrence   In regard to the deterrence hypothesis, the results indicated that amount and certainty of gain were more important than severity and certainty of punishment. This suggests that crime reduction might better be accomplished by lowering the payoff for crime and raising the payoff for legitimate behavior, than by deterrence. Newman (1973) has argued the effectiveness of architectural designs that make crime more difficult. Letkemann (1973) reports that alarm systems and credit purchasing have discouraged business burglaries, but that there has been a compensatory rise in armed robbery. A study by Short, Rivera, and Tennyson (1965) found that the "perception of *legitimate* opportunities is more strongly associated with delinquency rates than is perception of illegitimate opportunities" (p. 62). However, nearly one-third of the subjects in Carroll's study could be considered "deterrable" in that their judgments were dominated by certainty or severity of punishment.

The relative importance of the four dimensions of crime opportunities is the principal datum of interest for the deterrence hypothesis. However, the applicability of the results of Carroll's study depends on the match between the levels of the variables in the study and the characteristic levels of these variables in real-world settings.

The three levels of each dimension were selected to be illustrative of the ranges that might be found in real life. Little data are available suggesting what people perceive as normal ranges of these variables. Victimization data indicate that the success rate of property crimes (crimes committed/crimes attempted) ranges from 59% for robbery to 93% for personal theft (Hindelang et al., 1977, p. 358). Certainty of success for crime opportunities considered but rejected would presumably be lower. However, the values of 10%, 30%, and 80% used in Carroll's (1978) study appear low, if anything. The higher two values probably are more representative of crime opportunities.

The average gain from crimes reported to the police seems to be in the range of a few hundred dollars, with auto thefts and bank robberies going into the thousands (Hindelang et al., 1977, p. 507). Nonreported losses were probably of lesser magnitude. Carroll's use of the values of $100, $1,000, and $10,000 therefore seems high, although white-collar crimes and other non-Index crimes may have higher profits. However, the lower two values do not seem unreasonable by themselves.

Studies of the perceived certainty of punishment are also lacking. Waldo and Chiricos (1972) found that people generally estimated the chances of arrest for a theft of $100 to be between 20% and 50%. One of Letkemann's (1973) professional criminals stated: "you only get caught for one out of twenty things you do—sooner or later you pull a sloppy one" (p. 15). The official clearance rates for property crimes (percentage of reported crimes leading to an arrest for the crime) range from 15% for auto theft to 27% for robbery (Hindelang et al., 1977, p. 554). Given the underreporting of crimes, the "true" clearance rates are perhaps half as large. Of those adult offenders charged with property offenses, the conviction rates are in the rate of 60% to 70% (p. 587). Thus, the proportion of offenses actually leading to conviction is probably in the range of 5% to 10%, with considerable variation by crime, jurisdiction, and perpetrator. Naturally, crime opportunities not taken may have considerably higher risk of sanction.

Carroll's study labeled certainty of punishment as certainty of *capture*, which seems most closely related to certainty of arrest. In this case, the values of 5%, 15%, and 40% seem reasonable. However, if certainty were interpreted as certainty of conviction (all of the possible penalties included conviction), then only the lower two would seem representative.

If offenders are arrested, they are released about one out of three times (Hindelang et al., 1977, p. 587). Conviction results in probation about as often as it does in a sentence to serve time (p. 611). The average time of incarceration for juveniles in training schools, forestry camps, and so forth is about 8 months nationwide, 9 months in

Pennsylvania (p. 684). Adult prisoners released from federal institutions have actually served an average of 27 months for burglary, 19 months for theft, and 46 months for robbery (p. 724). In Pennsylvania as well, the median time served in prison is about 2 years. However, Pennsylvania prisons contain inmates whose offenses, records, and sentences are more serious, so that those offenders serving time in county jails rather than state prisons may be serving less time for the same type of offense.

If Carroll's (1978) crime sanctions are taken as certainty of *arrest*, and penalty if arrested, the penalties of probation, 6 months in prison, and 2 years in prison are unrepresentative. For juveniles, representative values would be release, probation, and 6 months in prison; for adults, release, probation, and 2 years in prison. If the sanctions are interpreted as probability of *conviction*, then different subsets of the three penalties appear valid for juveniles and adults. However, in this case, certainty of punishment would be too high.

In summary, it is nearly impossible to specify the subjective levels of inducements and sanctions with data currently available. Aggregate data appear to suggest that representative levels might be different from those used by Carroll (1978), although specifying representative *ranges* of these dimensions is even more difficult than identifying a central tendency. For this reason, it is probably better to compare specific levels of the dimensions rather than the general variance explained by each dimension. Thus, the mean difference between certainty of success of 30% and 80% was 7 units (on the response scale in Figure 3.1); between gaining $100 and $1,000 was 11 units; between certainty of punishment of 5% and 15% was 4 units; and between probation and 2 years in prison was 16 units. However, this type of analysis, while germane to the deterrence issue, does not substantially alter Carroll's principal finding that subjects focused primarily on *one* dimension with marked personal preferences.

TOWARD A MODEL OF THE DECISION
TO COMMIT A CRIME

The overall impact of the research summarized in this chapter is to suggest that the analysis of individual data is a promising approach to the deterrence issue and to the general issue of criminal behavior. The ideal type of data with which to pursue this approach would be data collected during decisional behavior (Payne, Braunstein, and Carroll, 1978). However, criminal behavior poses unique problems for on-the-spot research. Other possibilities include decisional behavior in simulated situations and retrospective accounts of actual decisions. These latter approaches suffer from well-known issues of validity (Nisbett and Wilson, 1977), although there is evidence that such data can be valid (Smith and Miller, 1978).

Available research has found support for a general lack of knowledge about the penalties and certainty of detection among the public, although "expert" criminals appear to have much greater knowledge. It is clear that people evaluate the benefits and risks differently depending on their experience with crime. Sociological studies seem to point toward professional criminals feeling that they can beat the system more frequently than can amateur criminals or good citizens; undoubtedly these feelings are accurate. It also appears that detection is itself a deterrent for most people committed to conventional lifestyles. Any involvement or suspicion is a threat to their access to the legitimate benefits of society. More experienced offenders are concerned with avoiding prison, as they have less stake in conventional society.

However, the very simplicity of the judgment processes uncovered by Carroll (1978) contrasts with the apparent knowledge and skill of offenders (Inciardi, 1975; Letkemann, 1973). Elaborate descriptions are available of offenders considering the risks and payoffs of crime opportunities. Reconciliation of these observations is possible in two ways. First, it could be argued that some offenders are *expert* and that expertise involves training in more complex decision-making. Carroll's data can identify offenders with long and short records, but this is not necessarily an index of expertise (Inciardi, 1975; Letkemann, 1973). The typology of offenders is not identified just by official records of offenses (Megargee, 1975).

A second and more appealing answer would propose that persons considering a crime opportunity examine one feature of the situation at any given time, but the decision process is *extended through time* in such a way that features are sequentially incorporated into decision behavior and criminal acts. For example, persons may decide that they should look for a good crime opportunity because legitimate opportunities are lacking, they need money, or they have used up their previous hauls. A target may be identified by the known presence of money or the likelihood of money. Then, a particular moment or technique may be selected to minimize risk.

For example, one of Letkemann's (1973) interviewees remarked: "When I was down to a certain level I would go out" (p. 22). Lack of money was one factor initiating a search for a good opportunity. Letkemann also provides an illustrative ordering of decision factors:

> Usually, the assessment of economic value precedes the assessment of risk. A safecracker may, while on legitimate business, spot a particu-

> larly "easy" safe. He may then assess the probable economic value of
> the safe's contents. Whether the value is high or low, if the risks are
> low, he may "make" the safe. On the other hand, if both are high, he
> may also attempt the job. (Letkemann, 1973, p. 151)

Thus, in this case, the order of considerations are certainty of success,
amount of gain (if high, try it; if low, examine risk), then risk.

This model is consistent with a large body of research documenting
the *limited rationality* of people (Simon, 1957). Complex situations
are typically dealt with through simplified strategies or heuristics
involving limited comparisons and judgments (Payne, 1973, 1975;
Slovic and Lichtenstein, 1971). As a result, human judgments often
appear nonoptimal or biased when contrasted with optimal responses (Fischhoff, 1976; Ross, 1977). Thus, at any one time, we may
expect decision-makers to be considering simple characteristics of a
situation, as in the results of Carroll (1978). Features of the situation
that are salient or concrete may dominate judgment (Nisbett et al.,
1976; Taylor and Fiske, 1978). However, if decision behavior can be
extended over time, involving many subdecisions interactively governing a sequence of behaviors, actions may be influenced by complex features of the situations.

This model also suggests a distinction between planned crimes,
spontaneous crimes, and crimes of passion. In planned crimes, decisions extend over a period of time, allowing consideration of multiple factors. In spontaneous crimes, the brief duration of precrime
deliberation insures that only one or a few features of the situation
(e.g., there's a car with keys in it, and no cops around) will be considered. Crimes of passion will have even more limited, if any, consideration of situational factors. Studies of the effects of emotional
arousal on judgment and behavior have shown that simple, well-
learned responses are enhanced, and complex new responses sup-
pressed, by higher arousal (Spence, 1956).

Interview studies of offenders substantiate this distinction. Letkemann reports of criminals that "they know that some crimes are
committed in a deliberate and rational manner, others, such as those
generated by frustration, may be done impulsively" (1973, p. 22).
Financial need may keep a criminal from examining crime opportunities in a leisurely manner. When money is acutely needed, "he
may deliberately need to find a spot, dispense with careful planning,
and proceed quickly and at high risk." Thus, "crimes committed
shortly after release from prison, when the exconvict is out of money,
are the most risky" (1973, p. 143). Financial resources may also determine the type of crime chosen: a bankroll can be used to impress
people in a confidence game or to simplify a crime, e.g., have a master
key made of a hotel (1973, p. 33).

Even if the sequence of decisions and actions occurs in the manner I have suggested, the decision process would still be responsive to the situation at hand. The criminal must be able to abort the crime or deal with a variety of occurrences that disturb the activity. Thus, in a bank robbery, should a customer about to enter the bank notice something wrong, the customer could not be prevented from leaving, and "becomes the first 'alarm.' When this happens, the doorman will call his men out immediately" (Letkemann, 1973, p. 95). Or again,

> Number 41 stated that he once entered a bank to rob it, and noticed a man standing behind the bank counter with his foot on a chair and his arms folded. He knew this man was a policeman, so he left the bank without robbing it. Number 41 went on to explain that a bank manager may sit on a table with his feet hanging down, or sit on a chair and have his feet on a desk, but "he will never stand with one foot on a chair!" (Letkemann, 1973, p. 149)

These events, triggered by the criminal's perceptual skills and knowledge of the nature of situations, act in the fashion of *interrupts* to ongoing decisional and behavioral processes (Simon, 1967). Clearly, then, in a comparison between the decision to commit a crime and administrative decisions in the criminal justice system, the former lacks the highly structured, or temporally and spatially delimited, nature of the latter. The decision to commit a crime can be a rapid one, or the moment before the person's behavior becomes illegal could be labeled the "decision." However, it appears that the decision to commit a crime and the choice of *which* crime to commit are often extended in time and interact with the changing environment in which they are embedded. For this reason, we are moving *toward* a model of this decision, and I hope this discussion has served to move our knowledge forward.

References

Abrahamsen, D. *The psychology of crime.* New York: Columbia University Press, 1960.

Becker, H. S. *Outsiders: Studies in the sociology of deviance.* New York: Free Press, 1963.

Becker, G. Crime and punishment: An economic approach. *Journal of Political Economy,* 1968, *76,* 169–217.

Blumstein, A., Cohen, J., & Nagin, D. (Eds.). *Deterrence and incapacitation: Estimating the effects of criminal sanctions on crime rates.* Washington, DC: National Academy of Sciences, 1978.

California Assembly Committee on Criminal Procedure. *The deterrent effects of criminal sanctions.* Sacramento: 1968.

Carroll, J. S. A psychological approach to deterrence: The evaluation of crime opportunities. *Journal of Personality and Social Psychology*, 1978, *36*, 1512–1520.

Carroll, J. S., & Payne, J. W. Judgments about crime and the criminal: A model and method for investigating parole decisions. In B. D. Sales (Ed.), *Perspectives in law and psychology*. Vol. 1: *The criminal justice system*. New York: Plenum, 1977.

Clark, R. *Crime in America*. New York: Simon and Schuster, 1971.

Claster, D. Comparison of risk perceptions between delinquents and non-delinquents. *Journal of Criminal Law, Criminology, and Police Science*, 1967, *58*, 80–86.

Clinard, M. B., & Quinney, R. *Criminal behavior systems: A typology*. 2nd ed. New York: Holt, Rinehart and Winston, 1973.

Cloward, R. A., & Ohlin, L. E. *Delinquency and opportunity: A theory of delinquent gangs*. New York: Free Press, 1960.

Ebbesen, E. B., Parker, S., & Konečni, V. J. Decisions involving risk: Laboratory and field analysis. *Journal of Experimental Psychology: Human Perception and Performance*, 1977, *3*, 576–589.

Feldman, M. P. Decision taking in a hypothetical criminal situation by approved school and secondary modern school boys. Unpublished manuscript, University of Birmingham, 1966.

Feldman, M. P. *Criminal behavior: A psychological analysis*. New York: Wiley, 1977.

Fischhoff, B. Attribution theory and judgment under uncertainty. In J. H. Harvey, W. Ickes, & R. Kidd (Eds.), *New directions in attribution research*. Hillsdale, NJ: Lawrence Erlbaum, 1976.

Henshel, R. L., & Carey, S. H. Deviance, deterrence, and knowledge of sanctions. In R. L. Henshel & R. A. Silverman (Eds.), *Perception in criminology*. New York: Columbia University Press, 1975.

Hindelang, M. J., Gottfredson, M. R., Dunn, C. S., & Parisi, N. *Sourcebook of criminal justice statistics—1976*. Washington, DC: U.S. Government Printing Office, 1977.

Inciardi, J. A. *Careers in crime*. Chicago: Rand McNally, 1975.

Jensen, G. F. Crime doesn't pay: Correlates of a shared misunderstanding. *Social Problems*, 1969, *17*, 189–201.

Krauss, H. H., Robinson, I., Janzen, W., & Cauthen, N. Predictions of ethical risk taking by psychopathic and non-psychopathic criminals. *Psychological Reports*, 1972, *30*, 83.

Letkemann, P. *Crime as work*. Englewood Cliffs, NJ: Prentice-Hall, 1973.

Manski, C. F. Prospects for inference on deterrence through empirical analysis of inividual criminal behavior. In A. Blumstein, J. Cohen, & D. Nagin (Eds.), *Deterrence and incapacitation: Estimating the effects of criminal sanctions on crime rates*. Washington, DC: National Academy of Sciences, 1978.

Megargee, E. I. *Crime and delinquency*. Morristown, NJ: General Learning Press, 1975.

Newman, O. *Architectural design for crime prevention*. Washington, DC: National Institute of Law Enforcement and Criminal Justice, 1973.

Nisbett, R. E., Borgida, E., Crandall, R., & Reed, H. Popular induction: Information is not necessarily informative. In J. S. Carroll & J. W. Payne (Eds.), *Cognition and social behavior*. Hillsdale, NJ: Lawrence Erlbaum, 1976.

Nisbett, R. E., & Wilson, T. D. Telling more than we can know: Verbal reports on mental processes. *Psychological Review*, 1977, *84*, 231–259.

Palmer, J. Economic analyses of the deterrent effect of punishment: A review. *Journal of Research in Crime and Delinquency*, 1977, *14*, 4–21.

Payne, J. W. Alternative approaches to decision making under risk: Moments versus risk dimensions. *Psychological Bulletin*, 1973, *80*, 439–453.

Payne, J. W. Relation of perceived risk to preferences among gambles. *Journal of Experimental Psychology: Human Perception and Performance*, 1975, *104*, 86–94.

Payne, J. W., Braunstein, M., & Carroll, J. S. Exploring predecisional behavior: An alternative approach to decision research. *Organizational Behavior and Human Performance*, 1978, *22*, 17–44.

President's Commission on Law Enforcement and the Administration of Justice. *The challenge of crime in a free society*. Washington, DC: U.S. Government Printing Office, 1967.

Reckless, W. C. *The crime problem*. 3rd ed. Appleton-Century-Crofts, 1961.

Rettig, S. Ethical risk sensitivity in male prisoners. *British Journal of Criminology*, 1964, *4*, 582–590.

Rettig, S., & Rawson, H. E. The risk hypothesis in predictive judgments of unethical behavior. *Journal of Abnormal and Social Psychology*, 1963, *66*, 243–248.

Rosett, A., & Cressey, D. R. *Justice by consent*. New York: Lippincott, 1976.

Ross, L. The intuitive psychologist and his shortcomings: Distortions in the attribution process. In L. Berkowitz (Ed.), *Advances in experimental social psychology*. New York: Academic Press, 1977.

Schrag, C. *Crime and justice: American style*. NIMH Publication HSM-72-9052. Rockville, MD: National Institute of Mental Health, 1971.

Shaver, K. G. *An introduction to attribution processes*. Cambridge, MA: Winthrop, 1975.

Short, J. F., Jr., Rivera, R., & Tennyson, R. A. Perceived opportunities, gang membership, and delinquency. *American Sociological Review*, 1965, *30*, 56–67.

Simon, H. A. *Models of man*. New York: Wiley, 1957.

Simon, H. A. Motivational and emotional controls on cognition. *Psychological Review*, 1967, *74*, 29–39.

Slovic, P., & Lichtenstein, S. Relative importance of probabilities and payoffs in risk taking. *Journal of Experimental Psychology Monograph*, 1968, *78* (3, pt. 2).

Slovic, P., & Lichtenstein, S. Comparison of Bayesian and regression approaches to the study of information processing in judgment. *Organizational Behavior and Human Performance*, 1971, *6*, 649–744.

Smith, E. R., & Miller, F. D. The limits on perception of cognitive processes: A reply to Nisbett and Wilson. *Psychological Review*, 1978, *85*, 355–362.

Spence, K. W. *Behavior theory and conditioning*. New Haven, CT: Yale University Press, 1956.

Stefanowicz, J. P., & Hannum, T. E. Ethical risk-taking and sociopathy in incarcerated females. *Correctional Psychologist*, 1971, *4*, 138–148.

Sutherland, E. H. *White collar crime*. New York: Holt, Rinehart and Winston, 1949.

Taylor, S. E., & Fiske, S. T. Salience, attention, and attribution: Top of the head phenomena. In L. Berkowitz (Ed.), *Advances in experimental social psychology*. New York: Academic Press, 1978.

Tittle, C. R., & Rowe, A. R. Certainty of arrest and crime rates: A further test of the deterrent hypothesis. *Social Forces*, 1974, *52*, 455–462.

Waldo, G. P., & Chiricos, T. G. Perceived penal sanction and self-reported criminality: A neglected approach to deterrence research. *Social Problems*, 1972, *19*, 522–540.

Zilboorg, G. *The psychology of the criminal act and punishment*. New York: Harcourt, Brace, Jovanovich, 1954.

Zimring, R., & Hawkins, G. *Deterrence: The legal threat in crime control*. Chicago: University of Chicago Press, 1973.

THE VICTIM'S DECISION
TO REPORT THE CRIME

Editors' Introduction

One view of criminal action focuses on legislative and judicial decisions. In this view crimes are defined as actions that violate state and federal penal codes (as interpreted and modified by higher-court rulings). Such a view assumes that the codification of criminal action is so detailed and at the same time so general that all actions are easily judged as either in violation of the codes or not. In so doing, this view ignores the role that the police, victims, and witnesses play in defining actions as crimes. Although writers frequently emphasize the fact that our criminal codes often consider the state of the defendant's mind in the test of whether and what actions constitute crimes (as, for example, in the distinction between involuntary manslaughter, manslaughter, and various degrees of murder), the rather obvious fact that the victim's state of mind also determines the criminality of actions is rarely discussed.

The victim can affect whether particular actions will be responded to as crimes by members of the criminal justice system in several different ways. At the most basic level, whether some interactions between people are considered crimes depends on the perceptions and intentions of the potential victim. This is clear in the case of sexual intercourse. The same physically abusive act of intercourse may be labeled rape by one woman and sexual gratification by another. Assault is another obvious example. A punch in the nose might be labeled a friendly argument or a vicious assault depending on the state of mind of the owner of the battered nose. Victims also determine whether actions that they perceive as criminal are brought to the attention of the criminal justice system. As the next chapter points out, many victims of criminal actions may choose not to report the crimes to relevant authorities. Even when victims do report crimes, they can determine how the case will be handled by the police and by the prosecutor's office. For example, in California, the Uniform Crime Charging Standards, written by the California District Attorneys Association, suggest that under appropriate circumstances it would be proper for the prosecutor to refuse to file criminal charges if the victim requests that no charges be filed. In short, if the victim of petty theft reports the crime and then later requests that formal charges not be filed against a defendant, it is likely that no charges will be filed.

Although it would be ideal to study victim decision-making in situ, the practical difficulties of conducting such research are both obvious and enormous. Unfortunately, surveys of potential victims and interviews with known victims provide data about victim decision-making that have obvious limitations. In an attempt to overcome both the practical and the methodological obstacles inherent in these approaches, Greenberg, Wilson, and Mills have devised an experimental paradigm that, while not entirely unobtrusive, brings us close to observing the reactions of real-world victims of a petty theft. The use of a true randomized experiment eliminates some of the obvious problems one encounters when drawing causal inferences from naturalistic, correlational data. On the other hand, although the findings from Greenberg, Wilson, and Mills's research concerning which factors govern victim reporting are tantalizing, they are necessarily limited in their generality to the particular circumstances created in the experimental situation. Nevertheless, their results provide yet another much-needed view of the decision-making of victims of criminal activity.

4

Victim Decision-Making:
An Experimental Approach[1]

Martin S. Greenberg, Chauncey E. Wilson, and Michael K. Mills

The criminal justice system can be viewed as a series of interconnected decision-makers (see Chapter 1, this volume). The decisions
made at a given stage of the system are, in part, a function of the
discretionary power exercised by those who have made decisions at
earlier stages. Thus, it can be argued that those who make the initial
decision exercise the greatest control over the system since they determine which individuals will be subject to the discretionary power
of those making decisions at subsequent stages. For this reason, the
police have traditionally been viewed as the "gatekeepers" of the
criminal justice system (see Chapter 6). Yet, when one considers the
fact that citizen notification accounts for about 85% of the crimes
investigated by police (Black and Reiss, 1967), it is the victim who
emerges as the true gatekeeper of the criminal justice system (Hindelang and Gottfredson, 1976). Ultimately, it is the victim who must
label an event as a crime and decide whether or not it should be
reported to the police. That victims do indeed exercise their discretionary power to report or not report crimes is demonstrated by recent
victimization surveys conducted jointly by the Law Enforcement Assistance Administration (LEAA) and the Census Bureau (*Criminal
Victimization in the United States*, 1977). These studies show that
less than half of the crimes surveyed are ever reported to the police.[2]
Thus, for certain classes of crime, such as larceny and rape, more

[1]This study was supported by PHS Research Grant No. MH 27526-01, NIMH (Center
for Studies of Crime and Delinquency).

[2]The surveyed crimes include rape, robbery, assault, burglary, personal and household larceny.

individuals are lost to the criminal justice system *prior* to entry than subsequent to entry. If the criminal justice system is to function more effectively as a means of prevention and control, more must be learned about the decision-making process involved in victim crime reporting.

In light of the pivotal role played by the victim in mobilizing the criminal justice system, it is important to identify methodologies that allow investigators to gain access to victims' decision-making process. In the following pages we will critically assess the utility of three methodological approaches to studying victims' decisions to notify the police. These include (1) naturalistic observation, (2) the self-report or survey approach, and (3) the experimental approach.

METHODOLOGICAL APPROACHES

Observations in naturalistic settings

A naturalistic observational approach is most appropriate when the investigator has the ability to monitor an individual's decision-making in a natural setting. It is ideally suited for studying a decision-making event for which the identity of the decision-maker is known in advance and which takes place at a predictable time and location. Thus, Ebbesen and Konečni (1975) have shown this approach to be an effective tool for investigating the bail-setting decisions of judges. The method is somewhat more costly to implement when only the decision-maker's identity is known in advance but not the time and location of the decision. In such a situation the investigator must be able to keep the decision-maker under surveillance until such time when the decision-making process is set in motion. Reiss (1971), for example, employed naturalistic observation to study decisions by police to detain, interrogate, and arrest a suspect. The investigator was able to do this by accompanying police officers on their patrol duties, which afforded him the opportunity to observe and record the interaction between the police and the suspect. While naturalistic observation has been shown to be an effective tool for studying decision-making by police and judges, it is ill-suited for studying victim decision-making. The identity of a potential crime victim is unlikely to be known to an investigator in advance. Nor is the time and place of occurrence of a specific victimization a predictable event. Even if such information were available to the investigator, there would be formidable ethical and legal constraints against allowing a crime to occur for the purpose of investigating victim decision-making. A more important disadvantage of the naturalistic observation method is that the investigator lacks control over the situation, which makes this approach less effective at eliminating plausible rival hypotheses and, therefore, weakens its effectiveness in identifying causal relations. For these reasons, naturalistic observation is not a suitable approach to studying causal relations in victim decision-making.

The self-report or survey approach

A logical alternative to naturalistic observation is to ask victims to recount their reasons for reporting or not reporting the event to the police. This is, in part, the rationale underlying the federal government's annual investment of over $10 million on victimization surveys. The surveys, which are conducted jointly by the LEAA and the Census Bureau, are designed to collect information on the incidence of criminal victimizations as well as a host of related variables, such as the time and place of occurrence, whether the incident was reported to the police, and the reasons for not reporting. These surveys involve periodic interviews with a random sample of the U.S. adult population about the extent of their victimization experiences during the preceding 6-month period. It is generally assumed that these surveys provide a more complete accounting of criminal victimizations than do the FBI's Uniform Crime Reports, which reflect only the rate of reported crimes.

Victimization surveys have proven particularly useful in the study of crimes such as rape, robbery, assault, burglary, and larceny (i.e., theft). The LEAA/Census Bureau surveys have yielded remarkably consistent data across time and geographical region. It has been consistently shown that less than half of the crimes surveyed are reported to the police—the rate varying with the particular category of crime (*Criminal Victimization in the United States*, 1976). Reporting is highest for commercial robbery (86%) and lowest for household larceny under $50 (15%). When those who did not report the incident to the police were asked to explain their behavior, the two most frequently cited reasons were that nothing could be done (i.e., lack of proof) or that the incident was not sufficiently important to warrant calling the police. The survey data further reveal that characteristics of the victim and the offender account for less of the variance in reporting than does the nature of the offense. Although victimization surveys have provided useful information regarding the incidence and reporting of crime, they nevertheless suffer from certain weaknesses that reduce their effectiveness as a device for understanding the causes of victims' decision-making. The weaknesses inhere in the particular instruments employed and in the general survey methodology.

That the LEAA/Census Bureau victimization surveys are unequal to the task of assessing the causes of victim reporting is the judgment of the Panel for the Evaluation of Crime Surveys (Penick and Owens, 1976), which was established by the National Academy of Sciences at the request of the U.S. Department of Justice. In the panel's judgment, "The NCS [National Crime Survey] at present can reveal little or nothing about local patterns of nonreporting, and it includes almost no measures that might help to account for different levels of reporting or changes in reporting behavior" (p. 45). Indeed, the LEAA/Census Bureau surveys include only two questions about reporting of victimization. The first reads: "Were the police informed of this incident in any way?" If the respondent indicates "No," a second question is asked: "What was the reason this incident was not reported to the police?" Respondents are provided with a list of eight reasons and told to mark all that apply. A ninth category, "Other," is also provided. Respondents are given no opportunity to elaborate on or to qualify their answers. If the respondent indicates that the incident was reported to the police, there is no parallel question asking why the incident was reported. Instead, the followup question reads: "Who told them?" The three response alternatives are not very informative: "Household member," "Someone else," and "Police on scene." Thus, the instrument fails to distinguish between victim reporting and reporting by another household member. As the Panel for the Evaluation of Crime Surveys noted in its report, "very little information is now obtained from respondents to help in explaining such things as nonreporting, as distinct from merely describing it" (p. 146).

Clearly, if such surveys are to provide more analytic, as opposed to descriptive, information about the determinants of victim reporting, many more questions need to be asked of respondents. However, the more detail that is sought, the more complex the questionnaire becomes. And, as Miller (1970) has noted, the longer and more complex the instrument, the lower the level of respondent cooperation. The problems discussed so far, while by no means minor, are technical in nature, and can conceivably be corrected in future victimization surveys. The problems to be discussed below are of a more serious and fundamental nature and are unlikely to be overcome by refinements in survey technology.

The fundamental weaknesses of victimization surveys are inherent in all methodologies that rely on self-reports to answer questions about "why." These weaknesses derive from several unsubstantiated assumptions, namely that (1) respondents *know* the reasons for their decisions, (2) they can accurately *recall* these reasons when asked to do so on subsequent occasions, and (3) they *are willing to disclose* these reasons to an interviewer. We would contend that all three are tenuous assumptions in survey attempts to explain victim decision-making. With regard to the first assumption, Nisbett and Wilson (1977) raise the question of whether people have direct, introspective access to higher-order cognitive processes. The authors propose that often people cannot report on the existence of critical stimuli and on the existence of their responses to these stimuli. They also suggest that people are often unaware that they *infer* answers to questions rather than know them. Thus, when persons are asked why they acted as they did in a situation, their reports may be based "on [their] implicit, a priori theories about the causal connection between stimulus and response" (p. 233). If, according to an individual's theory, a stimulus does not seem to be a plausible cause of the response, it is reported as noninfluential. Nisbett and Wilson contend that often when persons correctly infer the causes of their behavior, they do so not because of direct access to the reasoning process that they employed, but because of "the incidentally correct employment of a priori causal theories" (p. 233). In support of their theorizing, Nisbett and Wilson review data showing an inconsistency between what subjects choose to label as the cause of their behavior and what the experimenter believes the cause to be, based on the results of the experimental manipulations.

In the research discussed by Nisbett and Wilson, subjects were asked to reflect on the causes of their behavior only minutes after the behavior in question. How reliable are victims' self-reports when they are obtained 6 to 12 months after the victimization experience? Relevant data are provided by three LEAA-sponsored reverse-record surveys conducted prior to the development of the LEAA/Census Bureau surveys. The three studies involved interviews with a sample of known crime victims obtained from police files. In the first of these, 19% of a sample of Washington, D.C., crime victims were unable to "recall" their own victimization (*Victim Recall Pretest*, 1970). Further, recall accuracy varied with the elapsed time between the incident and the interview. Thus, when the incident occurred within 3 months of the interview, 14% failed to recall it. When the incident occurred 6 months before, the failure-to-recall rate rose to 20%; and after 11 months, the figure was 22%. It should be kept in mind that these figures relate to whether the victim was merely able to recall that the incident took place. When recall of more precise factual detail was required (e.g., the correct month), the error rate increased markedly. Reverse-record studies conducted in Baltimore (Yost and Dodge, 1970) and San Jose (*San Jose Methods Test*, 1972) yielded findings similar to those of the Washington, D.C., study. When the data from the three surveys were combined by Hindelang (1976), recall error was found to vary as a function of type of offense. Recall error was greatest for assault (53%), rape was second (33%), larceny was third (22%), robbery was fourth (20%), and burglary had the lowest recall error (12%). For all crimes combined in the three cities, the failure-to-recall rate was 27%.

The reverse-record checks may actually understate victim recall error, particularly for the crime of petty larceny. The results of these studies are based on a select sample of victims who reported their victimization to the police. It seems likely that these individuals would be more likely to recall the event, in part because the victimization experience may have been subjectively more serious for them (as compared to nonreporters), and partly because having reported details of the event to the police, the event may have gained greater salience. The selectivity of this population is all the more apparent in the case of larceny, where approximately 1 of 5 victims reported to the police (*Criminal Victimization . . .* , 1976). For these reasons, we would expect recall errors to be substantially higher if nonreporters were included in the sample. No data exist on the extent to which victim recall errors stem from victims' *inability* to recall as opposed to their *unwillingness* to recall. That victim unwillingness contributes to recall error is suggested by data collected in the San Jose reverse-record study. Crimes in which the offender was a relative or an acquaintance of the victim were less likely to be recalled than crimes in which the offender was a stranger. Presumably, victims are less inclined to disclose to an interviewer criminal incidents perpetrated by a relative or an acquaintance.

The discrepancy between police records and reverse-record surveys may result from victims' *relabeling* the incident as a noncrime rather than from either faulty recall or an unwillingness to disclose such information to an interviewer. The relabeling may occur for a variety of reasons having to do with changes in motivation, mood, and information. Thus, what was defined as "stolen" at time 1 may be defined as "missing" at time 2. The reverse may be true as well. An event that was not originally labeled as a crime and thus not reported to the police may subsequently be relabeled as a crime and reported in a victimization survey. Conceivably, participation in a victimization survey may encourage people to relabel as crimes events that were originally not so labeled. The relabeling process could thus cause victimization surveys to *overestimate* as well as *underestimate* the true incidence of crime. This analysis suggests that victims' definitions and the stability of these definitions are crucial for evaluating the accuracy of victimization surveys.

The arguments and supporting research presented in this section call into question the wisdom of relying exclusively on victims' self-reports as the basis for understanding the forces that affect their willingness to notify the police. Such reports, often obtained months after the incidents in question, may reveal more about victims' causal theories, rationalizations, self-disclosure motives, and definitions of crimes than about the true reasons for their actions. Despite these limitations, the survey approach remains, for *most* classes of victimization, the best source of information on victim discretion. However, for some classes of victimization, such as minor property crimes, there exists an alternative method that overcomes the shortcomings of the survey approach by permitting more direct access to the victim decision-making process. This alternative is the experimental approach.

The experimental approach

Instead of seeking insight about the determinants of victim decision-making via naturalistic observation and retrospective self-reports, this approach relies on the systematic manipulation of independent variables and observation of the effect of these manipulations on such decision-making. The generally agreed upon criteria for inferring a causal relationship include (1) covariation between presumed cause and presumed effect, (2) proper temporal order, with the cause preceding the effect, and (3) elimination of plausible alternative explanations for the observed relationship (Selltiz, Wrightsman, and Cook, 1976, p. 115).

In addition to allowing for these criteria to be met in an efficient way, the experimental approach has the unique advantage of permitting random assignment of subjects to conditions, thereby eliminating subject differences as a plausible rival hypothesis. Further, in exercising control over the situation, the experimenter is in an advantageous position to isolate variables and discover their impact on one or more dependent variables. Another advantage of this approach, which is particularly relevant to the study of victim reporting, concerns the predictability of the criminal event and the subsequent decision-making. Since investigators usually have no way of knowing when and where a crime is going to take place, the experimental approach allows for this event to be arranged at a time and place so that observation and measurement are possible. These remarks are not, however, meant to imply that causal relations can be investigated only by the experimental approach. As Campbell and Stanley (1966) have described in detail, causal hypotheses can be tested by nonexperimental methods as well. Still, as Blalock has noted: "It seems safe to conclude that the problem of making causal inferences on the basis of nonexperimental data is by no stretch of the imagination a simple one. A number of simplifying assumptions must be made, perhaps so many that the goal would seem almost impossible to achieve" (1964, p. 184). A frequently cited liability of the experimental approach concerns the generalizability of results. Whereas the experimental method may often allow for a higher degree of internal validity than do nonexperimental approaches, it often does so at the cost of reducing the generalizability of the results (i.e., external validity). For those who wish to generalize from experimental settings to real-life settings, the task is a very difficult one. It consists of maximizing the similarity between the experimental setting and the conditions of application while not jeopardizing the experiment's internal validity.

Whereas the experimental approach has been the major tool for investigating bystander decision-making (Bickman and Rosenbaum, 1977; Latané and Darley, 1970), there has been some reluctance to use the method to study victim decision-making. The causes of this reluctance are readily discernible. Experimental investigation of victims' reactions to staged criminal events poses formidable problems with regard to the ethics of such manipulations. The challenge to the investigator is one of creating a situation that is sufficiently real to subjects, yet is not so arousing as to cause them psychological or physical harm.

Subsequently, we initiated development of an experimental paradigm that satisfied these conflicting demands. We created our own theft "victims" in an off-campus laboratory setting and by so doing were able to create a standardized situation in which various conditions could be experimentally varied in order to test their effects. The value of studying responses to theft is that the LEAA/Census Bureau surveys indicate that it is the most frequently committed crime and yet the one that victims are least likely to report. Moreover, the costs of this crime are immense. Estimates based on reported larceny place the dollar loss to victims at close to $1 billion annually (FBI *Uniform Crime Reports*, 1976).

A DESCRIPTION OF THE EXPERIMENTAL PARADIGM

In order to provide a controlled setting for the theft, we created a fictitious research organization entitled Industrial Research Associates of Pittsburgh. A suite of offices was rented in a middle-class retail section of the city and was furnished with such props as desks, chairs, and file cabinets as well as human props such as a secretary, supervisor, and research participants. To lend an air of legitimacy to the enterprise, the organization's name was listed on the directory outside the building and in the entrance hall. The organization was given further legitimacy by the context of the other occupants of the building, which included a justice of the peace, a physician, and an attorney. In order to attract a diverse sample, participants were recruited via an ad placed in Pittsburgh's daily and weekly newspapers. The ad read:

> VOLUNTEERS—PAID
> Adults needed for research on
> work efficiency. $10 for 1½
> hours clerical work. Call . . . .

Respondents to the ad were told that the organization conducted research for local businesses on office management and work efficiency. They were told over the phone that, in addition to the $10, they would have an opportunity to earn more money. Prior to scheduling an appointment, respondents were screened for health problems (e.g., cardiac condition, high blood pressure). Only those who said they were free of such problems were given an appointment time.

Shortly after participants arrived for their appointment, they were joined by a young male participant who was, in fact, a confederate programed to play the role of thief. The supervisor then entered, paid them the money promised in the ad, and once again questioned participants about health problems, after reassuring them that the money could be kept regardless of how the question was answered. The supervisor then explained that the organization was studying clerical efficiency in office settings and that they would be asked to complete some questionnaires and then work on a clerical task. Subsequently, they were given the questionnaires, which assessed general demographic characteristics (e.g., age, education, occupation) and personality traits (the Crown–Marlowe need-for-approval scale and a shortened version of the F scale), and then seated in separate cubicles in order to protect the thief from an irate victim.

The clerical task was then described. It consisted of transferring numbers from a card to a work sheet and inserting the completed work sheet and card in an envelope. Participants were told that *immediately* after completing *each work sheet* they should place the envelope containing their completed work in their respective out boxes, located directly behind them. The out box rested on a shelf attached to the partition separating the participant from the confederate. This was accomplished by cutting away a portion of the glass partition. It was this opening in the glass that allowed the thief access to the participant's completed work.

Participants were then informed that in order to simulate real-life work conditions they would have an opportunity to earn additional money in the study. This was done by placing them in competition with the confederate and setting a monetary value of $3 on each completed work sheet. They were told that at the end of the work period their productivity would be compared, and the person who produced less would pay the other the appropriate amount from funds with which they would be provided. Thus, if one participant completed ten sheets and the other six, the one with the smaller production would have to pay the other $12 (a difference of four sheets at $3 per sheet). Each was then given $20 in small bills and was asked to sign a receipt for the money. They were thus led to believe that they could earn as much as $40 more in the study. This would occur if they outproduced the other by seven sheets, since at $3 per sheet they would win all of the other's money plus the $20 that they already had in hand.

There was, of course, no chance for participants actually to earn additional money since the confederate stole approximately 30% of the participants' work sheets from their outboxes during the work period. In order to facilitate discovery of the theft, participants, at the conclusion of the work period, were asked to check their work prior to its being scored by the secretary. The "evidence" of theft consisted of several empty envelopes in participants' stacks of completed work. In order to forestall participants' questioning why the empty envelopes were left behind, each was initially given visibly different color-coded envelopes. Participants were thus led to believe that if the thief had retained the stolen envelopes along with their contents, he would be caught with easily identifiable incriminating evidence. After the papers were picked up by the secretary and ostensibly scored, participants were informed over the intercom system that the confederate had completed seven more sheets than they did and, at $3 per sheet, they had lost their $20 to the confederate. After handing their money to the confederate, they were informed that the study was completed and that prior to leaving they should go to the secretary's office, one at a time, to sign some additional forms.

The meeting in the secretary's office comprised the setting for assessing the dependent variable—the participant's willingness to report the theft to the police. When they entered the secretary's office, few participants were aware that the empty envelopes were the result of a theft. Not having witnessed the theft, most participants later reported that they either believed they had made a clerical error or were, at most, mildly suspicious of the confederate. It remained for the secretary to provide conclusive evidence that a theft had occurred. After participants were seated in her office, she casually inquired, "Well, how did things go?" In 44% of the cases this question was sufficient to elicit a statement about the empty envelopes. When told of this, the secretary appeared surprised, volunteered to check the work sheets, which were located in another room, and left. If the participants failed to mention anything about the empty envelopes, the secretary expressed surprise that they had lost all of their money since "few participants ever do." She then volunteered to check the work sheets and left the room. Within minutes she returned with the evidence that enabled participants to label the event as a theft. The evidence consisted of four of the participant's work sheets that were ostensibly found in the confederate's work pile. The secretary called participants' attention to where their initials had been erased and the confederate's substituted. This evidence was sufficient to convince all but five participants that a theft had occurred. The secretary, who gave the impression of being new to the organization and of low status, then explained that her supervisor had left the office and that she could not provide financial compensation.

She subsequently proceeded to employ a series of prearranged prods of increasing intensity designed to induce participants to use her phone to call the police. The first prod read: "The least I can do is get the police's number so you can file a complaint with them. They can be here in a few minutes." Prod two read: "I think you ought to seriously consider calling the police." Prod three read: "The police should definitely be notified. I'll dial and you can speak to them." In this way it was possible to quantify participants' willingness to report the event to the police on a 6-point response scale ranging from a spontaneous request to call the police (scored 6) to a failure to label the incident as a theft (scored 1). A score of 5 was assigned if the participants agreed to call after the first prod, a score of 4 was assigned if they agreed to call after the second prod, a score of 3 if they agreed to call after the third prod, and a score of 2 if they resisted all prods. An assistant, who observed and listened to the interaction via a one-way mirror and a concealed microphone, recorded participants' responses on an observation form. The experiment was terminated immediately after participants agreed or failed to agree to call the police. For those who agreed to report the theft (i.e., they took the phone receiver), no actual report was made since the secretary's phone was not connected.

Participants then received a lengthy debriefing by the supervisor in which all of the deceptions and their rationale were revealed. Subsequently, the supervisor tested their recall of the events of the experiment and asked them to explain why they agreed or did not agree to phone the police. At the conclusion of the interview they were paid a bonus of $3 and were asked to sign a consent form and to complete anonymously a brief questionnaire assessing their reactions to the study. Approximately 2 months after their participation they were sent a photo of a simulated police lineup and asked to identify the confederate–thief if they saw him in the photo. Finally, their recall of specific details of the theft and their reasons for reporting or not reporting were assessed once more via a telephone interview.

Employment of the paradigm

The experimental paradigm enabled us to investigate victim reporting from a number of perspectives. First, we were able to manipulate systematically several features of the situation and to observe the impact of these manipulations on victims' willingness to notify the police. Second, since it was possible to observe directly the responses of our experimental victims as they labored over their decision, we conducted an observational study of victim decision-making. Third, because the paradigm allowed for a comparison among victim self-reports collected at three different times, we were able to measure the reliability of victim self-reports over a period of several months.

Independent variables

Three independent variables were factorially manipulated in a $2 \times 2 \times 2$ design. The three variables consisted of (1) magnitude of the theft ($20 versus $3), (2) race of the thief (black versus white), and (3) proximity of the thief at the time of the report opportunity (thief present versus thief absent). The variable of theft magnitude was chosen because survey studies have shown it to be correlated with victim reporting (Ennis, 1967; Schneider, Burcart, and Wilson, 1976). Inclusion of this variable was designed to provide a test of convergent validity as well as to permit the study of its interaction with the other two independent variables. We chose to look at the effects of the thief's race because the literature on racial stereotypes (Karlins, Coffman, and Walters, 1969) and the functioning of the criminal justice system (Chambliss and Seidman, 1971) suggest that race indirectly affects the likelihood of being arrested and convicted, as well as the severity of the sentence received. We were interested in learning whether the thief's race is related to victims' decisions to report the theft or not. The third variable, proximity of the thief, was chosen because survey results suggest that victims fail to report because of their belief that "nothing could be done." We expected it to interact with the other independent variables. More specifically, we predicted that when the magnitude of the theft is high ($20), victims would be highly motivated to report to the police regardless of the thief's proximity. When, however, the magnitude of the theft is low ($3), there would be greater reporting when the thief is present (and thus easier to apprehend) than when the thief is absent. While the thief's continued presence in the situation may facilitate apprehension by the police, presence may also serve to heighten fear. On the assumption that victims are more fearful of reprisal from a black thief, it was predicted that victims would be less likely to report a black suspect when the latter is still on the premises than when the thief has already left the scene. Thus, we expected an interaction between race of the thief and thief proximity, such that a black thief would be more likely to be reported when absent than when present, whereas a white thief would be more likely to be reported when present than when absent.

Magnitude of the theft was manipulated by giving participants either $20 or $3 and then having them lose the money as a result of the theft of papers from their out boxes. In the $3 loss condition each completed sheet was worth 50¢ compared to $3 per sheet in the $20 loss condition. Race of the thief was manipulated by employing four college-age male confederates (two black and two white) to play the role of thief. Proximity of the thief was manipulated by calling the participant in first to see the secretary (thief present) or by calling the participant in second, after the thief had supposedly departed (thief absent).

The participants

Of the 188 respondents to the newspaper ad, 40 were eliminated because of health problems. In the course of their participation an additional 28 participants were eliminated for the following reasons: suspicious ($n = 12$), failed to follow instructions ($n = 9$), refused to sign consent form ($n = 4$), experimenter procedural error ($n = 2$), became emotionally upset ($n = 1$).[3] The remaining 120 participants

---

[3]Identification of suspicious participants was made by the supervisor on the basis of his observation of participants' behavior immediately prior to and during the secretary's prodding. Although several participants voiced suspicion that this "might be a setup," most of them only entertained this as a tentative hypothesis and, as judged by their subsequent behavior, they abandoned it in favor of a crime interpretation. These participants were *not* labeled as suspicious. In every case, the supervisor's judgment was confirmed by participants during the debriefing session. Only those participants who persisted in verbally proclaiming their suspicions or who gave nonverbal displays of suspicion (e.g., smirks or snickers) were labeled as suspicious. Of the 9 participants who were omitted because they failed to follow instructions, 3 refused to compete with the confederate, and 6, upon being told to hand their money over to the confederate, either refused, thereby preventing completion of the theft, or left the experimental room prematurely in order to question the supervisor about the results. While most participants became aroused by knowledge of the theft, one person became unduly aroused (it appeared that this person was about to break into tears) and the supervisor, therefore, felt that it was wise to terminate the experiment prior to the secretary's prods. This person subsequently regained composure upon learning of the deceptions and willingly signed the consent form.

(94 females and 26 males) were randomly assigned to the experimental conditions. Participants ranged in age from 16 to 66 ($M = 32.6$) with 82.5% being white ($n = 99$) and 17.5% being black ($n = 21$). The racial composition of the sample resembled that of the city of Pittsburgh, where blacks comprise 20% of the population (U.S. Bureau of the Census, 1977). With respect to family income, 38% listed it as below $6,000; 30% between $6,001 and $12,000; 16% between 12,001 and $18,000; and 16% above $18,000. With regard to highest educational degree earned, 3% had completed grade school only, 52% had high school diplomas, 13% had degrees from technical schools, 26% had college degrees, and 6% had graduate degrees. In terms of occupation, 9% listed themselves as students, 40% held blue- and white-collar positions, 20% described themselves as homemakers, 30% were unemployed, and 1% were retired.

The impact of independent variables on reporting

Across all conditions, 31% ($n = 37$) of the participants were willing to notify the police (i.e., they had a report score of 3 or higher). An analysis of variance performed on the reporting scores showed that none of the main effects was significant. The analysis yielded a significant interaction between proximity of thief and magnitude of theft: $F (1,112) = 4.09, p <.05$. As hypothesized (see Table 4.1), when the theft was only $3, participants were more willing to report when the thief was present than when he was absent. Whereas we predicted no difference in reporting when the theft magnitude was $20, the data show that victims of a $20 theft were more likely to report when the thief was absent than when he was present. An alternative way of reading this table is that variations in theft magnitude have little impact on reporting when the thief is still present, whereas when the thief has fled the scene, reporting increases with the magnitude of the theft.

Although there was no main effect for participants' sex, there was a significant interaction between proximity of thief and sex of victim: $F (1, 112) = 6.37, p <.02$. As shown in Table 4.2, males were more likely to report when the thief was absent than when he was present, whereas the reverse was true for females.

One of the more important findings pertained to race of participant: black participants were more willing to call the police ($M = 3.0$) than white participants ($M = 2.36$), $t (118) = 2.86, p <.01$, regardless of the thief's race. This difference could not be accounted for by socioeconomic class differences or by differences on other demographic dimensions. Rather, the difference occurred despite the finding that

Table 4.1
Mean reporting scores as function of
proximity of thief and magnitude of theft

	Magnitude of theft	
Proximity of thief	$20	$3
Present	2.40	2.50
Absent	2.80	2.20

Table 4.2
Mean reporting scores as function of
proximity of thief and sex of victim

	Sex of victim	
Proximity of thief	Male	Female
Present	2.25	2.51
Absent	3.00	1.56

blacks expressed significantly more negative attitudes toward the police than did whites on three of four questionnaire items. Black participants felt that the local police do a poorer job of enforcing the law, t (113) = 2.05, $p <.05$; are less prompt in answering calls, t (111) = 5.02, $p <.001$; and provide poorer protection for people in their neighborhood, t (114) = 4.61, $p <.001$.

Arguments offered against notifying the police

In addition to measuring the effect of the independent variables on reporting, the paradigm offered a unique opportunity of observing the arguments participants gave the secretary for not wishing to report the incident to the police. Since the secretary's advice was to call the police, her prodding either elicited agreement or stimulated participants to verbalize their reasons for not wanting to call the police. For this reason the procedure did not allow us to assess the reasons participants offered for calling the police since responses to the secretary's prods were usually uninformative (e.g., "Okay, I guess I will"). Considering the first reason offered only by those who resisted all of the secretary's prods (i.e., the nonreporters), the most frequently cited arguments against calling the police were "Not important, not worth the time" (37%), "Not a police matter" (24%), "Police ineffectiveness" (20%), "Concern for the thief's welfare"

(10%, namely, "I didn't want to get him in trouble"), and "Fear of retaliation" (5%); 3% offered other reasons.

Participants' responses to the secretary's prods provided additional insights about the cognitive–emotional state produced by manipulation of the independent variables. Although there were no significant main effects in terms of reporting scores, there were differences in the reasons offered by nonreporters in the various conditions. Examination of all reasons (not just the first) given by nonreporters shows that 41% in the thief-absent condition cited police ineffectiveness as one reason for not wanting to report, as compared to 18% in the thief-present condition, $\chi^2 (1) = 3.95$, $p < .05$. Participants who resisted reporting a black thief more frequently cited fear of retaliation as a reason (26%) than those who resisted reporting a white thief (2.5%), $\chi^2 (1) = 7.26$, $p < .01$. In addition, there was a slight tendency for nonreporters who lost \$3 to cite the triviality of the theft (62%) as a reason for not reporting, compared to nonreporters who lost \$20 (44%), $\chi^2 (1) = 1.73$, $p > .05$. Inclusion of the reasons offered to the secretary for not wanting to call the police is not meant to imply that such reasons reflect the "true" motives for participants' actions. The data do not permit us to make that determination. Rather, they are included to provide the reader with an understanding of the kinds of arguments offered by participants in this situation. Such arguments, which may in part reflect participants' true motives, perhaps reveal more about the kinds of arguments they believed would be most convincing in responding to the secretary's prods.

Recall of the victimization experience

How reliable are participants' recall of the reasons initially offered for not reporting? The paradigm allows for measuring recall at two different times subsequent to the theft: about 20 minutes after the theft during the debriefing interview (immediate-recall measure), and approximately 2 months later (delayed-recall measure). Since written records were kept of the reasons offered by participants in response to the secretary's prods, it was possible to compare the recall measures with these responses and with each other. Telephone contact was made with 89 participants (74% of the sample) approximately 2 months after their participation. Of this number, there were 51 nonreporters who gave codable replies to the question: "What reason or reasons did you have for your decision not to call the police?" Table 4.3 shows the first reason given by nonreporters at the three different times of measurement. The results clearly show that the reason most often given at all three times was that the loss was so trivial, it would

Table 4.3
First reason given for not reporting at three different times

	Measure, %		
Reason	Report to secretary	Immediate recall	Delayed recall
Not important, not worth the time	37	35	53
Not a police matter	24	24	22
Police ineffectiveness	20	16	2
Concern for thief's welfare	10	9	12
Fear of retaliation	5	6	6
Other	3	10	6
	(n = 78)	(n = 80)	(n = 51)

not be worthwhile to report it. As indicated in Table 4.3, the percentage of nonreporters citing a particular reason was stable across the three measures. The one exception is the category "Police ineffectiveness," where the percentage declined from 20% to 16% to 2%. The category "Not a police matter" included a variety of responses. Some participants claimed that the organization was responsible for allowing the theft to occur and therefore should reimburse them, some preferred to consult with a friend or spouse, and still others (mostly females) preferred to confront the thief themselves rather than report him to the police.

Although the percentage of participants citing each reason is consistent over time, the data do not tell us whether *individuals* respond consistently over time. In order to ascertain individual consistency (as distinguished from group consistency), we calculated for each nonreporter whether the first reason given at each time corresponded with the first reason given at the other times. Results of this analysis show that the reason given during immediate recall matched our observation of the reason given to the secretary only 50% of the time. The first reason given during delayed recall matched the reason given the secretary in only 39% of the cases. Highest agreement was found between the immediate- and delayed-recall measures, the percentage being 57%. It would appear from these data that nonreporters were inconsistent in explaining their behavior. Only 20 minutes after their decision (immediate recall), half of the participants were already citing a reason that was at variance with the one initially given the secretary. What is striking about these data is that there is greater agreement between the immediate- and delayed-recall measures (an interval of about 2 months) than between the report to the secretary and the immediate-recall measure (an interval of about 20 minutes).

Somewhat better recall was found on the delayed measure when reporters and nonreporters were asked to recall specific details of the theft. Thus, all participants correctly recalled the thief's race and sex. Further, 95.5% correctly recalled whether the thief was present or absent during the report phase; 92% correctly recalled whether or not they agreed to call the police, and 63% correctly recalled the month the theft took place.

As a further test of recall accuracy, 2 months after the theft, participants were asked to identify the thief from a photo of a simulated police lineup. Returns were received from 77 participants (64% of the sample). Across conditions, 65% correctly identified the thief. Those who lost $20 tended to be more accurate in identifying the thief (76% correct) than those who lost $3 (54% correct), $\chi^2 (1) = 3.34$, $p < .10$. In order to obtain a more refined measure than the binary correct–incorrect measure so often used in eyewitness-identification research, an "accuracy" index was created by assigning a score of $+1$ to a correct identification and -1 to an incorrect identification and multiplying by participants' rating of confidence in their judgment (on a 9-point scale). An 18-point accuracy index was thus created, which ranged from $+9$ (confident and correct) to -9 (confident but wrong). An analysis of variance performed on these scores showed that $20 victims were more accurate in their identification than $3 victims, $F (1, 69) = 4.5$, $p < .05$. Victims of a $20 theft were probably more motivated to attend to the thief's characteristics than were victims of a $3 theft. Further analysis revealed that confidence and correctness were positively correlated, $r = .30$, $p < .01$. However, when this correlation was calculated separately according to the thief's race, an interesting difference emerged. When the thief was white, correctness and confidence were highly correlated, $r = .54$, $p < .01$; whereas when the thief was black, the correlation was insignificant, $r = .18$. The difference between the two correlations was only marginally significant, $p = .08$. The significant correlation obtained when the thief was white contrasts with the failure of most previous studies to find a significant relationship between correctness and confidence (Buckhout et al., 1974; Johnson and Scott, 1976). A major difference between the present study and previous research is that the earlier studies examined *bystander* accuracy, whereas the present study examined *victim* accuracy. In addition, participants in the present study had considerably longer exposure to the thief than did subjects in previous research. A combination of both factors may account for the difference in results.

A note of caution is in order concerning interpretation of the im-
mediate- and delayed-recall data. Since these data were collected
after the debriefing, participants knew when their recall was tested
that they were not victims of an actual theft. This knowledge may
have led many of them to view the event as less significant, thereby
producing poorer recall. Conceivably, the impact of the debriefing
may have varied across conditions (e.g., participants in the $20 con-
dition may have been more relieved than those in the $3 condition).
For these reasons care should be exercised in generalizing from the
present recall data to survey data.

CONCLUSIONS

Although victims are not usually thought to be part of the criminal
justice system, their decisions nevertheless have an immense impact
on its functioning. As the system's gatekeepers, victims, more than
any members of the system, determine the likelihood of who will be
arrested, prosecuted, and sentenced. Investigatory procedures that
may be appropriate for studying decision-making by members of the
system have been shown to be less suitable for studying victim decision-making. Rather than relying on naturalistic observation and self-
report procedures to infer why victims choose to report or not report
their victimization to the police, we have chosen instead an experimental paradigm to achieve this goal.

Among the more important results to emerge from this paradigm
is the finding that for thefts up to $20 an increase in the magnitude
of the theft enhances reporting only when the thief has already left
the scene. Contrary to expectations, the thief's race did not significantly affect reporting. Thus, while the decisions of some agents of
the criminal justice system may be correlated with the target's race,
the decisions of victims in our study apparently were not. Another
unexpected finding was that black victims were more likely to call
the police than white victims regardless of the thief's race. This finding is all the more perplexing in light of the finding that black participants expressed more negative attitudes toward the police. When
making their decision, black participants probably gave less weight
to their global attitudes toward the police than they did to yet-un-
identified situationally defined forces. At the very least, this apparent
contradiction represents still another instance of the frequently obtained inconsistency between attitude and behavior (Wicker, 1969).

One of the more significant findings to emerge from this research concerns participants' recall of their reasons for not calling the police. Participants offered different reasons at different times for their unwillingness to call the police. Such inconsistency casts doubt on the reliability of the self-report technique as a method for measuring the determinants of victim reporting. The fact that there was greater agreement between the immediate- and the delayed-recall measures than between the report to the secretary and the immediate-recall measure suggests that many participants reinterpreted the reasons for their actions shortly after their decision and that it was this interpretation that was recalled 2 months later.

Our advocacy of the experimental approach to the study of victim crime reporting by no means implies endorsement of all forms of experimentation such as a field experimental approach typically employed in studies of bystander reactions to a theft. The reservations about this approach derive primarily from our concern with participants' welfare since in such studies it is nearly impossible to screen potential participants for health risks or to give them a choice about participating. Nor does our advocacy of the experimental approach imply endorsement of experiments that employ paper-and-pencil measures of behavioral intentions as the dependent measure. While such "as if" techniques might prove useful when investigating responses to situations with which subjects are highly familiar, or situations in which the determining factors are blatantly obvious (e.g., "How would you respond if a robber stuck a gun to your head and asked for your money?"), they are likely to be poor measures when more subtle determining conditions are present. In our judgment, the decision to employ a laboratory experimental paradigm in a community setting involving the *behavior* of people from the community appears to represent the best balance in terms of *control, generalizability,* and *participant welfare.* Of necessity restricted to less serious categories of victimization, this approach offers researchers an excellent opportunity for rigorously testing causal hypotheses concerning the determinants of victim reporting.

We recommend that future research take a multimethod approach to the study of victim decision-making. The paradigm described in this chapter can provide a degree of balance in an area that is dominated by a single methodological approach. The survey and experimental approaches are, we believe, complementary. Each can provide information about victim reporting that the other appears unable to do. We contend that the results from our experimental paradigm can suggest issues and questions that can be examined in future victimization surveys, just as the survey results have suggested variables to be manipulated in the laboratory.

References

Bickman, L., & Rosenbaum, D. P. Crime reporting as a function of bystander encouragement, surveillance, and credibility. *Journal of Personality and Social Psychology,* 1977, *35,* 577–586.

Black, D. J., & Reiss, A. J., Jr. *Studies of crime and law enforcement in major metropolitan areas: Patterns of behavior in police and citizen transactions.* Field Surveys III, Vol. 2, President's Commission on Law Enforcement and the Administration of Justice. Washington, DC: U.S. Government Printing Office, 1967.

Blalock, H. M., Jr. *Causal inferences in nonexperimental research.* New York: Norton, 1964.

Buckhout, R., Alper, A., Chern, S., Silverberg, G., & Slomovits, M. Determinants of eyewitness performance on a lineup. *Bulletin of the Psychonomic Society,* 1974, *4,* 191–192.

Campbell, D. T., & Stanley, J. C. *Experimental and quasi-experimental designs for research.* Chicago: Rand McNally, 1966.

Chambliss, W. J., & Seidman, R. B. *Law, order, and power.* Reading, MA: Addison-Wesley, 1971.

Criminal victimization in the United States—1973. A national crime panel survey report #SD-NCP-N-4. Washington, DC: Law Enforcement Assistance Administration, December, 1976.

Criminal victimization in the United States: A comparison of 1974 and 1975 findings. A national crime panel survey report #SD-NCP-N-5. Washington, DC: Law Enforcement Assistance Administration, February 1977.

Ebbesen, E. B., & Konečni, V. J. Decision making and information integration in the courts: The setting of bail. *Journal of Personality and Social Psychology,* 1975, *32,* 805–821.

Ennis, P. H. *Criminal victimization in the United States: A report of a national survey.* Field Surveys II, President's Commission on Law Enforcement and the Administration of Justice. Washington, DC: U.S. Government Printing Office, 1967.

Federal Bureau of Investigation. *Uniform crime reports, 1971–1975.* Washington, DC: U.S. Government Printing Office, 1976.

Hindelang, M. J. *Criminal victimization in eight American cities: A descriptive analysis of common theft and assault.* Cambridge, MA: Ballinger, 1976.

Hindelang, M. J., & Gottfredson, M. The victim's decision not to invoke the criminal justice process. In W. F. McDonald (Ed.), *Criminal justice and the victim.* Beverly Hills, CA: Sage, 1976.

Johnson, C., & Scott, B. *Eyewitness testimony and subject identification as a function of arousal, sex of witness, and scheduling of interrogation.* Paper presented at 84th Annual Convention of American Psychological Association, Washington, DC, 1976.

Karlins, M., Coffman, T. L., & Walters, G. W. On the fading of social stereotypes: Studies in three generations of college students. *Journal of Personality and Social Psychology,* 1969, *13,* 1–16.

Latané, B., & Darley, J. M. *The unresponsive bystander: Why doesn't he help?* New York: Appleton-Century-Crofts, 1970.

Miller, D. C. *Handbook of research design and social measurement.* 2nd ed. New York: McKay, 1970.

Nisbett, R. E., & Wilson, T. D. Telling more than we know: Verbal reports on mental processes. *Psychological Review*, 1977, *84*, 231–259.

Penick, B. K. E., & Owens, M. E. B., III. *Surveying crime*. Washington, DC: National Academy of Sciences, 1976.

Reiss, A. J., Jr. *The police and the public*. New Haven, CT: Yale University Press, 1971.

San Jose methods test of known crime victims. Statistics technical report #1. Washington, DC: Law Enforcement Assistance Administration, 1972.

Schneider, A. L., Burcart, J. M., & Wilson, L. A., III. The role of attitudes in the decision to report crimes to the police. In W. F. McDonald (Ed.), *Criminal justice and the victim*. Beverly Hills, CA: Sage, 1976.

Selltiz, C., Wrightsman, L., & Cook, S. W. *Research methods in social relations*. New York: Holt, Rinehart and Winston, 1976.

U.S. Bureau of the Census. *Statistical abstract of the United States, 1977*. 98th ed. Washington, DC: U.S. Government Printing Office, 1977.

Victim recall pretest (Washington, D.C.) Prepared by the Demographic Surveys Division of the Bureau of the Census. Washington, DC: Law Enforcement Assistance Administration, 1970.

Wicker, A. W. Attitudes vs. actions: The relationship of verbal and overt behavioral responses to attitude objects. *Journal of Social Issues*, 1969, *25*, 41–78.

Yost, L. R., & Dodge, R. W. *Household survey of victims of crime, second pretest (Baltimore, Maryland)*. Prepared by the Demographic Surveys Division of the Bureau of the Census. Washington, DC: Law Enforcement Assistance Administration, 1970.

THE GATHERING OF EVIDENCE

Editors' Introduction

The next chapter is a comprehensive review of research findings in general, social, and legal psychology that are relevant to the issue of eyewitness identification and testimony. After a crime has been committed and either detected by police officers or reported to them by victims or witnesses, informal accounts of the circumstances of the crime given by the victims and/or witnesses may often influence the police officers' decision of whether or not to make an arrest, whom to arrest, and what to charge the person with. Subsequently, whether or not an arrested person remains in custody, whether or not the charges are modified by the police, whether or not the prosecutor decides to file a complaint, and what charges the complaint contains—all, in part and at least in some cases, depend on eyewitness identification carried out by victims and/or witnesses either informally (in interviews with police officers and examination of photographs in police files) or more formally (picking of suspects from lineups). When and if the case comes to trial, eyewitnesses' testimony regarding the identity and role of the accused in the crime is thought to carry a lot of weight in the fact-finding process, certainly more than other types of evidence (e.g., physical and circumstantial evidence).

Levine and Tapp review the psychological research that is concerned both with victims and witnesses as "data gatherers" and with witnesses' courtroom behavior (the psychology of testimony). They are thus dealing with some of the classical issues in legal psychology; indeed, these were the issues that seemed to first arouse the interest of experimentally trained psychologists in the legal process (as in Hugo Münsterberg's influential On the Witness Stand, published in 1908). In the folklore that surrounds the processing of alleged criminals, too, eyewitness identification and witness courtroom behavior seem to arouse fascination that is perhaps matched only by the mystique of the goings-on in the jury room.

From the decision-making orientation taken in this book, "gathering evidence" (which prominently includes eyewitness identification) can be thought of as a decision node that, on one hand, summarizes several "minidecisions" by the different participants in the criminal justice system (the victims' and witnesses' willingness and ability to provide a correct identification, police detectives' behavior in interviews with the witnesses regarding the composition of the lineups and instructions to the witnesses, etc.) and, on the other hand, influences the decisions of other participants (e.g., prosecutorial charging decisions; the behavior of the participants involved in subsequent stages of the process, such as juries and probation officers). Because the process of gathering evidence involves many participants and their decisions, and often lasts from before the arrest until the plea-bargaining and/or trial stage (and sometimes into the trial), our decision to place the chapter between the one dealing with the victim's decision to report the crime and those dealing with the behavior of the police was, of necessity, somewhat arbitrary.

5

Eyewitness Identification: Problems and Pitfalls[1]

Felice J. Levine and June Louin Tapp

The adjudication of disputes is a dynamic process that evolves through a complex network of interactions from initial event (e.g., crime, contractual arrangement, tort) to ultimate disposition (e.g., plea bargaining, negotiated settlement, court award). While the legal system is a structured, institutionalized forum for handling conflict, whether civil or criminal, decision-making does not result from the mechanical application of rules or procedures. In the criminal justice system, information delivered by the eyewitness, if there is one, is a crucial component of the decisional process. In actual practice, victims or other persons at the scene of the crime function as data-gathering sources whose construction of reality can significantly affect the fate of the alleged offender.

In this chapter we explore that decision-making role as it pertains to person identification. In criminal law, the victim is a complaining witness who—like other witnesses—provides evidence to the state. In comparison to circumstantial evidence, eyewitness reports tend to

---

[1]This chapter is an update and expansion of work on the psychology of criminal identification undertaken by the authors at the American Bar Foundation (see also Levine and Tapp, 1973). While the chapter was initially drafted in 1977, subsequent research over the past several years has generally supported our ideas and has further underscored the necessity of understanding the role of the eyewitness as data gatherer and particularly the impact of the legal system on witnesses coming to terms with the identification task. Some of this recent work is cited in the text and footnotes; for a comprehensive review of this literature, the reader is referred as well to Loftus (1979) and Yarmey (1979) and to the special issue on eyewitness behavior in *Law and Human Behavior*, edited by Wells (1980).

be accorded a high degree of credibility.[2] In fact, a positive identification is likely to be sufficiently persuasive to the police and the prosecutor to advance the case to the next decisional stage—charging, indictment, arraignment, and the like. An inconclusive identification, however, is likely to stall the proceeding or perhaps encourage law-enforcement officials to search for other suspects or evidence.

Because of the importance of information from eyewitnesses, our purpose here is to assess the role of victim or witness as data gatherer and some of the problems and pitfalls of that enterprise. To that end, we turn to the literature of psychology. First, we consider a number of areas in general and social psychology. In this effort we draw inferences about the dynamics of criminal identification from evidence that is relevant and transferable to, but not directly drawn from, legal contexts. Second, we examine the literature on legal psychology, a subfield of study where there has been extensive work, particularly on the psychology of testimony. While research applied specifically to legal settings is clearly the most germane, we have adopted a broader perspective in order to identify the range of considerations that might affect eyewitnesses as well as to raise questions about the certainty that seems to surround this form of identification.

In sum, although many crimes have no eyewitness, the importance of information provided by victims and bystanders suggests the value of attending to the quality (i.e., accuracy) of eyewitness input. Based on this analysis, we seek to advance the general contention that information processing within the criminal justice system is not an automatic set of events but a human activity with attendant fallibilities.

BACKGROUND OF THE PROBLEM

In the words of Judge McGowan, "the vagaries of visual identification [have] been thought by many experts to present what is conceivably the greatest single threat to the achievement of our ideal that no innocent man shall be punished" (1970, p. 238). Erroneous identification of criminal suspects has long been recognized as a crucial problem in the administration of justice (Frankfurter, 1927; Marshall,

---

[2]This issue is examined in greater depth in the next section of the chapter. The persuasiveness of eyewitness evidence has been frequently observed (Hammelmann and Williams, 1963; Sobel, 1972; Wall, 1965). Indeed, the analytic distinction between eyewitness reports and circumstantial evidence would suggest the attribution of greater certainty to the former than the latter. However, as Buckhout cautions, "the two types of evidence are similar: both contain areas of doubt which should be recognized" (1976, p. 91).

1966; Sobel, 1972; Wall, 1965; Wigmore, 1937). While numerous examples of convictions based on faulty identification have been documented (Borchard, 1932; Frank and Frank, 1957; Gardner, 1952; Wilder and Wentworth, 1932; Williams, 1963), the actual incidence of mistaken identification is of course impossible to determine because in most cases the error goes undetected. As the Michigan Supreme Court poignantly emphasized in *People v. Anderson*: "For a number of obvious reasons . . . including the fact that there is no on-going systematic study of the problem, the reported cases of misidentification are in every likelihood only the tip of the iceberg" (1973, p. 472).

In the fifth century B.C., Thucydides recognized the magnitude of the problem when he despairingly noted a "want of coincidence between accounts of the same occurrences by different eyewitnesses, arising sometimes from imperfect memory, sometimes from undue partiality for one side or the other" (1951, p. 14). Although we all know from our experience that people quite often do not see or hear things that are presented clearly to their senses, do see or hear things that are not there, do not remember things that have happened to them, and do remember things that did not happen, visual identification remains one of the most, if not the most, persuasive kind of evidence that can be presented in criminal cases. The problem of faulty identification is particularly important because potential jurors—and many law-enforcement officials and judges—seem to exhibit extraordinary confidence in eyewitness data. That people are unduly receptive to such testimony and may give it greater weight than they do alibis, character witnesses, or even physical evidence has been frequently observed by courts (*Manson v. Brathwaite*, 1977; *People v. Anderson*, 1973; *United States v. Wade*, 1967) and commentators alike (Borchard, 1932; Hammelmann and Williams, 1963; Sobel, 1972; Wall, 1965). This situation underscores the necessity of improving the quality of pretrial identification proceedings and thus reducing the number of faulty identifications transmitted for use in prosecutions.

A witness may be confronted by a range of opportunities for pretrial identification including photographs, voice tapes, showups (one suspect), and lineups. Indeed, a major problem in the implementation of justice is that often more than one procedure is employed, with earlier identifications affecting subsequent reports. Given such complexity, we endeavor to be inclusive in our consideration of identification procedures. Later in this chapter, however, we focus particularly on the lineup, which courts have held to be preferable to any single-suspect procedure or even photographic display (*People v.*

Cotton, 1972; *People* v. *Rowell*, 1968; *Simmons* v. *United States*, 1968; *United States* v. *Ash*, 1972; *United States* v. *Wade*, 1967). In fact, the lineup was developed by the British police in the 1920s because the showup, or formal one-to-one confrontation between witness and suspect, was considered grossly suggestive and unfair (Quinn, 1970; Wall, 1965). Research evidence, discussed subsequently, would seem to confirm that choice.

Despite the variable circumstances under which identifications occur, it may be useful at this point to describe briefly the lineup and its place in the criminal justice procedure. A lineup can occur from 1 or 2 days to weeks or even months after the crime. The witness, including a police eyewitness,[3] may be either the victim of the crime or a bystander. The witness typically will have been questioned by police soon after the crime, asked to describe the offender, and perhaps also requested to view photos for a possible identification. At that time the police probably will not have a particular suspect in mind unless either the description or the *modus operandi* struck a familiar chord, and therefore the potential for improper suggestion usually will be minimal. In the actual lineup, however, the police will almost always suspect a particular individual, and there is substantial potential for suggestion.

If witnesses identify a lineup participant as the perpetrator of the crime, they will ordinarily be asked to testify to this at the trial, if there is one. The last qualifying clause is crucial because only a very small percentage of criminal cases actually go to trial. The great majority are settled by plea bargaining, and, because of popular faith in eyewitness identification, it is probable that a positive identification often contributes to persuading the suspect and the defense attorney to accept a guilty plea. Without going to trial, witness testimony cannot be directly challenged by cross-examination from the defense, the one procedure that might call the identification into question.

As suggested by the above, the identification process is a complex phenomenon with substantial potential for mistakes. In evaluating

---

[3]See, e.g., *Manson* v. *Brathwaite* (1977, p. 130). More than 25 years ago, the lawyer–novelist Erle Stanley Gardner reported an empirical test of the inability of even trained, experienced state police officers to estimate accurately height, weight, and age. The respective variations were 5 inches, 20 pounds, and 15 years: "[A]nd it is to be remembered that these descriptions were furnished not by men who were excited because they were being held up, or by men who were getting a fleeting glimpse of an individual in a dim light—they were sitting there looking directly at [the subject] . . . and they were trained observers, men who made it their business to classify and describe" (Gardner, 1952, p. 82).

the quality of the "data" transmitted by the witness, we are concerned with two kinds of errors. The first, which has received the most attention, is identification of the wrong person as the criminal; the second is failure to identify the right person.[4] The first kind of error may be more common and, in a system of law and justice based on the presumption of innocence, is far more dangerous. But unfortunately the second type of mistake also occurs. The presumption of innocence is not incompatible with a desire to prevent crime. If there is a mistaken identification, the real criminal is still loose, and, whatever may be said about the morality or utility of punishment, the identification of offenders is essential to any system of criminal justice. Therefore, since both types of errors pose serious problems, procedures and standards should be developed that prevent both.

To promote the development of such procedures, the Supreme Court over a decade ago attempted to confront the "dangers inherent in eyewitness identification and the suggestibility inherent in the context of the pretrial identification" (*United States v. Wade*, 1967, p. 235). On June 12, 1967, the Court, in a trilogy of cases, *United States v. Wade*, *Gilbert v. California*, and *Stovall v. Denno*, dealt with the constitutionality of police practices and procedures in obtaining eyewitness identifications. The Court's primary concern was to evolve legal standards and remedies that would substantially reduce erroneous identification. Because of the risk of intentional and unintentional suggestion at lineups resulting in error and abuse in identifications, and because of the concomitant difficulty of reconstructing lineup events for purposes of discrediting a witness's testimony at trial, the Court designated the lineup a "critical stage" in the trial process, during which suspects were to be protected by the Sixth Amendment right to counsel.

While the *Wade* trilogy mandated reforms, subsequent decisions (*Kirby v. Illinois*, 1972; *Manson v. Brathwaite*, 1977; *Neil v. Biggers*, 1972) eroded its impact and revealed diminished judicial concern about protecting the fact-finding process from erroneous identification. This chapter seeks to revive that basic concern. Through an overview of empirical evidence—both direct and indirect—related to criminal identification, we seek (1) to illuminate the role of the witness or victim as a data gatherer and thereby (2) to stimulate further inquiry into how the accuracy of this information-processing stage might be increased.

---

[4]These two forms of identification error parallel the error that may emerge in hypothesis testing in statistical analysis. Type I error refers to invalid confirmation or a false positive. Type II error refers to invalid disconfirmation or a false negative.

GENERAL AND SOCIAL PSYCHOLOGY

Human limitations on identification

While the heavy reliance on eyewitness reports suggests that as a practical matter they are considered carbon copies of an objective reality, it is erroneous to assume that perceptual and memory processes yield photographic or exact records of events. There is ample research indicating that to function effectively these processes must be both flexible and selective (Gibson, 1968; Norman, 1976; Treisman and Geffen, 1969). Memory, cognition, and information processing are active, not passive, abilities that involve the meaningful organization of discrete elements of a situation.

Since perception consists of the coding of stimulus inputs, it may very well be limited or distorted by situational circumstances. What one perceives does not always correspond with what is before one. The length of time of the observation, the conditions of the observation (e.g., distance, lighting), the physical conditions of the witness (e.g., nearsighted, intoxicated), and the primary purpose of the witness at the time of the event are all important variables. For example, even leaving aside for the moment emotional or motivational factors that may distort perception, a witness to, or victim of, a crime may not concentrate on the perpetrator because the event itself may have gone unnoticed or seemed insignificant or because the person may need to focus on other aspects of the event (e.g., escaping).

In short, people can perceive only so much at one time and can code even less (Bruner, 1968). Thus, we develop what may be called *economical perception*, the ability "to concentrate on one thing at a time in the face of everything going on in the environment," so that "the information registered about objects and events becomes only what is needed, not all that could be obtained" (Gibson, 1968, p. 677). As Bruner put it, "organisms have a highly limited span of attention and a highly limited span of immediate memory. Selectivity is forced upon us by the nature of these limitations" (1958, p. 86).

The accuracy of memory depends in part on the accuracy of perception. To the extent that one perceives incorrectly what happens, remembering will be incorrect. But there are other factors (e.g., recency, primacy, contiguity, frequency) involved in memory that add to the possibility of inaccuracy. Because memory is an ongoing process that modifies or represents experience rather than simply registering it (Adams, 1967; Klatzky, 1975; Norman, 1976), the time span between initial event and later recognition is a particularly important situational variable.

The data on recognition memory—and eyewitness identification is one instance—generally show that retention weakens over time. Bahrick and Bahrick (1964), for example, found that recognition remained high after 2 hours, but deteriorated markedly after 2 weeks. Shepard (1967) tested for recognition of pictures after intervals of 2 hours and 3, 7, and 120 days and found respective median percent retentions of 100, 93, 92, and 57.[5] Not all research, however, confirmed these effects. Several studies on the relationship between time delay and face recognition did not find significant differences in recognition accuracy (Chance, Goldstein, and McBride, 1975; Laughery et al., 1974). But this work was conducted solely in the laboratory, and the time intervals used were generally quite short (typically a few days or a week).

The dominant finding for pictorial and verbal stimuli is that information is forgotten with increased time intervals. The processes involved in the weakening of recollections are quite complex. Intervening impressions can reduce the salience of a memory and inhibit completeness and accuracy. In addition, information or events relevant to the initial experience, but introduced subsequently (e.g., questioning, facial photos, police drawings), may also affect memory.[6] Thus, as a general rule, interpolated tasks, events, and materials are likely to affect the limits and nature of retention.

One final situational variable merits attention because of its impact on the human capacity to perceive and remember. Problems arising from (1) the unexpectedness, insignificance, and brevity of the event (reducing perceptual attention and readiness) and (2) the time span between the event and recognition are only compounded by the fact that a crime is a stressful situation. Research studies do not provide a simple equation for predicting whether emotional arousal will affect perception and memory positively or negatively. The evidence, however, suggests that moderate stress improves accuracy, whereas great or little stress hurts (Anastasi, 1964; Kubie, 1959; Redmount, 1959).

Two experiments well illustrate the point. Beier's research (1952) disclosed that considerable anxiety caused a loss of abstract abilities generally and, more specifically, a loss of flexibility in intellectual function and visual coordination. Smock (1955), too, reported that people in stressful situations were quicker to categorize ambiguous stimuli. The basic finding is clear: "[U]nder stress conditions or

---

[5]These and other studies on recognition were well reviewed by Adams (1967).

[6]For examples, Davies, Shepherd, and Ellis (1979) reported that subjects who searched through 100 facial photos after seeing a videotape of three men were much less accurate in their subsequent identification of the targets than were subjects in the other experimental and control groups.

under conditions of exigent motivation . . . the likelihood of erroneous perception increases" (Bruner, 1958, p. 91).

In sum, while mildly affective experience, either positive or negative, may be remembered better than neutral, insignificant experiences, with more pronounced trauma the effect is reversed. The implications of this are very relevant to the criminal-identification context. Although one cannot accept without qualification the argument that emotional strain distorts perception and memory, surely it can and frequently does.

The impact of social variables on perception and memory

As noted above, valid identification is necessarily restricted by human capacity. But this source of error does not account for all of the possibilities. Since perceptual processes necessarily involve an interaction between sensory (structural) and social (functional) inputs, the impact of such variables as needs, values, expectancies, and experiences must also be assessed (Allport, 1955; Tajfel, 1969).

Emotional state   Studies of person perception disclose that the significance of an object or an event to the viewer, including its emotional significance, can crucially affect the manner in which it is perceived (Tagiuri, 1969). Illustratively, in an experiment by Asthana (1960) using lenses that distort, subjects viewed a liked person (A), a disliked person (B), a stranger (C), physical objects (D), and the self-image in a mirror (E). The amount of experienced distortion, ranked from most to least, was B, D, C, A, and E. Positive emotional significance appeared to be crucial in offsetting or resisting perceptual distortion.

Studies on the perception of physical characteristics of persons demonstrate well the effects of emotions on perception (Ittelson and Slack, 1958). Although distortion may be reduced with stimuli that arouse positive affect or are familiar, these are categories into which a criminal suspect is not likely to fall. Both the events surrounding the crime and the persons involved are likely to evoke aversive reactions and thus reduce acuity. Under such circumstances, a witness may be more inclined to fill in or clean up "blurred" images in ways compatible with personal expectations or biases.

Motivational state   The processes by which viewers select from the evidence of their senses are extraordinarily complex. The early memory research of Bartlett (1932) isolated three basic steps in identification: perception, remembering, and reporting. Using a serial reproduction technique with storytelling and picture drawing,[7] Bartlett demonstrated experimentally that memory is a constructive, not a reproductive, process in which attitudes and expectations play a crucial role. Similarly, in their research on memory and on rumor, Allport (1955) and Allport and Postman (1947, 1958) found that perceptions are organized through the processes of leveling (reduction of detail), sharpening (bringing into prominence remaining detail), and assimilating (integrating representation in light of total experiences). In essence, persons condense or elaborate to achieve a simpler, more significant configuration congruent with their needs.

That needs affect perceptions does not suggest that people consciously distort reality in ways reflecting their biases. There is ample evidence that individuals do in fact see things in terms of what they want or need to see. Several studies, for example, have shown that subjects deprived of food for several hours responded to various meaningless or ambiguous stimuli with food association (Brozek, Guetzkow, and Baldwin, 1951; Levine, Chein, and Murphy, 1942; McClelland and Atkinson, 1948). Revealing the potency of personality needs, Shrauger and Altrocchi (1964) found that authoritarians described peers more favorably than nonauthoritarians, but with strangers the effect was reversed. On the basis of such data, Bruner concluded that "there is now enough evidence before us to suggest that not the *amount* of need but the *way* in which a person learns to *handle* his needs determines the manner in which motivation and cognitive selectivity will interact" (1958, p. 89; emphasis in original).

Prior experience Beyond emotional and motivational influences affecting perception, there is also considerable documentation regarding the relative inability of individuals to recognize persons from another group.[8] Malpass and Kravitz (1969) reported that subjects had greater acuity for faces of their own race. This pattern was generally confirmed in subsequent studies by Cross, Cross, and Daly (1971), Galper (1973), Luce (1974), Chance, Goldstein, and McBride (1975), and Brigham and Barkowitz (1978). The relationship of these differences to prior experience, however, is not yet clear. While one plausible explanation for the superior recognition of persons of one's own race is that familiarity provides necessary training, to date there

---

[7]For example, there would be a progression of pictures in which the form of an owl changed to that of a cat.

[8]Thus far, most of the research on prior experience has dealt with race. The effects of this variable have been of long-standing interest to those concerned about the problem of faulty identification. Increasingly similar consideration is being given to the effect of sex on same-sex and cross-sex recognition ability (see, e.g., Cross, Cross, and Daly, 1971).

is no empirical evidence that the amount of cross-race experience is positively related to cross-race recognition ability (Luce, 1974; Malpass and Kravitz, 1969).

Stereotypes and prejudice   Of the factors that can affect recognition of criminal suspects, prejudicial racial attitudes are among the most insidious. While not much research has been done on their effects, the results to date suggest that prejudice indeed has an adverse impact on perceptual abilities. For example, Seeleman (1940) found that prejudiced subjects, minimizing intergroup differences, were less accurate in recognizing individual blacks from photographs. Similarly, a study by Luce (1974) also suggested that attitudes (positive or negative) toward members of other races may affect cross-race identification (see also Katz, 1975).

Closely linked with racial attitudes is the relationship between stereotyping and identification bias. In a review of person perception studies, Secord (1958) found ample support for the proposition that people do stereotype by interpreting certain physiognomic characteristics to represent personality traits. Research undertaken by Allport and Postman in 1947 is a striking example of how expectations can result in misperceptions. These investigators conducted a series of now-classic experiments in which white subjects were shown a picture of a white man holding a razor and arguing with a black. More than half of the subjects reported that the black man was holding the razor, and many stated that he was brandishing it threateningly.

Such findings have particularly important implications when perception and recall combine two factors: (1) the values or emotions of the individual, and (2) cues too suggestive, too complex, or insufficient to permit an unambiguous decision. Since in particularly complex or ambiguous situations individuals will necessarily structure events to make them understandable, they may be guided in filling in details by past experiences, needs, and expectations. The Allport and Postman findings (1947, 1958), along with the literature on person perception (Secord, 1958; Shrauger and Altrocchi, 1964; Tagiuri, 1969), indicate that the effects of stereotypes on perception go far beyond the phenomenon of "they all look alike to me." To the extent that perceptions are edited to conform to personal interpretations of reality, fundamental perceptual and mnemonic errors may automatically and unknowingly occur.

The lineup as a social-psychological context

The social-psychological variables that affect perception and memory of a criminal event may again come into play during criminal justice procedures, further compounding the error-prone process of person perception. For example, the witness's motivational state at the time of the identification is a crucial component. The Supreme Court stated in *Wade* that "a victim's understandable outrage may excite vengeful or spiteful motives" (*United States* v. *Wade*, 1967, p. 230). It is also possible that the victim, as a function of emotional or physical needs, may simply want to bring the whole episode to a close as quickly as possible. Other powerful motives could be the desire to be a part of an important event or to avoid looking foolish by being unable to identify the "right" person—particularly when being questioned by apparent experts. Alternatively, witnesses may fear having to testify at the suspect's trial, may hesitate to contribute to sending anyone to prison, or may be reluctant to publicize all the facts surrounding the crime.

The above illustrates the wide range of factors potentially influencing a witness's decision-making. Whether conscious or unconscious, such factors can increase the danger of error, either the error of misidentification or the error of nonidentification. But other variables as well may inhibit an accurate identification process. The potential effects of such variables as social conformity, the legitimacy of authority, evaluation apprehension, and self-persuasion—garnered from research in other social contexts and applied to the lineup—are reviewed below.

Social conformity   Changes in perception occur readily in response to information from social sources. First Sherif (1936, 1958) and later Asch (1952, Chap. 16; 1958) demonstrated experimentally that the group can have an enormous suggestive power capable of modifying perceptions, attitudes, and norms. Sherif created the autokinetic phenomenon with subjects. When an individual is exposed to a fixed, pinpointed light under conditions of total darkness, an illusory movement occurs. Sherif found that the emergence of group norms resulted in concurring reports of this light movement.

In the Asch experiment, subjects were simultaneously presented with lines of different lengths and with blatantly incorrect judgments about equality in length expressed by the experimenter's confederates. Again there was a convergence of judgments. Only about 25% of Asch's subjects totally resisted group pressure and made no errors in judging length. According to Asch, some subjects were unaware that they had yielded, others presumed the group was correct, and yet others did not want to appear different or inferior.

Since the Asch and Sherif experiments there has been considerable research demonstrating the effects of conformity on the modification of judgments. As reviewed by Collins and Raven (1969), pedestrians were more likely to jaywalk, subjects were more likely to volunteer for an experiment, and people were more likely to violate a no-trespassing sign when they observed others doing so. It is clear from such studies that people tailor their responses by looking to what others do. And, in the case of criminal identification, this tailoring could occur among witnesses at the scene of the crime, in subsequent communication with or without police knowledge, and at the identification procedure itself.

Particularly in ambiguous, unusual, or threatening situations, people are prone to judge the appropriateness of their behavior in relation to others because they lack confidence in their perceptions or want to make contradictory perceptions fit together. In short, they turn to informational cues in order to construe the meaning of an event. As one might expect, the problems of influence and suggestibility are compounded by the fact that subjects are typically unaware of their yielding behavior (Wrightsman, 1960). To the extent that the lineup is characterized by extreme ambiguity for the witness, a similar reliance on others—especially expert police officers—might be expected. Perhaps if witnesses had greater clarity regarding what to expect and more accurate information regarding the identification process, procedure, and purpose as well as their role as data gatherers, the influence of other actors in the lineup context would be substantially reduced.

There are other steps that could be taken to diminish the tendency toward conforming responses. Deutsch and Gerard found that both public and private prior commitment (written judgments prior to group judgments) "markedly reduce the socially influenced errors in both . . . face-to-face and anonymous situations" (1955, p. 633). Also their experiment showed significantly less conformity when subjects expressed their judgments anonymously. Both field and experimental studies similarly confirm that anonymity leads to a decrease in judgmental shift (Raven and French, 1958; Zimbardo, 1969). These findings have important implications for identification procedures. Signed descriptions of suspects by witnesses as soon as possible after the crime might be required, and certainly anonymity, at least among witnesses, should be preserved.

Legitimacy of authority   While the opinion of another person or persons can markedly influence perception, suggestibility does not reside in numbers alone (Luchins and Luchins, 1961). Recognized or official power provides another substantial source of influence over individuals (Collins and Raven, 1969, p. 178). Milgram's now-classic experiment (1963, 1965) is a testament to the powerful effect of a legitimate authority conducting a legitimate "scientific" enterprise. In this research, subjects under request by an experimenter induced what they believed to be painful, dangerously high levels of shock to another subject who was actually a confederate of the investigator. This study is illustrative of a substantial body of research (e.g., Orne and Evans, 1965) demonstrating that the attribution of legitimacy to social roles and contexts can have a dramatic influence on individual behavior. Similarly, the police as a legitimate authority of the legal system may have a potentially critical impact on witnesses' judgments and on suspects' behavior.

Evaluation apprehension and expectancy   For almost two decades social psychologists have been actively involved in studying how the relationship between experimenter and subject may affect the validity of data gathered in social science research. Rosenthal (1963, 1964, 1966) has extensively investigated the various conditions that enhance "experimenter bias"; i.e., the subtle, unintentional communication of expectations from experimenter to subject. Dovetailing with Rosenthal's studies is considerable work that puts more emphasis on the subject side of the social interaction. Rosenberg (1969) views the subject of an experiment as an "active" actor who independently engages in information seeking, ambiguity reduction, and the development of interpretive hypotheses. His research on the conditions and consequences of evaluation apprehension (EA) is particularly useful for illuminating the lineup context.

For Rosenberg, evaluation apprehension is an anxiety-based concern on the part of subjects that they win a positive evaluation from the experimenter. When subjects, reponding to cues regarding what they are to do, believe that one mode of behavior is more "normal" or "competent" than another, data-biasing processes are likely to be triggered. Analogously, witnesses at a lineup know that they have been called in to make an identification and quite probably are concerned about performing well, being helpful, not looking foolish, or doing the "right" thing. In essence, victims or witnesses of crime do not want to be evaluated as atypical or abnormal in their ability to identify a suspect or in their performance as data gatherers. Therefore, they may be heavily oriented to gear their behavior to be congruent with their image of what a "competent witness" is able to do. To counterbalance such an effect, specific instructions alleviating apprehension may need to be given.

Self-persuasion   Another fruitful area for application to the lineup context has been the work on the false report and on self-persuasion. There is substantial evidence that an initially false statement may be distorted in a person's recall, engendering thereafter a belief that the erroneous statement is correct. Bem (1966, 1967) conducted an experiment in which subjects, after giving false information in response to certain cues, were asked to recall the correct answers. He found that subjects, under conditions normally associated in the subjects' experience with truthtelling, tended to recall the truth less accurately and to believe their erroneous confessions. These findings suggest that once a witness's report has been changed according to some minimum inducement and subtle pressure, self-persuasion regarding the truth of statements is likely to occur, and the error may be difficult, if not impossible, to rectify.

As we will consider in greater detail subsequently, the possibilities of error-producing suggestion in questioning are substantial. Bem's research clearly underscores the potential effect of both police reassurances to victims and other police procedures associated with truthtelling. Bem himself noted that self-persuasion can distort recall of small, vital details surrounding a crime, including distorting eyewitness accounts (1967, p. 25). Since the lineup is one stage of a three- or four-stage process and occurs after witnesses have been questioned at least once by police, the situation is fraught with self-persuasion possibilities. And the problem is compounded by the fact that repeated questioning is likely to strengthen commitment to a position.

What this and the above analyses suggest is that the victim or witness at a lineup is one "actor" in a complex social situation. Thus, viewing the lineup and all identification proceedings as a network of social interactions may offer a new dimension for analysis. Such a perspective has the important advantage of acknowledging that normative behavioral patterns may emerge as a function of the social structure itself. This, in essence, was the model the *Wade* Court adopted in saying: "We do not assume that these risks are the result of police procedures intentionally designed to prejudice an accused. Rather we assume they derive from the dangers inherent in eyewitnesses identification and the suggestibility inherent in the context of the pretrial identification" (*United States* v. *Wade*, 1967, p. 235).

LEGAL PSYCHOLOGY

Up to this point, we have applied general and social psychological research to illuminate the role of the victim or witness as a data gatherer. Work in legal psychology dating back to the beginning of the twentieth century is, however, of special relevance to our inquiry. Because of the emphasis—particularly until the 1970s—on the psychology of testimony, much of this research has focused on demonstrating (1) the unreliability of eyewitness reports, and (2) the impact of questioning on such reports. In this section of the chapter, we first review some of these early efforts and then conclude with an examination of contemporary research that has continued to emphasize such themes while also addressing other issues basic to accurate identification.

History of the field

Even before World War I, particularly in Europe, there was great interest in studying experimentally the role of memory, thinking, and emotion on witness behavior (for a review, see generally Rouke, 1957). The German jurist–criminologist Gross (1911) stressed the need for a scientific psychology of testimony. During that period, academic psychologists initiated experiments on the process of obtaining testimony in order to discern the impact of legal methods on perception, memory, and emotion (Binet, 1900; Münsterberg, 1908, 1914; Stern, 1903, 1938). Whipple's excellent summaries and comprehensive reviews (e.g, 1909, 1910, 1917) provide a complete description of scholarly inquiries into legal procedures being conducted at that time (e.g., Breukink's and Varendonck's experiments on the effects of leading questions).

Whipple was particularly laudatory of Stern's experiments on testimony (1903). In addition to using description-of-pictures tests developed by Binet to investigate pictorial fidelity (Peterson, 1925, pp. 126–132), Stern conducted reality experiments (also known as "event tests"). His work, demonstrating the unreliability of recall for unexpected events, has become the paradigm for subsequent experimental studies of eyewitness reporting (Berrien, 1944; Burtt, 1931, 1948; Marshall, 1966). In these reality experiments, subjects witnessed a close-to-real-life incident, unaware that it was carefully rehearsed, and then were asked to describe the events in detail. A typical incident involved two stooges in a scientific seminar arguing, drawing a gun, threatening to shoot, and then fleeing. Stern used two methods to test subjects' ability to report: (1) the narrative or free account, presumably spontaneous; and (2) the interrogatory or question-and-answer method, presumably affected by suggestion. He reported not only on the initial distortions of the original event but also on the suggestive effects of cross-examination.

The attractiveness and utility of the reality-experiment paradigm are apparent as well in Kobler's study of a legal society meeting (see Rouke 1957, p. 54). Kobler prearranged a quarrel between two audience members. Several weeks later two court panels—one of three psychologists and one of three judges—were examined. The results from both groups were similarly condensed, simplified, and somewhat distorted. Kobler concluded that excitement and emotion affect observation and that witness agreement may mean coincident erroneous testimony. Subsequent research on stress (Beier, 1952) supported his points.

In the United States the initial landmark effort on the psychology of testimony was made in 1908 by Münsterberg's *On the Witness Stand*. Two years after Freud (1906) counseled lawyers to use psychologists in ascertaining truth in courts of law, Münsterberg was one of the first psychologists to elucidate the discrepancies between the evidence of the senses and the evidence of the law and to argue for legal reforms based on scientific experimentation. His passionate interest in applying psychology to practical courtroom problems produced a series of classroom demonstrations illustrating that trained observers with generous advance warnings immediately disagreed on such "structural" sensory events as the pitch of a sound, the color of disks, and the shape of an inkblot (1908, pp. 21–31).

Also in the United States after World War I, the psychologist–lawyer Marston (1924) used an event test not just to study the accuracy of testimony but also to evaluate whether finders of fact (a judge, a jury of women, a jury of men) can determine what did and did not occur on the basis of testimonial evidence (see also Rouke, 1957, p. 57). As to the first purpose of the experiment, the results established that, of the various methods for eliciting testimony, free narration was somewhat less complete than direct examination or cross-examination (23% versus 31%, 29%) yet much more accurate (94% versus 83%, 76%). Also, direct examination was about as complete as cross-examination (31% versus 29%) but still more accurate (83% versus 76%). The study also indicated that, while the judge was better able to give complete findings than were the female and male juries (37%, judge; 27%, females; 23%, males), even the judge had a considerable margin of error (81%, judge; 78%, females; 67%, males).

The event-test paradigm was particularly popular in the classroom—for both teaching and research purposes. In an experiment by Brown (1935), three groups of students without warning saw a workman in a classroom briefly and two weeks later were asked if any of the men in a lineup was the workman. While approximately 70% of the students in two groups made correct identifications, 62.5% of a third group, which had received an instruction with some suggestion ("Which of the men . . . ?"), identified the wrong person from a lineup that excluded the actual workman. In a second classroom experiment by Vickery and Brooks (1938), students who witnessed a staged crime involving three persons gave grossly discrepant time estimates of the actual event (from 1 to 15 minutes) and the physical characteristics of the criminals (height from 4'8" to 7'; weight from 90 to 170 pounds; age from 11 to 20 years).

Beyond such research efforts, during the 1920s and 1930s, commentary and concern in legal psychology about the error-prone process of witness testimony continued to abound. In a series of articles, lawyer Hutchins and psychologist Slesinger (1928a, 1928b, 1929) reviewed legal rules of evidence in terms of psychological findings on perception, memory, and emotion, ultimately arguing for more interdisciplinary experimentation and application. Likewise, the very excellent integrative review of Gardner (1933) called for further exploration and experimentation to permit better evaluation of witness testimony. These issues as well as detailed information on behavioral processes as applied to the trial context were extensively presented in the major treatises of the period—by Brown (1926), Burtt (1931), and McCarty (1929).

Both of Burtt's texts (131, 1948) dealt with data related to sensory defects, distance perception, color vision, time perception, intelligence, attention, stress, and suggestion. In each instance Burtt tried to show that information possessed by psychologists about natural human processes and human interactions could be brought to bear on discrepancies in testimony. He systematically described numerous structural conditions affecting perception and memory. For example, about 4% of the male population and 1% of the female are color-blind; the absorbable number of simultaneous impressions is limited so that in one-tenth of a second most people read 4 or 5 digits and fail with 9; and set, or initial, cuing (i.e., advising a subject to concentrate on an event) results in witnesses giving better descriptions (1948, pp. 292–301). And, consistent with Kobler's conclusions, Burtt's experiment in a seminar on crime demonstrated that stress was a disorganizing condition operating against effective recall (1948, pp. 71–76).

Burtt also considered how the form of the questioning affects the accuracy of the information provided by the witness. Prior to Burtt, the most notable and extensive research on questioning had been conducted by Muscio (1915), who studied the effects of eight different questioning approaches on the accurate reporting of a movie. Consistent with Muscio's results, Burtt (1931, pp. 119–131) also found that expectative ("Was there a cat in the picture?") and implicative ("What color was the cat?") forms of questioning elicited more wrong responses than straightforward questions, that the objective form (no personal pronouns) was more suggestive than the subjective form (contains the word "you"), and that double negatives introduced confusion and inaccuracy. While Muscio found that the use of the definite article ("the") was more suggestive than the indefinite article ("a"), Burtt did not find such a difference.

As is apparent from the above, research conducted during the early decades of the twentieth century seemed to indicate that free narrative was more accurate than responses to specific questions (Marston, 1924; Stern, 1903; Whipple, 1909). Yet, the greater completeness of information obtained by questioning suggests the necessity of adopting an interrogatory format in investigatory contexts. The work by Muscio and by Burtt was particularly important because it began to address the complex problem of how to structure questioning so that completeness is preserved but accuracy enhanced. Related to these efforts were studies by Cady (1924) and Snee and Lush (1941) on the relationship between narrative and interrogatory methods of reporting. Their experiments showed that accuracy of testimony increased when interrogatory reports followed free-narrative accounts (see also Whitely and McGeoch, 1927). Such investigations dealt with difficult issues that continue to be addressed in current research (Lipton, 1977; Loftus, Altman, and Geballe, 1975; Marquis, Marshall, and Oskamp, 1972; Williams and Greenwald, 1975).

Contemporary research

After considerable work in legal psychology through the 1930s, scientific inquiry in this area markedly tapered off. Until the mid-1950s, with the writings of Weld (1954) and Berrien (1955) as well as the publication of a *Journal of Social Issues* symposium edited by Fishman and Morris (1957), there was no extensive updating or integration of efforts in this field. Berrien's short, but well-presented piece is particularly valuable in its recognition of the need for studying the "[s]pecial aspects of identifying persons in a line-up" (1955, p. 214). Nevertheless, more than a decade was to go by before a research response focusing on testimony generally or personal identification specifically was forthcoming.

The impact of questioning on testimony   Marshall's book, published in 1966, represents an admirable attempt to apply psychological studies to the problem of giving testimony and to conduct interdisciplinary research on the reliability of eyewitness reports. Using a movie of an alleged kidnapping, Marshall found that the recall of subjects from lower social classes was less accurate, that police trainees reported a greater number of nonexistent events, and that person—not action—items were least frequently recalled (1966, pp. 52–58). He correctly acknowledged the "selective process" and the "inventive reconstruction" of perception in all environments and stressed the need to attend to the "betting" predilections[9] in witness behavior in classroom, courtroom, and lineup situations (1966, pp. 9–25).

In the early 1970s Marshall and his associates, Marquis and Oskamp, dealt further with the psychology of testimony (1971; see also Marquis, Marshall, and Oskamp, 1972). In an effort to determine the effects of kinds of interrogation methods on the reliability of testimony, they showed a short film of an automobile accident followed by a scuffle. After giving a free report, subjects were questioned by one of several interrogation methods. Consistent with prior research, accuracy was slightly higher with spontaneous report. Further, the completeness of the testimony increased much more than accuracy decreased under all conditions of interrogation (1971, pp. 1624–1627). In other words, all forms of questioning produced a larger body of information. It should be noted, however, that in the case of person content the increase in information was attended by a more serious loss in accuracy than was the case for action, sound, or object content. Nevertheless, this experiment suggests that the effects of interrogation on the reliability of testimony are not uniformly negative.

Loftus, too, has considered the complex relationship between questioning and recall (1974, 1975). She and her associates have conducted a series of experiments focusing specifically on how the wording of questions may influence responses, both initial reports and subsequent accounts. In the tradition of the research paradigm developed by Muscio (1915) early in the century, Loftus and Zanni (1975) in two studies showed a short film of a car accident followed by questions differing in their use of the definite ("the") and indefinite ("a") articles. Whether or not the object referred to in the question in fact appeared in the movie, subjects who were asked definite questions were more likely to report in the affirmative than those asked indefinite ones. Related to this study, Loftus and Palmer (1974)— again using a car accident as the movie stimulus—conducted two experiments that altered the verb in asking how fast the vehicles were going when they "smashed" ("collided," "bumped," "contacted," or "hit") into each other. In both of these experiments wording affected estimates of speed. Further, in the second experiment subjects who

---

[9]According to Marshall: "Filling gaps in perception is a betting process. We select what we believe will be harmonious with those elements we have perceived and repress those that will create conflict for us. The elements that we choose or repress will depend on what bet, or what selection, we make as the likeliest explanation for what we see . . ." (1966, p. 19).

received the verb "smashed" were more likely a week later to report having seen broken glass when there was indeed none.

These results parallel the findings of another experiment by Loftus, Altman, and Geballe (1975) that dealt with witnesses' later recollections of a videotape of a classroom disruption. Immediately following the videotape, half of the subjects were asked "active" questions; half received "passive" questions. Active questions used more aggressive language. For example, "Did the professor shout something to the activists?" in contrast to "Did the professor say anything to the demonstrators?" A week later, in responses to a series of scales about the event, subjects previously receiving the active questionnaire rated demonstrators as significantly more noisy, violent, belligerent, and antagonistic.

A final set of four experiments by Loftus (1975) further underscores the potential impact of questioning on the reconstruction of memory. Three of the studies dealt with accidents; one, with a classroom disruption. The purpose of all four was to investigate systematically the effects on subsequent reports of introducing true or false presuppositions in the initial questioning. Whether or not the information introduced was correct, subjects were consistently and significantly more inclined to incorporate the presupposition into their conception of the event. All of these studies taken together provide strong evidence that new information regarding an event is indeed integrated into a person's original representation. As should be apparent, investigatory procedures may—unknowingly to all—influence witnesses in subtle and unintentional ways.

The dynamics of pretrial identifications   A reading of the above literature vividly demonstrates the unreliability of eyewitness memory and perception and the subtle but significant effects of questioning. These studies, however, did not systematically examine the impact of other potentially biasing variables on courtroom behavior or on the behavior of people at pretrial identifications. Recent efforts have begun to address a wider range of issues that affect the victim or witness as a data gatherer. While laboratory studies continue to focus on the relationship between the form and frequency of questioning and the accuracy of identification, work has expanded to include real-life contexts, different types of identification procedures (e.g., lineup, photographic display), and the suggestive conditions that can shape eyewitness reports (e.g., nonverbal communication of expectancies, bias in construction of lineups).

Buckhout (1974), for example, has been actively engaged in research on the error-prone nature of eyewitness data. He and his associates at the Center for Responsive Psychology at Brooklyn College designed a series of experiments to focus specifically on person identification. In an effort to link research on memory and perception to situations normally encountered by real witnesses, these investigators have endeavored to utilize diverse "events," including staged crimes, movies, actual lineup photographs, and television broadcasts. The findings from these studies clearly show that most people are likely to select *someone* when presented with a lineup, photospread, or the like. Further, and even more serious, the data consistently question the validity of eyewitness choices.

One of the most intriguing of Buckhout's studies (1975) was conducted as part of a local television news program. A film of a mugging followed by a 6-person lineup yielded accurate identifications from 14.1% of the 2,145 viewers who called after the program—only as many as would be expected by chance. Similarly, Buckhout and his associates' 1974 study revealed that, 3 weeks after a staged purse-snatching incident, only 13.5% of the 52 student witnesses were able to identify the assailant (without impeaching their choice) from two videotaped lineups. These results paralleled those from Loftus' simulated research (1976). She reported that there were 60% false identifications of a bystander when the offender was absent, whereas there were 83% correct identifications when the offender was present.

Buckhout and his colleagues have considered a number of conditions that may affect accurate identification. Illustratively, Williams and Greenwald (1975) studied two groups of subjects both of which had undergone verbal or written interrogation. The first group completed lengthy questionnaires (identical to the one used by the New York City police department); the second did not. Those in the questionnaire condition made significantly more lineup choice (88% versus 58%) and were significantly less accurate (11% versus 26%) than those questioned only by verbal or written format. These findings underscore the importance of initial questioning and its potential impact on subsequent recognition—an area being researched in depth by Loftus (e.g., 1975).

In making person identifications, witnesses may also be affected by the identification procedure itself. Egan, Pittner, and Goldstein (1977) found that lineups were far preferable to photographic displays (the latter producing less accurate information). In their laboratory experiment, subjects—after seeing a simulated crime—were asked to role-play eyewitnesses making an identification (live or photo). While in this experimental situation there was only a 14% difference in the "hit" rate (i.e., accurate identifications) between these two conditions, the researchers were cautious about the use of the photo procedure because it "can set the stage for a series of interlocking errors beginning with a witness who is 'positive' that the face in the mug book is *the* culprit . . ." (p. 205). Notably as well, these investigators also found a significant increase in false alarms (i.e., incorrect identifications) with increased time delay between the simulated crime and the identification (48% at day 2; 93% at day 56).

Beyond the type of identification procedure and the timing, there are other variables related to the pretrial identification context that can affect eyewitness judgments. In an experiment by Buckhout, Figueroa, and Huff (1975), 141 subjects, who had witnessed an assault 7 weeks earlier, were shown biased photos (i.e., the suspect had different facial expression and posture from the others in the photos) and/or were given biased instructions (i.e., subjects were told that the suspect was definitely among the photos). A substantial proportion of the students in the biased photo/instruction condition (61%) successfully identified the attacker. Further, when the same spread was shown to persons who had not even witnessed the assault, those under biased conditions were again most likely to make a correct positive identification (see Buckhout, 1974, 1976). Of equal concern, and congruent with Buckhout et al. (1974) and Loftus (1976) reported above, overall only 40% of the witnesses picked the correct person and 25% of them identified an innocent bystander from the photospreads.

A recent, related study by Malpass and Devine (in press) also underscores the negative impact of biased instructions. One to three days after witnessing a staged vandalism in a lecture hall, 100 undergraduates viewed a lineup with either biased or unbiased instructions *and* with the vandal either present or absent in the lineup. The data confirmed that the biased instructions induced a high rate of choosing, that identification errors were highest under biased instructions with the vandal absent, and that unbiased instructions resulted in fewer choices and fewer false identifications but no decrease in correct identifications. Importantly, unbiased instructions seemed to reduce choosing behavior without having adverse consequences for the number of correct identifications.

In addition to the potential for bias in explicit instructions, cuing may also occur through the nonverbal communication of expectancies from the presiding police officer to the witness. Fanselow's research (1975) persuasively indicates that subjects are affected by the nonverbal information they receive. Directly after seeing a film of a crime, 169 college students were asked to choose the assailant from pictures (under conditions of positive, negative, or neutral gestures by the experimenter). Under the biased conditions (i.e., nonverbal cues), subjects were significantly more likely to choose the target picture; under the neutral condition, they were more likely to make no choice.

Finally, three experiments utilizing real-life events vividly illuminate the potential for lineup bias and the necessity for carefully matching participants in terms of their physical attributes (e.g., height, weight, skin coloring). As part of Buckhout's program of research, Freire (1975) showed students a photo of an actual lineup and the initial description given by the witness. By chance, only about 16% of the subjects would be expected to select the defendant; however, 75% did. These data strongly support the contention that the suspect was the only participant in the lineup who matched the witness's original description.

Research by Doob and Kirshenbaum (1973) at the University of Toronto also demonstrated that subjects with no prior knowledge of an actual crime are still likely to identify the same suspect chosen by the witness. In the crime under study the witness, a bank cashier at a robbery, remembered only that the offender was "rather good-looking." Provided only with this information, subjects rated the suspect as significantly more attractive than the other 11 persons in the lineup photo. The investigators then replicated the experiment with subjects who were instructed to imagine that they were witnesses. In these circumstances as well, significantly more subjects than would be expected by chance picked the defendant. Doob and Kirshenbaum discussed how a witness's partial memory of an event may influence subsequent recognition. So too these partial memories may bias how law-enforcement officials, however unknowingly, construct identification proceedings.

Wells, Leippe, and Ostrom's research (1979) yielded related results. Using the description of a bank robbery and the robber as well as a picture of the lineup from an actual case, these investigators showed that 61% of the mock witnesses chose the "real" suspect. Wells and associates estimated that the functional size of this 6-person lineup (i.e., the number of lineup members resembling the criminal) was 1.64. This approach permits consideration of "whether a lineup with a functional size of 2 or 3 or any other low number might be judged as too close to a show-up to be acceptable" (1979, p. 291). Further, the fact that in all three studies persons who had not even witnessed a crime were likely to make the same identification as the real witness raises troublesome, complex problems about potential bias that necessitate both research and reform.

CONCLUSIONS

In the preceding sections we have systematically examined research findings important for understanding the role of the witness as a data gatherer. This analysis of the psychological dimensions of eyewitness identification has shown that the dangers from fallible sense perception and memory as well as from suggestive influences are overwhelming.[10] As we indicated earlier in this chapter, perception and memory are constructive rather than reproductive processes. Thus, in some cases very little can be done to improve the accuracy of either recall or recognition. But we must undertake to determine when these prepotent causes of erroneous identification cannot be eliminated. Further, we have discovered some of the psychological dynamics affecting witnesses during identification proceedings and the complexity of their effects. These suggestive and biasing influences (both internal and external to the witness) need also to be identified.[11] Only when such steps are taken, can we be more confident that faulty information is not transmitted to the next decisional stage in the criminal justice process.

---

[10]Furthermore and of considerable significance, current research suggests no overall relationship between a witness's confidence and accuracy. Witnesses to staged crimes who make a false identification are not notably less confident in their judgments than those who make an accurate identification (Gorenstein and Ellsworth, 1980; Leippe, Wells, and Ostrom, 1978; Wells, Lindsay, and Ferguson, 1979). Thus, witnesses are not likely to be aware of their erroneous inputs as data gatherers.

[11]In an important article, Wells (1978) emphasized the need for continued scientific study of *system* variables (those, like lineup features, that are under the control of the legal system) as well as *estimator* variables (those, like stereotyping, that are part of the naturally occurring situation). The value of examining system variables is well illustrated by Gorenstein and Ellsworth's recent study (1980) that showed the effects of subjects' prior commitment (selecting a face from mug shots) on their response to the "lineup" task.

References

Adams, J. A. *Human memory.* New York: McGraw-Hill, 1967.

Allport, F. *Theories of perception and the concept of structures.* New York: Wiley, 1955.

Allport, G. W., & Postman, L. J. *The psychology of rumor.* New York: Holt, 1947.

Allport, G. W., & Postman, L. J. The basic psychology of rumor. In E. E. Maccoby, T. M. Newcomb, & E. L. Hartley (Eds.), *Readings in social psychology.* 3rd ed. New York: Holt, 1958.

Anastasi, A. *Fields of applied psychology.* New York: McGraw-Hill, 1964.

Asch, S. E. *Social psychology.* New York: Prentice-Hall, 1952.

Asch, S. E. Effects of group pressure upon the modification and distortion of judgments. In E. E. Maccoby, T. M. Newcomb, & E. L. Hartley (Eds.), *Readings in social psychology.* 3rd ed. New York: Holt, 1958.

Asthana, H. S. Perceptual distortion as a function of the valence of perceived object. *Journal of Social Psychology,* 1960, *52,* 119–125.

Bahrick, H. P., & Bahrick, P. O. A re-examination of the interrelations among measures of retention. *Quarterly Journal of Experimental Psychology,* 1964, *16,* 318–324.

Bartlett, F. C. *Remembering: A study in experimental and social psychology.* London: Cambridge University Press, 1932.

Beier, E. C. The effect of induced anxiety on the flexibility of intellectual functioning. *Psychological Monographs*, 1952, 65 (Whole No. 365).

Bem, D. J. Inducing belief in false confessions. *Journal of Personality and Social Psychology*, 1966, 3, 707–710.

Bem, D. J. When saying is believing. *Psychology Today*, 1967, 1(2), 21–25.

Berrien, F. K. *Practical psychology.* New York: Macmillan, 1944.

Berrien, F. K. Psychology and the court. In G. J. Dudycha (Ed.), *Psychology for law enforcement officials.* Springfield, IL: Charles C Thomas, 1955.

Binet, A. *La suggestibilité.* Paris: Schleicher Frères, 1900.

Borchard, E. M. *Convicting the innocent: Errors of criminal justice.* New Haven, CT: Yale University Press, 1932.

Brigham, J. C., & Barkowitz, P. Do they all look alike? The effect of race, sex, experience, and attitudes on the ability to recognize faces. *Journal of Applied Social Psychology*, 1978, 8, 306–318.

Brown, H. B. An experience in identification testimony. *Journal of Criminal Law and Criminology*, 1935, 25, 621–622.

Brown, M. R. *Legal psychology.* Indianapolis: Bobbs-Merrill, 1926.

Brozek, J., Guetzkow, H., & Baldwin, M. V. A quantitative study of perception and association in experimental semi-starvation. *Journal of Personality*, 1951, 19, 245–264.

Bruner, J. S. Social psychology and perception. In E. E. Maccoby, T. M. Newcomb, & E. L. Hartley (Eds.), *Readings in social psychology.* 3rd ed. New York: Holt, 1958.

Bruner, J. S. On perceptual readiness. In R. Haber (Ed.), *Contemporary theory and research in visual perception.* New York: Holt, Rinehart and Winston, 1968.

Buckhout, R. Eyewitness testimony. *Scientific American*, 1974, 231(6), 23–31.

Buckhout, R. Nearly 2,000 witnesses can be wrong. *Social Action and the Law*, Newsletter, 1975, 2(3), 7.

Buckhout, R. Psychology and eyewitness identification. *Law and Psychology Review*, 1976, 2, 75–91.

Buckhout, R., Alper, A., Chern, S. Silverberg, G., & Slomovits, M. Determinants of eyewitness performance on a lineup. *Bulletin of the Psychonomic Society*, 1974, 4, 191–192.

Buckhout, R., Figueroa, D., & Huff, E. Psychology and eyewitness identification. *Social Action and the Law*, Newsletter, 1975, 1(4), 8–9.

Burtt, H. E. *Legal psychology.* New York: Prentice-Hall, 1931.

Burtt, H. E. *Applied psychology.* New York: Prentice-Hall, 1948.

Cady, H. M. On the psychology of testimony. *American Journal of Psychology*, 1924, 35, 110–112.

Chance, J., Goldstein, A. G., & McBride, L. Differential experience and recognition memory for faces. *Journal of Social Psychology*, 1975, 97, 243–253.

Collins, B. E., & Raven, B. H. Group structure: Attraction, coalitions, communication, and power. In G. Lindzey & E. Aronson (Eds.), *The handbook of social psychology.* Vol. 4. 2nd ed. Reading, MA: Addison-Wesley, 1969.

Cross, J. F., Cross, J., & Daly, J. Sex, race, age, and beauty as factors in recognition of faces. *Perception and Psychophysics*, 1971, 10, 393–396.

Davies, G., Shepherd, J., & Ellis, H. Effects of interpolated mugshot exposure on accuracy of eyewitness identification. *Journal of Applied Psychology*, 1979, 64, 232–237.

Deutsch, M., & Gerard, H. B. A study of normative and informational social influences upon individual judgment. *Journal of Abnormal and Social Psychology*, 1955, 51, 629–636.

Doob, A. N., & Kirshenbaum, H. M. Bias in police lineups—Partial remembering. *Journal of Police Science and Administration*, 1973, *1*, 287–293.

Egan, D., Pittner, M., & Goldstein, A. G. Eyewitness identification: Photographs vs. live models. *Law and Human Behavior*, 1977, *1*, 199–206.

Fanselow, M. S. How to bias an eyewitness (continued): Experimental evidence for the non-verbal bias factor in eyewitness identification testing. *Social Action and the Law*, Newsletter, 1975, *2*(2), 3–4.

Fishman, J. A., & Morris, R. E. (Eds.). Witnesses and testimony at trials and hearings. *Journal of Social Issues*, 1957, *13* (Whole No. 2).

Frank, J., & Frank, B. *Not guilty.* Garden City, NY: Doubleday, 1957.

Frankfurter, F. *The case of Sacco and Vanzetti: A critical analysis for lawyers and laymen.* Boston: Little, Brown, 1927.

Freire, V. A case history in suggestivity on a lineup. *Social Action and the Law*, Newsletter, 1975, *2*(2), 3–4.

Freud, S. Psycho-analysis and the ascertaining of truth in courts of law (1906). In J. Riviere (Trans.), *Collected papers.* Vol. 2. New York: International Psycho-analytic Press, 1953.

Galper, R. E. "Functional race membership" and recognition of faces. *Perceptual and Motor Skills*, 1973, *37*, 455–462.

Gardner, D. S. The perception and memory of witnesses. *Cornell Law Quarterly*, 1933, *18*, 391–409.

Gardner, E. S. *The court of last resort.* New York: William Sloane Associates, 1952.

Gibson, J. J. The theory of information pickup. In R. Haber (Ed.), *Contemporary theory and research in visual perception.* New York: Holt, Rinehart and Winston, 1968.

Gilbert v. California, 388 U.S. 263 (1967).

Gorenstein, G. W., & Ellsworth, P. C. Effect of choosing an incorrect photograph on a later identification by an eyewitness. *Journal of Applied Psychology*, 1980, *65*, 616–622.

Gross, H. G. A. *Criminal psychology.* Boston: Little, Brown, 1911.

Hammelmann, H. A., & Williams, G. Identification parades—II. *Criminal Law Review*, 1963, *1963*, 545–555.

Hutchins, R. M., & Slesinger, D. Some observations on the law of evidence—Memory. *Harvard Law Review*, 1928, *41*, 860–873. (a)

Hutchins, R. M., & Slesinger, D. Some observations on the law of evidence: Spontaneous exclamations. *Columbia Law Review*, 1928, *28*, 432–440. (b)

Hutchins, R. M., & Slesinger, D. Legal psychology. *Psychological Review*, 1929, *35*, 13–26.

Ittelson, W. H., & Slack, C. W. The perception of persons as visual objects. In R. Tagiuri & L. Petrullo (Eds.), *Person perception and interpersonal behavior.* Stanford, CA: Stanford University Press, 1958.

Katz, D. Eyewitness identification in black and white. *Social Action and the Law*, Newsletter, 1975, *2*(3), 8, 11.

Kirby v. Illinois, 406 U.S. 682 (1972).

Klatzky, R. L. *Human memory: Structures and processes.* San Francisco: W. H. Freeman and Company, 1975.

Kubie, L. S. Implications for legal procedure of the fallibility of human memory. *University of Pennsylvania Law Review*, 1959, *108*, 59–75.

Laughery, K. R., Fessler, P. K., Lenorovitz, D. R., & Yoblick, D. A. Time delay and similarity effects in facial recognition. *Journal of Applied Psychology*, 1974, *59*, 490–496.

Leippe, M. R., Wells, G. L., & Ostrom, J. M. Crime seriousness as a determinant of accuracy in eyewitness identification. *Journal of Applied Psychology*, 1978, *63*, 345–351.

Levine, F. J., & Tapp, J. L. The psychology of criminal identification: The gap from *Wade* to *Kirby. University of Pennsylvania Law Review*, 1973, *121*, 1079–1131.

Levine, R., Chein, I., & Murphy, G. The relation of the intensity of a need to the amount of perceptual distortion: A preliminary report. *Journal of Psychology*, 1942, *13*, 283–293.

Lipton, J. P. On the psychology of eyewitness testimony. *Journal of Applied Psychology*, 1977, *62*, 90–95.

Loftus, E. F. Leading questions and the eyewitness report. *Cognitive Psychology*, 1975, *7*, 560–572.

Loftus, E. F. Reconstructing memory: The incredible eyewitness. *Psychology Today*, 1974, *8*(7), 116–119.

Loftus, E. F. Unconscious transference in eyewitness identification. *Law and Psychology Review*, 1976, *2*, 93–98.

Loftus, E. F. *Eyewitness testimony*. Cambridge, MA: Harvard University Press, 1979.

Loftus, E. F., Altman, D., & Geballe, R. Effects of questioning upon a witness' later recollections. *Journal of Police Science and Administration*, 1975, *3*, 162–165.

Loftus, E. F., & Palmer, J. D. Reconstruction of automobile destruction: An example of the interaction between language and memory. *Journal of Verbal Learning and Verbal Behavior*, 1974, *13*, 585–589.

Loftus, E. F., & Zanni, G. Eyewitness testimony: The influence of the wording of a question. *Bulletin of the Psychonomic Society*, 1975, *5*, 86–88.

Luce, T. S. Blacks, whites, yellows: They all look alike to me. *Psychology Today*, 1974, *8*(6), 105–108.

Luchins, A. S., & Luchins, E. H. On conformity with judgments of a majority or an authority. *Journal of Social Psychology*, 1961, *53*, 303–316.

McCarty, D. G. *Psychology for the lawyer*. New York: Prentice-Hall, 1929.

McClelland, D. C., & Atkinson, J. W. The projective expression of needs: I. The effect of different intensities of the hunger drive on perception. *Journal of Psychology*, 1948, *25*, 205–222.

McGowan, C. Constitutional interpretation and criminal identification. *William and Mary Law Review*, 1970, *12*, 235–251.

Malpass, R. S., & Devine, P. G. Eyewitness identification: Lineup instructions and the absence of the offender. *Journal of Applied Psychology*, in press.

Malpass, R. S., & Kravitz, J. Recognition for faces of own and other race. *Journal of Personality and Social Psychology*, 1969, *13*, 330–334.

Manson v. Brathwaite, 432 U.S. 98 (1977).

Marquis, K. H., Marshall, J., & Oskamp, S. Testimony validity as a function of question form, atmosphere, and item difficulty. *Journal of Applied Social Psychology*, 1972, *2*, 167–186.

Marshall, J., Marquis, K. H., & Oskamp, S. Effects of kind of question and atmosphere of interrogation on accuracy and completeness of testimony. *Harvard Law Review*, 1971, *84*, 1620–1643.

Marshall, J. *Law and psychology in conflict*. Indianapolis: Bobbs-Merrill, 1966.

Marston, W. M. Studies in testimony. *Journal of Criminal Law and Criminology*, 1924, *15*, 5–31.

Milgram, S. Behavioral study of obedience. *Journal of Abnormal and Social Psychology*, 1963, *67*, 371–378.

Milgram, S. Some conditions of obedience and disobedience to authority. *Human Relations*, 1965, *18*, 57–76.

Münsterberg, H. *On the witness stand*. New York: Doubleday Page, 1908.

Münsterberg, H. *Psychology, general and applied*. New York: D. Appleton, 1914.

Muscio, B. The influence of the form of question. *British Journal of Psychology*, 1915, *8*, 351–386.

Neil v. *Biggers*, 409 U.S. 188 (1972).

Norman, D. A. *Memory and attention: An introduction to human information processing.* 2nd ed. New York: Wiley, 1976.

Orne, M. T., & Evans, F. J. Social control in the psychological experiment: Antisocial behavior and hypnosis. *Journal of Personality and Social Psychology,* 1965, *1,* 189–200.

People v. *Anderson,* 205 N.W. 2d 461 (1973).

People v. *Cotton,* 197 N.W. 2d 90 (1972).

People v. *Rowell,* 165 N.W. 2d 423 (1968).

Peterson, J. *Early conceptions and tests of intelligence.* Yonkers-on-Hudson, NY: World Book, 1925.

Quinn, J. R. In the wake of *Wade:* The dimensions of the eyewitness identification cases. *University of Colorado Law Review,* 1970, *42,* 135–158.

Raven, B. H., & French, J. R. P. Legitimate power, coercive power, and observability in social influence. *Sociometry,* 1958, *21,* 83–97.

Redmount, R. S. The psychological basis of evidence practices: Memory. *Journal of Criminal Law, Criminology, and Police Science,* 1959, *50,* 249–264.

Rosenberg, M. J. The conditions and consequences of evaluation apprehension. In R. Rosenthal & R. L. Rosnow (Eds.), *Artifact in behavioral research.* New York: Academic Press, 1969.

Rosenthal, R. On the social psychology of the psychological experiment: The experimenter's hypothesis as unintended determinant of experimental results. *American Scientist,* 1963, *51,* 268–283.

Rosenthal, R. Experimenter outcome-orientation and the results of the psychological experiment. *Psychological Bulletin,* 1964, *61,* 405–412.

Rosenthal, R. *Experimenter effects in behavioral research.* New York: Appleton-Century-Crofts, 1966.

Rouke, F. L. Psychological research on problems of testimony. *Journal of Social Issues,* 1957, *13*(2), 50–59.

Secord, P. F. Facial features and inference processes in interpersonal perception. In R. Tagiuri & L. Petrullo (Eds.), *Person perception and interpersonal behavior.* Stanford, CA: Stanford University Press, 1958.

Seeleman, V. The influence of attitude upon the remembering of pictorial material. *Archives of Psychology,* 1940 (Whole No. 258).

Shepard, R. N. Recognition memory for words, sentences, and pictures. *Journal of Verbal Learning and Verbal Behavior,* 1967, *6,* 156–163.

Sherif, M. *The psychology of social norms.* New York: Harper, 1936.

Sherif, M. Group influences upon the formation of norms and attitudes. In E. E. Maccoby, T. M. Newcomb, & E. L. Hartley (Eds.), *Readings in social psychology.* 3rd ed. New York: Holt, 1958.

Shrauger, S., & Altrocchi, J. The personality of the perceiver as a factor in person perception. *Psychological Bulletin,* 1964, *62,* 289–308.

Simmons v. *United States,* 406 F. 2d 456 (5th Cir. 1969).

Smock, C. D. The influence of psychological stress on the "intolerance of ambiguity." *Journal of Abnormal and Social Psychology,* 1955, *50,* 177–182.

Snee, T. J., & Lush, D. E. Interaction of the narrative and interrogatory methods of obtaining testimony. *Journal of Psychology,* 1941, *11,* 229–236.

Sobel, N. R. *Eyewitness identification: Legal and practical problems.* New York: Clark Boardman, 1972.

Stern, W. *Beiträge zur psychologie der aussage.* Leipzig: Verlag Barth, 1903.

Stern, W. *General psychology from the personalistic standpoint.* H. D. Spoerl (Trans.). New York: Macmillan, 1938.

Stovall v. Denno, 388 U.S. 293 (1967).

Strong, E. K. The effect of time interval upon recognition memory. *Psychological Review*, 1913, *20*, 339–372.

Tagiuri, R. Person perception. In G. Lindzey & E. Aronson (Eds.), *Handbook of social psychology*. Vol. 3. 2nd ed. Reading, MA: Addison-Wesley, 1969.

Tajfel, H. Social and cultural factors in perception. In G. Lindzey & E. Aronson (Eds.), *Handbook of social psychology*. Vol. 3. 2nd ed. Reading, MA: Addison-Wesley, 1969.

Thucydides. *The Peloponnesian war*. New York: Random House, 1951.

Treisman, A., & Geffen, G. Selective attention: Perception or response? In R. N. Haber (Ed.), *Information-processing approaches to visual perception*. New York: Holt, 1969.

United States v. Ash, 413 U.S. 300 (1972).

United States v. Wade, 388 U.S. 218 (1967).

Vickery, K., & Brooks, L. M. Time-spaced reporting of a "crime" witnessed by college girls. *Journal of Criminal Law and Criminology*, 1938, *29*, 371–382.

Wall, P. M. *Eye-witness identification in criminal cases*. Springfield, IL: Charles C Thomas, 1965.

Weld, H. P. Legal psychology: The psychology of testimony. In F. L. Marcuse (Ed.), *Areas of psychology*. New York: Harper, 1954.

Wells, G. L. Applied eyewitness-testimony research: System variables and estimator variables. *Journal of Personality and Social psychology*, 1978, *36*, 1546–1557.

Wells, G. L. (Ed.). Eyewitness behavior. *Law and Human Behavior*, 1980, *4* (Whole No. 4).

Wells, G. L., Leippe, M. R., & Ostrom, T. M. Guidelines for empirically assessing the fairness of a lineup. *Law and Human Behavior*, 1979, *3*, 285–293.

Wells, G. L., Lindsay, R. C. L., & Ferguson, T. Accuracy, confidence, and juror perceptions in eyewitness identification. *Journal of Applied Psychology*, 1979, *64*, 440–448.

Whipple, G. M. The observer as a reporter: A survey of the psychology of testimony. *Psychological Bulletin*, 1909, *6*, 153–170.

Whipple, G. M. Recent literature on the psychology of testimony. *Psychological Bulletin*, 1910, *7*, 365–368.

Whipple, G. M. Psychology of testimony. *Psychological Bulletin*, 1917, *14*, 234–236.

Whitely, P. L., & McGeoch, J. A. The effect of one form of report upon another. *American Journal of Psychology*, 1927, *38*, 280–284.

Wigmore, J. H. *Science of judicial proof*. 3rd ed. Boston: Little, Brown, 1937.

Wilder, H. H., & Wentworth, B. *Personal identification*. Chicago: T. G. Cooke, 1932.

Williams, G. L. The proof of guilt: A study of the English criminal trial. 3rd ed. London: Stevens, 1963.

Williams, L., & Greenwald, M. When witnesses think too much. *Social Action and the Law*, Newsletter, 1975, *2*(3), 5–6.

Wrightsman, L. S. Effects of waiting with others on changes in level of felt anxiety. *Journal of Abnormal and Social Psychology*, 1960, *61*, 216–222.

Yarmey, A. D. *The psychology of eyewitness testimony*. New York: Free Press, 1979.

Zimbardo, P. *The cognitive control of motivation*. Glenview, IL: Scott, Foresman, 1969.

POLICE ACTIVITIES:
ARRESTS AND COMMUNITY RELATIONS

Editors' Introduction

This chapter and the one that follows are concerned with police decision-making. This chapter, written by Grant, Grant, and Toch, examines an issue that grew out of the social unrest and consequent demands for government reform created in part by the American public's growing opposition to the Vietnam War, in part by what seemed like government interference in people's freedom to choose nonnormative lifestyles, and in part by charges that the police were acting as guardians of middle-class moral and political values rather than as detectors of and protectors from crime. From a broad perspective, the issue concerns police–community relationships. From a narrower perspective, the study deals with a special class of police behavior and, by inference, with citizen reactions to the attempts of the police to make arrests. In particular, the police have the discretion to charge an individual who does not comply with the arresting officer's orders with misdemeanor and/or felony violations (such as resisting arrest and assault on a police officer). Grant, Grant, and Toch use the frequency of these police charging decisions as an index of police–citizen conflict.

It is useful to keep several points in mind while reading the chapter. First, the charging decisions being examined represent only one potential consequence of police–citizen conflict and, more generally, only one form of the wide discretion that the police have in their day-to-day interactions with the public. For example, officers can respond to citizen disrespect and/or noncompliance by deciding to bring misdemeanor or felony charges in circumstances where an informal reprimand or citation would be more typical. Alternatively, officers can decide not to charge an individual even in situations where the law clearly has been violated. A second and related issue concerns the role that the police (as well as victims and witnesses—see Chapters 4 and 5, this volume) play in determining whether various citizen actions will be considered criminal. The wide discretion given to the police allows them to define whether a particular action is in violation of the law and which law is being violated. Thus, the decision-making of police officers plays as important a role in determining crime statistics as do victims. A third point to keep salient concerns the proportion of time that the police actually spend in crime-fighting activities. Several independent sources of evidence suggest that only a small proportion of police–citizen interactions are initiated because the officer intends to make an arrest. In many police departments, much of the time the police are on duty is spent on social-assistance activities—mediating conflicts, taking reports of crimes, directing traffic, and so on. In short, arrests and associated charging decisions index only a small part of police behavior. A fourth issue that emerges from the chapter deals with the effect, if any, that high-level policy changes in government organizations such as the police have on the day-to-day activities of low-level personnel. In the present case, the effects of a change in policy originated by a new chief of police are examined over time. Of particular interest is how a broadly defined policy change to improve police–citizen relationships affected one aspect of police–citizen interaction. Unfortunately, the practical problems inherent in observational studies dealing with police behavior prevent us from knowing how the policy change affected police activities that did not result in formal charges, such as mediational interventions in family and business disputes and responses to requests for health-related assistance.

The chapter by Stotland examines an issue related to the foregoing, namely, the effect that the "beat cop" can have on broad department policy if formal feedback networks are established. Although "bottom–up" influences on policy would seem to have beneficial consequences, the actual success of such feedback systems remains to be examined in real-world settings. Nevertheless, a full understanding of police decisions is likely to be incomplete unless both top–down and bottom–up influence channels are studied. With this in mind, Stotland suggests some reasonable mechanisms for ensuring bottom–up feedback.

6

Police–Citizen Conflict
and Decisions to Arrest

J. Douglas Grant, Joan Grant, and Hans H. Toch

It is obvious that an arrest is a fateful event in the life of a suspect, since it marks formal entry (or reentry) into the criminal justice system. But arrest decisions are also crucial events in the police agencies responsible for them and in the lives of the officers who make them. For the police agency, the overall arrest record may be regarded as the principal or exclusive measure of its productivity. For police officers, their record of arrests may help determine their chances of promotion, their standing among their peers, and their assessment of their own worth.

Though arrests form a relatively small proportion of police activity, their public character makes them loom large as a measure of police performance. It is important to remember that a police arrest is never *mandated*. It is, instead, *authorized*, and the language that lets officers decide when and when not to arrest is in practice ambiguous. Officers must decide whether a misdemeanor has occurred "in their presence" or whether they have "reasonable grounds" for assuming a felony. The greater the tendency to interpret such phrases generously, the greater the likelihood that citizens may view arrests as illegitimate exercises of police power.

This ambiguous nature of arrest authority provides the nexus for the link between arrests and police–citizen conflict. We will examine the nature of this link and the issue of productivity that is often invoked to explain it. We will then present some data collected during a four-year study of police–citizen conflict in the Oakland, California, police department. These data will show how officer arrest behavior is (and is not) influenced by changes in policy from above and finally how officer behavior can be changed by a peer-designed self-study intervention.

ARRESTS AND POLICE–CITIZEN CONFLICT

Police departments vary in the way in which they use their authority to arrest. Heaviest emphasis on arrest occurs in departments of the kind Wilson classifies as "legalistic":

> A legalistic department will issue traffic tickets at a high rate, detain and arrest a high proportion of juvenile offenders, act vigorously against illicit enterprises, and make a large number of misdemeanor arrests even when, as with petty larceny, the public order has not been breached. . . . The concept "legalistic" does not necessarily imply that the police regard all laws as equally important or that they love the law for its own sake. . . . The legalistic style does mean that, on the whole, the department will produce many arrests and citations, especially with respect to those matters in which the police and not the public invoke the law; even when the police are called by the public to intervene, they are likely to intervene formally, by making an arrest or urging the signing of a complaint, rather than informally, as through conciliation or by delaying an arrest in hopes that the situation will take care of itself. (Wilson, 1968, pp. 172–173)

Wilson points to one way in which legalism relates to citizen confrontations. Intensive enforcement, dispassionately applied, gravitates to "high-crime neighborhoods," which can contain disproportionate numbers of minority-group members. It is common for a legalistic department to face citizen resentment and widespread charges of harassment. "Harassment" here is not the arbitrary exercise of individual discretion, as it is elsewhere, in more lax organizations; it is, rather, the perceived role of the police agency. It is a corollary of generous deployment, *as a matter of policy*, of negative, "formal" enforcement sanctions, which may be unequally (though equitably when the area crime rate is considered) distributed.

Police officers also vary in the way they use arrest authority. As Stotland discusses at length in the following chapter, police officers exercise far more discretion than is generally realized in the decisions they make regarding how to behave on the job, including their decisions on who, when, how, and for what to arrest. Officers will thus vary in both the numbers and kinds of arrests they make. They will also vary in the extent to which their arrests are associated with violent encounters with citizens.

The police literature highlights two relationships between arrests and police–citizen conflicts. The first is the use of the arrest as a *weapon* in conflict; and the second, the invocation of the arrest as a self-protective measure when physical conflict has occurred. The first category refers to the propensity of officers to arrest a "disrespectful" rather than an "obsequious" suspect, when everything else is equal and discretion is available. This tendency was highlighted by Westley (1970), and has been confirmed in subsequent empirical work (Piliavin and Briar, 1964; Reiss, 1971). The magnitude of the effect is illustrated in a study by Hindelang (1976), who asked 69 sheriff's deputies to complete the sentence: "If a juvenile who has committed an arrestable violation, for which I would not normally make an arrest, verbally abuses me, I would . . . ." In response to the question, 56 of 69 officers indicated they would arrest, or probably arrest, the suspect. Whether or not the deputies would actually make an arrest in such a situation, they state that it is appropriate to vary the application of legal sanctions depending on how they are treated by a suspect.

The second issue is related to the first, since most police–citizen conflict is a manifestation of citizen disrespect or a reaction to it (Reiss, 1971; Toch, 1969; Westley, 1970). Out of intensive experience with civilians who claimed to have been assaulted by officers, Chevigny writes of the use of force by police:

> . . . most such acts arise out of defiance of authority or what the police take to be such defiance. A majority of the complaints about force (55 percent), whether authenticated or not, appeared on their face to involve defiance, and the overwhelming majority of the authenticated complaints were shown to involve such defiance (71 percent). (Chevigny, 1969, p. 70)

Though much police–citizen conflict may remain unrecorded (Reiss, 1971), officers may *arrest* their opponents *for the latter's role in conflict* or participation in the incident. One reason officers may arrest is to protect themselves from being sued or complained against (Chevigny, 1969). The least serious criminal charges the police may invoke can involve "interfering with an officer in the performance of duty" or "resisting arrest." Officers can also charge suspects with "assaulting a police officer" (themselves) in simple or aggravated fashion.

Arrests of this kind differ from other arrests because an unknown proportion of the total number represents the use of the criminal justice system to "cover" interpersonal conflicts between officers and civilians. Many incidents are unprovoked by police, but officers who are involved in a large number of conflicts raise questions about their own contribution to violence.

THE QUESTION OF PRODUCTIVITY

The use of arrests as a criterion of police productivity has been seriously challenged. The view of sophisticated police administrators is reflected by the National Advisory Commission on Criminal Justice Standards and Goals, whose position is the following:

> In evaluating performance, police departments rely heavily upon how many arrests officers make. Such a criterion, standing alone, is inappropriate as a measure of success in crime control unless factors such as the *quality of the arrest* or the *ultimate disposition of the case* are considered. Such a solitary standard may also distort measurement of the quality of policing on an individual level by ignoring such essential variables as an officer's use of discretion or his reputation for fairness and responsiveness to citizens. In no instance should the number of arrests be used as the only measure of an officer's productivity. Performance should be judged on the basis of criteria that reflect the necessary objectives, priorities, and overriding principles of police service. (National Advisory Commission, 1973, p. 151, emphasis added)

The American Bar Association Project on Standards for Criminal Justice states its concern even more strongly:

> The assumption that the use of an arrest and the criminal process is the primary or even the exclusive method available to police should be recognized as causing unnecessary *distortion* of both the criminal law and the system of criminal justice. (ABA, 1973, p. 12, emphasis added)

With specific regard to evaluation of police effectiveness, the ABA project on standards proposed:

> Traditional criteria such as the number of arrests that are made are inappropriate measures of the quality of performance of individual officers. Instead, police officers should be rewarded, in terms of status, compensation, and promotion, on the basis of criteria ... which directly relate to the objectives, priorities, and essential principles of police service. (ABA, 1973, p. 25)

These views are not shared by many police officers, and especially by those who have a record of many physical confrontations with citizens. The most frequent justification offered by such officers is that their encounters are a byproduct of high productivity (Toch, 1971). It logically follows, in fact, that officers with crime-ridden beats are more apt to risk violence than are officers making their redolent way through a shift in suburbia. And it similarly follows that officers concerned with ongoing offenses face more potential violence than officers who "ride by" them.

The issue of "riding by" is of very practical interest because, as Reiss (1971) points out, *most police violence occurs in "on-view" encounters*, in situations where officers approach citizens *on their own initiative*, rather than being dispatched or called. Such encounters (other than traffic offenses or outstanding warrants) do not involve identified offenders or perceived offenses. They consist, rather, of "field stops" or "field interrogations," in which the cues to suspicion cumulate *after* the contact, conversation, and observation have occurred (McCall, 1975). The citizen–officer contact is initiated in response to indicators that are not offense-relevant and have little evidentiary value, such as a person fleeing or "acting nervous" when being stared at or followed by a patrol car (Rubinstein, 1973).

On-view (proactive) police work raises the most delicate issue of *quality* in police productivity. It does so because the officer exercises maximum discretion, and the officer who is most actively involved may be the one most prone to "fishing expeditions" rather than the enforcer who is most sensitive to indicators of criminality. On-view contacts are also disproportionately viewed as illegitimate interferences by their targets (Reiss, 1971), who feel pounced upon. Field interrogations not infrequently result in responses such as "I don't have to tell you nothing," which entrap the officer in a zero-sum game (Toch, 1969). Such contacts may also eventuate in instructions by the officer (such as "Get your ass out of here") that invite escalation when the suspect refuses to comply (Reiss, 1971; Toch, 1969).

Quality issues also arise from dispatched calls in which a variety of interventions are possible, only some of which involve criminal sanctions. Officers who resolve most such occasions by attempting an arrest may add to their raw "productivity" score without demonstrating their effectiveness. In terms of criteria such as the ABA standards, such officers could be a liability rather than an asset to their department.

Whether a police agency views officers in terms of the quality of arrests hinges on the orientation and philosophy of the department in question. A legalistic agency is more apt to be concerned about the legality of arrests than about their appropriateness. The legalistic heroes tend to be officers with the largest scalp collections, without much concern about the quality or size of the scalps. By contrast, the legalistic deviants tend to be the phlegmatic old-timers, who are nostalgically oriented to a more relaxed (and slightly corrupt) behavioral pattern. In other types of departments—such as Wilson's (1968) "watchmen"—arrests are seen as last resorts. They are apt to occur with clear-cut and serious offenses or when the officers have been personally challenged or provoked. This results in a bimodal distribution, along a quality continuum, of the few arrests that take place. And in still other departments (classed by Wilson as "service-oriented"), quality may be defined in terms of the officers' ability to respond to their clients' needs and the officers' willingness to render positive services and enhance community relations.

The productivity–violence link is of most concern for legalistic departments, where the use of the arrest as the productivity index is stressed. Legalism frowns on violence, but smiles on productivity. The result is a double message for the officers, whose verbal reaction is that they are "damned if they do, and damned if they don't." The behavioral resolution of cross-pressures may vary from officer to officer. When productivity wins out, officers find that the "heat" from internal affairs is neutralized by the "warmth" of their sergeant and the regard of their peers. This may include supervisor collusion in "cover" arrests, and indulgences in reprimands. Chevigny notes:

> The New York Department seems to have made a decision, poorly articulated to be sure, that an officer is not to be disciplined for acts performed in the line of duty if those acts show initiative and an effort to maintain order. An angry reaction to defiance is thus felt to be one of the more minor of a policeman's failings. The effort to convict a prisoner is likewise to be commended, and shaving the facts a little to bring out that conviction is less reprehensible than avoiding the arrest altogether. The officer is at least showing initiative and the will to make arrests and obtain convictions—as far as the Department is concerned, virtues of a "good cop." (Chevigny, 1969, p. 67)

OAKLAND: A CASE STUDY

In 1969, two of the authors began work in the Oakland, California, police department around the issue of citizen–officer conflict.[1] The study had its roots in a concern with the anatomy of violent encounters, which we had studied first in prison inmates. We moved from this to a study of violent encounters between officers and citizens. Our concern was to demonstrate ways in which persons who represent a social problem can become involved in the study of the problem and in efforts to do something about it.

---

[1]Most of the data in this paper were developed under NIMH Grant MH 20757 ("Research on Violence Prevention by Police"). Initial work was carried out under Training Grant MH 12068 ("Training Police Officers for Violence Reduction"), described in Toch, Grant, and Galvin (1975). We are indebted to the Center for Studies of Crime and Delinquency, National Institute of Mental Health, for their support of these studies and to Chief Charles Gain and the Oakland, California, police department for their generous cooperation.

Oakland offered a particularly interesting example not only of the link between arrests and police conflict with citizens but of how police behavior can be changed over time. Oakland was one of three agencies described by Wilson (1968) as exemplifying the legalistic style of policing, an approach that began in the anticorruption decade of the 1950s. The picture changed in the late 1960s with the impact of an administration intent on furthering a due process model of police work. This move was responsive to citizen discontent, but was principally inspired by trends in the police field, described above, toward "well-rounded" and less "enforcement-oriented" policing. The new police chief, Charles Gain, pointed out:

> . . . there is a growing awareness of the need to improve our abilities in coping with people problems. . . . We have, then, discovered that a series of order maintenance activities which have grudgingly been performed in the past are important to our mission and that they should receive new recognition. They should be, and in some cases are now, given equal importance with crime prevention and control because of their frequency and significance to our clientele—the citizens we serve. (Gain, 1972, pp. 5–6)

The goals of his administration included:

1. Stress on the observance of suspect rights.

2. Increased attention to police–community relations.

3. Deemphasis of public-order crimes.

4. Introduction of new and improved service modalities.

5. Stress on "quality enforcement."

6. Reduction of police–citizen violence and conflict.

Chief Gain brought about a sharp policy change in the department. His tenure (he was appointed in 1967 and served until his retirement in 1973) was marked by a concern for improving the department's relations with the community, especially the minority community, through direct work with citizen groups, changes in department operation, and innovations in training. It was also marked by conflict with officers, resulting in a vote of no confidence by the Oakland Police Officers' Association. A major issue in this vote was disagreement with what was seen as the chief's effort to redefine the police role.

The change in the Oakland department's approach to policing gives us a laboratory in which to study what happens when change is mandated from the top. We will look first at what happened during

Gain's tenure to the incidence of police–citizen conflict, of injuries resulting from such conflict, and of citizens' complaints against the police. We will then look at some factors that may help explain incidence trends: the initiation of interaction with citizens, the arrest productivity of the department as a whole, and the productivity of individual officers. Finally we will look at one outgrowth of our own study, a change effort planned and implemented by officers.

The incidence of conflicts

Short of detailed and expensive observation (McCall, 1975; Reiss, 1971), conflict must be observed secondhand, through officer records of interactions with citizens. California has three charges referring to citizen–officer conflict: resisting arrest, a misdemeanor offense; battery or assault on a peace officer, a felony offense; and assault with a deadly weapon on a peace officer, also a felony offense. In the discussion below, these are referred to as "charged incidents."

Formal charges do not, of course, cover all instances of physical confrontations between citizens and officers. Many of these, in fact the majority, do not lead to a formal charge against the citizen; they become "invisible." In a special study undertaken by the Violence Prevention Unit of the department, all arrest reports were reviewed and coded for the presence or absence of physical confrontations.[2] In the discussion below, these are referred to as "not-charged incidents."

Table 6.1 shows the incidence of each of the three charges for the years 1970 through 1973 and of the not-charged incidents for 1971 through 1973. The total charged incidents show a decline from year to year over the four-year period; this holds for the not-charged incidents (over a three-year period) as well. It will be seen that the drop in charged incidents is due to the decrease in misdemeanor charges (resisting arrest) rather than in the two more serious felony assault charges. The latter, it might be argued, result from situations that offer less room for officer discretion in whether or not to make a formal charge. However, since the not-charged incidents decreased as well, it cannot be argued that the drop in resisting-arrest charges represents a shift from the charged to the not-charged category. Nor can it be argued that the recording of actual incidents became more lax. The chief, very concerned with reducing the number of citizen complaints, had made it clear that any behavior of which a citizen

---

[2] Elements of resistance, battery, or assault with a deadly weapon present in the arrest report but not charged by the arresting officer.

Table 6.1
Citizen–officer conflicts

Type of incident	1970	1971	1972	1973
Resisting arrest				
Total	630	489	469	326
Average/month	52.5	40.8	39.1	27.2
Battery				
Total	145	118	154	148
Average/month	12.1	9.8	12.8	12.3
Assault with deadly weapon				
Total	38	51	33	35
Average/month	3.2	4.2	2.8	2.9
All charged				
Total	813	658	656	509
Average/month	67.8	54.8	54.7	42.4
All not charged				
Total	NA	1,242[a]	1,007	724
Average/month	NA	103.5	83.9	60.3
All charged and not charged				
Total	NA	1,900	1,663	1,233
Average/month	NA	158.3	138.6	102.8

[a]The 1971 figures are extrapolations based on the data available for the last four months of that year.

might reasonably complain must be documented, whether with a formal charge or not, in the arrest report. The climate he set makes it reasonable to suppose that most, if not all, confrontations appeared in the department's records.

Injuries to officers and citizens

Physical confrontations between citizens and officers may be more show than substance, but they sometimes result in real injuries—to officers, to suspects, or to both. Table 6.2 gives data on injuries to each group over each of the four kinds of incidents reported in Table 6.1.

As would be expected, injuries resulted from the misdemeanor offenses far less often than from the two felony offenses, and injuries resulted from the not-charged incidents less often than from the charged offenses. Unlike the year-to-year decrease in number of

Table 6.2
Injuries to citizens and officers in citizen–officer conflicts

Type of incident	1970		1971		1972		1973[a]	
	Citizen	Officer	Citizen	Officer	Citizen	Officer	Citizen	Officer
Resisting arrest								
Total	23	48	24	32	26	33	8	12
Percent	3.7	7.6	4.9	6.5	5.5	7.0	3.2	4.7
Battery								
Total	38	37	44	28	50	39	13	11
Percent	26.2	25.5	37.3	23.7	32.5	25.3	11.2	9.5
Assault with deadly weapon								
Total	9	8	10	11	9	6	1	4
Percent	23.7	21.1	19.6	21.6	27.3	18.2	3.7	14.8
All charged								
Total	70	93	78	71	85	78	22	27
Percent	8.6	11.4	11.9	10.8	13.0	11.9	5.5	6.8
All not charged								
Total	NA	NA	12[b]	54[b]	21	44	0	9
Percent	NA	NA	1.0	4.3	2.1	4.4	0.0	2.0
All charged and not charged								
Total	NA	NA	90	125	106	122	22	36
Percent	NA	NA	4.7	6.6	6.4	7.3	2.6	4.2

[a]Injury data were not collected after the first three quarters of 1973. The number and percent of injuries are for the first nine months.
[b]The 1971 figures are extrapolations based on the data available for the last four months of that year.

incidents, the proportion of these in which injuries occurred to one or both participants showed no such clear-cut trend. The number of injuries to officers rose somewhat from 1970 to 1972; the number of injuries to suspects, at least in the misdemeanor and not-charged incidents, showed a slight decrease. Both dropped sharply in 1973; we have no explanation for this sudden change.

In reviewing resisting-arrest injuries, we find that, although it is the citizen who is being charged and arrested, the *alleged aggressors' injuries exceeded (consistently) those of the officer-complainants.* The same point holds—though not as surprisingly—for uncharged violence.

Complaints against the police

Under Gain's administration, the department encouraged the receipt of complaints by citizens. Complaints were accepted in any form, including those made anonymously, by a central complaint office. Case records were kept on all complaints; feedback was given routinely to the officers who were the subject of complaints and, on request, to the citizens who made them.

Table 6.3 shows the complaint data for each year from 1970 to 1973. The total number of complaints made by citizens can be taken as a gross measure of citizen dissatisfaction with police. The number of complaints sustained (i.e., the number in which the department formally found a valid basis for the complaint) can be taken as a measure of inappropriate officer behavior. The percent sustained may be considered a minimum measure of the legitimacy of the complaints made.

It will be seen that total complaints dropped dramatically from 1970 to 1971 and continued a downward trend after that time; the total in 1973 is one-third that of 1970. Despite encouragement to make complaints, this form of citizen dissatisfaction sharply decreased.

Table 6.3
Formal citizen complaints against officers

Complaints	1970	1971	1972	1973
Number sustained	96	77	44	23
Percent sustained	14.9	21.6	17.5	11.2
Total number of complaints	645	357	251	206

Note: χ^2 test (number sustained versus number not sustained over four years): $p < .01$.

The number of complaints that were found to have validity also decreased from year to year (differences are significant at the .01 level); the total sustained in 1973 is one-quarter that of 1970. The percent sustained rose from 1970 to 1971, a result of the fact that total complaints made dropped far more sharply than did number sustained. The first may indicate the chief's success in working with the community; the second, his success in working with his officers. The latter came more slowly. After 1971, however, the percent of complaints sustained decreased.

The initiation of interaction

As we have noted, a police officer may become involved with a citizen when dispatched on a call through the radio room, or the officer may initiate the interaction. In the former situation the officer's interaction is not a matter of choice. On-view incidents, on the other hand, are always "precipitated" by the officer in the sense of making a physical overture or contact. Table 6.4 shows the number of officer involvements in incidents in each type of citizen–officer conflict by the way in which the conflict was initiated.

The picture presented by Table 6.4 is striking and dramatic. In all categories, we see *a strong, consistent decrease in the proportion of violence resulting from on-view incidents.* In fact, we conclude that the time trends we have noted are disproportionately a function of on-view trends.

We also see that resisting-arrest incidents occurred more often with officer-initiated (on-view) activity than did felony-assault incidents; and of the latter two, assault on the officer occurred more often in officer-initiated actions than did assault on an officer with a deadly weapon. But for each of the three types of charge the ratio of officer-initiated to dispatched activities decreased from year to year over the four-year period. The same is true for the not-charged incidents.[3] Thus, it seems plausible to argue that the decrease in citizen–officer incidents reflected a decrease in field contacts or an improvement in field-interrogation conduct. In the resisting-arrest category, the number as well as the percent resulting from officer-initiated activity decreased; the number resulting from dispatched actions actually showed a slight increase.[4]

---

[3]Differences between the proportion of on-view and dispatched incidents over time are significant at the .005 level for all but "Assault with a deadly weapon."

[4]As noted in Table 6.4, 1973 figures are based on nine months only. Extrapolating to the full year would give 96 on-view and 523 dispatched incidents in the resisting-arrest category.

The type of arrest

To what extent is the amount of citizen–officer conflict simply an expression of how active officers are? In the extreme case, if officers snooze or drive aimlessly about, they will clearly have no difficulties with citizens. The more work they do, the more risk they take of physical involvement with citizens. Thus, the decrease in conflicts over this four-year period may simply reflect a decrease in the number of arrests made.

Table 6.5 both confirms and disconfirms this argument. This table presents the percent change in the number of arrests made for each year from 1970 to 1973. Offenses are divided for this purpose into the reporting categories used for the FBI Uniform Crime Reports. Part I offenses include the major felonies (criminal homicide, forcible rape, robbery, aggravated assault, burglary, larceny, and auto theft). Part II offenses include victimless crimes (e.g., drunkenness, vagrancy, disorderly conduct, and drug, gambling, and prostitution offenses), some white-collar crimes (forgery, fraud, and embezzlement), and a variety of others (e.g., arson, simple assault, family or child neglect or abuse, vandalism, carrying illegal weapons, receiving stolen property, curfew violations, and runaways).

The table shows that total arrests were down considerably—25%—over the four-year period from 1970 to 1973, but this decrease was almost solely due to a decrease in the Part II offenses. Productivity in the sense of major crime fighting showed relatively little change over the four years. There was a marked decrease in arrests for the less severe criminal offenses, with drunkenness constituting 30–40% of these over this time period. The concomitant decrease in citizen–officer conflict seems thus to be related to a change in police behavior toward troublesome but not seriously criminal citizen activity. Such change is, of course, precisely the thrust of antilegalistic police reform.

The arrest figures we have cited must be evaluated in two contexts. The first is change within the department: the advent of new activities—an increase in nonarrest productivity (including such service innovations as family crisis intervention and landlord–tenant intervention); the thrust for nonenforcement reactions to street situations formerly resulting in arrests (e.g., drunks, disturbance calls); and, to a lesser extent, the deployment of manpower into staff activities such as violence reduction, training, and other work concerned with re-orienting the department.

The second context is the crime picture. As we note in Table 6.6, Oakland experienced a slight, but consistent decrease in reported crime from 1970 on, due mostly to a drop in larceny-theft and auto-

Table 6.4
Initiation of citizen–officer conflicts

Type of incident	1970		1971		1972		1973[a]	
	No.	%	No.	%	No.	%	No.	%
Resisting arrest								
On-view[b]	474	50.1	383	42.6	352	41.5	147	27.2
Dispatched	415	43.9	458	50.9	449	52.9	392	72.6
Other[c]	57	6.0	58	6.5	47	5.5	1	0.2
Total[d]	946		899		848		540	
Battery								
On-view	116	46.2	90	38.3	144	38.4	53	20.5
Dispatched	113	45.0	121	51.5	205	54.7	206	79.5
Other	22	8.8	24	10.2	26	6.9	0	0.0
Total	251		235		375		259	
Assault with a deadly weapon								
On-view	21	35.6	33	34.7	26	28.6	17	22.1
Dispatched	31	52.5	53	55.8	59	64.8	58	75.3
Other	7	11.9	9	9.5	6	6.6	2	2.6
Total	59		95		91		77	
All charged								
On-view	611	48.6	506	41.2	522	39.7	217	24.8
Dispatched	559	44.5	632	51.4	713	54.3	656	74.9
Other	86	6.8	91	7.4	79	6.0	3	0.3
Total	1,256		1,229		1,314		876	

All not charged							
On-view	NA	846[e]	46.4[e]	784	38.8	425	35.2
Dispatched		906	49.7	1,174	58.0	781	64.6
Other		72	3.9	65	3.2	3	0.2
Total		1,824		2,023		1,209	
All charged and not charged							
On-view	NA	1,352	44.3	1,306	39.1	642	30.8
Dispatched		1,538	50.4	1,887	56.5	1,437	68.9
Other		163	5.3	144	4.3	6	0.3
Total		3,053		3,337		2,085	

Note: χ^2 test (on-view versus dispatch over four years):
  Resisting arrest: $p < .005$.
  Battery: $p < .005$.
  Assault with deadly weapon: NS.
  All charged: $p < .005$.
  All not charged: $p < .005$.
  All charged and not charged: $p < .005$.

[a] Data on initiation of conflict were not collected after the first three quarters of 1973. Thus the number and percent of incidents are for the first nine months.

[b] "On-view" refers to an officer-initiated interaction.

[c] "Other" refers to occasional situations in which the interaction neither is initiated by the officer in question nor results from a specific dispatch from the radio room; e.g., two officers may be dispatched on a call from the radio room, and a third makes a decision to join them on the call.

[d] Comparison with Table 6.1 will show larger "total" figures here. Figures presented here are for total number of officer involvements in incidents. Figures for Table 6.1 are for total number of incidents (which may have involved more than one officer).

[e] The 1971 figures are extrapolations based on the data available for the last four months of that year.

Table 6.5
Arrests by type of offense: percent change from preceding year

Type of offense	1970	1971	1972	1973	1970–1973
Part I					
Number	8,718	9,401	8,974	8,469	
Percent change	+ 12.8	+ 7.8	− 4.5	− 5.6	− 2.9
Part II					
Number	31,500	25,233	21,588	21,699	
Percent change	+ 0.2	− 19.9	− 14.4	+ 0.5	− 31.1
Total Part I and II					
Number	40,218	34,634	30,562	30,168	
Percent change	+ 2.7	− 13.9	− 11.8	− 1.3	− 25.0

theft offenses. An exception is aggravated assault, which spiraled steadily upward, doubling in number from 1970 to 1974. Thus, the decrease we find in police–citizen confrontations occurs against a backdrop of increased citizen–citizen conflict. This suggests an improvement in police response to assaultive citizens rather than a change in citizen behavior.

Individual productivity and violence

What of the individual officers? Is the amount of their arrest activity related to the frequency with which they have trouble with citizens? Does their involvement in incidents increase with their productivity or with certain kinds of productivity?

Some law-enforcement personnel feel that citizen–officer conflict is more likely to occur in situations of serious criminal activity, i.e., in association with felony arrests. The literature (Reiss, 1971; Toch, 1969; Westley, 1970) suggests that assaults are more likely to occur during misdemeanor arrests, in field contacts, and in police activity that might be construed as harassment.

To clarify this issue, a special study was undertaken to allow accumulation of arrest and conflict data for individual officers. The year selected was 1971. A count was made of the number of felony and of misdemeanor arrests for each of 489 officers and of the number of citizen–officer conflicts associated with each type. Officers were then classified as high or low in productivity for each type of arrest and for total arrests.

Table 6.6
Crimes known to police in Oakland, California

Year	Total Crime Index (using 1973 FBI formula)	Type of crime							
		Nonnegligent manslaughter	Negligent manslaughter	Forcible rape	Robbery	Aggravated assault	Burglary, breaking and entering	Larceny theft	Auto theft
1970	42,872	69	37	212	2,497	1,088	13,787	20,166	4,993
1971	42,699	89	26	220	2,932	1,224	14,311	18,528	5,395
1972	41,836	78	25	261	2,907	1,646	13,080	18,445	5,419
1973	41,595	100	11	220	2,879	1,853	14,734	17,063	4,746
1974	40,507	78	3	246	2,883	2,175	14,144	16,702	4,279

SOURCE: Federal Bureau of Investigation, Uniform Crime Reports, 1971–1975 (1976).

Table 6.7 presents the average number of citizen–officer conflicts during the year for officers classified as high and low in terms of various measures of productivity: number of felony arrests, number of misdemeanor arrests, number of total arrests, and ratio of number of felony arrests to number of misdemeanor arrests.[5]

It is clear from the table that officers with more citizen (arrest) contacts do have more conflict with citizens. This holds for felony, for misdemeanor, and for total arrests. The differences between the average number of conflicts for officers with high and low arrest productivity are significant beyond the .001 level for each type of arrest and for the two types combined. Thus, while the data in Table 6.5, which show a large drop in the number of arrests for less serious offenses over the period when citizen–officer conflicts were decreasing, tend to support the argument that conflict is more likely to occur in connection with misdemeanor than with felony arrests, the data in Table 6.7 support the reverse position. One explanation for the discrepancy may be exposure: those officers assigned to areas with a high amount of criminal activity and thus more arrestable behavior had more opportunity for conflict with citizens.

The felony/misdemeanor argument raises the question of the *quality* of arrest as distinct from arrest productivity. If the law-enforcement function of the police is seen as one of attending to greater as opposed to lesser crimes, then an officer whose arrests are primarily for felony as opposed to misdemeanor offenses might be considered more effective than one whose arrests are primarily for the latter.[6] Conflict may be more common among the less effective officers when effectiveness is defined in terms of the quality of arrests that they make.

As a crude measure of the quality of arrest, we calculated the ratio of felony to misdemeanor arrests for each of the 489 officers during 1971. The officers were then divided into those with a felony/misdemeanor ratio equal to or less than 1.0 (i.e., those who had no more felony than misdemeanor arrests during the year) and those with a ratio larger than 1.0 (i.e., those who had more felony than misdemeanor arrests). According to our argument, the latter would be said

---

[5]The data were compiled originally for a study of officers who participated, or were eligible for participation, in a Peer Review Panel, a program for officers with high numbers of citizen–officer conflicts. These constituted 171 of the total. The remaining 318 formed the criterion group for determining high and low productivity: high in each case being all numbers above the median for this group, low being all numbers at or below the median.

[6]It is recognized that this does not take into account the nature of an officer's assignment—its location and time of day—which may have an influence on the primary type of arrest the officer makes.

Table 6.7
Citizen–officer conflicts by officers with high and low productivity, 1971

Level of productivity (median split)	Different productivity indices			
	Felony arrests	Misde-meanor arrests	Total arrests: felony and misdemeanor	Felony/ misdemeanor ratio
High				
Number of officers	275	244	270	235
Average number of conflicts	3.2	3.3	3.1	2.8
Low				
Number of officers	214	245	219	254
Average number of conflicts	1.3	1.4	1.4	1.8
Total number of officers	489	489	489	489

Note: t-test (high versus low production)
  Felony arrests: $p < .001$.
  Misdemeanor arrests: $p < .001$.
  Total arrests: $p < .001$.
  Felony/Misdemeanor: $p < .001$.

to show more effective arrest quality and we would expect them to have fewer citizen–officer conflicts. They did not. The last column of Table 6.7 shows that the high felony/misdemeanor ratio group had an average of 2.8 citizen–officer confrontations during the year compared to 1.8 for the less effective (low felony/misdemeanor ratio) group. This difference is significant beyond the .001 level. Thus, citizen–officer conflicts were not associated with poorer rather than better quality of arrests (defined crudely by the felony/misdemeanor ratio). The data support the opposite position.

Let us look at the data again, however, across columns. Officers who made relatively few felony arrests tended to have relatively few conflicts with citizens. But officers whose number of felony arrests was low *in relation to the number of misdemeanor arrests they made* had substantially more conflicts. Officers who were high in felony-arrest productivity had a high number of citizen–officer conflicts; those whose number of felony arrests was high in relation to the number of misdemeanor arrests had somewhat fewer conflicts. This suggests that not all the variance in frequency of conflict is accounted for by a simple measure of arrest frequency, and that quality of arrest behavior contributes something to the variance in number of conflict incidents.

The Peer Review Panel

The data given above tend to support the position that administrative policy change *can* make a difference in officer behavior. We turn now to a program designed to deal directly with the problem of officers who have an unusually high number of physical conflicts with citizens.

The violence-reduction program in the Oakland police department (Toch, Grant, and Galvin, 1975) produced two organizational innovations. One was the Conflict Management Unit (earlier called the Violence Prevention Unit), which monitored police–citizen incidents, coordinated conflict–related police services, and participated in recruit and in-service training. The second was the Peer Review Panel, which located violence-involved officers and helped them review street incidents for remediable patterns.

The panel was designed and administered by officers. It reviewed departmental arrest reports and maintained full records on every officer on street assignment. When any officer's level of "incidents" became statistically unacceptable, the officer was scheduled for a review session in which the incidents were analyzed and inferences drawn about remediable patterns. The review session involved a rotating group of officers, with most being former panel subjects. Sessions were repeated if high incident levels persisted.

Though brief, there is evidence that panel experience had a positive effect on an officer's street behavior.[7] Table 6.8 compares panel participants with nonparticipants in the frequency of citizen–officer conflicts for the 5 months prior to instituting the review panel and the 26 months following. Only officers who were on street duty for the entire 31 months were used in the comparison.

Using the 5 months prior to the panel as a base, the average number of incidents expected for the next 26 months was determined. The actual number that occurred was less than the number expected for both the participants and the nonparticipants. The decrease was much greater, however, for the participating officers, their expected–observed discrepancy being 4½ times that of the nonparticipating officers. A covariance analysis shows that a difference of this magnitude has less than a .001 probability of occurring by chance. The original officer study of street conflicts led to the development of an intervention that significantly reduced the incidence of such conflict.

Though the review panel began in June 1970, participation in the panel was spread over the months following. The figures reported for

---

[7] The following analysis of panel data is drawn from Toch, Grant, and Galvin (1975), pp. 325–326.

Table 6.8
Total citizen–officer conflicts before and after panel participation: participants versus nonparticipants

Review panel	Before (Jan.–May 1970)	After (June 1970–July 1972)		Difference (expected versus observed)
		Expected[a]	Observed	
Participants (n = 72) Average incidents/ officer	2.39	12.48	7.90	4.58
Average/month/officer	0.48	0.48	0.30	0.18
Nonparticipants (n = 434) Average incidents/ officer	0.64	3.38	2.44	0.94
Average/month/officer	0.13	0.13	0.09	0.04

[a]Expected figures were obtained by multiplying the average number of incidents per month by the number of months in the June 1970–July 1972 period.

the participants for the "after" period in Table 6.8 include varying numbers of months prior to participation. More precise measures were obtained by taking each participant's average number of incidents for the actual months prior to and following participation in the panel. This analysis is reported in Table 6.9. The average monthly incidents for the participants dropped from .37 to .16 following participation. Monthly averages for the nonparticipants (using randomly assigned comparable time periods) dropped from .10 to .08. A covariance analysis shows that the differences among these averages have less than a .01 probability of occurring by chance.[8]

Residues of legalism

Organizational change is often obdurate. In a setting where change originates "from the top down," compliance may not necessarily purchase wholehearted commitment. This fact is critical, since results may end where pressure eases.

We have presented evidence that the police chief's efforts to modify officer behavior were successful and that the officers themselves could bring about an even further shift in behavior. Yet these efforts met with far from ready acceptance. We turn now to evidence that policy, as enunciated by the chief, was not necessarily policy as interpreted by his officers. What the chief said was good police work was not what the majority of officers said they would do.

---

[8]The preceding three paragraphs were taken from Toch, Grant, and Galvin (1975), pp. 325–326.

Table 6.9
Average monthly citizen–officer conflicts before and after panel participation: participants versus nonparticipants

Review panel	Before	After
Participants (n = 88)		
Average	0.37	0.16
Variance	0.13	0.02
Nonparticipants (n = 434)		
Average	0.10	0.08
Variance	0.03	0.02

Note: In contrast to the figures in Table 6.8, time before and after participation varied for each participant. Actual months on the street before and after participation were used to determine monthly averages. This allowed the inclusion of 16 additional officer-participants who could not be included in the analysis reported in Table 6.8 because they were not on the street for the full before and after periods.

Time is controlled for the nonparticipants by proportional random assignments, to correspond to the monthly proportions of participants.

Officers in the violence reduction program developed a "critical-incident survey" midway during the period we are reviewing. They solicited reactions to twelve "typical" incidents they saw as diagnostic of police discretionary problems. Three may suffice to show the pattern.[9]

The first incident (Table 6.10) depicted a standard on-view stimulus situation. In this incident, barely one-third of the personnel (29%) agreed with the chief that no police action was required. Two-thirds (71%) proceeded on the assumption that the citizen's actions warranted investigation, with the further assumption that a crime may have been committed. More than half (56%: responses 4, 5, and 6) would have attempted contact with the boy and detained him long enough for interrogation—an action of questionable legitimacy.

The second incident (Table 6.11) dealt with a field interrogation of a resistant subject. In this incident, only one-third of the personnel (34%) agreed with the chief that no action was required. Another one-third (37%: responses 5, 6, and 7) would have detained the subject—an action that is possibly illegal and likely to be resisted.

By contrast, the third incident (Table 6.12) featured a situation in which a nonenforcement intervention (arbitration) was possible. Responses here were almost equally divided among three alternatives: taking no action (40%), intervening by attempting a peacekeeping role (30%, including the chief), and intervening with the implied

---

[9]The incident data are excerpted from Toch, Grant, and Galvin (1975), pp. 385, 390, and 394.

Table 6.10
Responses to critical-incident item 2

Item: MN 15.[a] Officer observes subject loitering on corner. Officer stops car, gets out to approach subject. Subject runs 75 feet to a house and enters front door.

Response	Percent of all full-time personnel (n = 423)
1. No action.[b]	29
2. Check scene for crime, further action unspecified.	6
3. Ascertain from others if juvenile lives at address.	9
4. Check scene for crime, attempt to contact subject at his home, further action unspecified.	26
5. Question subject on reason for running, run F.C.,[c] etc., or instruct parent in control of juvenile, proper method of raising children, etc.	25
6. Demand explanation for behavior.	5

[a]Male Negro, 15 years old. This is standard terminology.
[b]Chief's response.
[c]Field check.

Table 6.11
Responses to critical-incident item 7

Item: MN in late 20's walking NB on 101st Avenue slowly in high frequency 10851 V.C.[a] area. Officer stops subject, asks for name and address. Subject identifies himself as John Smith of 1901–101st Avenue. Officer explains 10851 problem and says he wants to detain subject for further information. Subject says, "No, I gave you my name and address," and walks away.

Response	Percent of all full-time personnel (n = 423)
1. No action.[b]	34
2. Check area for signs of crime, observe area.	1
3. Make F.C. on present information, follow home.	18
4. F.C. unspecified.	9
5. Detain subject for further information, method of detaining unspecified, offer ride home, etc.	28
6. Detain subject forcibly if necessary to obtain information.	6
7. Detain subject forcibly to obtain information; if unsatisfactory, arrest subject.	3

[a]Vehicle code violation (stolen cars).
[b]Chief's response.

Table 6.12
Responses to critical-incident item 11

Item: MN and FN 25, 2 children FN 1 and 4. Wife obviously beaten by husband, refuses to sign complaint out of fear of further beating. Husband states, "It's all over now." Loudly and aggressively insists that officers leave at once.

Response	Percent of all full-time personnel (n = 423)
1. No action.	40
2. Talk to husband, give advice and/or warnings, make crime report, or talk to husband and wife, separate them.[a]	30
3. Attempt to talk to wife regardless of husband's wishes, make crime report, stand by.	15
4. Talk to wife, if necessary arrest husband, explain law to wife, preserve the peace.	6
5. Arrest husband.	8

[a]Chief's response.

use of force if necessary (29%: responses 3, 4, and 5). This last alternative would raise complications if the wife had made no actual complaint.

All three incidents suggest that legalistic police norms survived organizational change to some extent. In on-view situations, officers may have been more prone to intervene than the chief would have liked; given "service" opportunities, officers were less likely to exercise newly stressed "conflict-reduction options."

What people say they would do and what they in fact do may be quite different. We may be dealing with this kind of situation here. Officers may have been reporting that they would intervene in street situations far more than they actually do. Since our incident-behavior data are available over time and our critical-incident attitude data represent a cross-section in time, we do not know whether this is the case. It may be that the attitude data would have shown similar decreases over time had we been able to sample it repeatedly over the period we have studied. Were that the case, we might conclude that chief–officer discrepancies were a function of time lag and that it was taking officers a while to catch up with their chief's position.

CONCLUSIONS

Police have wide discretionary powers, and this discretion extends to how they use their power to arrest. There are differences among police professionals, and thus among police departments, in their use of arrest authority and in their view of arrests as a measure of good police work. Within a given department there are differences among officers in how policy is carried out.

We were fortunate to be allowed access to a large urban police department over a period of several years, to work with a small group of officers as costudents of a problem that had meaning both for them and for us, and to assist in their planning of interventions to cope with it. The problem for the department was the high number of physical confrontations between officers and citizens, leading to tensions with the community, and the concentration of those incidents among relatively few officers. The problem for us was the part played by officers in precipitating conflicts with citizens. We assumed that officers, by the use of their discretionary authority, contributed something to the occurrence of at least some incidents. We also assumed that the officers most seriously involved in the problem were the "experts" and were thus best-qualified to study the problem and propose solutions for it.

We have followed one kind of officer behavior, participation in physical conflict with citizens, over a period when the department was undergoing rapid policy and administrative change.[10] We have shown that police–citizen conflict can decrease sharply with a deemphasis of legalism and that citizen resentment (as expressed in complaints to the police) can also decrease. We have found that this decrease is associated with changes in kind of arresting behavior, with less emphasis placed on the less serious offenses and on-view stops. We found these changes occurring against a background of an increase in total assaultive crimes by citizens. We also found them occurring despite officer lack of commitment, at least on an attitudinal level, to the chief's change efforts.

We found a link between productivity and police–citizen conflict. This link is neither surprising nor disheartening. It confirms that productivity, even if refined, entails paying a price in violence. It tells us that a police force of any orientation must precariously balance its values. It must decide how much to prize arrests and how much to "trade" for them. Not all trade-offs are inevitable, and moderation in arresting—as elsewhere—pays decent dividends.

We found some evidence that frequency of conflict may be associated with arrest quality. This last is an issue that needs to be explored more fully. We need arrest-productivity indices (such as conviction rates) and ratings of nonarrest productivity. We need to

---

[10]Police departments do not commonly keep the kinds of records that allow systematic study of change efforts nor the tracking of individual officer behavior. The Conflict Management Unit, as part of its study of department operations, set up an information system that allowed study of the citizen–officer conflict problem over time. The data presented in this paper come from the work of that unit.

know more about different types of officers and about different patterns of productivity. We need to know how these patterns change when change is imposed from without and when it comes from within.

Finally, we found that officer behavior can be changed by an intervention designed and implemented by other officers. While incidents were decreasing in the department as a whole, officers who participated in the Peer Review Panel showed a larger decrease in incidents than officers who did not. The panel could not have been implemented without the background of change in the department, but its relative success is a testament to the importance of involving the object of change in change efforts.

References

American Bar Association Project on Standards for Criminal Justice. *Standards relating to the urban police function*. New York: American Bar Association, 1973.

Chevigny, P. *Police power: Police abuses in New York City*. New York: Pantheon, 1969.

Federal Bureau of Investigation. *Uniform Crime Reports, 1971–1975*. Washington, DC: U.S. Government Printing Office, 1976.

Gain, C. R. The state of the art. The police: What we know. Paper presented at California Justice Research Conference, San Francisco, 1972.

Hindelang, M. J. With a little help from their friends: Group participation in reported delinquent behavior. *British Journal of Criminology*, 1976, *16*, 109–125.

McCall, G. J. *Observing the law: Applications of field methods to the study of the criminal justice system*. Washington, DC: Center for Studies of Crime and Delinquency, National Institute of Mental Health, 1975.

National Advisory Commission on Criminal Justice Standards and Goals. *Police*. Washington, DC: U.S. Government Printing Office 1973.

Piliavin, L., & Briar, S. Police encounters with juveniles. *American Journal of Sociology*, 1964, *70*, 206–214.

Reiss, A. J., Jr. *The police and the public*. New Haven, CT: Yale University Press, 1971.

Rubinstein, J. *City police*. New York: Ballantine Books, 1973.

Toch, H. *Violent men: An inquiry into the psychology of violence*. Chicago: Aldine, 1969.

Toch, H. Quality control in police work. *Police*, 1971, *16*, 42–44.

Toch, H., Grant, J. D., & Galvin, R. T. *Agents of change: A study in police reform*. Cambridge, MA: Schenkman, 1975.

Westley, W. A. *Violence and the police: A sociological study of law, custom and morality*. Cambridge, MA: MIT Press, 1970.

Wilson, J. Q. *Varieties of police behavior*. Cambridge, MA: Harvard University Press, 1968.

7

The Police Feedback Cycle[1]

Ezra Stotland

One of the keys to understanding the actions of police officers either individually or as a group is the fact that they are more free to use their own judgment in deciding what to do—on the job—than their quasi-military public appearance would lead one to expect. In this chapter we will examine some of the reasons for this autonomy and some of the ways in which police officers obtain and process information in order to make decisions on how to act in given situations. We will see that there are a great many obstacles to officers' receiving all of the information about the community in which they work and about the criminal justice system—information they need to make the best possible decisions. One of the main factors determining such decisions concerns the officers' view and evaluation of themselves as effective officers and how this view corresponds to the views others have of them. These other people are other officers, especially those at the same level and rank in the department, and members of the community at large.

One way around the obstacles to the officers' gaining all the information they need might be to provide officers with research data on relevant matters. At present much information that is generated by research and evaluation agencies for the police is provided to the top levels of police departments, i.e., to the command officers who make policy decisions. However, the isolation of information from the semi-autonomous, decision-making officer does not allow this informa-

[1]The author is deeply indebted to the following for their many constructive criticisms and suggestions: John Berberich, Mike Brintnall, Ray Connery, Tony Gustin, and Stuart Scheingold.

tion to be maximally useful either to the total department or to the individual officer on the street. In some instances, the procedure of giving this information to the top echelon rather than to the officers on the street may have negative effects, especially on the officers' evaluations of themselves and their performances.

In the last part of this chapter, a solution to these problems is proposed. It is a solution that fits the recent trend of police departments to have a more decentralized organization. This decentralization stems in part from a recognition of the degree of autonomy of the officer on the street. It is proposed that both the process of gaining research data and its processing in the department also be decentralized. This proposal, called a Police Feedback Cycle, might help to solve the twin problems of gaining information and enhancing the evaluation that police have of themselves.

THE SEMIAUTONOMOUS POLICE OFFICER
AND THE HIERARCHY

A superficial, stereotyped view of police departments is that they are quasi-military hierarchical organizations—with military ranks of sergeant, captain, lieutenant, and major; with military-style uniforms; with formations, etc. It might be expected that the police is an authoritarian organization in its command structure, tight-knit, with basic decisions being made at the top and commands coming from the top echelons to the rank and file below.

Closer examination shows that the perception of a hierarchical military command structure implied by the stereotype does not correspond to reality. Instead, police officers on patrol have far more autonomy than soldiers generally do. Patrol officers are rarely under the supervision of their sergeants since they patrol mostly in pairs and most citizen calls for police service are answered by one car. Even if a second car is needed as a backup, it is rarely the sergeant's car that comes.

The hierarchy monitors the patrol officers primarily through their reports, citations, and arrests. But felony arrests occur so infrequently as to be rare events in the lives of patrol officers and therefore do not provide the hierarchy a way of monitoring the day-by-day conduct of the officers. Data from Reiss (1973) and Clark and Sykes (1971) indicate that more than 80% of police actions involve either no citations—receiving complaints only, traffic violations—or noncriminal citations. Contacts with other violators constitute no more than 20% of contacts; and only 6% of contacts result in any sort of an arrest. Nor do the officers' misdemeanor arrests, citations, reports, etc., provide a much better monitor. Reiss (1973) had civilian observers spend hundreds of hours riding in police cars and observing the officers' behavior. They found that in about half the cases in which police officers could make misdemeanor arrests they chose not to do so. Even when officers had probable cause, i.e., legal justification, for making arrests for felonies, they chose not to do so in 43% of the incidents. Davis (1975) reports that even in very serious assault cases, police officers will usually not make the arrests they can make legally if the victims do not indicate that they will press charges. Adams (1972) reports that more than half the police officers in his survey were willing to say that in deciding whether to make an arrest they take individual circumstances into account rather than the penal code or departmental policies. There is no definitive way for a supervisor to know the informational basis for making a decision, nor the weights that the officers give to such factors as the citizen's behavior and attitude to them, other events in the situation, the officers' time on the shift, state of fatigue, motivation to enhance their arrest records, acquaintance with the citizen, etc. The supervisor's lack of definitive knowledge results from the inevitably high degree of discretion, of individual judgment, that is left up to the officer, especially with respect to misdemeanors. McNamara (1967) found in a survey of the New York City police department that fewer than one-third of the officers felt that they were not given enough freedom to use their judgment. Most officers reported that supervisors would not reverse their decisions. Rubinstein, a reporter-turned-police-officer in Philadelphia, writes:

> Since every supervisor violates regulations to produce the conditions and circumstances which enable him to get the required work from his men, each must bear in mind the possibility of betrayal. No matter how rare its occurrence, it is both a barrier against petty tyranny and a brake on the capacity of the supervisors to enforce stringent control over their men. (Rubinstein, 1973, p. 43)

The high degree of discretion allowed the patrolling officers is an outcome of several facts of life in addition to the inability of supervisors to monitor closely what they do. It is impossible to write laws to encompass every instance in which they might be applicable. There are inevitable complications, inevitable novel situations. Should a person be cited for crossing the street against the light with no cars in sight and during a torrential downpour? Should the Chinese-American players in a traditional Chinese gambling game be arrested for violating the gambling laws? Furthermore, laws are written so that the officers can make their decisions not only by using information about the penal code, but also by using and appropriately weighting information about special circumstances. In deciding whether to cite a husband for beating his wife, officers can take into account not only the penal-code provisions, but also their observation that the wife has forgiven her husband. Judgment, reason, balance, flexibility must all be used by the police officer. Sometimes the reliance on such weighted decisions is so great that even the loose limits of law and due process are exceeded (Skolnick, 1967). As a retired deputy chief of the Los Angeles police department emphasizes (Fisk, 1974b), police officer decisions often entail weighing the need for legal order in society against the need to maintain democratic values. Police officers often will rely on their own view of the relative importance of these types of information as well as their perception of the community's view. The officers' problem is especially difficult when there is inconsistency or even conflict among the values held by different segments of the community (Ericson, 1974).

Finally, the police officers simply do not have the resources to react to every misdemeanor, or even felony, that comes to their attention. Officers cannot ticket every car that commits a moving violation; they would spend almost all of their time issuing traffic citations. Even detectives do not often have the time to investigate every burglary reported to them. Police officers have to decide which of the many laws on the books to enforce. In the case of archaic blue laws, the decision is clear. In the case of changing laws, such as those regarding marijuana, the decision is made on numerous and unstable types of information and changes of the weights of various types of information.

Thus, for numerous reasons, many, if not most, of the important decisions in police work are made at the street level. A police department is one of those organizations in which the total amount of power may be greater at the lower levels than at the top levels (Wilson, 1968). Not only do patrol officers make a great many important decisions as individuals and collectively, but other operational entities within police departments also have much decision-making power. Detectives often function as individual professionals, even keeping their own hours, their own files, and their own set of informers (Bittner, 1974). Precinct commanders collectively may have more power than chiefs. Gross (1975) describes how he and other precinct commanders in the New York City police department tended to work around rather than with the rules and policies coming down from above. Daley (1971) describes the great difficulties that a progressive and respected police commissioner like Patrick Murphy had in trying to impose his policies on his local commanders. The reasons for the downward shift of decision-making are basically the same as the case of the patrol officer.

The contrast and contradiction between the relative functional independence of the lower echelons and the presumptions of a supervisory hierarchy are not lost on police officers. Many of them are
quite ambivalent about the role of their higher-level supervisors
(Rubin, 1972). A retired deputy chief reports that patrol officers sometimes feel that the higher levels of command have forgotten what it
is like on the street and do not have the interests of the officers in
mind (Fisk, 1974a). They may perceive that the orders from above to
follow rules with respect to haircuts, shoe shine, report writing, etc.,
are not in keeping with their own need to make highly consequential
and literally vital decisions about the lives of others. Watson and
Sterling (1969), in their study of the attitudes of police officers, found
that only 50% believed the good police officers unquestioningly obey
their superior officers.

It is important to note that prosecutors, judges, probation officers,
jailers, and almost all other personnel in the criminal justice system
also exercise great discretion and make important decisions on the
basis of a great variety of sources of information, not all of which are
specified by law or by a supervisor's orders (Ebbesen and Konečni,
1975).

THE LOCKER-ROOM CULTURE

The picture we have presented may give the reader the impression of
individual, autonomous officers making decisions not only independently of their supervisors, but also independently of their colleagues. This picture is somewhat misleading, since the officer's peer
group is a major source of both informational input and of the weight
to be given to certain types of information. The patrol officers in
departments and even in precincts in large departments tend to develop their own set of standards and their own sources of information,
sometimes called the "locker-room culture" (often with a strong
"macho" flavor). Davis (1975) has described in detail this locker-room
culture in the Chicago police department, showing that it has great
power to "make rules" of police behavior that are often at odds with
the explicit policies of the higher echelons. The officers tend to take
the information and weighting practices of their peers very much into
consideration in making their decisions, although some authors have
claimed that this is, in actuality, limited to the rhetoric in the locker
room (Shellow, 1975).

The degree of influence of this culture on the decision-making of
police officers stems from the strength of the peer group formed in
the locker room and in the patrol cars. The strength of these peer
groups may derive from a number of sources:

1. The officers' ambivalence toward their supervisors.

2. The mutual dependency in the face of uncertainty and danger (Skolnick, 1967).

3. The suspiciousness concerning civilians, which is part of the police officers' working personality (Skolnick, 1967).

4. The perception that many segments of the public actively oppose the police (Skolnick, 1969).

5. The post-police-academy influence of the older officers to whom rookies are assigned.

6. The perception that civilians reject them socially because of the ever-present power to arrest and because of the peculiar shifts that police officers work.

7. The feeling that only other police officers can understand and appreciate the stress of the work.

8. The consequent pledge not to "snitch" on a fellow officer (Westley, 1953) or even inquire too closely as to how the officer works, although one study found that a sizable minority of police officers would report illegal behavior by other officers (Savitz, 1970).

In addition to these forces that make for the strong and cohesive in-groups of police officers, the very uncertainty involved in the police officers' exercise of their discretionary powers probably makes their relationships with their peers all the more significant. They may turn to each other for support, for confirmation of the propriety of their decisions. By a process of "social comparison" (Festinger, 1954), they check their actions against the standards expressed by their fellow officers. If they find that they measure up to the locker-room culture, they gain not only acceptance but also reassurance. Furthermore, they know that if they should be criticized later for any of their discretionary decisions, their peers would support them because they appreciate the risks involved in many such decisions (Goldstein, 1973).

Even within the total group in a department, patrol officers may form their own subgroup, separate from the others. Patrol officers are distinct for a number of reasons: they are the lowest-status group in the department; they are generally in uniform when working; very few are promoted out of their group; they generally face more dangers than others; they have to use more discretion under more stressful conditions than others.

Recently, the power of the locker-room culture has taken a quantum leap up through the development of formal organizations, unions, that build on the informal peer grouping that has existed for a long time. In San Francisco and in Chicago, patrol officers decided collectively to demonstrate their power and their anger at the public or at the mayors by ticketing every traffic violation they observed. They put a heavy brake on all the normal processes of urban living. These groups have increasingly been formally organized into police unions (Juris and Feuille, 1973; Levi, 1974). These unions not only fight for the usual bread-and-butter issues, like other labor unions, but also exercise considerable power with respect to policy. Levi (1974) describes how Police Commissioner Leary of New York City attempted to establish a fourth shift in order to provide more police during the hours when the crime rate is highest. This policy was resisted by the unions so strongly that it took an act of the state legislature to permit the establishment of the fourth shift. Ironically, even when this policy was finally established by the legislature, many of the local divisional and precinct commanders minimized the use of the fourth shift, partly out of fear of antagonizing the unions. In other instances, police unions have taken public stands on many policy issues, such as opposing citizen review boards, favoring "get-tough policies" in civil disturbances, and opposing court decisions, as reported, for example, by Juris and Feuille (1973). Olinos (1974) reports that in at least one of the two departments he studied, the establishment of unions was perceived by police "brass" as threatening the discipline in the departments. These authors speculate that the very fact that the unions are composed of police officers, who have so much authority in society, gives the police unions an aura of greater power and therefore actually greater power than they might otherwise have.

In the preceding chapter of this volume, Grant, Grant, and Toch describe the successful efforts of Chief Charles Gain, formerly of the Oakland, California, police department, to decrease the number of arrests made with respect to lesser crimes and to decrease the number of violent actions by the police. The effectiveness of his efforts may appear to contradict the above assertions that the departmental brass have less influence than might be expected in a quasi-military organization. A closer examination shows that the discrepancy is less great than it appears at first. As indicated by Grant, Grant, and Toch, the rank-and-file officers never accepted the viewpoint of the chief about when to make or not make arrests. This reaction to his efforts was also manifest in an overwhelming vote of no confidence in Chief Gain by the rank and file of his department. This vote and other related events no doubt contributed to his leaving the department. On the other hand, some of the programs that he supported to reduce violence by his officers were not dependent on his ordering them to avoid violence. Instead, these programs mobilized peer pressure on especially violent officers. Their effectiveness was a reflection of the power of an aspect of the locker-room society (cf. Toch, Grant, and Galvin, 1975). On the other hand, the maintenance of this program was dependent on Gain being chief. When he resigned, the program was discontinued, so that the locker-room culture not only remained unchanged throughout his regime but probably greatly influenced what happened after he left.

SELF-ESTEEM AS A FACTOR IN THE DECISION-MAKING OF POLICE OFFICERS

Thus far, we have considered social and organizational factors that determine the types of information and their weights that are used by police officers in making decisions. We need now to turn to one major individual factor that may very well enter strongly into the decision-making process. This factor is the evaluation that officers make of themselves, their self-esteem.

The self-esteem of police officers is not only important to them personally, it is also important because of its effects on the decisions they make. There is much evidence, summarized in Stotland and Cannon (1972), that people with high self-esteem cope with difficulties, with stress, in a more constructive, problem-oriented way. People with high self-esteem, for example, are better able to direct their hostility at appropriate targets, are less vulnerable to being upset by insults, are better able to solve problems, are more friendly to other people, and are more flexible in their thinking. They do not make decisions in which they give heavy weights to information that may influence their self-esteem. They do not need to protect their public image in order to protect their self-evaluation. Those police officers whose self-esteem is high would then be better able to cope with the conflicts and stresses of police work and would be expected to make decisions on the basis of information regarding the actual situation, rather than on the basis of how their decisions reflect on themselves (see Stotland, 1975, for an extended discussion). On the other hand, officers with low self-esteem could be expected to protect their esteem from still further reduction. The former deputy chief of the Los Angeles police department, James Fisk, writes about police officers:

> But when he exercises this power as a compensatory device because he feels a personal sense of inadequacy or as a response to a challenge

to his self-esteem, improper decisions are likely to result, decisions that are likely not only to alienate citizens but to generate counter-productive activity for the system. (Fisk, 1974a, p. 75)

Decisions to arrest are sometimes made on the basis of the attitude of the citizen toward the police. Citizens who show proper respect for officers are less likely to be arrested than those who do not (Piliavin and Briar, 1964). Data from studies of self-esteem in other settings would suggest that officers low in self-esteem are more likely to be sensitive to the citizen's attitude than those who are higher. As Westley (1953) found, police officers are most likely to be violent when their authority is threatened; and since police officers become closely identified with their authority, the threat to their authority is a threat to their self-esteem. It is likely that those with low self-esteem are more violence-prone, as a way of enhancing their image of themselves as people with power over others.

Police face a chronic threat to their self-esteem stemming from their lack of effectiveness in reducing crime, as well as for other reasons described later in this chapter. As a consequence, they may tend to act on the basis of stereotypes so as to shift the responsibility away from themselves for the problems of crime in society; they may become bureaucratized in their actions and overcontrol their "turf" by saturation patrols (Lipsky, 1969). As Rubinstein writes:

> Unable to prevent crime, they seek to ensure that nobody else can claim control of the street, which they view as belonging to themselves. If this dominance requires that the police saturate some neighborhoods, they will do so. The police can no more control the consequences of these actions than they can predict the impact of their unending experiments to show people that they are "doing something" about crime. (Rubinstein, 1973, p. 371)

THE POLICE AND THE COMMUNITY

Thus far we have examined a number of different factors that determine the decisions of police officers: their self-esteem, their locker-room culture, their supervisors. We have not yet turned to one of the most important determinants of what police officers do—the community in which they work.

Police departments do not function independently of their communities, policing them from the outside or from above like stern, omniscient guards. It is almost impossible for the police to be everywhere, to know everything, to be on top of every situation. We simply cannot afford to obtain enough police officers to do these things and, even if we could, the police would be highly likely to threaten our civil liberties. Instead, the police respond to reports from citizens— calls from victims and witnesses of crimes, from people who need help of all sorts. Thus, without the willingness of civilians to call the police, the police would rarely be able to function either as catchers of crooks, as helpers of the people, or as keepers of the peace. The police are dependent in other ways as well. They are dependent on the political establishment for funding, for pay raises, for money for equipment. They are dependent on legislatures and courts for statutory and case laws that govern their operations. They are dependent on community organizations, on political parties, on unions, and on churches to create an atmosphere in which civilians will report crimes, will be stand-up witnesses, and will support them politically.

These multiple dependencies are at the heart of a serious dilemma in police work. The very people and organizations in the community on which the police are dependent are sometimes the very people who should be subject to some sort of police action. For example, a good arrest of a drug pusher may stem from information from a competitive drug pusher. A good informant on burglaries may be a receiver of stolen goods, a fence. A political party that supports higher salaries for police may itself be rampant with corruption. The owner of the "greasy spoon," who both calls the police after a holdup and is willing to testify, may be the one who has been serving free meals to on-duty officers. A businessman who supports his local police may commit blatant consumer fraud. It is small wonder that the police are constantly having to make very difficult choices; it is small wonder that some of their initial idealism, self-esteem, and professionalism are undermined; and it is small wonder that they are often subject to pressures to become monetarily and morally corrupt. The dilemma of the police is a basic one: Many of their necessary sources of information in the community may themselves be illicit.

Of course, operational units presently attempt to obtain as much information about their areas as possible through contacts with ordinary citizens and informants and through general observation. Sometimes they may be encouraged to leave their cars, walk beats, talk with local business people, attend meetings. Nevertheless, information derived in this way is obviously incomplete and sometimes unreliable, for a number of reasons.

In their daily work, police officers often tend to encounter the public under negative circumstances. They rarely live in the community they police. Their ingrained and professionally functional suspiciousness of most civilians may overly color and distort what they might learn from their contacts (Skolnick, 1967). Their frequent dealings with deviant, negative, criminal groups may also color their outlook and their understanding of the community. The occasional adversary relationship with the "legitimate" community, such as in issuing traffic tickets, hardly encourages the sharing of information. If the police are viewed as an "occupying army," only the snitches will cooperate with them. The complaining witnesses who do call the police must be different in some ways from the many victims who do not report crime. Attendance at community meetings may be erratic and unrepresentative of the community. The more militant groups within the community may be the most vocal, but may not be representative (Kelly, 1975). Local business people can speak to the police for only part of the community, perhaps a small part. Police become acquainted more with restaurant and cafe owners, since they eat their lunches in these establishments, than with other business people or with factory workers. Groves and Rossi (1970) found that few ghetto officers got to know the important teenage leaders. Rubinstein (1973) reports that the officers' knowledge of their sector is determined and limited by their need to use their cars effectively. Furthermore, in large, urban areas it is very difficult for police officers to get to know their community, certainly more difficult than for small-town officers. The problem of getting to know the residents or business people or workers in high-rise buildings is a serious one. In central cities, police officers may develop the view that nothing much has improved in society, since they see little of middle-class life; in their work they do not follow the population movement out of the cities (Wilson, 1968).

THREATS TO THE SELF-ESTEEM OF POLICE

We do not mean to suggest that police should avoid contacts with the community because of the one-sided nature of these contacts or their potential for corruption. The police, as civil servants, as public employees, need to relate closely to the most legitimate groups and parts of the community. Yet, on occasion, relating to these groups can cause additional problems for the police and cause some threats to their self-esteem. For example, some community organizations—especially, but not only, those representing minorities—have been highly cognizant of the police as civil servants and have attempted to exert pressure on the police, not infrequently toward ends that are unquestionably valuable and laudatory in a democratic society, such as equal treatment under the law and respect for minorities.

However, a question may be raised as to whether such pressure from community groups does not sometimes have counterproductive effects. Such community pressure can present threats to the self-esteem of police officers and thereby render them more prone to be defensive or hostile. These pressures imply an attempt to reduce the status of the police, to reduce their ability to exercise their discretion; and we have already seen that such threats do not always lead to positive reactions. Kelly (1975) vividly analyzed an attempt to have a community "governing board" in a local police precinct in the ghetto of Washington, D.C., and found that the police reaction was not outstandingly positive (see also Shellow, 1975). The New York Police Benevolent Association campaigned long, hard, and successfully to destroy a police review board (Levi, 1974). In Philadelphia, the civilian review board was very cautious and restrained in its operation, and yet was essentially abolished, partly because of police pressure (Levi, 1974). Citizen complaints against police misconduct have not frequently been successfully pursued.

Some of the reactions of police may stem from the fact that the police probably have a special vulnerability to threats to their self-esteem, for a number of reasons. First, there are many other forces in the lives of police officers that may threaten their self-esteem. The above-average idealism with which they enter police work (Mills, 1969) is soon undermined by their perception of the ineffectuality of much of what they attempt: Criminals recidivate, crime rates rise, "stopping and frisking" accomplish little but increase public hostility (Reiss, 1973), traffic accidents do not decline, gambling and vice persist. Clark (1965) found that police officers saw a wide discrepancy between their ideals and the activity they experienced. Rubinstein (1973), McNamara (1967), and Sterling (1969) all report similar disillusionment and frustration.

The task of police officers is rampant with conflicting, inconsistent expectations from the community, from their department, from their locker-room culture, increasing their sense of uncertainty and ineffectiveness (Wilson, 1968). They have great difficulty in being certain that they made the "right" choice in the many ambiguous situations they face (Fisk, 1974a). The public's failure to report many crimes because of the belief in the ineffectiveness of the police is insulting to the police. Watson and Sterling (1969) found that 82% of police officers felt that the public regarded them as impersonal cogs in a governmental machine; 72% said they were not receiving support from the political powers of their cities. In Niederhoffer's (1967) study of New York police, it was found that the police believed that the newspapers were very negative toward them. Indeed, Neiderhoffer, as well as Hodge, Siegel, and Rossi (1964), found that police are not ranked high in status by the general populace, although they may be satisfied with their performance.

There are still other sources of threat to the self-esteem of officers. They hear of corruption among other police officers. They sometimes have to engage in demeaning activities such as acting as decoys for prostitutes, working "drug buys," tolerating the crimes of a good informant, and lying. Patrol officers are at the lowest level in a hierarchical organization that chooses not to acknowledge their great discretionary power. Felony cases, which patrol officers open, are turned over to detectives, who, in many instances, know their clearance rates are low.

It is small wonder that Niederhoffer (1967) reports that New York City police officers tend, during their first twelve years of service, to become increasingly cynical about the police department and its relationship to the community, although Lefkowitz (1973) found this to be less true in Dayton, Ohio, probably for a variety of departmental and regional reasons.

THE PLACE OF RESEARCH, EVALUATION, AND INTELLIGENCE IN POLICE AGENCIES

Obviously, what the police need in order to make wise use of their discretion is a way for them to gain information from the community that is not threatening or demeaning to them. The information needs to be valid and to come from a more representative range of sources than is now usually available to them. It needs to be available to the people who have to make crucial decisions on the street. It should also be available to groups of officers who share the locker-room culture. Finally, it should be available to the administration, the chiefs, and their assistants, who make overall policy decisions about employment of personnel, budgets, and the like.

Much of this information is available from research units, either in or out of the police departments. As in many other types of organizations, the people or groups who do the research and those who evaluate the effectiveness of programs and procedures typically report to the chief, the commissioner, or some other person high in the hierarchy, rather than to the operation units, such as precincts, teams, or detective squads. Crime-analysis units, which record the locations and types of reported crimes, generally report to the upper echelons. Intelligence units, which often attempt to keep track of the organized criminal elements, usually report to the chief. Operational research units, which evaluate procedures and programs, typically report to a deputy or an assistant chief.

The funneling of information into the top levels of police depart-ments is further enhanced by the development of law and justice planning offices (LJPOs), which often report to mayors, district at-torneys, county executives, or governors. These LJPOs often conduct their own research on crime and on the effectiveness of programs carried out by police departments. The data from these research proj-ects are sometimes very significant because these same LJPOs make decisions about the allocation of funds to police departments.

Because this information is funneled to the top of police depart-ments, it is separated from the lower levels of the hierarchy, from the operational units, which, as we have seen, often have a great deal of discretion and power. There are a number of probable reasons for this separation of operations from research:

1. The chiefs and their assistants obviously need such information to make budgetary, personnel, and logistical decisions.

2. The second probable reason is technical and administrative. Operational units, such as detective squads or shifts in a pre-cinct, usually have neither the time nor the technical skill to conduct research.

3. The operational units are presumed to be unlikely to report results of evaluations of their programs in a completely objective and fair manner. Some of this subjectivity may be a result not of dishonesty but of a natural human tendency to view oneself in the best light, without straying ridiculously far from reality. On the other hand, some of the lack of objectivity may lead to a deliberate distortion of the data. To reduce the rate of reported crime, some citizen crime reports may be ignored, or the re-ported events categorized as less serious crimes.

4. A fourth probable reason stems from the danger that the per-sonnel of an operational unit carrying out a program may change the goals to fit what the program is actually accomplishing rath-er than what it originally set out to do. A program for engraving one's driver's license number on property may turn from the goal of preventing burglary to the goal of increasing the chances of recovery of stolen goods. Sometimes these new substitute goals are simply procedural. The program to encourage people to engrave their goods might be evaluated on the basis of the number of citizen groups the police addressed, rather than on the basis of changes in the burglary rate. These substitute goals may, of course, be as important as the original goals. However, an outside agency, which is paying for the program, may or may

not be fully apprised of the shift, or the substitute goals may not be those within the agency's mandate or mission.

5. The researcher may probe into significant new areas that the operational unit could be reluctant to get into. Would a police juvenile squad be interested in the private attitude of juvenile delinquents toward themselves? Would a patrol unit be interested in the number of rats in a slum? These data might not have any simple, direct bearing on operations, but indirectly both of these might be related to juvenile delinquency and bitterness toward society and might even have operational implications.

THE EFFECT OF SEPARATING RESEARCH
AND OPERATIONS

Thus, there are probably many good reasons for providing information to top, rather than operational, levels. However, this creates a curious paradox. The people who make some of the most important decisions in police work do not have direct access to highly relevant research data. This is not to say that the research information does not sometimes ultmately reach the operational units and personnel. However, the separation between operations and research has at least three drawbacks:

1. The kinds of data that the research office develops may or may not be the types of data that are potentially the most useful to the operational units. The operational unit might, for example, find some value in knowing long before September what the expected racial distribution will be in a given high school. Or the operations unit might want to know exactly which ethnic groups within its patrol area are most fearful of being witnesses in criminal cses, to know the sources of this fear, and to explore what might reduce it. All of these types of information might affect the planning of vacations, the planning of transfers of minority officers, the communications of patrol officers with witnesses and their continued relationship with them. Yet, the research and evaluation units might or might not consider these to be important problems for research. Suggestions funneled up from the operational units to the research-and-evaluation units are just that, suggestions; and since research/evaluation has other constituencies besides the operational units, these suggestions may not be implemented. Furthermore, there is a danger that at least some of the research that is done, though inter-

esting and even intellectually fascinating, may be of no particular policy value to the operational units.

2. In many situations, research and evaluation efforts are dependent on operational units for their basic data: reports of crimes, number of citations, warrants, arrests, clearances. On the other hand, members of the operational units are often well aware of the influence that these data might have on the policies of the higher echelon and of outside agencies. Accordingly, there is pressure on operational units to report selectively and perhaps even distort information. The great freedom of the lower echelons to exercise discretion facilitates such selective reporting and slanting of the data. Gross (1975) reports that this was common practice when he was a precinct commander in New York City. Thus, officers might ignore citizen reports of certain crimes; in borderline cases, they might enhance or reduce the severity of a reported crime, for example, by reducing the estimated value of a stolen item in a larceny, so as to render the charge petty larceny rather than grand larceny. Such distortion of data obviously can lead to ill-founded policy and procedural decisions by top management. Police officers often become cynical about the validity of research data because of its great vulnerability to distortion.

3. When research is done to evaluate the performance of a professional unit, the research is often likely to present a direct threat to the self-esteem of the members of the operational units, especially if the evaluation is done by an agency outside that unit. Thus, evaluation of performance is a threat to the self-esteem of operational police officers, just as it is to professors, doctors, or lawyers. All of these professionals have resisted evaluation by outsiders—have resisted public evaluation and accountability.

THE POLICE FEEDBACK CYCLE

To provide better information for better decision-making at the operational levels and to avoid some of the problems just described, a procedure called the Police Feedback Cycle (PFC) is proposed and described in the remaining part of this chapter. The PFC is not designed to replace other forms of evaluation of programs or units by external evaluators. Obviously, evaluation of any publicly supported agency must be made by some representative of the public so as to assist in making judgments about the value of that agency to the public. What is questioned here is whether such evaluations need to be made solely by the external agency. There is no reason for the number of evaluations being limited to the one by an external agency. The unit being evaluated could have its own evaluation process, the PFC, at the same time that it is being evaluated externally. There are obvious advantages and disadvantages to each type of evaluation. The argument that there are not sufficient resources for both types of evaluation is not a convincing one, since, as will be argued below, the application of PFC should lead to a greater productivity of operational units and therefore should keep the total cost of the unit from rising excessively, relative to the benefits to society.

The PFC is also not designed as a replacement for extant procedures for gaining criminal intelligence and general information about the community. The PFC is intended to add significantly to the information pool, so that the police can attain their goals of reducing crime, keeping public order, and providing other public services. The focus of the PFC is also a method of growth and development, since it would provide a means for self-evaluation of performance.

The PFC is a variation of *action research*, a term originated by Lewin (1948) to describe research that is designed to measure the degree to which any program or activity achieves its goals. More recently, this idea has been applied to research on organizational development in industry (Bowers, 1973; Bowers and Franklin, 1972), although this application has beem limited to a survey of the attitudes of personnel toward their own organization. Campbell (1969) has presented a useful model in which public programs or reforms are treated as experiments whose outcomes can be tested.

Steps in the Police Feedback Cycle

Step 1: Select the unit with sufficient autonomy   The first step is either to identify or to create an operational unit within a police department that functions with sufficient autonomy to have its own goals and operating procedures. Such units might be a precinct, a division, a detective burglary squad, or a traffic division; in some cases, a whole, small department; or, as will be described below, a police team. Obviously, such units are not independent of the overall goals and policies of the department. The important point is that the information needed by the unit to carry out the overall policy be useful and relevant to this unit. The departmental policy might be to reduce juvenile burglary; a given precinct might try to acquire information relevant to that goal in its jurisdiction.

Nevertheless, the thrust of PFC would be to give more autonomy to individual operational units. Even if they work within the overall goals of the department, their use of the information relevant for them may lead to individual tactical policy decisions. And, obviously, if the operational unit sets up its own goals, it will be to some extent independent of top management in a medium- or large-sized department. It might be argued that such autonomy may lead to increased costs, but the research of Ostrom et al. (1973) has shown that smaller departments may in fact provide more satisfactory service to the citizenry at a lower cost. The same may be true of relatively autonomous units within police departments.

The increased autonomy of operational units is in line with the great power of the lower echelons in police work that was mentioned above and that is reflected in the rise of police unions. Furthermore, neighborhood and community differences within an overall urban environment demand flexibility of policy and goals. As Scheingold (1976) has pointed out, cultural, ethnic, and social-class differences among the various parts of a community may demand differences in policies adopted by the police. Justice may have to be attuned both to the local situation in the community and to the legal system.

Obviously, many police chiefs are reluctant to delegate power downward but, as we have pointed out above, the delegation of official, *de jure* power would simply give recognition to current realities. The need for more power at the lower echelons has recently been recognized by some police chiefs. Thus, Igleburger, the retired chief of the Dayton, Ohio, police department, proposes a centralized–decentralized organizational model for police departments in which support and staff functions, such as purchasing and training, would be centralized, whereas the operational units would be decentralized (Igleburger, Angell, and Pence, 1973). Some textbooks in police administration (e.g., Kenny, 1972) have advocated the downward delegation of authority. One of the academics most highly respected in police circles, James Q. Wilson (1968), has predicted more decentralization in future police organizations. The Los Angeles police department has inaugurated a Basic Radio Car Plan in which officers are responsible for community relations in their own sector (Davis, 1972).

In recent years, a common form of decentralized police administration has been dubbed Neighborhood Team Policing. It constitutes the most appropriate locus for the establishment of a PFC. In team policing, a number of officers are assigned exclusively, and more or less permanently, to a given neighborhood. In its ideal form, the team constitutes a kind of miniature police department just for that neighborhood. Thus, administrative decisions with respect to shifts, assignments, leaves, and so on, are handled at the team level. These decisions are made on the basis of the needs of the neighborhood police effort, not on the basis of any central policy, and can be changed depending on the changing neighborhood situation. The team leader is responsible for the neighborhood, even when not on duty. Many of the special jobs usually done by special detectives, for example, are done either by special officers who are part of the team, sometimes called investigators, or by all of the team members. Most importantly, the team is given the responsibility of relating as closely as possible to its neighborhood, to get to know it and its residents and social structure, and to interact with it as constructively as possible. Teams have been set up in a number of cities, although only rarely has a total city been turned over to team policing, and most of the teams do not fully match the descriptions just given. Such teams have been described in Elliott and Sardino (1971), Sherman, Milton, and Kelly (1973), Smith and Greene (1974), and others. It is very important to note that team policing is a way of getting a group of police officers to relate more closely to their communities, without at the same time turning power over to the communities. Flexibility and reactions to local conditions are the bywords, not local control of the police.

Step 2: Identify the types of information wanted   After an appropriate operational unit, such as a team, has been selected, the officers in that unit would be asked to identify the types of information they would like to have, which presently either are not available to them or are not reliable or complete. The information for which the officers would ask would be related to the goals of the unit or team (e.g., to reduce muggings in a given area). Hopefully, the unit will have set its goals before beginning the PFC process, so that the questions asked can be derived from these goals. However, if goals have not been established or articulated before the start of a feedback cycle, the beginning may entail asking the officers to formulate questions that might start the goal-articulation process. The research questions asked should be explicitly related to the goals. That is, the derived information should be either a measure of progress toward the goals or an indicator of which of several alternative operational procedures would be better to follow. The specific operational implications of the desired information should be worked out in advance of the attempts to get the information. In some cases, carrying out of one or more of the operational alternatives may require financial or policy support from a higher echelon. In such cases, the higher echelon should indicate in advance whether or not much support would be forthcoming for these alternatives. If the support would not be forthcoming, then these alternatives should not be considered in the PFC process.

The likelihood that a police chief would recognize the value of explicitly relating operational policy to the acquisition of data has been increasing recently. The police chief of Menlo Park, California, writes that the effectiveness of policy should be explicitly tied in with crime statistics (Cizanckas, 1973). He also found a survey of citizen attitudes toward the police to be very useful (Cizanckas and Feist, 1975). A police administrator, Hennessy (1974), emphasizes the importance of the impact of programs. Lieutenant Manning (1974) of the New York police department gives a detailed description of how police administrators can use data to evaluate their own agencies. The police department of San Diego has directly incorporated studies of the community into its training (San Diego Police Department, no date).

Some of the specific goals toward which the operational unit might work are the reduction of rear-entrance residential burglaries, the greater use of parks by the public, reduction in school vandalism, reduction in the number of fatal automobile accidents, better apprehension rate of armed robbers, reduction of "bunko" schemes with old people as victims, the increased proportion of arrests leading to prosecution and conviction, and increased influence of police on sentencing. It is very important that these goals be chosen, after some discussion, by the operational unit itself. The goals need to be relevant to the area of jurisdiction and both important and attainable. To evaluate the effectiveness of any program or procedure to attain these goals, the operational unit could use very specific information: how many rear-entrance burglaries actually occur; how many people actually use the parks; how satisfied citizens feel about non-crime-related contacts with the police; what the actual rates of prosecution and conviction are for various types of crimes or arrests.

Once the goals and the indices of movement toward the goals have been decided upon by the operational unit, the unit would then turn to questions of additional information that they need to help them make decisions on how to attain these goals most effectively. For example, if the goal is to reduce rear-entrance burglaries, then the unit would need to know first how much underreporting of such burglaries occurs and why it occurs. If, for example, citizens underreport because they do not see that the police can do anything about the burglaries, then a campaign to explain to the citizens what the police can do would be in order before any figures are obtained on the rear-entrance burglary rate itself. In another example, the operational unit's efforts to reduce school vandalism may be stymied by the unwillingness of the local community to turn in the vandals. The police would have to get some information about the basis of the reluctance before they could contribute to a permanent reduction of vandalism. If the goal is to increase the conviction rate, the police need to have information from prosecutors about the sources of difficulty in obtaining convictions.

The types of information that might be useful to the operational unit for the evaluation of progress are extremely varied: citizen and business use of public areas; citizen and business fear of crimes; citizen and business knowledge and use of anticrime procedures; citizen attitudes toward reporting crimes; attitudes about being a witness, especially against neighbors or neighborhood children; age, sex, educational level, size of household, exit and return patterns, and mobility of residents; size, functioning hours, and the like, of local businesses and schools; public stereotypes of police, perception of their effectiveness, value, availability, and rapport with the community; exact descriptions of unreported crimes; clearance rates per arrest (Block and Ulberg, 1974); prosecution and conviction rates per crime and per arrest; reasons for failure to convict; and reasons for lowering the level of criminal charges. It is important that these data not be acquired simply because they are interesting. The acquisition needs to be related to evaluation or to decision-making. Obviously, it would take time and training for the officers in the operational units to learn what sorts of questions they can ask and how to ask them.

Step 3: Use a professional survey organization   If the questions are internal to the criminal justice system, they would be referred to a research unit in the police department or elsewhere in the criminal justice system. If the research concerns the community, the questions would be referred to a professional survey organization, probably a private one. The reason for using a professional survey agency, rather than police-department personnel, is that people may be more open and honest, and less fearful in some areas, with citizen surveyors than with officers, even if they are out of uniform. This research organization would then design a formal study to obtain the data as rapidly as possible, since the data need to be current in most instances to be relevant to policy decisions.

Step 4: Check the research design   Before the research is actually carried out, the design would be checked with the operational unit to make certain that the researchers are getting at the information requested. In general, professional researchers would have to maintain good, close relations with the operational unit.

Step 5: Work out official sponsorship   In the case of the survey, the question of the official sponsorship (e.g., the mayor's office, police department) would have to be worked out with the appropriate public officials. Respondents would be guaranteed absolute anonymity, and their participation would, of course, be completely voluntary.

Step 6: Analyze results to achieve specific goals   The results would be analyzed so as to achieve specific goals. For example, reports of the location of unreported rapes would be precisely specified. The more specific the information, the more useful it would be to the operational police officers. Furthermore, to protect the police from premature political pressures, referred to earlier, the information would not be publicized at this time. Obviously, the data could not be kept away from a news reporter or from a citizen invoking the Freedom of Information Act, but they would not deliberately be publicized by the police.

Step 7: Use the information for change   The information could then be used, along with the usual forms of intelligence, by the operational unit. The unit could decide to change action procedures or policies, recommend changes to higher echelons, institute new procedures, and so on. The decision about how to use the information should be made at the operational level as much as possible. Furthermore, the decisions about any changes should be made as quickly as possible.

Step 8: Make a second study   At some predesignated period, after the initial research has been carried out, a second study would be done to determine whether any of the goals have been attained and whether there have been any changes in the criminal justice system or in the community. Have conviction rates gone up? Have actual crime rates, not just reported rates, declined? Have people become less fearful in given areas? The interval between research projects would depend primarily on the nature of the action the operational unit decided to take. For example, if the unit devoted its efforts to minimize a crime like burglary, it might wait a full year for the second survey, so that similar seasons of the year can be compared.

Step 9: Write up a report   A report would then be written up by the operational police unit in which the results of the first research study would be presented, the unit's use of and reactions to these data described, and, finally, the results of the second research study reported. The latter study, it is hoped, would show some positive consequences of the police reactions. This report would then be passed on to the appropriate office or official, such as police chief, police commissioner, city manager, or city council. In many cases, the information might be most valuable to the officer on patrol, such as information relevant to the willingness of witnesses to help the first officer on the scene of a crime.

Step 10: Use the second study as the basis for a new cycle   Needless to say, the second study could also serve as the first research effort of a new cycle of question-asking, response, and testing. Thus, the feedback cycle could be executed repeatedly, with the same or different sorts of questions asked in each cycle, depending on whether the situation and operational problems of the police remain the same or change over time.

Advantages of the Police Feedback Cycle

There are several advantages to this procedure:

1. Information could be gained that is unavailable or unreliable from the usual sources of police crime analysis and intelligence. For example, studies of the underreporting of crimes, such as rape and burglary, show that the police generally are able to react only to partial information from the community. A feedback cycle could in fact start with questions concerning those crimes that are most poorly reported to the police.

2. The police would be able to keep the process under their own control. They would determine the types of data needed and would write the final report. Their professional stature and integrity would be enhanced by the procedure. The delay in publicizing the results of the first survey would give the police a chance to function independently without public or official pressures, for at least a limited period, while at the same time maintaining public accountability.

3. The cycle would give the operational officers a chance to monitor their own performance and to evaluate themselves in ways other than arrest or citation counts. Also, they might have a better idea of how many good "pinches" the unit makes by getting an accurate conviction count. On the other hand, the PFC might give the operational police officer information on such important intangibles as the feelings of safety and security among the citizens. The pride that police officers have in their work would doubtless improve. And the cohesiveness and internal functioning of police teams would be enhanced greatly by getting feedback and other useful information. When movement toward a goal can be more or less objectively measured, when

decisions are made on the basis of facts rather than bias, then personal conflicts and "ego problems" within the teams would be reduced.

4. The police would receive important and credible information about and from the community (if the study involves gaining such information).

5. Police officers' sense of isolation from the rest of the criminal justice system and from the community might be reduced. Better knowledge of the fate of their arrestees might make them appreciate the prosecutors' dilemmas better. The police would be receiving information from the community in a way that is different from many of their usual community contacts, which often involve some negative reactions of the citizens. Studies have shown that police performance is viewed more positively by citizens than the police themselves believe to be the case. Radelet (1973) reports research in the 1950s that showed a generally positive image of the police. Even in the late 1960s, the overall rating by the population of the performance of the police was very high (Whisenand, 1973). The police might be convinced by a survey that more, not less, police protection is desired in the black ghetto and that police who are effective against crime, as well as respectful of civil liberties, would be most welcome in the ghetto (Block, 1970). The cooperation of the community in the PFC would communicate to the police that they are not as ostracized as they may have thought they were. Such implicitly positive feedback from the community would no doubt have a positive effect on the police. Criticism of the police that would be uncovered through research is more likely to be received in a nondefensive way, and the operational unit is more likely to react constructively to such criticism.

6. Increased information about the community would enable operational units and individual officers to exercise their discretion on the basis of more accurate and complete knowledge of the community, a step toward situational justice and a better recognition of the differences among subgroups within the total community. As Scheingold (1976) points out, there needs to be more recognition in police work of the "segmental" quality of our society and the need for more "segmentalized" justice.

7. The PFC would have an educational value for the rest of the criminal justice system and for the community in at least two ways. Knowledge that a given operational unit is using the PFC would enhance its status in the public eye, since its effort to

serve the public would be obvious. This was found to be the result of a survey in Menlo Park, California (Cizanckas and Feist, 1975). Also, some of the questions asked may prompt interviewees to think about certain issues or problems such as keeping cars locked and watching for daytime burglars.

Objections to the Police Feedback Cycle

There are several problems with a PFC system that may have occurred to the reader.

1. A PFC system entails the possibility of finding that a program has not attained its goals, that the actions taken after the initial study have not really had any beneficial effects by the time of the second study. There are several ways of minimizing this threat to the adoption and continued use of the PFC system. For example, the goals the unit sets up in the initial use of the PFC might be the more easily attainable, short-range goals—perhaps subgoals leading to the achievement of longer-range goals. By the use of more easily attainable, short-range goals, the probability of success in the initial use of the PFC can be enhanced. A few successes would make it easier to accept the inevitable failures. The operational unit can learn to view the failure as a way of learning what not to do. After a few successes, the unit would build up "credit" so that the higher echelon would not be so prone to criticize or even undercut the unit in the face of failures.

2. The members of the operational unit, as well as the hierarchy, would so much fear the uncertainty involved in a PFC as to reject it. If the initial goals set up by the operational unit are developed in the way described in the previous paragraph, some of the fears would undoubtedly be reduced. As the unit gains confidence in itself because of its use of the PFC, the fears of the unknown should decline.

3. It also may be objected that the expectations of goal attainment might be set too high, leading inevitably to disappointment. Again, the introduction of the PFC in the ways just described would reduce this problem.

4. The higher echelons (e.g., the chiefs) would not accept the degree of decentralization implied in a PFC, would not tolerate the possibility of disagreement from the lower echelons, and the

commander of the lower-level operational units or teams would therefore fear to assume the responsibility implicit in a PFC. The answer is that more and more chiefs are accepting such decentralization, as pointed out above. In fact, some may publicly take credit for the adoption of new management techniques. As political scientist Mike Brintnall has pointed out (personal communication), the establishment of a PFC might strengthen the decentralization process itself, once it has been started.

5. A final objection that might be raised is that most of the PFC program evaluation data would be of the "pre–post" type. As Campbell (1969) has pointed out, there are many methodological problems with this type of research design, mostly stemming from the fact that many other factors besides those in the programs would be at the root of any changes from the time prior to the programs to afterward. The objection can be met by pointing out, as Campbell has, that many of these other factors can be reasonably discounted on the basis of other data or general knowledge. Campbell presents many ways in which these extraneous factors can be dealt with in a methodologically sophisticated way. Furthermore, not all of the research done by using the PFC concerns program evaluation. Most generally, the problems in the whole area of policing are so great that they demand the best approach possible and should not be ignored because one approach falls short of an ideal.

References

Adams, T. F. Philosophy of police discretion. In T. J. Adams (Ed.), *Criminal justice readings*. Pacific Palisades, CA: Palisades Publishers, 1972.

Bittner, E. Esprit de corps and the code of secrecy. In J. Goldsmith & S. S. Goldsmith (Eds.), *The police community*. Pacific Palisades, CA: Palisades Publishers, 1974.

Black, D. J., & Reiss, A. J., Jr. *Studies of crime and law enforcement in major metropolitan areas: Patterns of behavior in police and citizen transactions*. Field Surveys III, Vol. 2, President's Commission on Law Enforcement and the Administration of Justice. Washington, DC: U.S. Government Printing Office, 1967.

Block, P. B., & Ulberg, C. *Auditing clearance dates*. Washington, DC: Police Foundation, 1974.

Block, R. L. Support for civil liberties and support for the police. In H. Hahn (Ed.), *Police in urban society*. Beverly Hills, CA: Sage, 1970.

Bowers, D. OD techniques and their results in twenty-three organizations: The Michigan I.C.L. study. *Journal of Applied Behavioral Science*, 1973, 9, 21–43.

Bowers, D., & Franklin, J. L. Survey-guided development: Using human resources measurement in organizational change. *Journal of Contemporary Business*, 1972, *1*, 43–55.

Campbell, D. T. Reforms as experiments. *American Psychologist*, 1969, *24*, 409–429.

Cizanckas, V. I. Perspectives on crime and crime prevention. *Crime Prevention Review*, 1973, *1*, 1010.

Cizanckas, V. I., & Feist, F. H. Community's response to police change. *Journal of Police Science and Administration*, 1975, *3*, 284–291.

Clark, J. P. Isolation of the police: A comparison of the British and American situation. *Journal of Criminal Law, Criminology, and Police Science*, 1965, *56*, 307–319.

Clark, J. P., & Sykes, R. E. Some determinants of police organization and practice in a modern industrial democracy. In E. Glaser (Ed.), *Handbook of criminology*. Chicago: Rand McNally, 1971.

Daley, R. *Target blue*. New York: Delacorte Press, 1971.

Davis, E. M. Basic radio car plan. In D. G. Pursuit, J. D. Gerletti, R. M. Brown, Jr., & S. M. Ward (Eds.), *Police programs for preventing crime and delinquency*. Springfield, IL: Charles C Thomas, 1972.

Davis, K. E. *Police discretion*. St. Paul, MN: West, 1975.

Ebbesen, E. B., and Konečni, V. J. Decision making and information integration in the courts: The setting of bail. *Journal of Personality and Social Psychology*, 1975, *32*, 805–821.

Elliott, J. F., & Sardino, T. J. *Crime control team*. Springfield, IL: Charles C Thomas, 1971.

Ericson, R. V. The police bureaucracy and decision making. In J. Goldsmith & S. S. Goldsmith (Eds.), *The police community*. Pacific Palisades, CA: Palisades Publishers, 1974.

Festinger, L. A theory of social comparison processes. *Human Relations*, 1954, *7*, 117–140.

Fisk, J. G. *The police officer's exercise of discretion in the decision to arrest: Relationship to organizational goals and societal values*. Los Angles: Institute of Government and Public Affairs, UCLA, 1974. (a)

Fisk, J. G. Some dimensions of police discretion. In J. Goldsmith & S. S. Goldsmith (Eds.), *The police community*. Pacific Palisades, CA: Palisades Publishers, 1974. (b)

Godfrey, E. D., & Harris, D. R. *Basic elements of intelligence*. Washington, DC: Law Enforcement Assistance Administration, 1971.

Goldstein, H. Police policy foundation: A proposal for improving police performance. In T. J. Sweeney & W. Ellingsworth (Eds.), *Issues in police patrol*. Kansas City, MO: Kansas City Police Department; and Washington, DC: Police Foundation, 1973.

Gross, S. Bureaucracy and decision making: Viewed from a patrol precinct level. *Police Chief*, 1975, *42*, 59–64.

Groves, W. E., & Rossi, P. H. Police perceptions of a hostile ghetto. In H. Hahn (Ed.), *Police in urban society*. Beverly Hills, CA: Sage, 1970.

Hennessy, J. J. The evaluation of program impact. *Police Chief*, 1974, *41*, 36–37.

Hodge, J., Siegel, R., & Rossi, P. Occupational prestige in the United States 1925–1963. *American Journal of Sociology*, 1964, *70*, 286.

Igleburger, R. M., Angell, J. E., & Pence, G. *Changing urban police: Practitioners' view*. Washington, DC: Law Enforcement Assistance Administration, 1973.

Juris, H. A., & Feuille, P. *Police unionism*. Lexington, MA: Lexington Books, 1973.

Kelly, R. M. Generalizations from an OEO experiment in Washington, DC. *Journal of Social Issues*, 1975, *31*, 57–86.

Kenny, J. P. *Police administration*. Springfield, IL: Charles C Thomas, 1972.

Lefkowitz, J. Attitudes of police toward their job. In J. R. Snibbe & H. M. Snibbe (Eds.), *The urban policeman in transition.* Springfield, IL: Charles C Thomas, 1973.

Levi, M. A. *Conflict and collusion: Police collective bargaining.* Cambridge, MA: MIT Press, 1974.

Lewin, K. *Resolving social conflicts.* New York: Harper & Row, 1948.

Lipsky, M. Toward a theory of street-level bureaucracy. Presented at American Political Science Association, New York, 1969.

McNamara, J. H. Uncertainties in police work. In D. J. Bordua (Ed.), *The police: Six sociological essays.* New York: Wiley, 1967.

Manning, R. T. Feedback . . . Information for management. *Police Chief,* 1974, *41,* 44–46.

Mills, R. B. Use of diagnostic small groups in police recruit selection and training. *Journal of Criminal Law, Criminology, and Police Science,* 1969, *60,* 238–241.

Municipal Police Administration. Washington, DC: International City Management Association, 1969.

National Advisory Commission on Criminal Justice Goals and Standards. *Report on the police.* Washington, DC: U.S. Government Printing Office, 1973.

Niederhoffer, A. *Behind the shield.* Garden City, NY: Doubleday, 1967.

Olinos, R. A. Some effects of police unionism on discipline. *Police Chief,* 1974, *41,* 24–29.

Ostrom, E., Bargh, W., Guarasci, R., Parks, R., & Whitaker, G. D. *Community organization and the provision of police service.* Beverly Hills, CA: Sage, 1973.

Piliavin, I., & Briar, S. Police encounters with juveniles. *American Journal of Sociology,* 1964, *70,* 206–214.

Radelet, L. A. *The police and the community.* Beverly Hills, CA: Glencoe, 1973.

Reiss, A. J., Jr. *The police and the public.* New Haven, CT: Yale University Press, 1973.

Rubin, J. *The police and the community.* Baltimore: Johns Hopkins Press, 1972.

Rubinstein, J. *City police.* New York: Farrar, Straus, and Giroux, 1973.

Savitz, L. Dimensions of police loyalty. In H. Hahn (Ed.), *Police in urban society.* Beverly Hills, CA: Sage, 1970.

Scheingold, S. Cultural cleavage and criminal justice. Paper presented at meeting of American Political Science Association, Chicago, 1976.

Shellow, R. Evaluating an evaluation. *Journal of Social Issues,* 1975, *31,* 87–94.

Sherman, L. W., Milton, C. H., & Kelly, T. V. *Team policing.* Washington, DC: Police Foundation, 1973.

Skolnick, J. H. *Justice without trial.* New York: Wiley, 1967.

Skolnick, J. H. *Politics of protest.* New York: Simon and Schuster, 1969.

Smith, L., & Greene, J. W. The Tacoma police team. *Police Chief,* 1974, *41,* 42–45.

Sterling, J. *Changes in role concepts of police officers during recruit training.* Washington, DC: International Association of Chiefs of Police, 1969.

Stotland, E. Self-esteem and stress in police work. In W. H. Kroes & J. J. Hurrell, Jr. (Eds.), *Job stress and the police officer.* Washington, DC: Department of Health, Education and Welfare, 1975.

Stotland, E., & Cannon, L., *Social psychology: A cognitive approach.* Philadelphia: Saunders, 1972.

Toch, H., Grant, J. D., & Galvin, R. T. *Agents of change: A study in police reform.* Cambridge, MA: Schenkman, 1975.

Wambaugh, J. *The blue knight.* New York: Dell, 1972.

Watson, N. A., & Sterling, J. *Police and their opinions.* Washington, DC: International Association of Chiefs of Police, 1969.

Westley, W. A. Violence and the police. *American Journal of Sociology,* 1953, *59,* 34–41.

Whisenand, P. M. *Police supervision: Theory and practice.* Englewood Cliffs, NJ: Prentice-Hall, 1973.

Whisenand, P. M., & Ferguson, R. F. *The managing of police organizations.* Englewood Cliffs, NJ: Prentice-Hall, 1973.

Wilson, J. Q. *Varieties of police behavior.* Cambridge, MA: Harvard University Press, 1968.

THE BAIL DECISION

8

An Analysis of the Bail System

Ebbe B. Ebbesen and Vladimir J. Konečni

An important legal dilemma arises shortly after an individual has been charged with committing a crime. The due process right of the accused to be considered innocent of criminal charges until proven guilty is in conflict with the fact that at least one part of the criminal justice system—the police—believe that sufficient legally obtained evidence exists to prove the accused guilty of a crime. The dilemma results from the fact that in the present criminal justice system it takes considerable time to achieve the numerous steps due process has come to involve (e.g., a fair trial), partly as a consequence of long delays made necessary by crowded court calendars. The dilemma facing the court is how the accused is to be treated during the period before the court can dispose of the case. If accused individuals are simply released, some of them might leave the area before their cases could be disposed of and some might commit additional crimes. If accused individuals are detained in jail, they are being punished for crimes they may not have committed.

FEATURES OF THE BAIL SYSTEM

The bail system is intended to provide a partial solution to the above dilemma.

Pretrial options of the court

In most jurisdictions, accused individuals are released a few days after arrest in exchange for a monetary bond—a promise to pay a stated amount of money if they fail to appear at any of the court proceedings dealing with the case. If defendants are unable to deliver the required bond amount to the court because their financial resources are not sufficient to cover the bond or the fees (usually between 10–30% of the bond) of a professional bondsman who acts as surety for the bond, the court generally orders the defendants detained in jail until the bond amount is obtained or until the proceedings are completed. In some jurisdictions, accused individuals are released without paying a cash sum to the court if they sign a promise to pay the bond, should they fail to appear. In other jurisdictions, accused individuals are allowed to pay some fraction of the bond amount provided they sign a promise to pay the rest. The court may, of course, choose not to set any bail bond and release the defendants on their own recognizance. Finally, failure to appear is considered a criminal action in many jurisdictions, so that the prospect of additional criminal charges serves as another deterrent against not appearing at scheduled court proceedings.

Potential adverse consequences of the bail system

Although the bail system seems to provide a means for the court to avoid punishing individuals prior to their being found guilty of a crime and still insure that potential criminals are not allowed to escape appropriate legal proceedings and sanctions, a number of studies have concluded that the bail system contains many potential and actual injustices (Ares, Rankin, and Sturz, 1963; Foote, 1958; Foote, Markle, and Woolley, 1954; Freed and Wald, 1964; Friedland, 1965; Goldfarb, 1965; Rankin, 1964; Wald, 1964). Besides the obvious fact that a monetary bail system discriminates against the poor, the President's Commission on Law Enforcement and the Administration of Justice had the following to say about the bail decision:

> The importance of this decision to any defendant is obvious. A released defendant is one who can live with and support his family, maintain his ties to his community, and busy himself with his own defense by searching for witnesses and evidence and by keeping close touch with his lawyer. An imprisoned defendant is subjected to the squalor, idleness, and possible criminalizing effect of jail. He may be confined for something he did not do; some jailed defendants are ultimately acquitted. He may be confined while presumed innocent only to be freed when found guilty; many jailed defendants, after they have been convicted, are placed on probation rather than imprisoned. The community also relies on the magistrate for protection when he makes his decision about releasing a defendant. If a released defendant fails to appear for trial, the law is flouted. If a released defendant commits

crimes, the community is endangered. (President's Commission, 1967, p. 131)

Consequences of judicial bail decisions may extend beyond their immediate effects on defendants. In particular, the treatment that defendants receive from other participants in the criminal justice system (e.g., judges, prosecutors, and probation officers) may depend on their pretrial status (Konečni and Ebbesen, Chapter 11, this volume; Landes, 1974; Rankin, 1964). For example, probation officers may not react as sympathetically to defendants when the presentence interview is conducted in jail, rather than in the officers' own office.

Given the obvious impact that the bail decision can have on a defendant's pretrial activities and its potential for affecting the outcome of decisions at other points in the criminal justice system, it is important that the rules that seem to govern judicial bail decisions be discovered and examined in light of the functions that the bail system is supposed to serve. Therefore, in the remainder of this chapter we will first explore the constitutional and statutory functions of the bail system. Next, we will examine empirical evidence concerning the extent to which these functions are achieved by the bail system. Then, we will present the results of research on the decision rules used by judges when setting bail. Finally, the best-fitting decision rules that emerge from this research will be examined in light of the apparent purposes of the bail system.

FUNCTIONS OF THE BAIL SYSTEM

Even though the bail system can and does produce many injustices, these inadequacies are tolerable if the functions of the bail system are reasonable and can only be accomplished in a manner consistent with the current operation of the bail system. Unfortunately, there is widespread disagreement about the exact purposes of the bail system and whether it is successful in performing these functions. Critics of the bail system often recognize the right of the court to guarantee the appearance of defendants at required court proceedings, but object to bail being set at such high levels (e.g., in major felony cases) that defendants cannot possibly afford to pay the bond (e.g., Beeley, 1927; Foote, Markle, and Woolley, 1954). Such *sub rosa* preventive detention is seen as an abuse of the court's legitimate discretionary power. On the other side are those who argue that an equally, if not more, important function of high bail bonds is to protect the community, witnesses, and jurors from harm that a potentially dangerous criminal might inflict if released.

Dicta for the former view can be found in several places. For example, in a Supreme Court case of 1951, it was stated: "Since the function of bail is limited, the fixing of bail for any individual defendant must be based upon standards relevant to the purpose of assuring the presence of that defendant" (*Stack* v. *Boyle*, at p. 4). In short, bail should serve the function of assuring the attendance of the accused at court proceedings and not as a preventive measure against predicted offenses. However, in a case before the Supreme Court in the same year (*Carlson* v. *Landon*), the Court suggested that there was not a constitutional right to bail and that "apprehension of hurt" could be considered in the setting of bail. The concept of apprehension of hurt refers to the danger that a defendant might commit additional crimes if released in the community and/or threaten or harm witnesses, jurors, or other individuals involved in the case.

Although there is considerable constitutional and *dicta* uncertainty regarding the exact purposes of the bail system, a functional feature common to most views is that bail should counteract the defendant's tendencies to engage in specified pretrial behaviors (e.g., nonappearance at court proceedings and/or criminal actions). The higher the apparent likelihood of these behaviors, the more the court would be expected to order actions designed to counteract such behavioral tendencies. Although current *dicta* routinely fail to specify exactly how the court is to determine the likelihood of relevant pretrial behaviors on a case-by-case basis, most state statutes and administrative guidelines seem to require that the court consider one or more case and defendant factors in making this decision.

Table 8.1 lists those case and defendant factors that in 1976 were most often cited in state statutes, along with the number of states that cited each. As can be seen, states differ in the types of factors that are to be considered in the bail-setting decision.[1] Of the factors listed, some state statutes require that as many as fifteen separate factors be taken into account, while other states do not specify any (not even in the form of administrative guidelines). Nevertheless, three broad categories of factors are mentioned most frequently: the nature and severity of the current crime, the defendant's prior record, and the defendant's community ties. By emphasizing community ties, some states seem to accept the idea that one function of bail is to counteract

---

[1]It is of interest to note that the factors listed in Table 8.1 vary in terms of specificity. For example, the prior-arrests factor presumably refers to the number (and possibly severity) of prior arrrests on the accused's FBI and/or state "rap sheet." In contrast, it is quite unclear which facts in a case are to be used in evaluating the danger-to-self factor. In a real sense, the latter expresses a vague policy rather than a specific factor that can be associated with specific features of the case. How, exactly, is danger to self to be determined? In short, some states list factors that are easily determined by examining the facts of the case, while other states list "factors" that can only be the result of an unspecified judgment process.

Table 8.1
Factors to be used in bail and pretrial release decisions that were listed in state statutes, 1976

Category	Factor	Number of states
Current crime	Nature of present charge	28
	Probability of conviction	13
	Possible penalty	2
Prior record	Prior criminal record	25
	Prior record of court appearance	15
	On pretrial release for previous charge	3
	On probation or parole when presently charged	1
	Prior arrests	1
Community ties	Financial resources of defendant	22
	Family living in area	16
	Length of residence in area	15
	Employment history	15
	General community ties	2
	Persons to aid defendant in appearing	2
Character of defendant	Character of defendant	16
	Mental condition of defendant	12
	Reputation of defendant	3
	Past conduct	1
Dangerousness	Danger to community (in general)	6
	Danger to others	4
	Dangerousness of defendant	2
	Danger to self	2
	Likelihood of violating law if released	3
Risk	Risk of nonappearance	13

Note: Many of the states not included in this summary table list factors to be used in bail setting in places other than state statutes, e.g., state constitutions and administrative guidelines. Although these states were not included in this table, their inclusion would not substantially alter the list of factors nor the number of states that endorsed the various factors.
SOURCE: Goldkamp (1977).

nonappearance and that the degree to which a defendant is tied to the local community is predictive of nonappearance. In contrast, other states seem to assume that previous and current criminal activity is predictive of nonappearance and/or that the control of pretrial criminal activity is the primary function of bail and can best be predicted by prior criminal activity.

Factors that predict appearance

Unfortunately, the predictive relationship between such factors and defendant pretrial behavior has received little empirical attention, and what evidence does exist is inconsistent with some of the intuitions that seem to guide state statutes. In particular, one study (Landes, 1974), based on a 1971 sample of 307 individuals who were released during their pretrial period in New York County, examined (among other things) the relationship between a large number of predictors—community ties (e.g., residence, employment, and income), current charge (nature and severity of charges), size of bond, and prior record (e.g., number of prior felony arrests, number of prior misdemeanor arrests, and prior parole and probation violation history)—and whether the defendant failed to appear. Only three factors were significantly related to appearance. These were size of bond,[2] whether there was an outstanding detainer for the defendant, and whether resisting arrest was included in the current charge. Factors such as nature of charge, penalty if convicted, prior record, residence, employment, and so on, were unrelated to the likelihood of nonappearance. In short, in the sample studied, community ties did *not* predict whether defendants would appear.

In a study of a 1973 sample from Charlotte, North Carolina, Clark, Freeman, and Koch (1976) also found that employment and income were unrelated to nonappearance. (Residence was not included as a variable since almost all defendants lived in the Charlotte area.) Besides the time that had elapsed since the bail hearing, Clark and coworkers found that the form of pretrial release and the extent of the prior arrest record *were* related to nonappearance, however. With regard to the latter, individuals with more extensive arrest records were less likely to appear. The effect of the form of pretrial release was slightly different from that reported by Landes. In particular, defendants whose release was secured through the aid of a bail bondsman were *less* likely to appear than (1) defendants who were selected and supervised during the release period by a formal pretrial release program (and who signed an unsecured appearance bond), and (2) defendants who paid their own bail bond.[3] Clark and asso-

---

[2]This relationship between bond amount and appearance is complicated, however, by several factors. One of the most important is that the effect appears to be due primarily to whether any bond, regardless of amount, was set. Of those released without any bond, 33% failed to appear, whereas only 12.5% of those with some bond failed to appear. In other words, requiring that some bond amount be paid seems to be associated with a reduced nonappearance rate but, given that a bond is set, the role of size of bond is ambiguous.

[3]Too few defendants were released on their own recognizance for their appearance rates to be evaluated in a meaningful way.

ciates did not examine the relationship between appearance and size of bond.

The findings from these studies are not necessarily incompatible with the view that community ties (and other factors) play an important role in determining the pretrial behavior of defendants. If the community ties for those defendants who were *not* released were much weaker than those who were, and if the former defendants would have been much less likely to appear had they been released, then community ties would prove to be a potentially important factor in pretrial behavior. On the other hand, Landes (1974) did report that the community-ties variables were not significantly related to the likelihood that a defendant obtained pretrial release. In other words, although Landes did not study this question directly, it is unlikely that this alternative explanation is correct for Landes' data set.

In a third study, Gottfredson (1974) examined the predictive utility of the criteria suggested by the Vera Institute of Justice (1972) for releasing defendants on their own recognizance. He also compared these criteria to the predictive utility of other defendant characteristics. Briefly, the Vera method is to devise a score by giving points for various defendant characteristics that are thought to predict appearance. Four major categories of information are typically collected and scored: residence (e.g., length of time in area, property owned), family ties (e.g., relatives living in area, marital status, children in area), employment (e.g., currently employed, history of employment), and prior record (e.g., number of prior arrests, history on previous probations). The resulting scores are used to determine whether to release the defendants on their own recognizance. An unusual feature of Gottfredson's study was that it contained two samples of defendants from the Los Angeles area who were released on their own recognizance. One sample consisted of those defendants whom the project staff recommended for release on the basis of the Vera score, and the other sample consisted of defendants whom the staff did not recommend for release but who were released anyway by special arrangement with the courts. When the rates of nonappearance were compared across the two samples, it was found that they did not differ to a great extent: 15% of those recommended for release failed to appear, compared to 26% of those not recommended. Although this difference was statistically significant, many prediction errors were made by the project staff.

When the predictive ability of other factors (e.g., age, sex, prior record, severity of current charge) was examined for the entire sample of defendants, Gottfredson found that although it was possible to account for a significant portion of the variability in appearance with a multiple regression equation, when this equation was used to predict the appearance of an independent sample of defendants, it accounted for less than 4% of the variance in the new sample. Thus, prior record, severity of crime, community ties, and other defendant characteristics, even when collected by a trained staff who attempt to verify most of the information, seem unable to predict, to any reasonable degree, whether defendants will appear at appropriate court proceedings.

In summary, the results from several studies tentatively suggest that community ties may be a less important factor in predicting appearance than is generally believed. The roles that crime (its type and severity) and prior record play are even less clear. Landes (1974) reported that neither factor was significantly related to appearance. Clark, Freeman, and Koch (1976) reported that although severity of current crime was not related to appearance, extent of prior record was. Finally, Gottfredson (1974) found that both factors were related to appearance, but when the obtained prediction equation was used on a validation sample (a step neither Landes nor Clark et al. took), it failed to adequately predict appearance.[4]

Factors that predict pretrial criminal activity

The same three studies also attempted to determine which factors predict pretrial criminal activity (other than failure to appear). Landes (1974) accomplished this by comparing defendants who had pending charges against them with those who did not.[5] On the other

---

[4]Of course, these different results might be due to differences in factor definitions and/or sampling procedures. For example, none of the defendants in Gottfredson's sample was released on *bail*, whereas many of those in the other studies were. The definitions of severity of crime, prior record, and so on, varied considerably across the studies. Furthermore, the samples in the Landes study and the Clark et al. study did not contain any defendants who could not afford the bond or who were detained for other reasons. Since amount of bond was related to severity of crime in Landes' New York sample, and probably in the Charlotte sample as well, it is conceivable that whatever effects severity might have had on appearance were counterbalanced by bond amount. Finally, Gottfredson's sample eliminated all defendants who had been charged with certain violent offenses (e.g., homicide, sexual assault, robbery, and assault). Despite these differences, it does appear, when these studies are taken together, that the community-ties factor does *not* predict appearance and that if prior record and severity of crime do predict appearance, they account for a very small portion of the variance.

[5]Because Landes did not have data on the pretrial criminal activity of the defendants, he was forced to use this procedure even though it meant that the two samples were not equated in terms of the time when they received bail. This procedure would present a biased picture of the relationship between various factors and pretrial criminal activity if the police arrest and charging policies were influenced by the defendants' prior records. (For example, the police might seek out known felons as potential suspects of particular crimes.)

hand, both Clark et al. (1976) and Gottfredson (1974) directly examined the likelihood of defendants being arrested for a new offense while released on their own recognizance or on bail. Although there were some differences, the agreement in findings between the studies was much closer than that obtained with the appearance measure. In particular, all three studies found that indicators of the severity of the current charge and of prior criminal activity were related to the likelihood of the defendant being arrested while awaiting trial for another crime. In addition, other defendant characteristics (e.g., age, sex, race, income, marital status) were consistently unrelated to pretrial arrests. However, although neither Landes nor Clark and associates reported that the community-ties factor was related to pretrial arrests, Gottfredson found a very weak, but significant relationship. Nevertheless, when Gottfredson examined, on a new sample, the predictive ability of his best-fitting multiple regression equation that included all of these factors, he again found that only a very small percentage of the variance (2%) in rearrests could be predicted.

Although there is good agreement across the available studies regarding those factors that predict the defendant's criminal activity while awaiting disposition of another charge, several points should be noted. First, in agreement with other studies (e.g., Thomas, 1974), only a small minority of those defendants who were released (around 15%) were arrested or charged with serious crimes during the pretrial period, despite the fact that Chief Justice Warren E. Burger claims that "bail crime" is one of the major failures of the current judicial system's attempts to deter crime (San Diego *Evening Tribune*, February 4, 1980). Second, the interpretation of the consistent results from these studies is partially hampered by the fact that individuals who failed to appear may have fled the area and therefore could not be arrested by the local authorities, even though they may have committed crimes before leaving the area. Third, in the one case in which the prediction equation was validated on a new sample, the shrinkage in the accounted-for variance was very large. Finally, although nature of the crime and extent of prior record were significantly related to the likelihood that additional crimes would be committed (even in the validation sample), these factors by no means accounted for all of the variation in the data. Therefore, the use of these factors as predictors would not necessarily decrease the total number of prediction errors below that which would occur if judges simply assumed that no defendant would be arrested for additional crimes and therefore simply released all defendants on their own recognizance or set a small bail amount (Meehl and Rosen, 1955; Nagel and Neef, 1976).

The effect of bail amount on pretrial behavior

One very important issue about which virtually nothing is known concerns the effect that the size (as well as the form) of the bail bond has on the pretrial behavior of defendants. Aside from the obvious effect that being detained (as a result of an inability to afford bail) has, the *amount* of bail that is needed to counteract whatever tendencies defendants might have to fail to appear and/or to commit additional crimes is not known. Furthermore, except for the suggestive evidence obtained by Clark, Freeman, and Koch (1976), the extent to which other forms of pretrial release (e.g., supervision by probation officers, promissory notes, the addition of severe criminal sanctions against nonappearance and rearrest, property in lieu of monetary bonds, and so on) might prove to be equally or even more effective methods of controlling pretrial behavior has received little attention. Unless it is shown that size of the bond has an effect on the pretrial behavior of defendants, then the only consequence of a bail bond would be to cause some defendants to be detained. This consequence can be achieved without the bail system by giving judges two options: release on own recognizance and pretrial detention.

Even if size of the bond is related to the pretrial behavior of defendants, as Landes (1974) has argued, there is still the question of whether the effect it has depends on case and defendant characteristics. For example, is a higher bond needed for defendants with extensive prior records than for defendants with minimal records in order to produce equivalent pretrial behavior, or is the effect of the bond amount independent of such factors? Until answers to this and similar questions are obtained, it will be impossible to determine whether the bail system is serving the appearance and/or the crime-control functions that most observers argue it should serve.

FACTORS THAT JUDGES USE IN SETTING BAIL

Quite independent of the factors that predict and control the pretrial behavior of defendants is the issue concerning the factors that are causal in judicial bail-setting decisions. Judges may or may not base their bail-setting decisions on factors that actually predict the pretrial behavior of defendants. Judges might adopt a particular decision strategy because it is consistent with state or administrative guidelines or because it intuitively follows from their beliefs about the function that bail should serve regardless of the actual effectiveness of that strategy.

Factors producing predictively ineffective decision strategies

It is quite reasonable to expect that judicial decisions are made on the basis of factors that are poor predictors of pretrial behavior. The feedback that judges receive from incorrect decisions is necessarily biased given the nature of the bail system. For example, assume that judges use prior record as a factor to decide how much bail should be set. Defendants with extensive prior records would then find it more difficult to pay the higher bonds that are set for them and would consequently be more likely to be detained in jail. Being detained in jail, these defendants would be unable to demonstrate to the judges that if they had been released, they would have appeared when scheduled and would not have been rearrested. In short, unnecessary detentions will be undetected by judges. Furthermore, the use of *any* decision factor that eventually increases the number of defendants who are detained almost guarantees a reduction in the total number of individuals who are rearrested, even if the factor has no relationship to the pretrial behavior of defendants. Defendants who are detained in jail cannot be rearrested for additional crimes. Finally, judges in crowded urban courts do not usually receive any feedback concerning their decisions. A given defendant is not handled by the same judge for each court proceeding. The judge who sets bail may never know how the defendant behaved during the pretrial period, much less how the case was disposed of. Thus, the nature of the feedback that judges receive concerning the adequacy of their bail-setting decisions will not, in general, tend to reinforce decision factors that are accurate predictors of pretrial behavior.

Other facts that tend to militate against decision strategies that are based on predictively accurate factors are:

1. The data available to judges in most jurisdictions concerning the defendant's background and the crime are meager.

2. The reliability of what data do exist is often unknown.

3. As with many legal decisions, the decision-maker must rely on other people for the "facts."

4. As the previous section suggested, it is unclear whether the potential predictors of pretrial behavior that are available to judges (e.g., Table 8.1) *can* predict who will appear and/or who will commit additional crimes even if they could be measured in a perfectly reliable manner.

With regard to the latter point, it may be that the factors which account for most of the variation in pretrial behavior have little to do with community ties, prior record, and severity of crime. Even the pioneering efforts of the Vera Institute of Justice (Ares, Rankin, and Sturz, 1963) to provide judges with more reliable information about community ties through the use of an extensive prebail interview schedule have not improved, to any substantial degree, the predictive ability of the community-ties factor (Gottfredson, 1974).

Although the efforts of the Vera Institute to show that more reliable information can be provided to judges have had a major impact on many jurisdictions, it is still the case that the information made available often depends on the self-reports of the defendant, whether and how strongly a defense attorney argues for lower bail, and the information that the police have presented to the prosecutor regarding their investigations and the nature of the criminal activity. In fact, in one study conducted in England (which has a bail system very similar to that in the United States), Bottomley (1970) found that the court often set bail and remanded accused individuals to custody knowing *only* the offenses with which the defendants were charged!

Case factors and bail decisions

Several studies have examined the relationship between various case and defendant characteristics (including community ties) and judicial bail decisions in an attempt to discover the decision strategies that judges do use (Ebbesen and Konečni, 1975; Foote, 1958; Foote, Markle, and Woolley, 1954; Landes, 1974; Suffert, 1966). It is quite clear from these studies that the amount of bail increases as the severity of the current crime increases and, to a lesser degree, as the extent of the prior record increases. Other factors—age, sex, community ties, and so on—seem to be only very weakly related to bail amount, if at all. In short, most studies have found that the amount of bail (and the decision to remand the defendant to custody with no bail) are related to two factors: severity of the current crime and extent of prior record.

Social influence and bail decisions

It would be premature to conclude from this evidence, as many have, that severity of crime and prior record are the *direct* causes of judicial bail decisions. It is conceivable, for example, that these two factors are related to some other, unmeasured factor or factors that are the direct causes of judicial decisions. One class of such factors, often ignored in most studies of bail setting, is *social influence*. As with many legal decisions, in bail hearings the judge is often presented with arguments and recommendations for action from several different sources. Three different actors are potentially important: the defense attorney, the district attorney, and the probation officer. The probation officer often is responsible for collecting and verifying community-ties and prior-record information, which is then made available to the court usually in a written form. In some jurisdictions, the probation officer also recommends whether defendants should be released on their own recognizance. In the bail hearing the district attorney often proposes a particular bail amount and attempts to support this recommendation with a series of brief arguments. The defense attorney then usually makes a recommendation for a lower bond amount and attempts to support it with a different series of arguments. It is conceivable that judicial decision strategies are, at least partly, based on these recommendations. That is, rather than directly considering prior record, nature of current crime, community ties, and other factors, a judge might simply base the bail decision on the recommendations that are received from other individuals.

For example, as part of the Manhattan Bail Project conducted by the Vera Institute, Suffert (1966) examined the interaction patterns between the judge, the prosecutor, and the defense attorney at bail hearings. He found that in 49% of the hearings a judge simply proposed a bond amount that was not opposed by either attorney. That is, both attorneys quietly agreed with the judge's decision. In another 38% of the cases, one or the other attorney suggested that bail be set at a particular amount, and then the judge imposed bail without disagreement from either attorney. Rarely was the imposed amount the same as that recommended, however. The remaining cases involved some form of counterargument and counterproposal from one, the other, or both attorneys before the judge imposed bail. Analysis of the cases in which the prosecuting attorney suggested a higher bail and/or the defense attorney suggested a lower bail than either the judge's or the other attorney's initial recommendation led Suffert to conclude that the district attorney's recommendations had a greater impact on the judge than did the defense attorney's recommendations. This conclusion was based on several results:

1. The judges were more likely to raise the bail amount over a previous suggestion in response to a district attorney's request than to lower the bail amount in response to a defense attorney's recommendation.

2. Defense attorneys made fewer recommendations than prosecuting attorneys.

3. When prosecutors recommended that defendants be released on their own recognizance, the judges *always* followed this suggestion; whereas when similar recommendations were made by defense attorneys, they were followed in only about 60% of the cases.

Although aspects of Suffert's results are consistent with the view that the prosecutor's recommendation is influential in judicial bail decisions, there is another explanation for the findings: The judge's and the prosecutor's decision strategies may be more similar to each other than are the judge's and the defense attorney's strategies. That is, judges may agree with prosecutors because they base their decisions on the same case and defendant characteristics that the prosecutors use to construct their recommendations. Unfortunately, Suffert did not present his data in a manner that allows this issue to be examined. In summary, there is a reasonable degree of uncertainty concerning which factors are *direct* causes of judicial bail decisions. Severity of crime, prior record, prosecutor recommendation, defense attorney recommendation, and possibly community ties are likely candidates, but which, if any, are direct causes of the judicial decision remains to be determined. If both case and social-influence factors prove to be causal, the relative importance of these different factors in the final outcome needs to be determined as well.

A causal analysis of case and social influence

These empirical issues led us (Ebbesen and Konečni, 1975) to consider different methods that might be used to determine which factors were direct causes of judicial decisions. One method, unusual for legal research, but common in social-psychological research, was an experimental simulation of the bail-setting process. This method allowed us to examine the impact of different potential causes of judicial decisions unconfounded by other potential causes. If some of the previously studied factors are related to bail decisions only because they are associated with the actual causes of bail decisions and therefore are not themselves direct causes, then, in an experimental analysis, these factors should have no effect on bail decisions.

While experimental designs provide an unambiguous method of determining which factors are direct causes *in the simulation*, they have other difficulties. In particular, the causal process that controls judicial decisions in the simulation need not be the same as that which controls bail setting in actual court proceedings (Ebbesen and Konečni, 1980; Konečni and Ebbesen, 1979; also Chapter 2, this volume). The simulation may differ from the situations being simulated in any number of potentially important respects. If any of these differences influence the nature of the decision processes that judges use, then incorrect conclusions could be drawn from simulation research. To counteract this difficulty, it is necessary to examine the extent to which simulation results are consistent with evidence from the situations being simulated.

An experimental simulation Eighteen municipal and superior-court judges who had recently been or were currently involved in bail hearings in San Diego County participated in the simulation. The judges were given "case records" designed to simulate the type of information typically available in bail hearings. To reinforce this idea, the judges were told that the cases had been selected from San Diego County Court records. Each case described the defendant as an unmarried, male Caucasian between the ages of 21 and 25 (the ages were varied within this range to enhance the appearance that these case records were derived from actual past cases). The criminal charge against the defendants was held constant across all cases: robbery. Although the details of the criminal activities leading to this charge were varied from case to case (e.g., two TV sets from an appliance store, cash and liquor from a liquor store, gems from a jewelry store, cash from a restaurant), the value of the stolen property did not exceed $950 nor go below $850. A plea of "not guilty" was always entered.

The levels of four different factors were systematically varied: the district attorney's bail recommendation (in dollars), the defense attorney's bail recommendation (in dollars), the extent of the defendant's prior record, and the strength of the defendant's community ties.[6] The levels of these factors were chosen to be representative of the range of values that usually occurred in robbery cases. Three levels of district attorney recommendation (around $1,500, $2,400, and $6,000) and three levels of defense attorney recommendation (release on own recognizance, $500, and $1,000) were used. The two levels of prior record were: no previous arrests versus several previous felony convictions along with the fact that the defendant was on probation for one of the prior convictions at the time of the hearing. The two levels of community ties were: the defendant had lived in San Diego for 4 to 6 years, was currently employed, and had a family that lived in the San Diego area versus the defendant had lived in the area for only 1 to 2 months, was unemployed, and had a family that

---

[6]Because the judges were unwilling to spend a great deal of time on this study, we reduced the number of cases they had to judge by holding severity of crime constant.

lived in Northern California. To conform to typical courtroom procedure, prior-record information was presented with the district attorney's recommendation, while community-ties information was presented along with the defense attorney's recommendation.

Each judge read eight case histories and was told to set bail as if they were real cases. A $3 \times 3 \times 2 \times 2$ analysis of variance of the amount of bail set as a function of the above conditions showed that three of the four factors had significant effects on the judges' bail decisions: community ties, $F(1,198) = 22.38$, $p < .0001$; district attorney recommendation, $F(2,108) = 7.05$, $p < .01$; prior record, $F(1,108) = 5.91$, $p < .05$. Community ties accounted for the most variation, district attorney recommendation the next most, and prior record the next most. The effect of the defense attorney recommendation was not significant: $F < 1$. There were no interactions among the factors: $F_{max}(2,108) = 2.22$, $p > .05$. The effect of any one factor did not depend on the level of other factors. The mean amounts of bail that were set (collapsed over the one nonsignificant factor: defense recommendation) are shown in Table 8.2. As can be seen, the judges seemed to conform to the American Bar Association (1968) and Vera Institute recommendations that high bail be set when the community ties of the defendant are weak. In addition, higher bail bonds were set for defendants wih prior felony records than for those with no previous records. Finally, consistent with Suffert's (1966) findings, the bond amount increased as the amount of the prosecutor's recommendation increased.

Several conclusions follow from these results. The failure of the defense attorney recommendation to have a significant impact on bond amount suggests that the defense recommendation is not a

Table 8.2
Mean bail set (in dollars) by judges as function of prior record, community ties, and prosecuting attorney recommendation

Prior record	Community ties	Prosecuting attorney recommendation		
		1,600	2,250	6,250
No	Strong	1,208	1,375	1,600
	Weak	1,958	2,437	3,142
Yes	Strong	2,121	1,462	2,492
	Weak	2,175	2,750	4,437

SOURCE: Adapted from E. B. Ebbesen and V. J. Konečni, Decision making and information integration in the courts: The setting of bail. *Journal of Personality and Social Psychology*, 1975, *32*, 805–821. Copyright © 1975 by the American Psychological Association. Reprinted by permission.

direct cause of the judge's bail decision. The significant effects of prior record and of the prosecutor's recommendation suggest that none of the previous findings relating prior record and prosecuting attorney recommendations to the amount of bail is artifactual. Apparently, prior record and the district attorney recommendation are both *direct* causes of bail decisions. On the other hand, it is curious that the one factor that accounted for most of the variation in the amount of bail was the strength of the defendant's community ties. As we noted earlier, previous research has not found this factor to be strongly related to judicial bail decisions.

Several explanations for the latter anomaly are possible. One that comes readily to mind is that the bail-setting procedures may have been different in California (at the time of the study) than in the jurisdictions where the previous data were collected. For example, several studies prior to ours were based on samples from New York. Although neither New York nor California includes community ties in state statutes, California differs from New York in that its statutes require that the risk of nonappearance be considered. It is conceivable that the judges in our sample were accomplishing this by attending to the community-ties factor. Another explanation for the difference in results is that the simulation methodology did not tap the decision process that judges normally use when setting bail (Ebbesen and Konečni, 1980; Konečni and Ebbesen, 1979).

An analysis of actual bail decisions   In order to examine the utility of these two alternative explanations, we obtained naturalistic data from five of the eighteen judges who participated in the simulation by unobtrusively observing them set bail in actual bail hearings. Trained observers attended a total of 177 bail hearings. Using specially prepared data sheets, the observers recorded the following for each case:

1. The sex, approximate age, and race of the accused.

2. The type of crime charged against the accused.

3. Whether a defense attorney was present.

4. The defendant's plea (guilty or not guilty).

5. The defense attorney's dollar recommendation.

6. The prosecuting attorney's dollar recommendation.

7. The accused's prior record (when it was mentioned by one of the participants).

8. Whether the accused was employed.

9. Whether and how long the accused had lived in the San Diego area.

10. Whether the accused had relatives living in the area.

11. The amount of bail that was set.

Of the cases observed, 35% were not used in the analyses described below because one or more of the major classes of information were missing. Since 96% of the defendants were males between the ages of 18 and 30 who pleaded not guilty, sex, age, and plea were ignored in the final analyses.

The reliability of these data was assessed by comparing the records of two independent observers who simultaneously coded 23 cases. Comparison of the records indicated that the two observers agreed with each other on all major categories of data for all of the cases, indicating near-perfect reliability.

The analyses of the data that are of most relevance to the present concern were conducted using five predictors of the judges' decisions. One was the severity of the current criminal charge. Seven levels were created by categorizing the charges into the following classes:

1. Victimless crimes (possession of drugs, AWOL).

2. Nonviolent crimes with nonspecific victims (forgery, sexual perversion).

3. Nonviolent minor crimes with specific victims (burglary, petty theft, theft).

4. Nonviolent major crimes with specific victims (sale of drugs, robbery).

5. Crimes with the potential of violence or death (armed robbery, possession of a deadly weapon).

6. Violent crimes not resulting in death (kidnapping, rape, and assault).

7. Homicide.

The ordering of these categories from least to most severe matches that derived from our own (Ebbesen and Konečni, 1976) and previous judgmental work (Coombs, 1967).

Another factor was prior record. Four levels were created: (1) No prior arrests. (2) A minor record consisting of traffic violations. (3) A moderate prior record consisting of no more than one nonviolent felony conviction. (4) A severe record consisting of more than one felony conviction or one violent felony conviction. Those defendants with severe prior records were also typically on parole at the time of the hearing.

The third factor was community ties. Three levels were defined: (1) A defendant with weak ties had not lived in the San Diego area for more than 1 month. (2) One with moderate ties had lived in the area for more than 1 year but was unemployed at the time of arrest. (3) A defendant with strong community ties had lived in the area for more than 1 year, had been steadily employed, and had relatives living in the area.

The remaining two factors, defense and prosecutor recommendations, were coded in terms of dollar amounts: (1) The defense attorney recommendation ranged from $0 (release on own recognizance) to $25,000 in one homicide case. (2) The prosecuting attorney recommendation ranged from $0 to a recommendation that the bail request be denied (also in one homicide case).

The judges' final bail decisions were also coded in dollars. They were obtained when the judge announced the final bail amount so that the court stenographer could record it.

The results of an initial analysis of the relationships between the judge's bail recommendation (treating release on own recognizance as $0) and each of the aforementioned factors are presented in Table 8.3.[7] It shows these relationships in terms of separate regression equations for each factor. Prior record was the only factor that was not at least marginally related to the amount of bail. For the remaining factors, bail increased as the severity of the crime and the two attorney

Table 8.3
Regression equations relating severity of crime, prior record, community ties, defense attorney recommendation, and prosecuting attorney recommendation to amount of bail set

Source	Constant	Beta	r
Severity of crime[a]	− 1744	1319.0	.47[b]
Prior record[a]	1575	296.7	.07
Community ties[a]	3678	− 878.3	− .16[b]
Defense attorney recommendation	664	2.6	.84[b]
Prosecuting attorney recommendation	− 464	.9	.96[b]

[a]·Scaled arbitrarily: 1–6, 1–4, and 1–3, respectively.
[b]·$p \leq .05$.

[7]Four homicide cases were eliminated from the analyses since no bail was set for three of them and an unusually high bail was set for the fourth one.

recommendations increased and as the strength of the community ties decreased.

When all five factors were considered together in a multiple regression analysis, the resulting equation was able to account for slightly over 94% of the variance in the bail amount. When all possible two-way *linear* interactions (Ebbesen and Konečni, 1975) between pairs of factors were included in the model, the new model accounted for a significant amount of additional variance, F (10,86) = 5.12, p < .0001, and explained about 97% of the total variation in bail. To determine the contribution that each of the factors made to this excellent fit, the *additional* sum of squares that each factor added to the remaining factors was examined. The results of this analysis are presented in Table 8.4. We found that only the two attorney recommendations and the severity of the crime each added significantly to the amount of "main-effect" variation in the amount of bail that could be explained by the remaining four factors. Thus, the previously noted relationship between bail and community ties could be explained by the fact that the strength of a defendant's community ties was correlated with the remaining three factors. In fact, when the community-ties and prior-record factors were removed, the remaining three factors accounted for virtually the same amount of variation in bail as all five factors taken together: residual $F < 1$. The effects that these three significant factors had on the amount of bail that was set are shown in the following best-fitting linear equation:

$$\text{Bail (in dollars)} = -91.49 + .82 \text{ (prosecutor)} + .52 \text{ (defense)} - 122.13 \text{ (crime)}$$

When a similar analysis was performed to determine which interactions were contributing to the overall two-way interaction variance, we found that two interactions were sufficient to explain all of the "interaction-effect" variance. One was between severity of crime and the defense attorney recommendation, and another was between the two recommendations. The first of these interactions was examined by dividing the data into minor crimes (categories 1–3) and major crimes (categories 4–6) and then examining the relationship between the judges' decisions and the defense attorneys' recommendations. Table 8.5 presents the zero-order correlations between the judicial decision and the defense recommendation (and for comparison purposes correlations between the judge and the prosecutor and between the judge and the crime) for minor crimes and for major crimes. As can be seen, the relationship between the defense attorney and the judge was higher (p < .05) when the defendant was charged with a more severe crime. In contrast, the correlations between the judge and the prosecutor and between the judge and the severity of

Table 8.4
Multiple regression analyses of judge's actual bail decision

Source	df	F
All main and two-way interaction effects	15	155.77[a]
Main effects only	5	319.90[a]
Two-way interactions only (residual)	10	5.12[a]
Main effects (additionals)		
Severity of crime (A)	1	4.26[b]
Prior record (B)	1	1.61
Community ties (C)	1	<1.0
Defense attorney recommendation (D)	1	23.63[a]
Prosecuting attorney recommendation (E)	1	523.81[a]
Two-way linear interaction effects (additionals)		
A × B	1	1.45
A × C	1	2.78
A × D	1	10.59[a]
A × E	1	<1.0
B × C	1	<1.0
B × D	1	<1.0
B × E	1	2.19
C × D	1	<1.0
C × E	1	<1.0
D × E	1	15.08[a]
Mean square error	86	.83[c]

Note: These analyses were based on data from 102 cases. Four homicide cases were eliminated because of extreme values. Severity of crime, prior record, and community ties were scaled as in Table 8.3.
[a]p < .01.
[b]p < .05.
[c]Mean square error; should be multiplied by 10^5 to obtain the true value.
SOURCE: Adapted from E. B. Ebbesen and V. J. Konečni, Decision making and information integration in the courts: The setting of bail. Journal of Personality and Social Psychology, 1975, 32, 805–821. Copyright © 1975 by the American Psychological Association. Reprinted by permission.

Table 8.5
Correlations between judge's bail decision and defense attorney recommendation, prosecuting attorney recommendation, and severity of crime for minor and major crimes

Judge with:	Severity of crime	
	Minor (n = 52)	Major (n = 50)
Defense attorney recommendation	.43	.84
Prosecuting attorney recommendation	.88	.97
Severity of crime (within category)	.58	.63

the crime remained fairly stable across the two data sets. In short, the judge seemed to have been more responsive to the defense attorney recommendation when the crime was more severe.

The linear interaction between the defense attorney and the prosecutor suggests that the judges' recommendations were higher than might be expected from either the defense attorney recommendation or the prosecutor recommendation considered alone when *both* attorneys recommended that higher bail bonds be set. That is, the impact of either attorney's recommendation was enhanced by the presence of a similarly high recommendation from the other attorney.

These results paint quite a different picture of the bail decision from that obtained in the simulation study. Recall that the major causal factor in the simulation was the same factor used by the Vera Institute and recommended by the American Bar Association: the strength of the defendant's community ties. In the present, real-world data, however, community ties did not seem to play a meaningful role in the judges' bail decisions. Before rejecting the simulation results as unrepresentative of causal processes in actual bail decisions, however, we explored several *methodological* explanations for the different results. These were: (1) The ranges of the factors were much larger in the naturalistic data than in the simulation data. (2) The scale values used in the multiple regressions may have been quite different from the subjective scale values that the judges used in deciding on bail. (3) Some unmeasured factor or factors not included in the multiple regression analyses may have produced the pattern of results. Although the last of these alternative explanations is virtually impossible to reject, it is hard to imagine what such a factor or factors might be in the present setting. Even if such factors were found, the resulting picture of the bail-setting process would still be different from that obtained in the simulation experiment and therefore would not provide a satisfying account of the differences between the two studies.

To provide some evidence relevant to the first two explanations for the differences in results, 63 cases were selected from the real-world sample so that their range of values on the four factors that were varied in the simulation did not exceed those values used in the simulation and so that the levels of these factors matched, as closely as possible, the levels used in the simulation. Three levels of prosecuting attorney and of defense attorney recommendations, two levels of prior record, and two of community ties were coded, using Overall and Spiegal's (1969) dummy-variable coding procedure. Then a dummy-variable multiple regression (a technique that can be identical to least-squares analysis of variance and therefore does not scale the levels of the factors; e.g., Applebaum and Cramer, 1974; Cohen, 1968) was used to analyze these data. We reasoned that if the results of this analysis were the same as those from the simulation, then one or more of the previous methodological explanations were probably correct. As it turned out, these analyses did not substantially alter the conclusions from the naturalistic data. The district attorney recommendation was the most important predictor of bail, $F (2,43) = 17.91$, $p < .01$, just as in the entire naturalistic sample, and neither prior record nor community ties was significantly related to the bail amount ($p > .05$). The defense attorney recommendation was only marginally related to the bail amount ($p < .10$) in this restricted sample, however. These results implied that the differences between the simulation study and the naturalistic study were not due to simple artifactual problems in our methods of analysis. Apparently, the judges in the simulation were using a decision strategy that was not identical to the one they used when setting bail in actual cases.

In fact, a number of important differences in results emerged. Within the range of values studied, the simulation data implied that judges combined, in a noninteractive fashion, three sources of information in deciding on the amount of bail to set: community ties, prior record, and the prosecuting attorney recommendation. In contrast, the full range of naturalistic data implied that community ties and prior record were not relevant factors and that the prosecuting attorney recommendation was far more influential than the other factors. These and other differences suggested that the causal process controlling judicial decisions in the simulation was not the same as that in real bail hearings. (See Chapter 2, this volume, for an expanded discussion of this issue.) Therefore, we were not able to use the simulation results as we had originally intended, namely, to clarify the causal relationships among the studied factors and judicial decisions. Nevertheless, we used some features of the naturalistic data to assess the plausibility of several alternative causal models.

Any one of several different causal models might describe the influence that the five factors (crime, prior record, community ties, defense recommendation, and prosecutor recommendation) have on judges' bail decisions:

1. In an *independent-judgment model,* all of the factors are assumed to act as *direct* (though correlated) causes of judicial bail decisions. Given the results that we have already described, neither community ties nor prior record is likely to be a direct cause of the bail decision. Nevertheless, severity of the crime and the two attorney recommendations could all act as direct causes of judicial decisions.

2. In contrast to the independent-judgment model, we can assume that the factors are related to each other in a causal chain. One

reasonable chain assumes that the direct causes of the judges' decisions are the recommendations of the two attorneys and that the remaining factors (including prior record) have only *indirect* causal effects on bail. In this complete *social-influence model*, severity of crime, prior record, and community ties have no direct effects on the judges' decisions. Thus, some subset of these case factors or all of them have only indirect effects on judicial decisions.

3. In the *case-factors model*, all three actors are assumed to reach independent decisions. Thus, the decisions of one actor are assumed to have no effect on the decisions of any other actor. Instead, the three case factors (or some subset of them) are assumed to have direct causal effects on the decisions of all three actors. One could explain the agreement between the attorney recommendations and the judges' decisions that we described previously by assuming that all of the actors used similar decision strategies. Focusing on the judges, this causal model assumes that they make their decisions on the basis of the case factors only.

4. A *prosecutor-only model*, suggested in part by Suffert's (1966) study, assumes that the only direct cause of the judges' decisions is the prosecutor's recommendation. Case factors are assumed to influence both of the attorney recommendations, but only the prosecutor is assumed to have a direct causal effect on the judges. A slightly modified version of this model assumes that the defense attorney is also directly influenced by the prosecutor's recommendation rather than by the case factors.

5. A *defense-only model* reverses the role of the prosecutor and the defense attorney in the previous model.[8]

The prosecutor-only and defense-only models make similar types of predictions. If one or the other attorney recommendation is the only direct cause of judicial bail decisions, then the relationships between the remaining variables and the judges' decisions should disappear when the appropriate recommendation is held constant. Stated differently, the other factors should not explain a significant amount of *additional* variance in bail over that already explained by

---

[8]It is also possible that the judge has a causal influence on attorney recommendations. This seems especially reasonable in light of the fact that discussion among the attorneys and the judge sometimes occurs. Unfortunately, an adequate test of the fit of this and other mutual causality (or nonhierarchical) models was not possible in the current case.

the relevant attorney recommendation. We examined this prediction for both attorney recommendations using the error term from the "main-effects" model (described earlier). Although both the prosecutor and the defense attorney recommendations each accounted for large portions of the variance in bail (see Table 8.3), the additional variance accounted for by the remaining four factors (one attorney recommendation and the three case factors) was highly significant in each case: prosecutor-only residual F (4,96) = 5.03, p < .0001; defense-only residual F (4,96) = 100.13, p < .0001. These results are inconsistent with both the prosecutor-only and the defense-only models.

Although neither attorney recommendation can be considered the sole direct cause of judicial bail decisions, it is possible that both attorney recommendations when taken together are sufficient to explain the relationships between the case factors and judicial decisions. Using the same additional-variance logic outlined previously, we found that the two attorney recommendations were capable of accounting for virtually all of the "main-effect" variance in bail: residual F (3,96) = 1.19, p = .32). Thus, the present results are not inconsistent with the complete social-influence model.

To test whether the complete social-influence model or the case-factors model provided a better account of the results, we examined the additional variance that the two attorney recommendations added to the variance that the three case factors could explain by themselves. We reasoned that if the case-factors model was correct, the addition of the two attorney recommendations should not significantly increase the variance that we could account for, since according to the case-factors model the only reason the three actors' decisions correlate with each other is that they all respond to the same case factors in a similar manner. From a different perspective, this analysis tested whether the multiple correlation between the judge and the two attorneys was due to all three decisions having a common set of causes—the three case factors. As it turned out, the two attorney recommendations considerably improved our ability to account for variation in the judges' bail decisions, F (2,96) = 603.06, p < .001, suggesting that the complete social-influence model is to be preferred over the case-factors model.

It is conceivable that one or two of the remaining case factors rather than all three of them act directly on the judge in addition to their having effects on the two attorney recommendations. If this were so, we would expect the addition to the attorney recommendations of one or two of the case factors to significantly increase the variance in judicial bail decisions. Only one of the three case factors came close, severity of crime: F (1,96) = 2.37, p = .13.

Taken together, these results suggest that the complete social-influence model provides the most parsimonious account of the real-world judicial decision data.[9] The model that assumes that the judge is independently influenced by the various case factors and by the two attorney recommendations was not supported by the results of the previous analyses. On the other hand, the previous results do not exclude the possibility that one or more of the case factors have *indirect* effects on the judges' decisions. It is conceivable, for example, that the judges respond to the attorney recommendations because they know that the attorneys are basing their recommendations on precisely those case factors that the judges would have taken into account had the attorneys been absent from the proceedings.

We examined which of the three case factors had significant effects on the prosecuting attorney and on the defense attorney in separate regression analyses. When the relationships between each case factor and one of the recommendations were examined, we found that severity of crime and community ties were both significantly related to the prosecutor's recommendation ($r = .52$ and $-.167$, respectively), but only severity of crime was significantly related to the defense attorney's recommendations ($r = .44$). The multiple main and interaction effects of these variables on the two recommendations are shown in Table 8.6. Each main and interaction "effect" represents the significance of the additional variance that each factor (or interaction) added to the remaining factors (or interactions).

As can be seen, for the prosecutor's recommendation, severity of crime is capable of accounting for the previously noted main effect of the community-ties factor. Given that the crime is known, the addition of community ties does not improve our ability to predict the prosecutor's recommendations: $F(1,99) = 1.11$. On the other hand, severity of crime and community ties did seem to interact significantly. Our analysis of the mean bail that the prosecuting attorney recommended for each level of crime within the various levels of the community-ties factor provided a picture of this interaction. Table 8.7 shows these results collapsed across several levels of crime category to increase the number of cases in each cell. The form of this

---

[9]Other explanations for the pattern of results are possible. Some would assume differential reliability of our measures. Others would point to the greater variance in the recommendations than in the case factors. Still others might attack our assumptions about error (e.g., that the errors in measurement of the different factors were uncorrelated with each other and/or with any of the measured factors) or about the lack of "third-factor causes." Finally, others might point to the lack of power in our statistical tests because of the extreme multicollinearity in our small sample. Nevertheless, the present findings still suggest that bail is not set in the real world in a manner consistent with the simple independent-judgment model that emerged from the simulation study.

Table 8.6

Results of multiple regression analyses of severity of crime, prior record, and community ties on recommendations of the prosecuting attorney and defense attorney

		F values	
Source	df	Prosecuting attorney	Defense attorney
Regression (all main and two-way interaction effects)	6	8.42[a]	4.26[a]
Regression (main effects only)	3	12.89[a]	7.93[a]
Additional (two-way interactions only)	3	9.35[a]	2.02
Main effects (additionals)			
Severity of crime (A)	1	36.99[a]	14.26[a]
Prior record (B)	1	< 1	< 1
Community ties (C)	1	1.31	< 1
Two-way linear interaction effects (additionals)			
A × B	1	1.26	< 1
A × C	1	9.05[a]	1.92
B × C	1	< 1	< 1
Mean square error	99	.15[b]	.02[b]

[a]$p < .01$.
[b]Mean square error.
SOURCE: Adapted from E. B. Ebbesen and V. J. Konečni, Decision making and information integration in the courts: The setting of bail. *Journal of Personality and Social Psychology,* 1975, *32,* 805–821. Copyright © 1975 by the American Psychological Association. Reprinted by permission.

Table 8.7

Mean bail recommended (in dollars) by prosecuting attorney as function of severity of crime and community ties

	Community ties		
Severity of crime	Weak	Moderate	Strong
Low[a]	1,000 (n = 13)	1,111 (n = 9)	738 (n = 19)
High[b]	1,999 (n = 9)	3,283 (n = 23)	5,404 (n = 29)

[a]Consisted of the two lowest levels described in the text.
[b]Consisted of the remaining levels, with the exclusion of the homicide cases.
SOURCE: Adapted from E. B. Ebbesen and V. J. Konečni, Decision making and information integration in the courts: The setting of bail. *Journal of Personality and Social Psychology,* 1975, *32,* 805–821. Copyright © 1975 by the American Psychological Association. Reprinted by permission.

interaction was quite unexpected. For less severe crimes the prose-cutors tended to recommend less bail as the strength of the defend-ants' community ties increased—exactly as recommended by the American Bar Association. On the other hand, for more severe crimes, the prosecutors acted in opposition to the ABA guidelines and actually recommended higher bail bonds as the strength of the defendants' community ties increased! Thus, being tied to the area was actually detrimental to defendants charged with more severe crimes.

Interestingly enough, even though one might expect the defense attorneys to be most responsive to the community-ties factor, severity of crime seems to control their recommendations as well as that of the prosecutors. In fact, as Table 8.6 shows, severity of crime is the only factor one needs to know in order to account for the defense attorney recommendations.

The causal processes that are most consistent with the results of these analyses can now be summarized. The judges seemed to be directly influenced by the prosecutor and the defense attorney rec-ommendations. The causal path from the prosecutor to the judge (standardized beta = .83) was considerably higher, however, than that from the defense attorney to the judge (standardized beta = .17). With the possible exception of severity of crime, none of the case factors studied appeared to have direct causal effects on the judges' decisions. Severity of crime seemed to play some role by moderating the causal relationship between the defense attorney and the judge, however. In particular, the causal influence of the defense attorney seemed greatest when the defendant was charged with a more severe crime. Finally, the impact that either attorney recommendation had on the judge increased as the recommendation of the other attorney increased.[10] It was almost as if the judges expected an own-recogni-zance recommendation from the defense attorney, and when the defense attorney recommended that some bail be set, the judges assumed that some bail amount was necessary (otherwise, the defense would have recommended own recognizance). In our sample, judges never set less bail than was recommended by the defense attorney.

Although severity of crime, prior record, and community ties did not seem to have direct causal effects on the judge, severity of crime and community ties did seem to have indirect effects by controlling

---

[10]It is possible to formalize the decision rule that the judges appear to have followed. In particular, as we discuss later, a weighted averaging model in which the weight given to the defense attorney recommendation is assumed to increase with the amount of the recommendation provides a satisfactory account of the pattern of results.

the recommendations of the two attorneys. Severity of crime interacted with community ties to determine the prosecutor recommendations. On the other hand, the defense attorney responded solely to
severity of crime. Neither attorney seemed to respond to prior record,
as we coded it, however.[11]

In sum, except for the weak role of prior record, our results were
quite consistent with previous studies. Both case and social-influence factors were important in judicial bail decisions. Thus, bail
seems to be set in San Diego in a manner quite similar to the way it
is set in other large urban areas. Severity of crime seems to be the
primary cause, although apparently it has its effects on the judge
indirectly by influencing both the prosecutor and the defense attorney recommendations, which in turn directly determine the judge's
decision.

CONCLUSIONS

The dependence of causal relations on methodology

The fact that the causal model which best described the simulation
results was different from that which described the real-world results
can be looked at from several different perspectives. It might be
argued, for example, that our simulation was not very good and that
had we designed a better (more realistic?) simulation, it would have
yielded results that were more comparable to the naturalistic data.
Although this argument may prove correct, it is important to note
that when we designed the simulation, we felt that it was quite
realistic and that it would yield results similar to those obtained
from the actual bail hearings. The point is that results from experiments that seem to have mundane realism or face validity may not
generalize. Had we not collected the real-world data, we would never
have known that the results from the simulation were caused by
a process other than that which seems to govern real-world decisions.

From a somewhat different perspective, one could attempt to minimize the differences in results from the two procedures and search

---

[11]In a more recent sample in which prior-record information was obtained from
court records rather than from the hearings, prior record was weakly related to bail
amount. Apparently, the prior-record information discussed in the hearing is not a
perfectly reliable indicator of the prior-record information that is available to the judge
(e.g., in a file that is in front of the judge) when the bail decision is made. In short, the
information about particular case factors that emerges in public court proceedings
may be different from the information in the court files that are available to the judge
but not made public. This raises the possibility that our results from the real-world
study represent the public part of the bail-setting process only.

for commonalities. This is the approach we took in our initial discussion of this work (Ebbesen and Konečni, 1975). In particular, we
argued that the same general decision model, namely, a weighted
averaging model in which the weight (or relative importance) of the
defense attorney recommendation was monotonically related to the
size of that recommendation, could explain aspects of results from
both studies. Although it was clear that the weights that best fit the
factors and the scale values that best fit the levels within the factors
had to be different across the studies, we still felt that the fact that
some type of weighted averaging model could account for both sets
of results was worth emphasizing. After all, it could have been the
case that, say, a multiplying model explained the data from one study,
but a configural model worked best for the other study. If a similar
decision process did underlie both data sets, it suggested that something useful would be found by conducting the kinds of simulation
studies that are so common in social psychology.

Since our original report, however, we have changed our position
on this issue. It is clear that had we behaved like most social psychologists and conducted only the simulation (relying on our belief
in its mundane realism), we would not have concluded that a
weighted averaging model was the likely decision process. This
model was suggested to us by the pattern of results in the real-world
data. After the fact, a weighted averaging model is general enough to
account for a wide range of findings, including those that we obtained
from the simulation. In short, the fact that one model can be found
to explain the results from both studies should not be taken as evidence that simulation research will lead to the same general conclusions as do its real-world counterparts. On the other hand, the fact
that a weighted averaging model can explain the behavior of judges
in the real world is a finding worth emphasizing, especially if it is
realized that the model only describes part of the entire causal
process that determines how bail is set.

The multimethod approach to social research emphasized by
Campbell and his associates (Campbell and Stanley, 1966; Webb et
al., 1966) assumes that all methods have biases, that through the use
of different methods the different biases will (hopefully) cancel each
other out, and that what remains is as good an approximation of the
truth as we can get. This argument applies equally well to the measurement of unobservable states such as attitudes, values, and feelings and to the assessment of causal processes. Applying this
approach to the results from the two studies that we have reported
here (and to our research on other decision-makers in the legal system; see Chapter 11, this volume) is difficult, however. We have
already noted that a weighted averaging model can describe both data

sets. On the other hand, the only factor common to both models is the prosecutor recommendation. It would seem silly to conclude both that judges set bail by taking a weighted average of several different sources of information and that only one source of information causes the judges' decision! We prefer, in part for reasons that we have outlined elsewhere (Konečni and Ebbesen, 1979; and Chapter 2, this volume), to assume that our real-world data, even with its own peculiar biases, provides a far more accurate and useful view of the bail-setting process than do the data from the simulation or even than the view that emerges from the common features of both studies. Underlying this assumption is our belief that our simulation and most others are likely to have more biases and sources of error than carefully done observations of the real world. But in addition, we worry that the types of conclusions that may "fall out" of attempts to combine results from different methods will be so general as to be of little practical use.

Even if one wishes to conclude from our work that a basic decision process, a weighted averaging integration rule, underlies judicial bail decisions (say, by adding the defense attorney recommendation to the model), this conclusion has no applied significance until the weights of the factors and the scaling of levels within the factors are specified. Until they are specified, prediction of judicial behavior is not possible. As should be obvious from the previously described results, quite different estimates for weights and scale values are obtained from the simulation than from the real-world study. These different estimates imply quite different models of bail setting. For example, from the simulation we concluded that judges respond primarily to the strength of the defendant's community ties, that prior record and prosecutor recommendation both have significant weights but are of low magnitude compared to the weight given to community-ties information, and that the defense attorney recommendation is unimportant. In contrast, from the real-world study we concluded that the prosecutor recommendation was the most important factor, that the effect of community ties was indirect (had no direct effect on the judges) and interacted with severity of crime, that the defense attorney recommendation was *not* ignored by the judge, and that severity of crime rather than community ties was the primary factor controlling the recommendations by the two attorneys. Thus, the simulation results are largely consistent with the Vera Institute and American Bar Association guidelines and suggest that judges believe the primary function of bail is to insure the appearance of defendants at pretrial court hearings. In contrast, the real-world results are inconsistent (and in the case of severe crimes directly opposite to) Vera Institute and ABA guidelines and suggest that judges believe the primary function of bail is either to protect the community and court personnel from predicted criminal activities and/or to punish the defendant for current criminal activities.[12] In short, even though one might argue that the "same" basic process underlies judicial bail-setting decisions no matter how measured, the details of the picture of bail setting that one obtains from the two studies are quite different and lead to very different conclusions about the policy that seems to guide judicial bail decisions.

An evaluation of the bail system

An evaluation of the utility of judicial bail-setting and pretrial-release strategies can be made in light of the particular functions that the bail system should serve.[13] If it is agreed that the function of bail is to increase the likelihood of appearance, then deciding how much bail to set on the basis of factors that do not predict the likelihood of appearance—even though these factors might predict the likelihood of rearrest—would not seem to be a useful strategy. On the other hand, the identical decision strategy could be quite useful if the principal function of bail were to reduce the likelihood of criminal activity during the pretrial interval.[14]

If decision strategies can only be evaluated in the context of particular functions of bail, then it is important to ask how the function of bail should be determined. Unfortunately, there is no clear method. As already noted, Supreme Court decisions provide conflicting views. Even the judges who set bail daily do not generally agree on what the function of bail should be. For example, as part of our project, we interviewed judges and asked them their views on this topic.

---

[12] Another conclusion consistent with the real-world data is that judges believe that the primary function of bail is to insure appearance but also incorrectly believe that the best predictor of appearance is severity of the crime rather than strength of community ties.

[13] To the extent that the bail decision is seen as an attempt to control *predicted* behaviors of defendants, the pretrial decision has much in common with the civil commitment of persons believed to be mentally ill. In both cases, the function of the decision is to prevent (or cause) certain predicted behaviors. In fact, in some states dangerousness to self and others—common criteria in civil commitment cases—are proposed as factors relevant in the bail decision (see Table 8.1).

[14] If bail is designed to control predicted criminal behavior, one wonders to whom these predictions ought to apply. If accurate predictions of criminal behavior are possible and if aspects of the current crime play little role in these predictions, then one might apply the same prediction model to anyone, whether currently charged with a crime or not. In short, if one function of bail is to control predicted criminal behavior, it is important to ask what criteria should be used to decide whether a given individual belongs in the sample of people that the court considers for bail or detention.

Although the majority of the judges stressed appearance as the primary function, others suggested that the control of pretrial criminal activity was either a primary or a secondary function of the bail system. Even if there had been greater agreement among the judges' verbal reports, we would not know what to make of the agreed-upon function. As we have emphasized (see Chapters 1 and 2, this volume), the reports that judges (and others) give about their decision-making may not reflect the causal processes that seem to best describe their actual decisions. Whether these reports are designed to reflect the way judges believe the decisions ought to be made or merely reflect the fact that judges are reporting noncausal aspects of their decision-making is not known. In fact, it is quite reasonable to suppose that judicial decisions might be guided by considerations that are rarely verbalized, even informally. Some judges may use a decision strategy that coincides with what they believe the public or other members of the legal system view as a reasonable strategy, even though that strategy may not satisfy the function these other groups believe it does. For example, the public may believe that the severity of a crime is a good indicator of the likelihood that the accused will commit additional crimes and therefore expect that high bail bonds will be set in such cases. Thus, even though there is little evidence linking the severity of the current charge with the likelihood of rearrest, a judge's decisions might be considered useful because they coincide with public demands. Appeasing public outcries for protection against *potentially* dangerous individuals may be an important function of bail decisions, even though such decisions might be considered contrary to due process rights.

As we have emphasized, attempting to discover what the judges regard as the function of bail by conducting simulation experiments is likely to yield results that are not much better than those obtained from simple interviews with the judges. One wonders, in fact, whether the multiattribute-utility approach used so frequently by decision analysts (e.g., Edwards, Guttentag, and Snapper, 1975) to help decision-makers choose among complex alternatives can provide any better picture of the values and goals of decision-makers than can experimental simulations. In such applied research, the decision-maker is often asked which goals or attributes of the alternatives are important and what the relevant weights of these goals are. When we have done similar things (although admittedly not in as formal a manner as is typical of decision analysts), we have found that the goals elicited and weights obtained depend, at least to some extent, on the method used to obtain them (Ebbesen and Konečni, 1976; Konečni and Ebbesen, 1979). In short, attempts to characterize the function of bail by asking relevant "experts" what the function should be may yield as method-specific an answer as we argue is obtained from experimental simulations. Goals and values may be as labile as causal processes (Fischhoff, Slovic, and Lichtenstein, 1980).

Reaching agreement concerning the function that the bail system should serve is not the only issue making evaluation of the bail system difficult, however. It is conceivable that procedures other than the setting of bail bonds can better achieve that function. For example, Clark, Freeman, and Koch (1976) suggest that shortening the delay between arrest and disposition will tend to have a much larger impact on appearance and rearrest than imposing bail (unless the latter leads to detention). It is also possible that some forms of posting bail are more effective than others. For example, Landes (1974) reported that the amount of bail was related to appearance, but only when the defendant had to deposit the entire amount of bond with the court. In those cases in which a written promise to pay, along with a small fraction of the total bond, was given to the court, the size of the bond was unrelated to the likelihood that the defendant would appear. In the Clark et al. (1976) study, bonds paid by bail bondsmen did not seem to be as effective in controlling appearance as bonds paid by the defendants themselves. In short, when one focuses on the effectiveness of different procedures for controlling the pretrial behavior of the defendant, one must conclude that at present the utility of bail is unknown.

Prediction errors also play an important role in an evaluation of the bail system. Not only should the total number of prediction errors be examined, but a system for weighting different types of errors needs to be established. Is it worse to detain defendants who would not have been rearrested and would have appeared had they been released on their own recognizance, or is it worse to release defendants who commit additional crimes and/or do not appear? Since it is likely that the selection of high-risk defendants will never be perfectly accurate, it is essential to have a decision system that not only minimizes errors (e.g., Nagel and Neef, 1976), but also defines acceptable trade-offs between different types of errors. Trade-off functions that weight errors not only according to type but also according to defendant characteristics might even be developed. For example, incorrectly detaining a mother of a 1-month-old child might be considered worse than incorrectly detaining an unemployed male with no living relatives. Finally, bail decisions may well have multiple consequences, some of which have little to do with the pretrial behavior of the defendant. There is evidence, for example, that being detained increases the likelihood that a defendant will be convicted of a crime (Rankin, 1964; Single, 1972) and if convicted will receive a prison sentence (Friedland, 1965; Chapter 11, this volume). Such consequences should be included in the evaluation of a particular strategy. Until these and similar issues are resolved, evaluation of the usefulness of the bail system will be difficult if not impossible, except along dimensions that everyone would agree should characterize discretionary decisions, such as equal treatment for equal cases (see Chapter 13, this volume).

Given the research that has been done thus far, the amount of variation in both nonappearances and rearrests that is accounted for by aspects of the current crime, prior record, and community ties seems minimal, at best. Therefore, any judicial bail-setting strategy based only on these factors is bound to result in many decision errors. Too much bail will be set in some cases, and too little in others. Thus, the important role that severity of crime seems to play in determining the amount of bail set is in no way consistent with the predictive utility of this factor. It is of interest, therefore, to ask why severity of crime plays the role it does when its predictive validity is so poor. Judges may be unaware of the lack of predictive validity of this factor, they may realize the problem but not know how to improve the situation, or they may not see their decisions as prediction errors because they believe bail serves a different function from those specified here, for example, a partial punishment for the current charge.

Adequate knowledge of the kinds of prediction errors that different decision strategies are likely to produce is not yet available because identification of errors depends on having agreement about the function that bail should serve and knowing what role particular case factors should play in that function. Much future research should be directed at discovering factors that predict and control the pretrial behavior of defendants on the assumption that most agree that a primary function of bail is to control pretrial behavior. As the work by Gottfredson (1974) shows, an essential aspect of such research is that it include validation-sample assessments of the predictive ability of different models.

The determination of the extent to which judges are employing a useful decision strategy (given agreement about the function of the decision node), also needs to be accomplished carefully. As our work on bail suggests, simulation procedures must be evaluated with much more care than is typically done. As another example, Ebbesen and Konečni (1981) described results concerning individual differences among judges in their sentencing decisions. They found that the same *causal model* (see Chapter 11, this volume) seemed to apply to each judge, even though many simulated judicial-sentencing studies (e.g., O'Donnell, Churgin, and Curtis, 1977) have suggested that judges differ widely in their sentencing decision strategies. Judges' motivations may be quite different in simulation studies than in the courtroom.

In our bail research, one explanation for the pattern of results in the simulation is that the judges were attempting to present themselves as behaving consistently with Vera Institute guidelines. An alternative explanation is that the judges may *believe* that they make bail decisions largely on the basis of community ties. Then, when asked to make simulated decisions, the judges may respond to each case by asking themselves how they *would* respond had this been a real case. If judges spend some proportion of their time in each real case thinking about the community ties of the defendant without these thoughts having any causal effect on the final decision, then the judges might determine what they would have done by remembering what they think about in real cases. In short, the simulations may have tapped the judges' phenomenology about their own decision processes. There is no need to assume, however, that this phenomenology accurately describes the causal process guiding their decisions in the real world.

Social influence in the bail system

Although additional research is clearly required, the fact that judges seem to be strongly influenced by the recommendations of the prosecutor and the defense attorney is of considerable interest. The bail hearing has an adversary tone, much like a trial. The prosecutor and the defense attorney often disagree about the way to treat a defendant during the pretrial period. These disagreements arise from legitimate differences in the goals of the two attorneys. Defense attorneys are probably attempting to protect their clients and to obtain the best possible treatment for them. Prosecutors, on the other hand, are probably trying to insure that the defendant will be sanctioned appropriately for the current charge as well as trying to prevent the defendant from committing additional crimes. If, as our results suggest, judges are more influenced by prosecuting attorney recommendations than by defense attorney recommendations, then the court is siding with the prosecutor's motivations rather than acting as an independent fact finder or as an unbiased arbitrator.

On the other hand, the court is generally ill-equipped to serve either of the latter two functions. Fact finding is an essential part of arbitration, yet the time given to bail hearings (they rarely last more than a few minutes), the lack of knowledge concerning which facts might be relevant, and the method by which the facts are obtained (from the reports of the two adversaries) virtually prevent the court from being a successful fact-finding arbitrator. The court is virtually forced to rely on the recommendations of the two attorneys, although both are clearly biased.

Although the court must gather its information from others, it is not necessary that it be more influenced by one as opposed to another class of individuals. It is unclear why prosecutors have more influence on the bail decision than do defense attorneys. One possible explanation is that the prosecutor's recommendations are more likely to agree with what the public expects; i.e., potentially dangerous criminals should be treated harshly (even if such treatment violates due process). Along similar lines, the judge may consider that setting bail too high is less worrisome than setting it too low. The latter can result in community harm, the former hurts only the defendant.

Alternatively, in line with our previous comments about the detection of errors, unnecessarily high bail recommendations by the prosecutor are not likely to be discovered by the judge or anyone else, because in such cases defendants often are unable to obtain the bond amount and are detained in jail. On the other hand, unnecessarily low bail recommendations by the defense attorney can be detected if the defendant does not appear when scheduled or is arrested for additional crimes after being released. In short, prosecuting attorney recommendations may be seen as more accurate, and therefore more reasonable, than defense attorney recommendations, even though the relative accuracy of the two recommendations is more or less equal.

Another factor that could bias the judge in favor of the prosecutor is that the variability of defense recommendations is necessarily less than the variability of prosecutor recommendations. The range of defense recommendations is limited at the upper end by the prosecutor's recommendation and at the lower end by release on one's own recognizance. The defense cannot have a differential effect when low prosecutor recommendations are given. The only reasonable response available to the defense if the prosecutor recommends, say, $1,000 bail, is release on one's own recognizance. However, the defense cannot recommend negative bail when the prosecutor only recommends, say, $500. Release on one's own recognizance is still the best that the defense can do. Thus, the prosecutor's recommendation will tend to control variation in the judge's decision when the recommendation is low enough that the defense attorney's only response is release on one's own recognizance.

The fact that prosecutors seem to have more influence on the amount of bail set than do defense attorneys is not a sufficient explanation for the role that severity of the crime seems to play in bail setting. It will be recalled that the defense attorney recommendation was also best predicted by severity of the crime. Community ties simply did not predict defense recommendations.

These results are of special interest because defense attorneys typically supported their recommendations not by focusing on aspects of the current crime and/or prior record, but rather by emphasizing positive features of the defendant's community ties. In short, even though defense attorneys seemed to speak mostly about community ties, they apparently based their own recommendations on severity of the crime. One wonders whether defense attorneys are aware of this discrepancy in their behavior. Could it be that the arguments they present are for the defendant's ears, rather than the court's?

References

American Bar Association. Project on *Standards for Criminal Justice. Standards Relating to Pretrial Release.* New York: American Bar Association, 1968.

Applebaum, M. I., & Cramer, E. M. Some problems in the nonorthogonal analysis of variance. *Psychological Bulletin,* 1974, *81,* 335–343.

Ares, C., Rankin, A., & Sturz, H. The Manhattan Bail project: An interim report on the use of pretrial parole. *New York University Law Review,* 1963, *38,* 67–95.

Beeley, A. *The bail system in Chicago.* Chicago: University of Chicago Press, 1927.

Bottomley, A. *Prison before trial: A study of remand decisions in magistrates' courts.* London: Bell, 1970.

Campbell, D. T., & Stanley, J. C. *Experimental and quasi-experimental designs for research.* Chicago: Rand McNally, 1963.

Carlson v. Landon. 72 U.S. 525 (1952).

Clark, S. H., Freeman, J. L., & Koch, G. G. Bail risk: A multivariate analysis. *Journal of Legal Studies,* 1976, *5,* 341–386.

Cohen, J. Multiple regression as a general data-analytic system. *Psychological Bulletin,* 1968, *70,* 426–443.

Coombs, C. H. Thurstone's measurement of social values revisited forty years later. *Journal of Personality and Social Psychology,* 1967, *6,* 85–90.

Ebbesen, E. B., & Konečni, V. J. Decision making and information integration in the courts: The setting of bail. *Journal of Personality and Social Psychology,* 1975, *32,* 805–821.

Ebbesen, E. B., & Konečni, V. J. Fairness in sentencing: Severity of crime and judicial decision making. Paper presented at 84th Annual Convention of American Psychological Association, Washington, DC, 1976.

Ebbesen, E. B., & Konečni, V. J. On the external validity of decision-making research: What do we know about decisions in the real world? In T. S. Wallsten (Ed.), *Cognitive processes in choice and decision behavior.* Hillsdale, NJ: Lawrence Erlbaum, 1980.

Ebbesen, E. B., & Konečni, V. J. The process of sentencing adult felons: A causal analysis of judicial decisions. In B. D. Sales (Ed.), *Perspectives in law and psychology.* Vol. 2: *The jury, judicial, and trial process.* New York: Plenum, 1981.

Edwards, W., Guttentag, M., & Snapper, K. Effective evaluation: A decision theoretic approach. In C. A. Bennett and A. Lumsdaine (Eds.), *Evaluation and experiment:*

Some critical issues in assessing social programs. New York: Academic Press, 1975.

Fischhoff, B., Slovic, P., & Lichtenstein, S. Knowing what you want: Measuring labile values. In T. S. Wallsten (Ed.), *Cognitive processes in choice and decision behavior.* Hillsdale, NJ: Erlbaum, 1980.

Foote, C. A study of the administration of bail in New York City. *University of Pennsylvania Law Review,* 1958, *106,* 693–730.

Foote, C., Markle, J., & Woolley, E. Compelling appearance in court: Administration of bail in Philadelphia. *University of Pennsylvania Law Review,* 1954, *102,* 1031–1079.

Freed, D. J., & Wald, P. M. *Bail in the United States: 1964.* Washington, DC: U.S. Department of Justice, 1964.

Friedland, M. L. Detention before trial: A study of criminal cases tried in the Toronto magistrates' courts. Toronto: University of Toronto Press, 1965.

Goldfarb, R. L. *Ransom.* New York: Harper & Row, 1965.

Goldkamp, J. S. *Bail decisionmaking and the role of pretrial detention in American justice.* Unpublished Ph.D. dissertation, State University of New York at Albany, 1977.

Gottfredson, M. An empirical analysis of pretrial release decisions. *Journal of Criminal Justice,* 1974, *2,* 287–304.

Konečni, V. J., & Ebbesen, E. B. External validity of research in legal psychology. *Law and Human Behavior,* 1979, *3,* 39–70.

Landes, W. M. Legality and reality: Some evidence on criminal procedure. *Journal of Legal Studies,* 1974, *3,* 287–338.

Meehl, P., & Rosen, A. Antecedent probability and the efficiency of psychometric signs, patterns, or cutting scores. *Psychological Bulletin,* 1955, *52,* 194–216.

Nagel, S., & Neef, M. Bail, not jail, for more defendants. *Judicature,* 1976, *60,* 172–178.

O'Donnell, P., Churgin, M. J., & Curtis, D. E. *Toward a just and effective sentencing system: Agenda for legislative reform.* New York: Praeger, 1977.

Overall, J. E., & Spiegal, D. K. Concerning least squares analysis of experimental data. *Psychological Bulletin,* 1969, *72,* 311–322.

President's Commission on Law Enforcement and the Administration of Justice. *The challenge of crime in a free society.* Washington, DC: U.S. Government Printing Office, 1967.

Rankin, A. The effect of pretrial detention. *New York University Law Review,* 1964, *39,* 641–653.

Single, E. W. The unconstitutional administration of bail: Bellamy v. the judges of New York City. *Criminal Law Bulletin,* 1972, *8,* 459–471.

Stack v. Boyle, 342 U.S. 1 (1951).

Suffert, F. Bail setting: A study of courtroom interaction. *Crime and Delinquency,* 1966, *12,* 318–331.

Thomas, D. A decade of bail reform. Unpublished manuscript, 1974, cited in *An evaluation of policy-related research on the effectiveness of pretrial release programs.* Washington, DC: National Center for State Courts, 1975.

Vera Institute of Justice. *Fair treatment for the indigent: The Manhattan Bail Project. Programs in criminal justice reform: Ten-year report, 1961–1971.* New York: Vera Institute, 1972.

Wald, P. M. Pre-trial detention and ultimate freedom: A statistical study. *New York University Law Review,* 1964, *39,* 631–648.

Webb, E. J., Campbell, D. T., Schwartz, R. D., & Sechrest, L. *Unobtrusive measures: Nonreactive research in the social sciences.* Chicago: Rand McNally, 1966.

THE DECISION TO PROSECUTE

Editors' Introduction

Prosecutors occupy a central and multifunctional position in the U.S. criminal justice system. Prosecutors can decide to initiate investigations of persons or organizations suspected of criminal activity (for whatever reasons the particular prosecutor believes are relevant). Charges brought by the police against defendants can be dismissed, reduced, increased, or elaborated by prosecutors. Prosecutors recommend whether and how much bail ought to be set, interview witnesses, prepare and evaluate evidence, control plea and sentence bargaining, argue their cases at probable cause hearings, occasionally represent the state in trials, and make recommendations concerning the sentence convicted offenders should receive. In short, prosecutors are often involved in many of the major decision nodes in the criminal justice system.

At certain of these nodes, prosecutors make the decision that determines how a case will progress through the rest of the system, for example, by filing a felony complaint or recommending that the charges include only misdemeanor violations. At other nodes, prosecutors act to influence the decisions of others. This chapter examines that part of the prosecutor's activities that have a direct influence on the disposition of cases: namely, the screening process. Unlike other frequently studied decisions, both in and out of the legal system, Gelman argues that the screening decision takes place over a long period of time and can best be conceptualized in terms of several decision stages.

To show the usefulness of the stage model, Gelman examines the differences in the rates of different types of dispositional decisions in two U.S. cities. This strategy of studying gross (base-rate) statistics across different jurisdictions is of interest for several reasons. First, such data clearly reflect the real-world operation of the criminal justice system. In fact, the differences in the use of various types of dispositions from one jurisdiction to another supports the need for more real-world studies of legal decision-making. The generality of findings concerning such decisions may be limited not only by the methodology that is used (e.g., simulations versus observations of real-world events) but also by the jurisdiction(s) from which the data are obtained. It seems unlikely that a simulation (as typically done) would be capable of discovering such jurisdictional differences.

A second feature of Gelman's approach is that although it does not provide direct evidence concerning the reasons for the differences across the jurisdictions studied, it highlights the possibility that a number of different kinds of causal processes might be acting at once on prosecutor decisions. In particular, it is likely that broad administrative policies, differences in organization within departments, case loads, political pressure, the types of crimes that are prevalent in a jurisdiction, and local attitudes toward various types of illegal activities may determine how various case factors are subjectively evaluated, weighted, and combined to determine the screening decisions of prosecutors. Although work is currently being done at the Institute for Law and Social Research to examine such issues, relevant data were not available when Gelman wrote his chapter. Therefore, Gelman's chapter focuses primarily on the fact and type of jurisdictional differences in screening decisions. Hopefully, future research will clarify the reasons for such differences in decision-making.

9

Prosecutorial Decision-Making:
The Screening Process

Arthur M. Gelman

The dominant figure in the criminal justice system, the person with the greatest responsibility for enforcing the laws that make up our system of justice, is the prosecutor. Throughout the past several years there has been an increasing awareness of the power of the prosecutor: the power to decide against whom charges will be filed, the power to decide what charges will be filed, the power to decide who will plead guilty to committing what illegal act. Moreover, there is a burgeoning, though implicit, effort to grant prosecutors even more power: the ability to directly influence the sentencing decision. Recent legislation passed in a number of states has apparently shifted at least some sentencing discretion from trial judges to prosecuting attorneys (Alschuler, 1978).[1]

LEGISLATIVE AND JUDICIAL INTERVENTION:
THE NATURE OF PROSECUTOR DISCRETION

Perhaps the most surprising development in prosecutors' dominance of the system is that the legislative and judicial branches of government have avoided confrontation with prosecutors over the exercise of their authority. In regard to the legislature, it seems as if there are two explanations for this reluctance: first, legislators are fearful of

---

[1]This is especially true in states having statutes that prescribe mandatory minimum terms for convicted offenders, e.g., New York (drug laws) and Massachusetts (possession of a weapon). However, similar results are likely under presumptive sentencing reforms.

sponsoring or supporting legislation that may result, even inaccurately, in their being labeled as "soft on crime"; second, the political image of prosecutors as leaders in society's effort to enforce its laws has provided them with a protective shield.

The judiciary has also exercised a good deal of restraint in this area. This seems atypical because the courts have consistently intervened in the exercise of discretionary powers by the police—powers comparable to those exercised by prosecutors.[2] The courts have found the doctrine of separation of powers to be applicable to prosecutors' conduct and have therefore consistently refused to review prosecutorial decisions. One of the most prominent examples of a case that reached that conclusion was United States v. Cox (1965), in which the Court of Appeals for the Fifth Circuit overturned a contempt citation issued against a United States Attorney who refused to file charges after a grand jury wanted to indict two individuals. The court stated:

> Although as a member of the bar, the attorney for the United States is an officer of the court, he is nevertheless an executive official of the Government, and it is as an officer of the executive department that he exercises a discretion as to whether or not there shall be a prosecution in a particular case. It follows, as an incident of the constitutional separation of powers, that the courts are not to interfere with the free exercise of the discretionary powers of the attorneys of the United States in their control over criminal prosecution. (United States v. Cox, 1965, p. 171)

A second case that illustrates the judiciary's restraint, and perhaps an even more important one because the opinion was rendered by then Circuit Court Judge Warren Burger, is Newman v. United States (1967). In that case, the court was to decide whether there had been a denial of Newman's constitutional rights when a prosecutor accepted a plea from a codefendant for a lesser included offense (under the indictment), but refused to consent to a similar plea from Newman despite the fact that both individuals appeared to have engaged in similar behavior. Burger ruled that the exercise of discretion by the executive branch in deciding whether to file charges against an individual and whether to dismiss those charges later did not easily lend itself to judicial review. He stated that it was the responsibility of the President, as the Chief Executive, to supervise

---

[2]See, e.g., the following topic areas in which the U.S. Supreme Court has rendered opinions: Chimel v. California (1969), search incident to an arrest; Katz v. United States (1967), electronic surveillance; Miranda v. Arizona (1966), interrogations; Neil v. Biggers (1972), pretrial identification procedures; Terry v. Ohio (1962), search and seizure; United States v. Russell (1973), entrapment.

and discipline his subordinates and that it was "not the function of the judiciary" to review the exercise of that discretion regardless of whether it was exercised by the President or his delegate.

However, the *Cox* and *Newman* decisions should not be interpreted as placing an absolute prohibition on the power of the judiciary to review prosecutors' screening decisions. There are some narrowly defined circumstances in which the courts, relying on the equal protection clause, have shown an interest in granting relief to a defendant who can establish that the prosecutor acted in bad faith. Indeed, the landmark case in this area dates back to 1886, when the United States Supreme Court held that the practice of enforcing certain municipal ordinances against only those persons of Chinese origin represented a violation of the equal protection clause (*Yick Wo v. Hopkins,* 1886).[3]

It was not until 1953, however, that the Supreme Court elaborated on that decision, stating that there must be a showing of "systematic or intentional discrimination" before relief can be granted (*Edelman v. California,* 1953). Nine years later, the Court further narrowed the standard by articulating the principle that the exercise of some selectivity in prosecution was not, in and of itself, a violation of the Constitution. To show such a violation, the defendant had to establish that the selectivity was motivated by an improper factor (*Oyler v. Boles,* 1962). Thus, a two-pronged test to establish discriminatory prosecution emerged. First, one had to demonstrate that other members of the same or a similar class had not been prosecuted; second, one had to prove that the discrimination was based on an unjustifiable standard. Statistics are generally available to certify the first element of the test; however, it is very difficult to prove that an unjustifiable standard was in fact utilized (Cox, 1976).

In 1973, the Seventh Circuit sought to make the task somewhat easier by shifting the burden of proof to the prosecutor when a defendant who alleges discriminatory prosecution presents enough factual evidence to create a strong inference that an unjustifiable standard was applied (*United States v. Falk,* 1973).[4] Nevertheless, even

---

[3]In holding that the duty to provide equal protection of the laws applied to the executive branch of government as well as to the legislative branch, the Court stated: "Though the law itself be fair on its face and impartial in appearance, if it is applied and administered by public authority with an evil eye and unequal hand, so as practically to make unjust and illegal discriminations between persons in similar circumstances, material to their rights, the denial of equal justice is still within the prohibition of the Constitution." (*Yick Wo v. Hopkins* [1886], at 373–374)

[4]It should be noted, however, that *Falk* involved a combination of three elements: massive nonenforcement of a (Selective Service) statute, an infringement of First Amendment rights, and an improper prosecutorial motive to chill those rights. The court did not resolve the question of whether the existence of massive nonenforcement alone would be enough to invalidate a prosecution (Work, Richman, and Williams, 1976; Note, 1974).

creating a strong inference is difficult; consequently, there have been few successful challenges to prosecutorial charging decisions.[5]

The screening process, though, involves more than just deciding what charge, if any, should be filed in a given case. Clearly, those postfiling decisions that affect the prosecutor's ability to dismiss a case are important steps in the process (Work, Richman, and Williams, 1976). On the federal level, Criminal Procedure Rule 48(a) requires leave of court before dismissal of an indictment, information, or complaint. Furthermore, since dismissals under this rule are without prejudice, the defendant's consent must be obtained before a dismissal may be filed after a trial has begun.

Despite the leave-of-court requirement, and the explicit recognition that the trial judge has the discretion to determine whether the dismissal of charges is in the public interest, the judiciary has been reluctant to exercise its authority. Although some of the District Courts have expressed the concern that the trial judge not be a "rubber stamp" to a government motion to dismiss an indictment,[6] neither the Supreme Court nor the Circuit Courts have given any indication that they would support a policy that closely scrutinized these postfiling decisions. For example, the Fifth Circuit ruled that the judiciary should not usurp or interfere with a good-faith effort on the part of the executive to ensure that the laws are faithfully executed:

> The executive remains the absolute judge of whether a prosecution should be initiated and the first and presumably the best judge of whether a pending prosecution should be terminated. The exercise of this discretion with respect to the termination of pending prosecution should not be judicially disturbed unless clearly contrary to manifest public interest. (*United States* v. *Cowan*, 1976, p. 513)

The court reasoned that a policy of nonintervention would protect the synchronized, interactive relationship of the three branches of government—a relationship it viewed as essential to maintaining a balanced system of government.[7]

---

[5]The primary obstacle faced by a defendant is obtaining the information needed to create a reasonable doubt as to the purpose of a particular prosecution. However, at least three commentators note that the development and use of computerized information systems will make it easier to access that information (Work, Richman, and Williams, 1976).

[6]The court stated that not only did it have to protect the defendant from "harassing motions" but it also had the responsibility of "protecting the interests of the public on whose behalf the criminal action is brought." That was especially true when the matter came before the court on indictment rather than information.

[7]The court reasoned that Rule 48(a) was not promulgated to shift absolute power from the executive to the judiciary. Instead, the rule was intended to support the premise that power should check power.

On the state level, most jurisdictions, either by statute, court rule, or judicial decision, have also authorized the trial judge to decide whether to grant a dismissal of a pending criminal prosecution.[8] The usual standard to be applied in making that determination is whether the dismissal is "in the public interest." However, judicial decisions interpreting that standard are rather sparse. One of the few courts to make any attempt to define which dismissals would be in the public interest could only state that a case-by-case approach that considered the effect of the dismissal on the general welfare of the public should be utilized (*State v. Kenyon* [1978]).

PREVIOUS STUDIES OF PROSECUTORIAL DECISION-MAKING

Despite the reluctance of the other branches of government to closely monitor the working of the prosecutor, the office has not escaped the watchful eye of numerous commentators and national commissions. Most of the literature on prosecution can be characterized as falling within at least one of three broad categories:

1. *Descriptive:* detailing the workings of a prosecutor's office in a case (Abrams, 1975; Kaplan, 1965; Miller, 1969) or empirical study (Brosi, 1979; Cole, 1970; Greenwood et al., 1973; Rabin, 1972).

2. *Theoretical:* presenting various philosophies that attempt to distinguish between and explain the workings of various prosecutors' offices (Abrams, 1971; Friedman, 1978; Jacoby, 1977; LaFave, 1970).

3. *Suggestive:* proposing various reforms or standards to help structure the exercise of prosecutive discretion (Abrams, 1971; American Bar Association Project on Standards for Criminal Justice, 1971; Davis, 1969; National Advisory Commission on Criminal Justice Standards and Goals, 1973; National District Attorneys Association, 1977; Noll, 1978).

---

[8]See, e.g., *People ex rel. Kuntsman v. Shinsaku Nagano* (1945); *Denham v. Robinson* (1913); Arizona Rules of Criminal Procedure, 15.5; Georgia Code Annotated (1972); Washington Criminal Rules, 8.3. But see, e.g., Louisiana Code Criminal Procedures Annotated (1979): "The district attorney has the power, in his discretion, to dismiss an indictment or a court in an indictment, and in order to exercise that power it is not necessary that he obtain consent of the court."

Descriptive studies

The first type of study, the descriptive, has sought to detail the screening process as it is actually conducted in a jurisdiction. Although no two prosecutors' offices follow exactly the same procedures, it does seem that a large majority of offices can be classified as utilizing some variant of two basic models.

In the first model, the initial screening decision is often made by a relatively inexperienced prosecutor within hours of an arrest. The information on which that decision is based usually consists of the arresting officer's written and oral report of the circumstances of the arrest and some, perhaps unverified, information concerning the offender's prior criminal record. The decision is then subject to review by an experienced supervisory attorney. The postfiling decision to *nolle prosequi* is generally made by a more experienced attorney, although it may still be subject to some sort of internal review. In addition, as previously noted, the court must approve the prosecutor's request to *nolle prosequi* (Abrams, 1975; Brosi, 1979; Miller, 1969).

The second model relies more on decision-making by experienced attorneys, who may be rotated, at periodic intervals, into the filing stage of the screening process. Some offices may even utilize a specialization technique, with individual prosecutors focusing on certain types of crimes (e.g., drug cases or sex offenses). The prosecutor will usually make a decision after meeting with either the arresting officer, a detective assigned to the case, or both. When dealing with a detective, however, the prosecutor may have the option of asking for an additional investigation. Depending on office practices, the initial charging decision, along with any later decisions, may be subject to review by a supervisory attorney. The meeting, and hence the charging decision, are not likely to occur until at least 24 hours after the arrest and may not take place for a week. Moreover, in some jurisdictions, the prosecutor will not even receive the case until a probable cause hearing has already been conducted in a lower court (Abrams, 1975; Brosi, 1979; Miller, 1969).

Theoretical studies

Two of the more significant theoretical studies in this area were conducted by Abrams (1971) and by the Bureau of Social Science Research (Jacoby, 1977). Abrams wrote that "substantive prosecutorial policy" may take three different forms: nonprosecution; complete enforcement; and intermediate, or selective, enforcement. He acknowledged that the first policy, nonenforcement, is generally limited to three circumstances:

1. Those few crimes for which the attitude of the community has dramatically shifted since the enactment of the statute.

2. Those situations in which there is some doubt as to the constitutionality of the statute.

3. Jurisdictions in which civil remedies are available or an effective alternative enforcement authority exists, such as another court system.

The second policy is one of complete or strict enforcement of all cases in which the evidence supports a particular charge. Abrams comments that in carrying out this policy, the prosecutor, when in doubt as to whether the evidence is sufficient to justify a prosecution, would err in favor of filing charges against a defendant. The third policy, the one in effect in most prosecutors' offices, involves selective prosecution. Under this policy, prosecutors rely on their own intuition, training, and values, and on any published policy guidelines when deciding whether to file charges in a given case.

More recent work conducted by the Bureau of Social Science Research (Jacoby, 1977) identifies four major charging policies operating in prosecutors' offices. These policies have different labels and definitions from those cited earlier by Abrams (1971). Under the Bureau's first policy, a legally sufficient standard is applied by the prosecutor in determining whether the elements of a crime are present. If a positive determination is made, the case is referred for prosecution. The second policy, one frequently found in large urban offices, operates as a system efficiency model. Under this policy, the emphasis is on the speedy processing of cases by any available disposition. Consequently, prosecutors utilize various referral alternatives and diversion programs to help move cases through the system. The third policy focuses on the rehabilitation of the defendant. Here, prosecutors make extensive use of resources in the community to keep the offender out of the criminal justice system. Under the fourth policy, trial sufficiency, prosecutors accept a case only if the available evidence is likely to result in the conviction of the defendant. This policy assumes that any accepted case will go to trial.

The Bureau, however, wisely places two important limitations on its findings: first, it recognizes that other policies do exist and therefore, it makes no claim of exhaustiveness; second, it rejects the notion that any policy will always exist in pure form in every prosecutor's office.[9] Thus, the Bureau is completely cognizant of the inherent difficulties faced in an evaluation of the screening process.

Suggestive studies

Certainly, two of the more influential bodies to put forth proposals for reforming the screening process have been the American Bar Association and the National District Attorneys Association. In its *Standards Relating to the Prosecution Function*, the ABA explicitly states that the prosecutor "should establish standards . . . for evaluating complaints to determine whether criminal proceedings should be instituted" (American Bar Association Project on Standards for Criminal Justice, 1971, §3.4). However, the ABA is of the opinion that because too many uncertainties exist that might necessitate a decision outside a norm, the exercise of discretion could not be reduced to a narrow or rigid formula. It then goes on to list eight broadly defined characteristics of a case that a prosecutor would want to evaluate in making a charging decision.[10]

Six years later, the National District Attorneys Association took a similar position, also calling for some flexible mechanism (e.g., guidelines) that would assist prosecutors in making the charging decision. In addition, the NDAA listed 15 factors that it felt should be considered in making the screening decision. For the most part, these factors were consistent with those previously delineated by the ABA.[11] Unlike the ABA, however, the NDAA supported an "informal"

---

[9]The Bureau notes that "*a prosecutor cannot be judged by one measure alone (e.g., a dismissal rate, or rejection rate or by a simple comparison to other prosecutors) but rather that he be judged in terms of what he hopes to achieve (his policy) and how closely case dispositions approximate the goal of his policy*" (Jacoby, 1977; emphasis in original).

[10]Those factors include:

"(i)   the prosecutor's reasonable doubt that the accused is in fact guilty;
(ii)   the extent of the harm caused by the offense;
(iii)   the disproportion of the authorized punishment in relation to the particular offense or the offender;
(iv)   possible improper motives of a complainant;
(v)   prolonged non-enforcement of a statute, with community acquiescence;
(vi)   reluctance of the victim to testify;
(vii)   coooperation of the accused in the apprehension or conviction of others;
(viii) availability and likelihood of prosecution by another jurisdiction."

[11]Those factors include:

"1. Doubt as to the accused's guilt;
2. Undue hardship caused to the accused;
3. Excessive cost of prosecution in relation to the seriousness of the offense;
4. Possible deterrent value of prosecution;
5. Aid to other prosecution goals through non-prosecution;
6. The expressed wish of the victim not to prosecute;
7. The age of the case;
8. Insufficiency of admissible evidence to support a case;

in-house procedure for reviewing and, if appropriate, modifying prosecutorial screening decisions.[12]

Many commentators might take issue with such a limited review
procedure. While most have called for some type of explicit policy
guidelines to oversee the exercise of prosecutorial screening decisions (Abrams, 1971; American Bar Association, 1971; Beck, 1978;
Comment, 1969; Kress, 1976; National Advisory Commission, 1973;
National District Attorneys Association, 1977; Vorenberg, 1976), a
number of them, including Davis (1969), have also called for some
form of judicial review.[13] These individuals feel that in addition to
examining the merits of prosecutors' decisions, a review would help
ensure the equal treatment of similarly situated offenders.

The decision-making process

Most of the literature has generally overlooked the basic decision-
making process undertaken by the prosecutor. This chapter will focus
on that process at the screening stage of the criminal justice system.
Although at first glance seemingly limited in importance, the screening decision, because of its direct bearing on eventual conviction, is
the most significant decision that prosecutors make and could be

---

   9. Attitude and mental state of the defendant;
  10. Possible improper motives of a victim or witness;
  11. A history of non-enforcement of the statute at issue;
  12. Likelihood of prosecution by another criminal justice authority;
  13. The availability of suitable diversion programs;
  14. Any mitigating circumstances; and
  15. Any provisions for restitution."

[12]The NDAA comments that an opportunity for an appeal (through the prosecutor)
of a charging decision should be provided concerned citizens or law-enforcement
officials.

[13]Davis argues: "The reasons for a judicial check of prosecutors' discretion are
stronger than for such a check of other administrative discretion that is now traditionally reviewable" (Davis, 1969, pp. 211–212, emphasis in original; see also Noll,
1978; Comment, 1974; National Advisory Commission, 1973). But Abrams argues that
the "ready availability of judicial review could interfere with the rapid development
of the desired type of internal controls": "Making judicial review available to correct
abuses in the initiation of prosecutions would mean that every defendant could claim
that his prosecution violates existing policy, express or implied, and also that the
policy itself is not a valid exercise of discretion. Despite the fact that few defendants
would be likely to succeed on such issues, the claims would be raised anyway since
the criminal defendant is already in court and his motivation is strong to make any
argument that either delays the process or provides even the remotest chance of success. Consequently, considerable prosecutorial and judicial resources would be
expended litigating about policy, resources that would be much better spent in the
formulation and development of policy. This expenditure of resources would
obviously be required if significant benefits to the individual defendant or the administration of criminal justice could be anticipated from such review. My judgment is
that the clogging of the system which would result far outweighs the possible benefits"
(Abrams, 1971, p. 52). See Note (1974), which cites two difficulties inherent in judicial
review of prosecutorial decision-making: the need for prosecutive secrecy and solic-
itude for the accused.

considered the most important decision made in the entire criminal justice system. The decision, however, is not an isolated event occurring at one particular moment. Instead, it is a series of decisions made at various points throughout the official, and even the unofficial, disposition process. Thus, from the perspective of the prosecutor, screening is best defined as incorporating any decision that, based on available information, has the potential to effectively terminate the possibility of government intervention in the life of a particular individual. This definition attempts to broaden the spectrum of the screening process to include all decisions made by a representative of the prosecutor's office that may result in the full and complete dismissal of a case.

The initial step in examining the screening process is to distinguish between the two types of decisions that are made. First, there are those decisions made on the policy level. In most jurisdictions, these decisions are not a conscious, explicit statement of the philosophical basis for the exercise of prosecutorial discretion. More often than not, policy is simply the implicit product of the implementation of those criteria that are used in making the second type of decision, the case-by-case decision. Consequently, the case-by-case decisions are *forming* policy rather than policy *informing* the case-by-case decisions.

Studies have failed to clearly differentiate between these two types of decisions. For example, as noted earlier, the Bureau of Social Science Research (Jacoby, 1977) puts forth four different "policies" that were observed by its researchers in an on-site study of prosecutors' offices. Although the Bureau defines four important factors that seem to have a role in decision-making during the screening process, I must take issue with the labeling of those factors as "policies." A policy must have an objective; i.e., it is something more than the criteria by which a decision-maker operates. Therefore, I would suggest that those policies are, in fact, standards that, depending upon the prosecutor's office, may guide the application of a yet-undefined policy.

I would argue that in most offices the actual policy probably closely resembles the punishment philosophy that prevails at other stages of the criminal justice system (Ebbesen and Konečni, 1975; Chapter 11, this volume; Gottfredson et al., 1975; Wilkins et al., 1978).[14] Under that philosophy, the government (after following proper procedures)

---

[14]I base this statement on the findings of empirical studies of other decision points in the criminal justice system. These studies indicate that the two most important factors affecting decisions are seriousness of the crime and prior record. See, e.g., Ebbesen and Konečni (1979) and Chapter 8, this volume, on judicial bail decisions; and Wilkins et al. (1978) and Chapter 11, this volume, on judicial sentencing decisions; Gottfredson et al. (1975) on parole decisions (although the second dimension was labeled as the probability of recidivism, a majority of the salient factors included in the dimension were related to the prior record of the incarcerated offender).

has the authority, if not the duty, to punish those individuals who have committed an illegal act. That philosophy also tells us that a system of proportionality guides the choice of punishment: *the more serious the wrongdoing, the more severe the sanction* (von Hirsch, 1976). Thus, the standard that guides the application of the screening policy may be primarily concerned with the seriousness of the criminal behavior and the likelihood that the defendant committed the crime.

The choice of punishment, however, is not necessarily limited to those dispositions that flow from the criminal justice system. Punishment can be any governmental action that has the potential to (or actually does, in some way) infringe upon one's liberty. Indeed, most of the sanctions imposed outside the criminal justice system (e.g., attending special classes, writing essays) are not unpleasant in nature (or at least not as unpleasant as incarceration) because they have a rehabilitative focus. Yet, for the most part, these sanctions are not the product of a purely rehabilitative model, the purpose of which is to help the individual. Instead, they appear to result from the application of the punishment model, which requires that some sanction be imposed in the case.

Applying the foregoing logic to the screening decision, one would expect to find that the more serious the offense, the greater the likelihood that the case will be accepted at screening. An essential component of this model, though, is the dichotomization of the screening decision into "accept" or "reject" outcomes. If an individual's case has not been effectively terminated, i.e., if some form of government action is possible against the individual as a result of a prosecutor's decision, then the case has been accepted at that point of the screening process.

The present model is schematically presented in Figure 9.1. As can be seen, an "accept" decision is not necessarily limited to just those followup actions that result in the continued processing of the case, and hence the individual, in the criminal justice system. This is not to say, however, that the defendant is being set free or that no conviction will be obtained. Although there will not be a local felony conviction, defendants could have their cases referred to authorities for prosecution in a lower (misdemeanor or municipal) court or in another jurisdiction (e.g., another state court or the federal court). The "accept" category also includes outcomes that take place in other media. For example, the case may be diverted pending the successful completion of some "formal" though nonadjudicative program, such as drug treatment or unsupervised probation. In addition, the case may be dropped or consolidated with another case as part of a plea bargain. Even under this arrangement, however, the case is not totally forgotten, since the prosecutor or judge who is making decisions

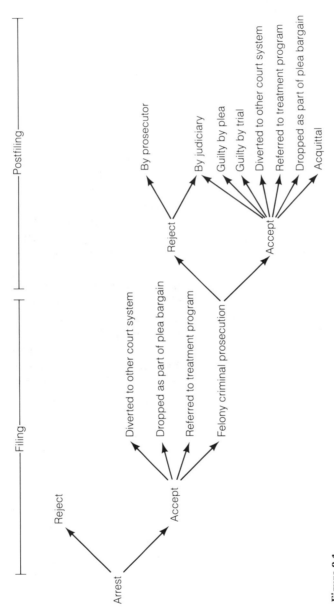

Figure 9.1
Model of the screening decisions of prosecutors and other participants in the criminal justice system. Of particular importance is the dichotomization of prosecutorial decisions into reject and accept categories and the fact that the accept category need not consist only of continued felony prosecution.

about the handling of the offender in other pending cases will likely be presented with and consider information about all alleged criminal activity engaged in by the defendant regardless of whether a conviction has been obtained.[15] Consequently, the prosecutor can be fairly confident that dropping the case will not necessarily result in defendants escaping without any infringement on their liberty.

The key to understanding the screening decision, then, is to ascertain what standard is being applied in making the initial "accept" or "reject" decision and to determine what other standards are being utilized in making the secondary, yet critically important, decision as to whether an accepted case will be processed in the criminal justice system. Perhaps the first, if not the best, place to look for the answer to those questions is in the empirical data bases that have already been assembled. Not only will those data help us identify the criteria being used, they will also provide an in-depth look at the results of various prosecutive screening decisions.

SCREENING DECISIONS IN LOS ANGELES COUNTY AND THE DISTRICT OF COLUMBIA

PROMIS Data

One of the best data sources in the area has been PROMIS, a management information system that was designed to assist prosecutors in better managing their offices. INSLAW, a research and development corporation based in Washington, D.C., developed the PROMIS technology in the early 1970s. The Law Enforcement Assistance Administration has funded the implementation of PROMIS in over 50 jurisdictions throughout the United States since its original implementation in January 1971 in the Washington, D.C., prosecutor's office (Hamilton, 1979).

PROMIS data were compared on a multijurisdictional basis by Brosi (1979). In her report, Brosi used data for the first six months of 1977 to describe the screening decision in five different prosecutors' offices.[16] Relevant data were particulary rich in two of the jurisdic-

---

[15]A judge may legally consider such information. See *United States* v. *Bowdach* (1977) and *United States* v. *Weston* (1971) on prior arrests; *Henry* v. *State* (1974) and *Kean* v. *State* (1976) on allegations of criminal conduct; *City of Dickinson* v. *Mueller* (1977) on pending charges. One can assume that a court would issue similar rulings in terms of the prosecutor.

[16]The five jurisdictions were Cobb County, Georgia; the District of Columbia; Salt Lake County, Utah; New Orleans County, Louisiana; and Los Angeles County, California.

tions, Los Angeles County and the District of Columbia. Therefore, the offices in those sites will be the focus of this discussion. Table 9.1 presents the disposition rates in these two jurisdictions.

Brosi found that the overall prosecutor rejection rate of cases at the initial screening review varied considerably in the two offices, ranging from 22% in the District of Columbia to 64% in Los Angeles County. However, as Table 9.1 shows, those figures included two types of rejections, in addition to outright dismissals: (1) cases referred to another jurisdiction for prosecution (e.g., the local court of limited jurisdiction or the federal courts), and (2) defendants diverted to special agencies or facilities (e.g., drug or alcoholic treatment centers). In accordance with the model of decision-making in the screening process depicted in Figure 9.1, those rejections would actually be characterized as "accept" decisions, since the government could, in some fashion, still restrict the individual's liberty. Therefore, taking into account only "pure" dismissals, the rate of rejection by the prosecutor at the initial screening review remains 22% in the District of Columbia, but is more accurately stated as 40% in Los Angeles County.

Those percentages still reflect a significant amount of variation between the sites, however. Moreover, the reasons given for rejecting a case do not reveal any clear pattern that might account for the differences. The large majority of cases were rejected because of evidence problems (e.g., insufficient evidence to corroborate the offense or to establish a necessary element of it) or witness problems (e.g.,

Table 9.1
Percent of different dispositions in Washington, D.C., and in Los Angeles County of all cases, January–June 1977.

Type of disposition	Washington, D.C.	Los Angeles County
Rejected by prosecutor at filing	22	40
Rejected by prosecutor during postfiling	18	2
Rejected by court during postfiling	8	8
Accepted by prosecutor, but diverted by court	<1	1
Accepted by prosecutor, but diverted at filing	<1	24
Accepted by prosecutor, but diverted at postfiling	1	1
Accepted by prosecutor; conviction by guilty plea	40	17
Accepted by prosecutor; conviction by trial	6	4
Accepted by prosecutor; acquittal by trial	2	1

SOURCE: Adapted from Brosi (1979).

witness refusal to pursue the case, inability to qualify witnesses, and witness credibility questions).[17]

One might suggest that the differences in the two sites can be traced to the quality of police arrests. Unfortunately, only a limited amount of the available empirical evidence can be used to evaluate police arrests. While we can determine whether the case was rejected for an evidentiary problem, we have no way of ascertaining whether the problem was caused by faulty police work or whether it simply reflected a realistic assessment of the merits of the case based on all possible evidence, which the police had, in fact, properly gathered. The only category that sheds any light on the quality of police arrests is rejections related to due process, since these rejections tend to imply that evidence, be it physical or testimonial, was available but was improperly collected by the police.

Rejections for due process reasons varied in the two sites, with less than one half of 1% of rejections falling in this category in the District of Columbia, compared with 8% in Los Angeles.[18] Those figures appear to imply that the law-enforcement agencies in Los Angeles County are not as conscientious as those in the District of Columbia in assuring the quality of their arrests. However, I would like to attach two caveats to any such decision. First, the fact that so few of the rejections in the District of Columbia were for due process reasons makes one question the validity of those statistics: perhaps the prosecutors there just did not feel comfortable recording that particular code when rejecting a case. Second, the percentage of rejections for due process reasons was relatively small; in neither site did it account for more than 8% of all rejections.[19]

Thus, one can reasonably assume that differences in the overall rejection rates are the result of the application of differing policies or standards. As to the former conclusion, it must be pointed out that filing is only the first stage of the screening process. The judiciary and the prosecutor have later opportunities to decide on the merits of a case. Therefore, any assessment of policy is best delayed until the final disposition is known for every case.

Table 9.1 indicates varying postfiling rejection rates in the sites. As might be expected from its low rejection rate at filing, the District of Columbia had the higher postfiling rejection rate: 26% of all the cases

---

[17]PROMIS data, January–June 1977. For examples of other studies with similar findings, see Greenwood et al. (1973), Vera Institute of Justice (1977), Williams (1978).

[18]PROMIS data, January–June 1977.

[19]Consequently, it is possible that the vast amount of attention given to due process issues in the prosecution of criminal offenders has conditioned us to thinking that such problems are more extensive than they really are.

in which a felony arrest had occurred. The rate in Los Angeles County was substantially lower; 10% of all arrests were rejected at some point in the process between filing and trial. Included in these figures for both sites are prosecutor- and court-initiated actions (i.e., *nolles* and dismissals). Before we draw any conclusions about the effectiveness of prosecutorial decision-making, however, it is necessary to break down those figures to determine how many rejections are prosecutor-initiated and how many are court-ordered.

In Washington, D.C., prosecutors *nolled* 11% of all arrests; 1% of these cases, though, were not pure rejections and thus are classified as "accept" decisions. They fell into one of the "accept, but divert" categories (e.g., referrals to other agencies or lower courts, or consideration of plea bargains). The remaining *nolles* were pure rejections; that is, they resulted in the complete cessation of government action against the individual.

The overall *nolle* rate in Los Angeles County was substantially lower; only 2% of all cases were rejected by the prosecutor's office during the postfiling stage. Another 1% of the cases were *nolled*, but resulted in some form of "accept" decision. Reasons for these rejections (in both sites) once again focused on evidence- and witness-related problems. Because data were often missing, however, no firm conclusions can be drawn.

Court-ordered dismissals also took two forms: (1) pure rejections and (2) diversion rejections, in which the case was disposed of without a formal adjudication of guilt or innocence but which could result in the facts of the current offense being considered by government or judicial authorities when processing other pending cases involving the same defendant. In Los Angeles County, 9% of all the cases were dismissed by the court during this pretrial period: 8% of these were pure rejections; the other 1% were accept decisions that fell into a diversionary category.

A similar percentage of cases (8%) were rejected by the judiciary in the District of Columbia. Unfortunately, however, we do not know how many of these dismissals were pure rejections and how many actually resulted in some form of accept decision. At least 20% of the court rejections appear to have resulted in the complete termination of the case, but in the other 80% the exact reason for dismissal is unknown.

Looking next at cases that were actually adjudicated—i.e., involving the full and complete prosecution of the case and an official determination of guilt or innocence—there is a significantly higher percentage of guilty pleas in the District of Columbia than in Los Angeles: 17% of all arrests resulted in a plea of guilty (or *nolo contendere*) in Los Angeles, compared with 40% in the District of Columbia. Trial dispositions were somewhat similar, however: in the District of Columbia, 6% of the arrestees were convicted after a trial, and 2% were acquitted; in Los Angeles, the corresponding figures were 4% and 1%.

Therefore, prosecutors in Los Angeles, perhaps because of enormous case loads or because excellent outside resources for diversion programs are available, have acknowledged in their screening decisions that not all cases must be processed in the highest levels of the local criminal justice system. Los Angeles prosecutors accepted 58% of all cases presented to them, yet disposed of nearly half of those accept decisions, 25%, by some vehicle that did not result in even the possibility of a Superior Court felony conviction (e.g., diverted to another court system). Of that 25%, 24% were terminated at filing; the other 1% left the system after filing. On the other hand, in the District of Columbia, only 1% of all cases were accepted, but diverted from the "official" process of the Superior Court during screening. Thus, an extra 24% of all cases remained in the criminal justice system to be disposed of later.

If, however, one looks at the dispositions of only those arrests that the prosecutor charged at filing, which are presented in Table 9.2, conviction and *nolle*/dismissal rates are remarkably similar for the two sites. In Los Angeles, 62% of these cases eventually resulted in a conviction; in the District of Columbia, the figure was 61%. *Nolle*/dismissal rates were 35% for Los Angeles and 36% for the District of Columbia.

Discussion of the data

The data have provided us with a detailed look at the screening process in two different jurisdictions. At the filing stage, Los Angeles County prosecutors reject 2 out of every 5 arrests. In contrast, the rejection rate at the same stage in the District of Columbia is approximately half that, 22%. However, the figures are more than reversed

Table 9.2
Percent of different dispositions in Washington, D.C., and Los Angeles County of only those cases in which prosecutor filed charges with the court

Type of disposition	Washington, D.C.	Los Angeles County
Convicted by plea or trial	61	62
Nolle prosequi or dismissed	36	35
Acquitted by trial	3	3

when compared for postfiling prosecutor rejections. An additional 18% of all arrests were rejected by District of Columbia prosecutors *after* filing, compared with only 2% in Los Angeles County. Consequently, despite some obvious differences in the decision points at which cases are being rejected, the overall prosecutor rejection rate for the screening process in these two jurisdictions is similar: 42% of all arrests in Los Angeles County and 40% of all arrests in the District of Columbia. In addition, as previously noted, conviction rates for filed cases are nearly identical. Therefore, one could reasonably argue that these two offices are following the same screening policy. Whether that policy is the punishment philosophy described earlier, though, remains to be determined.

Nevertheless, the point at which the rejection takes place varies significantly in the two jurisdictions. Thus, it is apparent that Los Angeles County prosecutors are using a higher standard to screen cases at initial filing than are prosecutors in the District of Columbia. By the time a case is actually ready for trial, though, the two jurisdictions appear to be using a similar standard.

One can make use of the available data in speculating as to what the first standard is. Perhaps the best indicator in this regard would be the percentage of cases rejected by the judiciary before trial that were previously accepted at filing by the prosecutor. Surprisingly, that figure is 14% in both jurisdictions. That probably means that neither site is using a standard of "beyond a reasonable doubt" to screen cases, as a judicial rejection rate of 14% would be highly unlikely if such a rigorous standard were being utilized. Consequently, the judicial rejection rate also indicates that the prosecutor is effectively using some lower standard to evaluate cases, a standard that is at least as stringent as probable cause. One could therefore theorize that the District of Columbia prosecutors are using "probable cause" as the standard at filing and a higher standard, perhaps "clear and convincing," at postfiling decision points. In contrast, prosecutors in Los Angeles County appear to be utilizing a more rigorous standard, perhaps "clear and convincing," at all decision points. Notwithstanding that explanation, at least one question remains: Why are the judicial rejection rates identical if the prosecutors are using different standards? One would expect that these rates would be higher in the jurisdiction using the lower standard (District of Columbia). That does not appear to be the case, and one can only speculate as to why the rates are the same.

Once a case is accepted, different standards are again applied in making decisions concerning the processing of the case. As noted in Figure 9.1, there appear to be at least four major paths for accept decisions to take:

1. They could continue to be processed in the criminal justice system at the Superior Court (felony) level.

2. They could be diverted to the criminal justice system at a lower level (courts of limited jurisdiction) or to the criminal justice system of another jurisdiction (state, county, federal).

3. They could be dropped as part of a plea bargain.

4. They could be referred to various treatment programs outside the criminal justice system.

Los Angeles County prosecutors apply a standard for those second-stage decisions that means processing 25% of their accept cases outside the Superior Court system. Unfortunately, there has been a tendency to brush off these diversionary dispositions as decisions made in consideration of case-load or system pressures. However, that does not tell us which cases are diverted or rejected. The data provide some indication that seriousness of offense might be a consideration in reaching these followup decisions. In addition, studies examining other decision-making points in the criminal justice system have usually found that some characteristics of the offender (e.g., prior record and social stability) may influence decisions. The availability of alternative programs is undoubtedly another major factor. Unfortunately, no data were available to test these assumptions, and one cannot say for certain whether they are actually affecting the screening decisions made by prosecutors.

CONCLUSIONS

While many commentators have acknowledged the broad discretionary powers exercised by the prosecutor in screening cases, few have attempted to detail the process used in making those decisions. I have attempted to redefine screening in terms of dichotomized decision-making. Although the available data did not permit an extensive study of screening in these terms, they did permit the documentation of differences and similarities in the screening processes of two large urban jurisdictions. Further studies should attempt to identify the policy used by prosecutors and the specific standards by which this policy is implemented. Once policies and standards have been accurately identifed, prosecutors can be provided with feedback as to the degree of success of their screening decisions. However, that feedback must consist of more than raw percentages of convictions. If it is to be useful, it must be conscious of jurisdictional constraints and the availability of alternative dispositions, since both appear to greatly affect screening decisions.

References

Abrams, N. Internal policy: Guiding the exercise of prosecutorial discretion. *University of California Los Angeles Law Review*, 1971, *19*, 1–58.

Abrams, N. Prosecutorial charge decision systems. *University of California Los Angeles Law Review*, 1975, *23*, 1–56.

Alschuler, A. W. Sentencing reform and prosecutorial power: A critique of recent proposals for "fixed" and "presumptive" sentencing. *University of Pennsylvania Law Review*, 1978, *126*, 550–577.

American Bar Association Project on Standards for Criminal Justice. *Standards relating to the prosecution function and the defense function.* New York: American Bar Association, 1971.

Arizona Rules of Criminal Procedure. St. Paul: West Publishing, Supp. 1979–1980.

Beck, L. E. The administrative law of criminal prosecution: The development of prosecutorial policy. *American University Law Review*, 1978, *27*, 310–380.

Brosi, K. *A cross-city comparison of felony case processing.* Washington, DC: U.S. Government Printing Office, 1979.

City of Dickinson v. Mueller, 261 N.W.2d 787 (N.D. 1977).

Chimel v. California, 395 U.S. 752 (1969).

Cole, G. F. The decision to prosecute. *Law and Society Review*, 1970, *4*, 331–343.

Comment. Curbing the prosecutor's discretion: *United States v. Falk*. *Harvard Civil Rights and Civil Liberties Law Review*, 1974, *9*, 372–397.

Comment. Prosecutorial discretion in the initiation of criminal complaints. *Southern California Law Review*, 1969, *42*, 519–545.

Cox, S. J. Prosecutorial discretion: An overview. *American Criminal Law Review*, 1976, *13*, 383–434.

Davis, K. C. *Discretionary justice: A preliminary inquiry.* Baton Rouge: Louisiana State University Press, 1969.

Denham v. Robinson, 72 W.Va. 243, 77 S.E. 970 (1913).

Ebbesen, E. B., & Konečni, V. J. Decision making and information integration in the courts: The setting of bail. *Journal of Personality and Social Psychology*, 1975, *32*, 805–821.

Edelman v. California, 344 U.S. 357 (1953).

Federal Rules of Criminal Procedure. St. Paul: West Publishing, 1975.

Friedman, M. The prosecutor: A model for role and function. *Washington University Law Quarterly*, 1978, *1978*, 109–139.

Georgia Code Annotated. Norcross: Harison Publishing, 1978.

Gottfredson, D. M., Hoffman, P. B., Sigler, M. H., & Wilkins, L. T. Making paroling policy explicit. *Crime and Delinquency*, 1975, *21*, 34–44.

Greenwood, P., Wildhorn, S., Poggio, E. C., Strumwasser, M., & DeLeon, P. *Prosecution of adult felony defendants in Los Angeles County: A policy perspective.* Santa Monica, CA: Rand, 1973.

Hamilton, W. H. Highlights of PROMIS research. In W. McDonald (Ed.), *The prosecutor.* Beverly Hills, CA: Sage, 1979.

Henry v. State, 273 Md. 131, 328 A2d 293 (1974).

Hirsch, A. von. *Doing justice: The choice of punishments.* New York: Hill and Wang, 1976.

Jacoby, J. E. *The prosecutor's charging decision: A policy perspective.* Washington, DC: U.S. Government Printing Office, 1977.

Kaplan, J. The prosecutorial description—A comment. *Northwestern Law Review,* 1965, *60,* 174–193.

Katz v. United States, 389 U.S. 347 (1967).

Kean v. State, 340 So.2d 102 (Alabama App. 1976).

Kress, J. M. Progress and prosecution. *Annals,* 1976, *423,* 99–117.

LaFave, W. R. The prosecutor's discretion in the United States. *American Journal of Comparative Law,* 1970, *18,* 532–548.

Louisiana Code Criminal Procedure Annotated. St. Paul: West Publishing, 1977.

Miller, F. W. *Prosecution: The decision to charge a suspect with a crime.* Boston: Little, Brown, 1969.

Miranda v. Arizona, 384 U.S. 436 (1966).

National Advisory Commission on Criminal Justice Standards and Goals. *Courts.* Washington, DC: U.S. Government Printing Office, 1973.

National District Attorneys Association. *National prosecution standards.* Washington, DC: National District Attorneys Association, 1977.

Neil v. Biggers, 409 U.S. 188 (1972).

Newman v. United States, 382 F. 2d 479 (D.C. Cir. 1967).

Noll, D. Controlling a prosecutor's screening discretion through fuller enforcement. *Syracuse Law Review,* 1978, *29,* 697–738.

Note. Reviewability of prosecutorial discretion: Failure to prosecute. *Columbia Law Review,* 1974, *75,* 130–161.

Oyler v. Boles, 368 U.S. 448 (1962).

People ex rel. Kuntsman v. Shinsaku Nagano, 309 Ill. 231, 59 N.E. 2d 96 (1945).

Rabin, R. L. Agency criminal referrals in the federal system: An empirical study of prosecutorial discretion. *Stanford Law Review,* 1972, *24,* 1036–1091.

State v. Kenyon, 85 Wis. 2d 36, 270 N.W. 2d 160 (1978).

Terry v. Ohio, 392 U.S. 1 (1962).

United States v. Bowdach, 561 F. 2d 1160 (5th Cir. 1977).

United States v. Cowan, 524 F. 2d 504 (5th Cir. 1975), cert. denied, 425 U.S. 971 (1976).

United States v. Cox, 342 F. 2d 165 (5th Cir.), cert. denied, 381 U.S. 935 (1965).

United States v. Falk, 479 F. 2d 616 (7th Cir. 1973).

United States v. Nederlandsche Combinatie Voor Chemische Industrie, 428 F. Supp. 114 (S.D.N.Y. 1977).

United States v. Russell, 411 U.S. 423 (1973).

United States v. Weston, 448 F. 2d 626 (9th Cir. 1971).

Vera Institute of Justice. *Felony arrests: Their prosecution and disposition in New York City's courts.* New York: Vera Institute, 1977.

Vorenberg, J. Narrowing the discretion of criminal justice officials. *Duke Law Journal,* 1976, *1976,* 651–697.

Washington Criminal Rules. St. Paul: West Publishing, 1961.

Wilkins, L. T., Kress, J. M., Gottfredson, D. M., Calpin, J. C., & Gelman, A. M. *Sentencing guidelines: Structuring judicial discretion.* Washington, DC: U.S. Government Printing Office, 1978.

Williams, K. M. *The role of the victim in the prosecution of violent crimes.* Washington, DC: Institute for Law and Social Research, 1978.

Work, C. R., Richman, L. D., & Williams, D. L. Toward a fairer system of justice: The impact of technology on prosecutorial discretion. *Criminal Law Bulletin,* 1976, *12,* 189–300.

Yick Wo v. Hopkins, 118 U.S. 359 (1886).

THE JURY TRIAL

Editors' Introduction

As we pointed out in Chapter 2, jury decision-making has been one of the most exhaustively investigated topics in legal psychology. However, the vast majority of the studies have been simulations in which student "jurors" or, at best, research participants chosen from the same source from which actual jurors are selected (jury rolls), make what are, by definition, inconsequential decisions on the basis of fictitious cases in which certain variables, often of primarily psychological, rather than legal, interest are experimentally manipulated. In the introductory portion of this chapter, Kerr ably discusses these problems.

The ultimate defense by the proponents of mock-jury simulations has been that, whatever their problems, experimental simulations are better than no studies at all (since jury deliberations, by law, cannot be observed or recorded). We disagree on the grounds that information that cannot be properly validated has a high potential for being misinformation and thus worse than no information at all, especially when the conclusions have an aura of scientific respectability and may quite literally affect people's lives. Be that as it may, it remains unclear why researchers claiming to be interested in this decision node of the criminal justice system have done so little work on the events taking place in the courtroom during jury trials. The public has access to these proceedings, and it is not unreasonable to expect that the events taking place during a trial might affect the jury's verdict. Although jury trials are relatively rare occurrences in the criminal justice system, as has been pointed out in this volume, Kerr convincingly discusses several reasons why jury trials are important and should be extensively studied. In addition to the reasons he mentions, it might be noted that jury trials are important in that they are more likely to result in appeals and it is generally the appellate courts that set precedents.

To the best of our knowledge, the work described by Kerr is the first relatively thorough attempt to examine simultaneously the organismic, dispositional, and behavioral characteristics of the various participants in a trial (with the exception of the jurors themselves), during the trial itself, as predictors of juries' verdicts (or, rather, of juries' "punitiveness," as expressed by a conviction ratio). In addition to the various characteristics of the participants in trials, a number of derived variables were also coded, such as the ethnic similarity between the jury and the defendant, the relative skill of the defense attorney vis-à-vis the prosecutor, and the judge's relative favoritism toward the two attorneys.

The research Kerr describes resulted in a number of interesting and counterintuitive findings, even though the percent of variance explained by the coded variables was quite modest. As Kerr points out, some factors that probably account for a great deal of variance, such as the strength of the evidence presented in a trial, were not coded. It should be emphasized that the data Kerr analyzed had been collected for a different purpose and that he had no control over the construction of the coding instrument. Despite these problems, we think that Kerr took a major step in reaching a better understanding of the role that trial events play in jury decisions. In addition to providing important substantive information, his work helps to "demystify" the trial process. In time, work of this type may yet succeed in altering the gross misconceptions that the general public has about the trial process and the criminal justice system as a whole—misconceptions of the Perry Mason variety, for which the media can be held largely responsible.

10

Trial Participants' Behaviors
and Jury Verdicts:
An Exploratory Field Study

Norbert L. Kerr

The traditional method of determining guilt or innocence in U.S. criminal cases has been trial by jury. However, the proportion of all prosecuted cases that are currently tried before a jury is relatively small, due primarily to the high percentage of cases disposed of by plea bargaining.[1] Nevertheless, the empirical study of jury behavior is important for several reasons. The cases that are tried by juries are likely to be those in which the issue of guilt is least clear-cut because very weak prosecution cases are likely to result in dropped charges whereas very strong prosecution cases are likely to prompt plea bargaining and an eventual guilty plea. Juries also represent an interesting class of decision-making group because the consequences of jury verdicts are among the most serious entrusted to a group. Furthermore, the use of juries is based upon a number of assumptions about human behavior; e.g., jurors can and will ignore personal biases and rationally evaluate the available evidence, jurors can accurately recall testimony, jurors can comprehend the legal rules given to them and act within their constraints (Marshall, 1969). The degree to which juror behavior actually satisfies such assumptions is pertinent to the ongoing debate on the relative merits of the jury system vis-à-vis its alternatives.

This chapter describes an exploratory field study of jury behavior. This methodological approach is sufficiently rare in jury research to warrant some discussion.

---

[1] Ebbesen and Konečni (1976) report that for 1974, of 2,504 felons brought to trial in the San Diego Superior Court, 215 (or 8.6%) were tried before a jury. Kalven and Zeisel (1966) report that the proportion of misdemeanors tried before a jury is even smaller than the proportion for felonies.

RESEARCH METHODOLOGY AND THE STUDY
OF JURY BEHAVIOR

Although a great deal of jury research has been carried out since the University of Chicago Jury Project spurred interest in the topic more than two decades ago, only a small portion of this research has examined the jury *in situ*. There are many good reasons for this. By law, jury deliberations may not be observed or recorded. Even if juries could be observed, the complexity of each trial makes very difficult the acquisition of unconfounded replications under any particular set of conditions (Strodtbeck, 1962). And even if similar trials could be identified, their length tend to make data acquisition prohibitively expensive and time-consuming. In light of such difficulties, many investigators have chosen to examine jury behavior within simulated (mock) jury trials, usually carried out in the laboratory. Experimental control and opportunity for observation are optimized with this research strategy. Large numbers of exact replications can be obtained quickly and inexpensively. The high internal validity that is attainable in such simulations permits strong causal inference. The many virtues of this research method have frequently been put to good advantage, producing a sizable literature (for comprehensive reviews, see Davis, Bray, and Holt, 1977; or Kerr and Bray, in press).

As the experimental literature on juries has grown, so has concern for its external validity. Most experimental studies have differed in several respects from the actual courtroom setting to which one would hope to generalize. One potentially serious problem is the choice of mock jurors. Most have been college students, chosen primarily for their accessibility (Bray and Kerr, in press). One cannot readily allude to the "typical juror" because juror characteristics vary with the method of jury-panel composition, jury-duty exemption rules, and regional demographic patterns. Still, college-student samples generally are not highly representative. Some research has suggested that this may be important. For example, Simon and Mahan (1971) found that college-student jurors and juries were much less likely to convict a defendant charged with homicide than was a sample of subjects drawn from a pool of actual jurors. Others have also reported age or educational-background effects (Nemeth and Sosis, 1973; Sealy and Cornish, 1973; Simon, 1967). The basis for such effects is unclear, and it is unknown whether they represent only relatively uninteresting main effects, reflecting somewhat different evaluations of input, or whether they signify more fundamental differences in choices and processing of information.

Occasionally, mock jurors have been drawn from a pool of actual, prospective jurors (Simon, 1967), but still other difficulties typically remain. For example:

1. In many studies the verdicts were without consequence.

2. Cases have typically been presented via audiotape, videotape, trial transcript, or brief trial summaries.

3. Deliberation time has usually been constrained and short.

4. Subjects may have been repeatedly questioned or eavesdropped upon.

5. Procedural rules (e.g., admissibility of evidence) have sometimes been violated to achieve experimental ends.

6. Subjects are often asked to make judgments that may not correspond to reaching a verdict (e.g., making ratings of guilt on continuous scales) or that are infrequently entrusted to jurors (e.g., sentencing).

7. Often no group deliberation has taken place (Bray and Kerr, in press).

The importance of such differences is clearly an empirical question that has only recently begun to receive attention. The pattern of the research to date is far from conclusive, but points to potential problems. For example, Bermant et al. (1974) contrasted four modes of case presentation: (1) an audiotape with accompanying slides of court participants, (2) the audiotape only, (3) a transcript, and (4) a summary of evidence. Comparing predeliberation verdicts of undergraduate mock jurors, they found a negative relationship between rate of conviction and verisimilitude of the simulation. Two studies have obtained significant differences in verdicts between role-playing and actual jurors. Diamond and Zeisel (1974) compared actual juries with juries composed of those excused during *voir dire* (jury selection) and with a third group of juries composed by random selection from the jury pool. For 10 actual cases, each real jury heard and deliberated its case as usual. One jury from each of the other conditions observed each trial as members of the audience and subsequently engaged in mock deliberation. Diamond and Zeisel's actual juries were less likely to convict than the other two types of jury. In a laboratory study, Wilson and Donnerstein (1977) again contrasted typical role-playing student jurors with students who were told that their verdicts would actually decide a student discipline case. In contrast to Diamond and Zeisel's results, Wilson and Donnerstein found that conviction was more likely with the real jurors in two out of three experiments; the third produced nonsignificant results. More importantly, in one study they found that an effect that had been reliably obtained in previous simulation studies (namely, fewer convictions for a defendant with an attractive character) did not obtain for their "real" jurors.

It should be reiterated that these studies are far from conclusive; each has several plausible, competing explanations. For example, it is unclear in the Bermant et al. study (1974) whether the results should be attributed to the mode of presentation or to the amount of information available. Diamond and Zeisel's matched triplets of juries almost certainly differed in other ways than the significance of their decisions. And Wilson and Donnerstein's results could very well have been due to "real" jurors' seeing through the experimental cover story. Furthermore, there are also a few studies in which simulation variables have not shown any effects. To illustrate, Miller (1975) has found little difference between mock jurors' responses to videotape and live presentations of a trial; and Kerr, Nerenz, and Herrick (1979) found no differences between simulated and actual student jurors (using a manipulation similar to Wilson and Donnerstein's, except with greater care taken to ensure the credibility of the cover story).

A final aspect of the generalizability problem is the question of whether effects obtained in simulated trials of a particular offense (e.g., rape) will obtain for other charges. For example, the effects of juror sex (Sealy and Cornish, 1973) and defendant attractiveness (Sigall and Ostrove, 1975) have been found to vary with the type of offense tried.

In summary, although the empirical issue of the external validity of phenomena discovered in laboratory simulations is far from resolved, there is clearly good reason to hesitate in generalizing such phenomena to real juries. While we have learned a good deal about the factors that affect the behavior of mock jurors in particular types of cases, we still know distressingly little about the extent to which this knowledge represents a valid or complete description of most actual juries. One worthwhile way to address this problem is to continue to experimentally examine the importance of various simulation features (role playing, mode of presentation, etc.). Another strategy is to do field studies of the behavior of actual juries. This was the approach of the research reported here. Despite the many serious difficulties mentioned earlier that are inherent in this approach, such research can both supplement and complement the experimental research. To be sure, when one is interested only in the application of one's research, jury field data are the ultimate criteria of the validity of any research hypotheses.

THE JURY AS A DECISION-MAKING BODY:
TRADITIONAL AND NONTRADITIONAL VIEWS

This volume conceptualizes the operation of the legal system in terms of the behavior of decision-makers at key nodes in a decision network. The jury in a criminal case is a single, frequently bypassed node in that network. Like the decision-makers at every other node, the jury must select and assimilate information, then interpret, weigh, and integrate that information to produce its decision (verdict). Viewed in this way, the identification of salient inputs to the jury's decision-making process becomes a central concern.

The traditional legal view of jury functioning makes definite assumptions about a jury's decision-making processes. The jury is presumed to restrict its attention to the admissible evidence presented during the trial. The jury must interpret this evidence, deciding what is and is not factual. Having done so, the jury compares its interpretation of the evidence with the legal criteria for conviction as described by the judge and reaches its verdict. In this traditional view, the other principal actors in the trial (e.g., judge, attorneys, witnesses) serve primarily to elicit evidence and guide the jury's understanding of it and of the law.

While the traditional emphasis on evidentiary information is probably appropriate, it is most likely too limited a view of the jury's decision-making process. Many legal professionals have observed that jurors are often quite sensitive to the character and behavior of the defendant, victim, attorneys, or judge (e.g., Clarence Darrow, quoted in Sutherland, 1966; Percy Foreman, quoted in Smith, 1966; Jerome Frank, 1949). Frequently these factors are extralegal; i.e., the law presumes they are irrelevant to the jury's verdict. As far as defendant and victim characteristics are concerned, much experimental jury research is corroborative (Efran, 1974; Jones and Aronson, 1973; Kerr, 1978; Landy and Aronson, 1969; Sigall and Ostrove, 1975). The effects of the characteristics and behavior of the judge and attorneys have not been studied extensively. This is unfortunate because they are usually far more active participants in the trial than either the defendant or the victim.

THE RESEARCH PLAN

The research reported here is an exploratory attempt to identify and gauge the relative salience of some trial features that may affect a jury's verdict. Examination of extralegal factors was stressed, particularly those involving the attorneys and the judge. Data were acquired on a large number of personal characteristics and behaviors

of the principal characters in a sample of felony trials. The power of
these variables, separately and in combination, to predict the pattern
of verdicts of criminal trial juries was the principal criterion for identifying salient variables. Of course, the demonstration of such predictive links does not establish any simple causal relationships. And
since the set of variables studied is neither exhaustive nor without
common reliability and validity problems, one must concede that
salient inputs to deliberation may have been overlooked and that the
relative salience of the variables identified are conditional on the
total set examined. Nevertheless, this approach may help identify
unsuspected inputs to the decision-making process of juries. Furthermore, such research may extend the external validity of experimental jury research.

A secondary goal was also addressed. Since many of the judges'
and attorneys' behaviors were observed, it was also possible to examine their mutual influence. One might also consider the attorneys
and the judge as decision-makers; their behavior during a trial may
be viewed as the result of a series of decisions: Should I object?
Should I sustain or overrule? Should I pursue this or that line of
questioning? It's quite likely that these decisions are based primarily
on evidentiary, procedural, and legal factors, but, again, it is of interest to examine the extent to which such decisions are reliably related
to another actor's behaviors or characteristics.

THE RESEARCH METHOD

Data collection

The data described in this chapter were obtained by students in the
Judicial Administration Program of San Diego State University and
were generously made available to me by the administrators of that
program, along with detailed descriptions of the program's operation,
on which the following summary is based.[2]

The Judicial Administration Program's primary purpose is educational: to familiarize students with the functioning of the criminal
courts. To this end, each student attended several court sessions in
local courtrooms.[3] The number of sessions attended partially determined the course grade. At the beginning of the semester each stu-

---

[2]I wish to express my deep appreciation to Frank Eddy, Greg Newell, and Ivar Paur
for making these data available, and to Charles Uhl for his help in the reduction and
analyses of these data.

[3]Sessions were defined as morning or afternoon judicial session, generally lasting
from 3 to 4 hours.

dent was required to attend at least four of five "core" sessions (misdemeanor trial, felony arraignment, felony preliminary hearing, felony trial, and federal trial). After completing these core sessions, students could choose additional sessions according to their interests. Thus, students were not required to attend every session of a particular trial, and rarely did so.

A secondary goal of the program was the collection of data on a continuing basis. The students not only informally observed the functioning of the court, but also recorded a variety of data on prepared forms. Since this chapter is concerned only with jury trials, only the Trial Form will be described.[4] Several objective data were recorded on this form: offenses charged, final verdicts, sentences and/or fines, defense attorney status (privately retained or court-appointed), defendant's status (bail bond, released on own recognizance, or custody), number of objections held for prosecution and defense,[5] number of privileged conferences,[5] and names of the attorneys and the judge. The students also made several subjective ratings: the frequency with which defense attorney and prosecutor utilized materials, cited cases, and raised objections; each attorney's knowledge of the evidence and degree of rational and emotional appeal; the rapport between attorneys; the judge's courtesy and motor mannerisms favoring either attorney; and overall impressions of the impartiality of the judge and the convincingness of either side's arguments. Students also tallied the number of supportive and negative reactions of the court officers (judge, prosecutor, and defense attorney) to one another.[5,6] Finally, the race, age, sex, hairstyle, attire, interest, nervousness, respectfulness, and aggressiveness of the judge, defendant, attorneys, victim, and jury members were coded. The criteria to be used for coding each of these variables were described in detail to the students at the course orientation and printed in the course materials. Furthermore, the importance of adherence to these criteria and of accurate coding was emphasized repeatedly.[7] In summary,

---

[4]Separate Preliminary Examination and Arraignment forms were used by students when appropriate.

[5]These frequency counts were transformed to rates by dividing the duration of the session, which was also coded on the Trial Form.

[6]These were broadly defined. Any outward signs of either negative or supportive voice intonations, physical mannerisms, facial expressions, or simply hostile or affable signals were to be tallied.

[7]These precautions probably helped increase the reliability of the observers' responses. Unfortunately, it was not possible to obtain meaningful reliability coefficients for this data set. It was very rare for many students to attend the same court session. For the few instances when this occurred, it was usually the case that pairs of students attended several sessions together. It is possible that friends who did this might sometimes copy each others' ratings, artificially inflating the apparent reliability. Averaging across student observations within each trial tended to reduce the effect of nonsystematic errors of observation for those cases with several student observers.

each student attended between 1 and 14 trial sessions and completed a Trial Form for each session. The choices of trial sessions and the number attended were largely up to the student; therefore, the number of observations obtained varied a good deal from trial to trial. Thus, for some popular trials there were many observers at each of several sessions; for other trials, very few observations were obtained.[8]

It is clear that in several respects the manner in which the data were collected was not optimal for the purposes of the present analysis; e.g., observers were not trained or monitored extensively, checks of observer reliability were not possible, the choices of behaviors and characteristics to be coded were not guided by previous research. It should be kept in mind that the program was designed primarily to serve educational functions and that no specific research objectives, certainly not the present ones, guided the design of the Trial Form. Nevertheless, there were several positive features of this data set that are worth noting. One attractive feature of this data source for the present purposes was the large number and variety of behaviors observed. This increased the likelihood not only of detecting significant factors but also of uncovering confounds and alternative hypotheses. Another attractive feature is the extent of observation on the contesting attorneys and the judge. As noted above, relatively little research has examined the impact of their behaviors and characteristics on jury verdicts. Finally, the data set may well be unique; I know of no other set of systematically collected observations of trial participants' in-court behaviors, at least not for a sizable sample of criminal trials.

Data set

The results reported in this chapter were based on 1,296 separate Trial Forms describing 113 criminal jury trials in the San Diego County Superior Court. These data were compiled during the 1974–1975 and 1975–1976 academic years. In each of the trials, one or more defendants were charged with one or more felonies from the California Penal Code or Health and Safety Code. A total of 379 charges were filed, representing a broad range of offenses.[9] For each variable on the Trial Form, a trial average was computed across all

---

[8]Most trials had more than one observer, although a few (17) were attended by only one student at one session.

[9]Robbery was the modal charge (55 counts in all), with drug-related charges (48), assault (31), homicide (13), rape (17), burglary (29), receiving stolen property (22), and grand theft (18) also fairly common.

observers who attended that trial. For many variables (e.g., age of attorney), it was reasonable to assume no variation across sessions; while for others (e.g., frequency of objections by the defense attorney), it seemed much less reasonable. To determine empirically for which variables this assumption was justified, the 49 trials observed during one semester (fall 1974) were considered. For each trial, a one-way analysis of variance was performed on each variable with sessions as the single factor. If a variable consistently failed to produce significant between-session effects across trials, or if it was necessarily constant across sessions (e.g., judge's age), then the trial average was the simple average of every observation on that variable during that trial. For all other variables, the data were first averaged within each session, and then these session averages were averaged.

Jury verdict criteria   The primary concern of this chapter is how these averaged ratings were related to juries' verdicts. Since it was frequently the case that there was more than one defendant and/or more than one charge, juries often had to reach more than one verdict. For this reason, the ratio of the number of guilty verdicts to the total number of verdicts reached (i.e., the conviction ratio, or CR) was taken as an index of jury punitiveness. Of course, other indices of jury decision-making might have been used. For example, the proportion of defendants in a trial who were convicted of at least one charge and, similarly, the proportion of defendants in a trial acquitted of at least one charge were considered as criteria. However, these were so closely related to the CR ($r = .93$ and $-.89$, respectively) that they were rejected in favor of the more conceptually simple CR.

Before we discuss the results, a description of the decision-makers themselves is in order. The jurors in the present sample of Superior Court trials were likely to be white, middle-aged, and female. The distributions of these characteristics in the present sample as well as in the general community are presented in Table 10.1. These jurors were not highly representative of the general population from which they are drawn; for each of the three juror characteristics, the obtained distribution differed significantly from the population distribution (for age $\chi^2_7 = 662.1$, $p < .001$; for sex $\chi^2_1 = 17.2$, $p < .001$; and for ethnic group $\chi^2_3 = 184.4$, $p < .001$).[10] Similar nonrepresentativeness has also been reported elsewhere (Beiser, 1973; Mills, 1969). The jury pool in San Diego County is composed by random selection from the current voter registration list. To then serve on a

---

[10]It should be noted that some of the jurors classified as white may have been Chicano; juror ethnic classification was based only on visual inspection in most cases.

Table 10.1
Distribution of jurors' demographic characteristics

		Ethnic group (n = 1,351)			
		White	Black	Chicano	Other
Jurors	f	1,269	39	28	15
	%	93.9	2.9	2.1	1.1
County	%	79.4	4.6	12.8	3.2

		Sex (n = 1,350)	
		Male	Female
Jurors	f	609	711
	%	45.1	53.6
County	%	51.8	48.2

		Age (n = 1,336)							
		20–24	25–34	35–44	45–54	55–59	60–64	65–74	75 +
Jurors	f	36	227	339	475	141	83	33	2
	%	2.7	17.0	25.4	35.6	10.6	6.2	2.5	.16
County	%	19.0	20.2	17.7	17.1	6.6	5.6	8.6	5.3

Notes: 1. Countywide distributions were based on 1970 census figures for San Diego County.
    2. Two jurors were judged to be less than 20 years old. Since census figures for 18–20-year-olds were not available, this category was excluded from the table.
    3. n < 1,356 (= 113 juries × 12 persons/jury), because of occasional failures to code juror characteristics.

jury, one must meet the statutory requirements[11] and pass the *voir dire* examination. Further, during the period these data were collected, some potential jurors could be excused by request or by law because of their occupations (e.g., physicians, students, police) or because of special hardship that would result from jury service. Clearly, the selection of jurors is a multistaged process, and the nonrepresentativeness of the jury is probably attributable in part to selection biases at each stage.[12]

[11]Jurors must be 18 or older, county residents for a least a year, sufficiently knowledgeable of the English language, and "in possession of his [sic] natural faculties and of ordinary intelligence and not decrepit" (Sec. 198, California Code of Civil Procedure). A potential juror's satisfaction of these requirements in San Diego County is determined by the Jury Commissioner from responses to a mailed questionnaire.
[12]Interestingly, Leslie's (1975) data show no significant race differences between seated and prospective jurors, suggesting that the *voir dire* may not strongly affect this aspect of juror representativeness. However, it seems likely that this effect would be strongly influenced by the extensiveness of the *voir dire* examination and the nature of the case. Other data indicate that the use of voter registration lists to construct the jury panel may be a major source of unrepresentativeness (Ginger, 1975, pp. 168–170).

RESULTS

The plan of data analysis and inferential limitations

In the preliminary analyses of these data, a simple model was assumed, namely, that the Trial Form variables have simple linear relationships with the juries' conviction ratios. Nonlinear effects, as well as interactive effects, were not considered. Simple correlation coefficients were computed between all Trial Form variables and the juries' CRs. The large number of predictor variables (relative to the total number of cases) and the exploratory nature of the inquiry governed the choice of this simple approach. Also, in testing the significance of these correlations, $\alpha = .10$ was employed. This, along with the large number of coefficients tested, increases the possibility of Type I errors. In light of the exploratory intent, this was judged preferable to a high Type II error rate. After the strongest predictors of the CR were identified, they were considered jointly to identify the most powerful, yet most parsimonious, predictive model.

It should be emphasized that any number of other variables, observed and unobserved, may mediate or qualify the relationships reported here. One such unobserved variable should be noted explicitly because of its potential relevance for several of the relationships described below. That variable is the weight of evidence. The most naive theory of jury decision-making assumes that the jury bases its verdict solely on the facts of the case (Frank, 1949), and most will agree that the weight of evidence plays a central role in jury deliberation. Since the student observers did not attend every session of a trial, an accurate assessment of this variable was not possible.[13] There are two ways in which this variable may be responsible for effects reported in this chapter. First, the behaviors of the judge, attorneys, and defendant may be systematically altered by the relative strengths of the contesting adversaries. For example, suppose that the prosecutor's case is extremely strong and the defense's is rather weak. It is possible that the judge's attitude would be adversely affected when a case with a very weak defense is added to the crowded docket. In anticipation of a result to be described below, the rated surliness of the judge was associated with juries' CRs in just this manner. A second, related possibility is that regardless of whether the weight of evidence affects the behaviors of trial participants, it may have

---

[13]The closest approximations on the Trial Form to a measure of the weight-of-evidence variable were the ratings of how convincing the arguments by the prosecutor and the defense attorney were. Because these were often based on very few observations of very few court sessions, they are suspect as valid measures of the weight-of-evidence variable.

affected the student observers' perceptions of those behaviors. These speculations are less clearly applicable to some of the obtained relationships than others, but without a satisfactory measure of the weight of evidence, they remain tenable.

The results may best be comprehended by considering the characteristics and behaviors of each trial participant separately. They will be ordered in rough correspondence to the importance for juries' verdicts that has traditionally been attributed to each participant. Thus, we will consider in turn (1) the defendant, (2) the defense attorney, (3) the prosecuting attorney, (4) the judge, (5) the victim, and (6) a nonsocial class of "participants," characteristics of the case. The original Trial Form variables associated with each of these participants, plus a few new variables derived from the original set, are listed in the Appendix at the end of this chapter.

The defendant

As noted earlier, the most frequently confirmed result in experimental mock-jury research is that a characteristic of the defendant can affect a mock juror's verdict (Dane and Wrightsman, in press). The observations of judges (Kalven and Zeisel, 1966, Chap. 15) and lawyers (Darrow, quoted in Sutherland, 1966) also attest to the importance of the jury's perception of and reaction to the defendant.

Seven defendant characteristics/behaviors were included in the Trial Form (see the Appendix). With an $\alpha = .10$, none of these variables correlated significantly with juries' CRs.[14] (See Chapter 11, this volume, for similar results for the sentencing of defendants.) There was a weak trend for higher CRs for younger defendants ($r = -.155$, $p < .11$).[15] The nonsignificance of the sex variable may have been attributable to its restricted range in this sample (only 5 of the 113 cases involved a female defendant).

Some experimental research has shown that juror–defendant attitudinal similarity may induce greater leniency (Griffitt and Jackson,

---

[14]All tests of significance of correlation coefficients were two-tailed.

[15]There is some evidence that defendant age is sytematically related to the frequency of arrest and type of offense charged (Sutherland and Cressey, 1974, p. 123). Arrests for serious, violent crimes (homicide, rape, robbery, aggravated assault) more likely involve a relatively older suspect (25 and over); while a number of less serious crimes (larceny, burglary, auto theft) more likely involve a relatively younger suspect. If obtaining a conviction is more difficult for the more serious crimes, as some laboratory research suggests (McComas and Noll, 1974), then the trend for defendant age may not be due to jurors' attitudes toward age. (However, see footnote 19.)

1973), especially when the jurors are highly authoritarian (Mitchell and Byrne, 1973). It was possible to examine a similar hypothesis with respect to three of the defendant's demographic characteristics: race, age, and sex. Indices of defendant–juror similarity were computed and correlated with the CR.[16] Again, none of these variables produced significant correlations. There were two weak trends, however. As might be expected from the defendant-age trend and the juror-age data, age dissimilarity predicted higher CRs ($r = .156$, $p < .13$). Also, ethnic dissimilarity predicted higher CRs ($r = .145$, $p < .14$).

To summarize, none of the defendant characteristics or behaviors available from the Trial Form was significantly associated with the juries' CRs, even using a rather liberal level of significance.

The defense and prosecuting attorneys

The outcome of any trial under an adversary system is clearly dependent on the skill of the contesting attorneys. Many observers of the courts suggest that juries often "try the lawyers" as much as or more than they try the defendant (Frank, 1949). Balzac went so far as to define the jury as twelve men chosen to decide who has the better lawyer. But which skills make one lawyer better (i.e., more effective) than another? With respect to the goal of arriving at a just verdict, such individual differences should ideally reflect an ability to bring important evidence to light and to state one's case clearly and persuasively. However, some of the most successful lawyers suggest that effectiveness is partially based on lawyers' ability to recognize and exploit any of the jurors' biases, to elicit the jury's sympathy and preference for themselves and their clients, or merely to entertain the jury. Handbooks on trial tactics abound with references to such skills (Keeton, 1954; Owen, 1973). Unfortunately, the widespread conviction that such skills are important is not based on systematic investigation, but on such sources as lawyers' personal experiences and "gut reactions," informal observation, and the folklore accumulated by generations of trial practitioners. The present data set permitted

---

[16]The proportions of white and female jurors in each jury were computed. Then the absolute values of the differences between these proportions and the defendant's race (coded as 0 = nonwhite, 1 = white) and sex (0 = male, 1 = female) were used as the indices of similarity. Age similarity was indexed by the difference between the jury's average age and the defendant's age. If there was more than one defendant, and the defendants differed with respect to race, age, or sex, the case was dropped from the analysis.

a tentative, empirical search for the behaviors of the effective criminal lawyer and prosecutor.

The defense attorney   On the Trial Form 17 characteristics or behaviors of the defense attorney were coded, and 2 more variables were derived from these (see the Appendix). Of these variables, 3 were significantly correlated with juries' CRs. The correlation with the rate of supportive reactions directed to the prosecutor ($r = -.17, p < .07$) indicated that the more often the defense attorney was supportive toward the prosecutor, the lower the proportion of convictions. This might reflect an intentional (an effective) tactic, a cordiality bred of an advantageous position, or perhaps personality traits (e.g., sociability) that communicate confidence and assurance to the jury. The other two significant variables were the rating of the defense attorney's working knowledge of the evidence and the rating of how convincing the arguments were ($r = .18$, $p < .06$; and $r = -.216$, $p < .03$, respectively). Not surprisingly, these two variables were themselves highly related ($r = .44$) and displayed similar relationships to several other variables as well. For example, both the knowledgeable and the convincing defense attorneys dealt with a relatively courteous, impartial, and respectful judge who favored the defense somewhat in motor mannerisms; both also had relatively respectful clients; and both were perceived as delivering appeals that were both highly rational and emotional.

Although not significant, two other variables also indicated some association with CR. Defense attorneys who were perceived as more indifferent were likely to suffer a relatively high CR ($r = .15, p < .12$). Also, it seemed that frequent negative reactions toward the prosecutor signaled fewer convictions ($r = -.14$, $p < .15$). This is somewhat puzzling in the light of the previously noted effect of supportive reactions to the prosecutor. Perhaps the magnitude of the defense attorney's reactivity is more important than its polarity.

One relationship is conspicuous in its absence. The defense attorney's status (privately retained versus court-appointed) was not significantly associated with juries' verdicts.[17] It bears noting that this result relates only to trial performance and not to other areas of the defense counsel's responsibility (e.g., plea bargaining).

---

[17] For this analysis, the conviction ratios for each defendant were classified as being high (CR > .67), moderate (.34 ≤ CR ≤ .67) or low (CR ≤ .34). This was done because occasionally codefendants did not share an attorney. The χ^2 test of association between attorney's status and this categorical verdict index was nonsignificant ($\chi^2 = 3.48$, $df = 2$).

The prosecuting attorney   The set of variables describing the prosecutor paralleled those used to describe the defense attorney (see the Appendix). Three of these variables were significantly correlated with juries' CRs. The rate of supportive reactions of the prosecutor to the defense attorney was inversely related to CR ($r = -.16$, $p < .09$); prosecutors were actually less successful when they were supportive toward opposing counsel, exactly opposite to the relationship obtained for the defense attorney. The other two variables were the prosecutor's interest/indifference and respectfulness/surliness ($r = .186$, $p < .06$; and $r = .180$, $p < .06$, respectively). Surprisingly, the prosecutors who were perceived as being more interested and respectful tended to win fewer convictions. On average, prosecutors were seen as highly interested ($\overline{X} = 1.8$, $s = .97$, on a 7-point scale) and respectful ($\overline{X} = 2.4$, $s = .92$, on a 7-point scale). These behaviors may have been interpreted by jurors as overeagerness (for interest) and oversubmissiveness (for respectfulness). Although these two variables were positively related ($r = .39$), the best predictor of each was the corresponding rating of the defense attorney ($r = .69$ for interest/indifference; $r = .57$ for respectfulness/surliness). So while the contesting attorneys tended to be perceived as interested and respectful to similar degrees, the significance of these variables was different for each. Strong interest in the case tended to signal success for the defense attorney, but failure for the prosecutor; the defense attorney's respectfulness/surliness was unrelated to success, while successful prosecutors were relatively less respectful.

Prosecutor–defense attorney relationships   One Trial Form variable and three derived variables compared the contesting attorneys (see the Appendix). None of these variables was significantly associated with CRs. There was a weak trend for fewer convictions when the defense attorney was relatively younger than the prosecutor ($r = -.14$, $p < .14$).

The judge

Judges command a special role of authority in the courtroom, particularly for the jurors. The judges supervise their selection, rule on what they should and should not consider relevant, explain the relevant law to them, and may even insert their own evaluation of the evidence. It is to be expected that jurors are particularly reliant on the judges and sensitive to their sentiments, even though jurors are routinely instructed not to be so influenced.

Of the 20 original or derived variables concerned with the judge (see the Appendix), two produced significant effects. They were (1) the judge's respectfulness/surliness ($r = .16$, $p < .10$), and (2) a summary index of the judge's relative favoritism for the contesting attorneys ($r = -.17$, $p < .08$); the CR was lower when the judge was respectful and relatively favorable toward the defense. These two variables were themselves correlated ($r = -.42$, $p < .001$), suggesting that the judge's surliness was usually perceived as being directed more strongly at the defense than at the prosecution. Other relationships are corroborative. For example, the surly judge was also judged to be relatively less impartial and more responsive to the prosecution in motor mannerisms. Furthermore, the respectfulness/surliness of the judge was more strongly correlated with ratings of courtesy ($r = -.59$) and impartiality ($r = -.54$) for the defense attorney than for the prosecutor ($r = -.31$ for courtesy; $r = -.22$ for impartiality). The latter relationships do indicate, however, that the surliness variable signifies more than favoritism, since the surly judge tended also to be relatively less courteous toward the prosecutor than was the respectful judge. It is interesting to note that the judge's surliness also signaled surliness on the part of the defense attorney ($r = .42$), defendant ($r = .42$), prosecutor ($r = .52$), and victim ($r = .32$). Precisely which (if any) of these variables were causes and which effects cannot be determined from these correlational data. Finally, judges tended to be less respectful when either the prosecutor ($r = -.20$, $p < .05$) or the defense attorney ($r = -.25$, $p < .01$) was relatively young. This might reflect impatience with inexperienced or unfamiliar attorneys, or a more general age bias.

Besides the two significant predictors, four other characteristics of the judge displayed predictive trends:

1. The rate at which objections were held for the prosecution tended to be positively related to the CR ($r = .154$, $p < .11$).

2. The CR tended to be high when the rate of negative reactions by the judge to the prosecutor was high ($r = .15$, $p < .13$).

3. The CR also tended to be high when the rate of supportive reactions by the judge to the defense attorney ($r = -.154$, $p < .11$) was low.

4. Finally the higher the judge's ratings on the interest/indifference scale, the higher the CR ($r = .15$, $p < .12$).

To summarize the judge's respectfulness/surliness and relative favoritism were significantly associated with the CR. The latter relationship may be interpreted straightforwardly; the basis for the prior relationship is less obvious. One intriguing possibility is an emotional modeling process. The surly judge may serve as an emotional model for the jurors, and the defendant may become the victim of the jurors' poor humor.

The victim

Except for a few obvious exceptions (e.g., rape, claims of self-defense), the character and behavior of the victim are presumed to be legally irrelevant to the question of whether or not the defendant violated the law. However, a growing body of psychological, socio-logical, and clinical evidence suggests that victim characteristics may be crucial for the attribution-of-responsibility process (Lerner and Simmons, 1966; Ryan, 1970). In addition, lawyers (Smith, 1966) and judges (Kalven and Zeisel, 1966, Chap. 17) have also suggested that juries' verdicts may reflect their reaction to the victim. Some labo-ratory evidence also exists on these issues (Jones and Aronson, 1973; Landy and Aronson, 1969; Scroggs, 1976). For example, Kerr (1978) found that mock jurors were more likely to convict a defendant charged with stealing the car of a physically attractive victim than one whose victim was physically unattractive. This effect obtained only when the victim was blameless in the crime; when the victim's carelessness made the crime easier to commit, there was no victim attractiveness effect.

The number of victim characteristics available from the Trial Form was small; there were 7 original and 3 derived variables (see the Appendix). Furthermore, the number of cases available for this analy-sis (67) was smaller than in the previous analyses (113), due either to the absence of the victim at every observed session or to the vic-timless nature of the offense(s) being tried. Two of the Trial Form's victim characteristics were significantly correlated with the CR. Sur-prisingly, conviction was more likely if a victim was male ($r_{pb} = .22$, $p < .10$); and the older the victim, the greater the likelihood of con-viction ($r = .275$, $p < .03$).

Several explanations for these counterintuitive findings were explored. For example, relatively older victims were generally more similar in age to the jurors. However, the correlation between CR and the jury–victim age similarity ($r = -.28$, $p < .03$) was not much larger than that produced by the victim's age alone. Another possi-bility was that the age and/or sex of the victim was systematically related to the type of offense, and the type of offense was related to CR. For example, younger victims might have been relatively more likely to be victims of violent crime,[18] and it may have been more difficult to obtain a conviction for such serious offenses.[19] A perusal of our data showed no such pattern.[20] However, another pattern did emerge. In every case in which the defendant's only charge was a sex crime against a female victim (namely, rape, assault to rape, child molesting), no convictions were obtained.[21] These victims were also relatively young on average within the total sample of victims. When the 7 cases that involved such victims were dropped from the analysis, the victim sex–CR correlation vanished ($r_{pb} = .014$) and the victim age–CR correlation was drastically attenuated ($r = .13$, n.s.). Thus, there was little evidence for a general effect of victim age and sex on jury verdicts in this data set.

Case factors

With respect to case characteristics, 4 variables were culled from the Trial Form (see the Appendix). All are extralegal as far as jury verdicts are concerned. None of these variables was significantly correlated with juries' CRs. There was a weak trend for a higher conviction rate

---

[18]Recent data on victimization in San Diego evidence such a pattern (National Criminal Justice Information . . . , 1975). For example, an association between victim's age (over 24 versus under 24) and seriousness of the crime (personal crimes of violence versus personal crimes of theft) indicates that relatively more young persons were victims of violent crime than nonviolent crime ($\chi^2 = 31.3$, $df = 1$, $p < .001$). It should be noted that these data are based on victims' self-reports and do not necessarily represent the pattern for crimes that actually come to trial before juries.

[19]There is some laboratory research that confirms this hypothesis (McComas and Noll, 1974; Vidmar, 1972); however, the data on actual juries are less supportive. For example, the rank-order correlation between Coombs' (1967) seriousness scaling and the conviction rates reported in U.S. District Courts in 1972 (Annual Report . . . , 1973) is nonsignificant ($r = .39$, $n = 10$ offenses common to both sources).

[20]Cases were dichotomized into those that included a violent crime against the person (murder, rape, assault, battery) and those that did not. Victim age was not significantly correlated with this seriousness classification ($r_{pb} = .02$). Similarly, there was not a significant relationship between victim sex and seriousness of the crime ($\phi = .15$).

[21]There exists some other statistical evidence that the conviction rates for such offenses are low. Kalven and Zeisel (1966, p. 42) showed rape charges as having the third-highest acquittal rate in their sample of 15 major crimes. Conviction rates of defendants charged with rape in U.S. District Courts are also quite low; in one year, rape charges resulted in the eighth-highest jury acquittal rate out of 71 offense classes (Annual Report . . . , 1973). I suspect that this pattern is due primarily to the difficulty of satisfying the burden-of-proof requirements of such charges (e.g., proving beyond a reasonable doubt that the victim in no sense consented, proving that force or threat of force was involved, overcoming reasonable doubt on the basis of a victim's uncorroborated testimony).

when the number of dropped charges was large ($r = .14$, $p < .14$). This might reflect the elimination of weakly substantiated charges by the judge, leaving the cases with more substantial evidence for the jury.

The predictive utility of the Trial Form variables

In all, 10 variables correlated significantly ($\alpha = .10$) with juries' CRs.[22] Of these, 8 were included in a multiple regression analysis to assess their collective and relative predictive power. Victim age and sex were omitted from this analysis since their effects seem due solely to the difficulty in obtaining convictions for certain sex offenses.

Collectively, the eight predictors resulted in a multiple $R = .338$ when regressed on juries' CRs. Thus, approximately 11.4% of the total variation in CR could be accounted for in this sample using these 8 predictors. When Wherry's shrinkage formula was applied, the estimated proportion of variance accounted for dropped to approximately 4%. These variables were also entered in a stepwise multiple regression analysis. The results of this analysis are reported in Table 10.2. Nearly all (79%) of the predictable variance was accounted for by the first 3 variables to enter the regression equation (namely, convincingness of defense attorney, supportive reactions of defense attorney for prosecutor, and prosecutor's respectfulness/surliness). The remaining 5 variables increased the percent of variance accounted for by less than 1% each and by only 2.4% collectively. Further, the test for the significance of R was nonsignificant ($\alpha = .10$) after the fourth variable was entered. This analysis does not necessarily indicate that the variables entering in the later steps are less important for the juries' decisions than those entering in the early steps. It does signify, however, that the late-entering variables are redundant with the first three for the prediction of juries' CRs in this sample of cases. The multiple R obtained with the 3-predictor equa-

---

[22]   1. Defense attorney's knowledge of evidence.
    2. Defense attorney's convincingness of argument.
    3. Supportive reactions of defense attorney for prosecutor.
    4. Supportive reactions of prosecutor for defense attorney.
    5. Prosecutor's interest.
    6. Prosecutor's respectfulness/surliness.
    7. Judge's relative favoratism.
    8. Judge's respectfulness/surliness.
    9. Victim's sex.
  10. Victim's age.

Table 10.2
Summary of stepwise regression analysis

Step	Variable	R^2 after this step
1	Defense attorney's convincingness	.047
2	Defense attorney's supportive reactions for prosecutor	.072
3	Prosecutor's respectfulness/surliness	.090
4	Prosecutor's interest/indifference	.098
5	Prosecutor's supportive reactions for defense attorney	.106
5	Judge's relative favoritism	.113
7	Defense attorney's knowledge of evidence	.114
8	Judge's respectfulness/surliness	.114

tion, when corrected for shrinkage, indicated that 6.2% of the total variability in CR was accounted for.

DISCUSSION

The demographic and behavioral characteristics of the defendant and the victim provided by the Trial Form were not generally related to the jury's conviction rate, the one exception being the low conviction rate for cases involving isolated sex offenses toward a female victim.[23] Of course, caution must always be exercised when one fails to reject a null hypothesis (Greenwald, 1975); unreliable measurement, variables with restricted ranges (e.g., defendant's and victim's sex), or tests with low power (a more serious problem for the present tests of victim characteristics) may all obscure real relationships. One must also consider the strong likelihood that even if such characteristics do affect juries' verdicts, the effects are quite likely to be weak ones. It seems likely that defendant and victim characteristics are secondary to evidentiary considerations in most juries' deliberations. Hence, only when the evidence is highly equivocal (probably the exception rather than the rule), should such characteristics have much effect on

---

[23]One ought not to conclude that these results contradict the sizable experimental literature that has reported a myriad of effects due to defendant and victim characteristics. With few exceptions (e.g., Nemeth and Sosis, 1973), the experimental research has not examined the demographic variables that were studied here. Instead, most of the experimental work has focused on variables that have been linked to interpersonal attraction in previous research (e.g., physical attractiveness, defendant–juror similarity).

verdicts. Thus, we are probably not likely to account for much of the variance in jury behavior using such characteristics; if our interest is exclusively predictive, they are probably not very useful. Of course, if our interest extends to the fitness of juries to carry out their responsibilities, even small or infrequently applied juror biases may be important, particularly when they are based on extralegal factors.

A curious pattern emerges from the analyses of the attorneys' behaviors. Those behaviors that were related to success in winning acquittals by the defense attorney seemed to make good sense. When defense attorneys displayed a good working knowledge of the evidence and made convincing arguments against conviction, they tended to win more cases. Also, the effective defense attorneys tended to react in a positive manner to the prosecutor. The impression of an effective defense attorney one is left with is of interpersonal cordiality, careful preparation, and well-developed rhetorical skills. The data suggest a different, more counterintuitive impression of the effective prosecutor. When prosecutors reacted favorably toward their opponent, they were less likely to win—a reversal of the pattern for defense attorneys. The reason for this result is not clear; perhaps when the prosecutor reacts in a friendly, supportive way to the defense, the jury comes to view the defendant in a more positive, sympathetic light. Finally, a prosecutor who appeared to be especially interested or respectful won fewer convictions than one who was less so. There are many plausible ways one might interpret this result. For example, if the prosecutor was relatively unsympathetic toward the defendant, the jurors may have adopted a similar attitude. Observers may have translated the prosecutor's indifference to the fate of the defendant into high ratings on the prosecutor's interest/ indifference scale. Likewise, a harsh, punitive attitude toward the defendant by the prosecutor might result in a relatively high score on the respectfulness/surliness scale. This interpretation is consistent with the results for the prosecutor's supportive reactions to the defense. Alternatively, as suggested earlier, the jurors may have seen high prosecutor interest as overeagerness for a conviction, and the high prosecutor respectfulness as obsequiousness. The impression of the effective prosecutor that emerges from these analyses is of an unemotional and relentless accuser. Although the impressions of effective defense and prosecution tactics offered here are admittedly speculative, the data clearly demonstrate that the moods, styles, and skills of the contesting attorneys in a criminal trial are associated with the trial's outcome.

In an adversary system of justice, it doesn't surprise us greatly that the jury's evaluation of the advocates may also affect its evaluation of the cases being advocated. However, it is more unexpected and, perhaps, disturbing to find that the in-court behavior of the judge may also influence a jury's verdict. Under our adversary system, the judge of a jury trial is charged with enforcing the rules of evidence and declaring the law to the jury. In a few instances, judges may even express opinions on the case, although whenever this is done the jurors are told that they may reject this opinion if they choose. But while judges preside over a jury trial they are supposed to maintain a strict neutrality toward the two contesting parties. However, the present data suggest that judges are sometimes perceived as favoring one side over the other and, furthermore, that when this occurred, the favored side was more likely to prevail. This perceived favoritism is conveyed in different ways: through courtesy, through a greater responsiveness in motor mannerisms to one side, and through the apparent impartiality with which issues were decided. Furthermore, the less respectful the judge was perceived to be, the higher the conviction ratio tended to be. In line with this result, such judicial surliness seemed to be directed more strongly at the defense than at the prosecution. Thus, the judge's surly attitude may have communicated to the jurors, perhaps inaccurately, an impression that the judge saw less merit in the defense's case. Another interesting possibility raised previously is that judges may serve as emotional models for the jurors. Regardless of their biases, the present results suggest that much greater care may be required from judges if they are to successfully fulfill their roles as neutral arbiters. Stronger warnings to the jury about disregarding any overt or implicit indications of opinion by judges may also be warranted, although the ability of jurors to understand and follow judicial instructions remains in doubt (Elwork, Sales, and Alfini, 1977; Kerr et al., 1976). Another procedural safeguard would be to increase the number of peremptory challenges of judges allowed to the attorneys.

The significance of the present results does not lie in the identification of an exhaustive and powerful set of predictors of jury verdicts. The proportion of variance of verdicts accounted for by the best of the predictors was small (estimated to be between 4% and 6%, depending on the number of predictors included). Other limitations of this study have been touched on earlier: e.g., the high risk of Type I errors (i.e., some of the significant correlations may be attributable to chance); the inability to obtain data on many potentially interesting variables (e.g., defendant and victim physical attractiveness, weight of evidence); the disregard of high-order interaction effects; the ambiguity about direction or existence of causality; and the possibility that problems in reliability of measurement may have obscured the importance of various measures. The significance of such limitations for qualifying the results can be determined only through further research.[24]

Despite these limitations, the methodology and the results of this study are noteworthy in several regards. The data demonstrate that at least some of the salient inputs to the jury decision-making process may be captured without continuous observation through the entire length of a trial; the observations of irregularity attending audience members can reveal interesting relationships. Furthermore, the observers may not need special training or expertise in the law or in psychology; the student observers had no noteworthy qualifications. This is not to say that long-term scrutiny by expert observers may not be an even more productive source of information, but rather that student observers, working under the observational constraints of this study, may detect some of the factors that influence jurors' decision-making.

The most interesting aspect of this study is the particular kinds of factors that were revealed. Many of the obtained relationships (e.g., those involving judges' respectfulness/surliness and attorneys' supportive reactions to one another) have not, to my knowledge, been reported elsewhere and may represent the first concrete, empirical demonstrations of an association between the in-courtroom behavior of the officers of the court and juries' decision-making. They also suggest that these behaviors may often be subtle ones of mood or nonverbal behavior. Those relationships that suggest the operation of extralegal factors are particularly interesting. Some of the obtained relationships clearly do not fall within this category; for example, the

---

[24]Additional research should take a two-pronged approach. First, the factors suggested by the correlational analysis should be examined further within an experimental setting. The effect of most conceivable confounding legal factors can thereby be controlled. For example, videotaped simulated trials could be constructed in which the judge's respectfulness/surliness and favoritism were manipulated orthogonally, while the evidential content of the case was kept constant across all versions. An experimental approach also seems the most efficient for determining which, if any, of the obtained significant results were, in fact, Type I errors. Second, more extensive field research should be undertaken to examine the reliability and scope of the results obtained in the present study. Several important changes in the research methodology seem advisable. Observers should be scheduled so as to permit reliability checks on all measures. Also, having an observer at every session of each trial observed would not only produce a more complete, and hence valid, summary of trial-long behavior, but it would also permit an assessment of the overall weight of evidence. It is also important to check to what extent the obtained effects depended on the type of offense. The effects of victim age and sex illustrated how offense-specific effects could produce a significant result in the entire sample. The desired analysis could be accomplished by obtaining much larger samples, so that many replications existed for specific offenses. A related alternative, which is more economical, would be to restrict attention to a few carefully chosen and representative offenses.

convincingness of defense attorneys' arguments and their knowledge of the evidence may be straightforwardly interpreted as legally sanctioned manifestations of a strong defense case. It is also possible that some of the other relationships may be due to a confounding of legal and extralegal factors. For example, as mentioned earlier, the weight of evidence and judges' respectfulness/surliness may be related, with the former and not the latter affecting juries' verdicts. It is conceivable that a few of the other obtained correlations are spurious for similar reasons (e.g., those involving judges' favoritism, and the trends involving number of dismissed charges and the relative ages of the contesting attorneys). However, several of the relationships do not seem to readily lend themselves to any straightforward "legal" interpretation (e.g., the effects of prosecutors' interest and respectfulness). Again, more research is needed to determine the degree of confounding between legal and extralegal factors.

APPENDIX: PREDICTOR VARIABLES
FROM THE TRIAL FORM

Defendant variables

1. Race (1 = white, 0 = nonwhite)

2. Age

3. Sex (1 = female, 0 = male)

4. Awareness (1 = interested, 7 = indifferent)

5. Mannerisms (1 = calm, 7 = nervous)

6. Attitude (1 = respectful, 7 = surly)

7. Conduct (1 = aggressive, 7 = passive)

Derived variables

8. Ethnic similarity of jury and defendant (= |proportion white jurors − defendant race|)

9. Sex similarity of jury and defendant (= |proportion female jurors − defendant sex|)

10. Age similarity of jury and defendant (= |average age of jurors − defendant's age|)

Defense attorney variables

1. Status (1 = court-appointed, 2 = privately retained)

2. Utilizes materials in court (1 = never, 7 = frequently)

3. Cites cases and raises objections (1 = never, 7 = frequently)

4. Appears to have working knowledge of evidence (1 = poor, 7 = excellent)

5. Rate of negative reactions to judge

6. Rate of negative reactions to prosecutor

7. Rate of supportive reactions to judge

8. Rate of supportive reactions to prosecutor

9. Degree of emotional impact utilized (1 = weak, 7 = strong)

10. Degree of rational appeal utilized (1 = weak, 7 = strong)

11. Makes convincing argument against conviction (1 = poor, 7 − excellent)

12. Overall impression of impartiality afforded defendant's case (1 − poor, 7 − excellent)

13. Age

14. Awareness (1 = interested, 7 = indifferent)

15. Mannerisms (1 = calm, 7 = nervous)

16. Attitude (1 = respectful, 7 = surly)

17. Conduct (1 = aggressive, 7 = passive)

Derived variables

18. Skill (average of defense attorney variables 2, 3, 4, 11)

19. Emotionalism (average of defense attorney variable 9 and variable 10 [with polarity reversed])

Prosecutor variables

1. Utilizes materials in court (1 = never, 7 = frequently)

2. Cites cases and raises objections (1 = never, 7 = frequently)

3. Appears to have working knowledge of evidence (1 = poor, 7 = excellent)

4. Rate of negative reactions to judge

5. Rate of negative reactions to defense attorney

6. Rate of supportive reactions to judge

7. Rate of supportive reactions to defense attorney

8. Degree of emotional impact utilized (1 = weak, 7 = strong)

9. Degree of rational appeal utilized (1 = weak, 7 = strong)

10. Makes convincing argument for conviction (1 = poor, 7 = excellent)

11. Overall impression of impartiality afforded prosecutor's case (1 = poor, 7 = excellent)

12. Age

13. Awareness (1 = interested, 7 = indifferent)

14. Mannerisms (1 = calm, 7 = nervous)

15. Attitude (1 = respectful, 7 = surly)

16. Conduct (1 = aggressive, 7 = passive)

Derived variables

17. Skill (average of prosecutor variables 1, 2, 3, 10)

18. Emotionalism (average of prosecutor variable 8 and variable 9 [with polarity reversed])

Prosecutor–defense attorney relationships

1. Rapport between contending attorneys (1 = hostile, 7 = amiable)

Derived variables

2. Relative skill (defense attorney's skill − prosecutor's skill)

3. Relative emotionalism (defense attorney's emotionalism − prosecutor's emotionalism)

4. Relative ages (defense attorney's age − prosecutor's age)

Judge variables

1. Reacts courteously to defense attorney (1 = never, 7 = frequently)

2. Reacts courteously to prosecutor (1 = never, 7 = frequently)

3. Rate of holding for defense on objections

4. Rate of holding for prosecutor on objections

5. Rate of urging others to hurry

6. Rate of privileged conferences with opposing attorneys

7. Appears to decide issues impartially (1 = never, 7 = frequently)

8. Rate of negative reactions to prosecutor

9. Rate of negative reactions to defense attorney

10. Rate of supportive reactions to prosecutor

11. Rate of supportive reactions to defense attorney

12. By motor mannerisms, appears to be more responsive to presentations of either adversary (1 = defense, 7 = prosecutor)

13. Age

14. Awareness (1 = interested, 7 = indifferent)

15. Mannerisms (1 = calm, 7 = nervous)

16. Attitude (1 = respectful, 7 = surly)

17. Conduct (1 = aggressive, 7 = passive)

Derived variables

18. Favoritism for defense attorney (average of judge variables 1 and 12, appropriately scaled)

19. Favoritism for prosecutor (average of judge variables 2 and 12)

20. Relative favoritism $\left((8.0 - \#17) \times (\#18 - \#19) \right)$

Victim variables

1. Race (1 = white, 0 = nonwhite)

2. Age

3. Sex (1 = female, 0 = male)

    4. Awareness (1 = interested, 7 = indifferent)

    5. Mannerisms (1 = calm, 7 = nervous)

    6. Attitude (1 = respectful, 7 = surly)

    7. Conduct (1 = aggressive, 7 = passive)

Derived variables

    8. Ethnic similarity of jury and victim (= |proportion of white jurors − victim race|)

    9. Sex similarity of jury and victim (= |proportion of female jurors − victim's sex|)

    10. Age similarity of jury and victim (= |average age of juror − victim's age|)

Case variables

    1. Number of defendants

    2. Number of charges

    3. Number of charges dismissed

    4. Mean number of charges per defendant

References

Annual report of the director of the Administrative Office of the United States Courts, 1972. Washington, DC: U.S. Government Printing Office, 1973.

Beiser, E. Are juries representative? *Judicature*, 1973, 57, 194–199.

Bermant, G., McGuire, M., McKinley, W., & Salo, C. The logic of simulation in jury research. *Criminal Justice and Behavior*, 1974, 1, 224–233.

Bray, R. M., & Kerr, N. L. Methodological issues in the study of the psychology of the courtroom. In N. L. Kerr and R. M. Bray (Eds.), *The psychology of the courtroom.* New York: Academic Press, in press.

Coombs, C. Thurstone's measurement of social values revisited forty years later. *Journal of Personality and Social Psychology*, 1967, 6, 85–91.

Dane, F., & Wrightsman, L. Effects of defendant and victim characteristics on juror judgments. In N. L. Kerr & R. M. Bray (Eds.), *The psychology of the courtroom.* New York: Academic Press, in press.

Davis, J. H., Bray, R., & Holt, R. The empirical study of decision processes in juries: A critical review. In J. Tapp and F. Levine (Eds.), *Law, justice and the individual in society: Psychological and legal issues.* New York: Holt, 1977.

Diamond, S. S., & Zeisel, H. A courtroom experiment on juror selection and decision-making. *Personality and Social Psychology Bulletin*, 1974, 1, 276–277.

Ebbesen, E. B., & Konečni, V. J. Fairness in sentencing: Severity of crime and judicial decision-making. Paper presented at annual convention of American Psychological Association, Washington, DC, 1976.

Efran, M. G. The effects of physical appearance on the judgment of guilt, interpersonal attraction, and severity of recommended punishment in a simulated jury task. *Journal of Research in Personality*, 1974, 8, 45–54.

Elwork, A., Sales, B. D., & Alfini, J. J. Juridic decisions: In ignorance of the law or in light of it? *Law and Human Behavior*, 1977, 1, 163–190.

Frank, J. *Courts on trial: Myth and reality in American justice*. Princeton, NJ: Princeton University Press, 1949.

Ginger, A. F. *Jury selection in criminal trials: New techniques and concepts*. Tiburon, CA: Lawpress, 1975.

Greenwald, A. Consequences of prejudice against the null hypothesis. *Psychological Bulletin*, 1975, 82, 1–20.

Griffitt, W., & Jackson, T. Simulated jury decisions: The influence of jury–defendant attitude similarity–dissimilarity. *Social Behavior and Personality*, 1973, 1, 1–7.

Jones, C., & Aronson, E. Attribution of fault to a rape victim as a function of respectability of the victim. *Journal of Personality and Social Psychology*, 1973, 26, 415–419.

Kalven, H., Jr., & Zeisel, H. *The American jury*. Boston: Little, Brown, 1966.

Keeton, R. *Trial tactics and methods*. Boston: Little, Brown, 1954.

Kerr, N. L. Beautiful and blameless: Effects of victim attractiveness and responsibility on jurors' judgments. *Personality and Social Psychology Bulletin*, 1978, 4, 479–482.

Kerr, N. L., Atkin, R., Stasser, G., Meek, D., Holt, R., & Davis, J. H. Guilt beyond a reasonable doubt: Effects of concept definition and assigned decision rule on the judgments of mock jurors. *Journal of Personality and Social Psychology*, 1976, 34, 282–294.

Kerr, N. L., & Bray, R. M. (Eds.). *The psychology of the courtroom*. New York: Academic Press, in press.

Kerr, N. L., Nerenz, D., & Herrick, D. Role playing and the study of jury behavior. *Sociological Methods and Research*, 1979, 7, 337–355.

Landy, D., & Aronson, E. The influence of the character of the criminal and his victim on the decisions of simulated jurors. *Journal of Experimental Social Psychology*, 1969, 5, 141–152.

Lerner, M., & Simmons, C. Observer's reaction to the "innocent victim": Compassion or rejection? *Journal of Personality and Social Psychology*, 1966, 4, 203–210.

Leslie, R. Minorities and the petit jury system. Unpublished report of San Diego County Human Relations Commission, 1975.

McComas, W. C., & Noll, M. E. Effects of seriousness of charge and punishment severity on the judgments of simulated jurors. *Psychological Record*, 1974, 24, 545–547.

Marshall, J. *Law and psychology in conflict*. Garden City, NY: Doubleday, 1969.

Miller, G. R. Jurors' responses to videotaped trial materials: Some recent findings. *Personality and Social Psychology Bulletin*, 1975, 1, 561–569.

Mills, E. Statistical profile of jurors in a U.S. District Court. *Law and the Social Order*, 1969, 1, 329.

Mitchell, H., & Byrne, D. The defendant's dilemma: Effects of jurors' attitudes and authoritarianism on judicial decisions. *Journal of Personality and Social Psychology*, 1973, 25, 123–129.

National Criminal Justice Information and Statistical Services. *Criminal victimization surveys in thirteen American cities.* Washington, DC: U.S. Government Printing Office, 1975.

Nemeth, C., & Sosis, R. A simulated jury: Characteristics of the defendant and the jurors. *Journal of Social Psychology*, 1973, *90*, 221–229.

Owen, I. *Defending criminal cases before juries: A common-sense approach.* Englewood Cliffs, NJ: Prentice-Hall, 1973.

Ryan, W. *Blaming the victim.* New York: Pantheon, 1970.

Scroggs, J. Penalties for rape as a function of victim provocativeness, damage, and resistance. *Journal of Applied Social Psychology*, 1976, *4*, 360–368.

Sealy, A., & Cornish, W. Jurors and their verdicts. *Modern Law Review*, 1973, *36*, 496–508.

Sigall, H., & Ostrove, N. Beautiful but dangerous: Effects of offender attractiveness and nature of the crime on juridic judgment. *Journal of Personality and Social Psychology*, 1975, *31*, 410–414.

Simon, R. *The jury and the defense of insanity.* Boston: Little, Brown, 1967.

Simon, R., & Mahan, L. Quantifying burdens of proof: A view from the bench, the jury, and the classroom. *Law and Society Review*, 1971, *5*, 319–330.

Smith, M. Percy Foreman: Top trial lawyer. *Life*, 1966, *60*, 92–101.

Strodtbeck, F. Social processes, the law, and jury functioning. In W. M. Evan (Ed.), *Law and sociology: Exploratory essays*, New York: Free Press, 1962.

Sutherland, E. *Principles of criminology.* Philadelphia: Lippincott, 1966.

Sutherland, E., & Cressey, D. *Criminology.* 9th Ed. Philadelphia: Lippincott, 1974.

Vidmar, N. Effects of decision alternatives on the verdicts and social perceptions of simulated jurors. *Journal of Personality and Social Psychology*, 1972, *22*, 211–218.

Wilson, D. W., & Donnerstein, E. Guilty or not guilty? A look at the "simulated" jury paradigm. *Journal of Applied Social Psychology*, 1977, *7*, 175–190.

THE SENTENCING DECISION

11

An Analysis of the Sentencing System

Vladimir J. Konečni and Ebbe B. Ebbesen

Sentencing occupies a central position in the administration of criminal justice. Decisions made at this stage have not only important consequences for offenders, but they also affect the entire criminal justice system. Judges and magistrates are given enormous power over the lives of individuals. The proper exercise of that power is a matter of concern to offenders, to the agencies and individuals responsible for law enforcement and the treatment of offenders, and to the public at large. (Hogarth, 1971, p. 3)

The sentencing decisions taken by magistrates and judges occupy a central place in the penal process, not only in the obvious chronological sense, but more significantly because of their direct and indirect influences upon the police and pretrial stages which precede them, and upon the subsequent implementation of the penal measures imposed upon convicted offenders. [I]n ... most ... jurisdictions ..., magistrates and judges possess wide discretionary powers in the choice of sentence . . . . (Bottomley, 1973, p. 130)

There is no decision in the criminal process that is so complicated and so difficult to make as that of the sentencing judge. (President's Commission . . . , 1967, p. 141)

Sentencing is almost universally viewed as the apex of the criminal justice process, the culmination of protracted investigatory, prosecutorial, defense, administrative, and fact-finding efforts. As can be seen from the quotations above, writers agree that sentencing has a central position in the criminal justice system—temporally, administratively, and in the size of its impact on both the preceding and the subsequent stages. It is commonly thought that sentencing decisions are very complex and difficult to make and that they require much training, experience, and wisdom. (Judges would, of course, be quick to agree with such an opinion, skeptics like Judge Frank [1949] notwithstanding.) Furthermore, all observers readily acknowledge that in most jurisdictions the sentencing judges have extensive and wide-ranging discretionary powers both in the choice of sentence and in the decision rule used in that choice.

Typically, judges have vigorously defended this state of affairs, especially since the advent of the concept of "individualized justice," on the grounds that their discretionary powers in sentencing represent their very *raison d'être* and affirm their alleged independence from political pressures and passing social mores. As Bottomley (1973) has pointed out, sentencing decisions are supposedly more open to public scrutiny than are all other decisions within the criminal justice system.[1] The facts that sentencing decisions are visible, occasionally have an impact on public opinion, and for many people epitomize society's control over its aberrant members make sentencing a highly important social issue.

A great deal has been written about sentencing. The bulk of the nonempirical literature is devoted to discussions of the purpose of sentencing and a formalization of philosophies of sentencing (ranging from simple retribution, to deterrence of the offender and others, to rehabilitation, and to various combinations thereof). More recently, the issue of disparity in sentencing has received a considerable amount of both theoretical and empirical attention (Bottomley, 1973; Carter and Wilkins, 1967; Diamond and Zeisel, 1975; Ebbesen and Konečni, 1981; Green, 1961; Hagan, 1975; Hogarth, 1971; Hood, 1962). Explanations offered for sentencing disparity have been in terms of differences among judges in personality, values, and various types of attitudes (Hogarth, 1971), differences among probation officers along similar lines as among judges (Carter and Wilkins, 1967), and case-load factors, i.e., that different judges get different types of cases assigned to them (see Ebbesen and Konečni, 1981, for a dis-

---

[1]The visibility of sentencing decisions sometimes has as a corollary that these decisions are used as indicators of a particular judge's character, personality, and even ability to hold public office. Eville Younger's handing down of a relatively mild sentence to a convicted rapist came to haunt him many years later when he ran, in 1978, for the office of Governor of the State of California. The incumbent Governor Edmund G. Brown, Jr., saw fit to focus on this one sentencing decision from Younger's long record as a judge. Presumably in an attempt to exploit politically the public's indignation about rape and to characterize Younger's personality and values as undesirable to both women and law-and-order voters, the sentencing decision in the rape case was described in some detail in a frequently broadcast radio announcement paid for by the Brown reelection committee.

cussion of this issue). The literature is also replete with attempts to minimize disparity by providing guidelines for sentencing judges (Gottfredson, Wilkins, and Hoffman, 1978; American Law Institute, 1962; President's Commission . . . , 1967).

In contrast to the previous work, our objective in the domain of sentencing has been to discover empirically the factors that sentencing judges consider in making their decisions and the relative weights that they assign to these factors. In other words, we have attempted to discover judges' decision strategies and to develop a causal model of sentencing. As we have pointed out elsewhere (Ebbesen and Konečni, 1981), once sentencing is viewed from this perspective, the issue of disparity becomes secondary.

Our work in this area follows the general decision-making orientation and methodological guidelines we described in our earlier chapters in this volume. Many aspects of our work on sentencing have already been described elsewhere (Ebbesen and Konečni, 1981; Konečni and Ebbesen, 1979); a condensed description of the methodology, main findings, and conclusions will suffice for the purposes of this volume.

Before we turn to these matters, however, it is necessary to describe briefly (1) some of the events that precede the actual pronouncement of the sentence in the modal adult felony case in San Diego County (where the research was done), (2) the sentencing hearing itself, and (3) the sentencing options available to the judge. This will also clarify the relationship of the sentencing decision to other decision nodes in the criminal justice system that are dealt with in other chapters of this volume.

In 1976 and 1977, there were more than 24,000 felony arrests in San Diego County (see Figure 2.1 in Chapter 2, this volume, for more details). Of these, only about 20% reached the Superior Court. (The remaining cases were resolved by actions such as release by the police, dismissal in lower-court review, the prosecutor's refusal to file a felony complaint, or a misdemeanor conviction in a lower court.) Of the cases that did reach the Superior Court, 7.44% were dismissed by a judge, 1.22% acquitted by a jury, and 91.17% convicted. The vast majority of convictions were obtained through a plea of guilty (85.54% or a no-contest plea (6.12%); 8.15% were convicted as a result of a trial (by a jury, 6.77%; or by a judge, 1.38%). One consequence of the very high frequency of plea bargaining is that charges for which offenders are convicted often bear little resemblance to charges for which they were arrested. Another consequence is that in a typical case the sentencing judge has a very limited familiarity with the case (as there has been no trial).

The sentencing hearing occurs several weeks after the defendant has been convicted of a felony. In the meantime, a probation officer investigates the case and presents to the judge an 8–15-page report. The report typically contains a wealth of information, varying from the description of the crime, arrest, charges, and postarrest events (bail, plea-bargaining activity, etc.), to a summary of the interview with the defendant and information obtained from other sources (family members, employers, neighbors, psychologists), to an evaluation by the probation officer of the totality of the facts of the case. The report, significantly, concludes with a detailed recommendation regarding the sentence to be imposed.

Sentencing hearings themselves are typically very brief and consist of an informal discussion among the judge, the prosecutor, and the defense attorney (the defendant and the probation officer are also present, but rarely speak). Judges typically explain the sentence to the defendants, after insuring that the defendants understand their rights (especially when a plea of guilty is involved).

At the time when the research to be discussed later was carried out, California had an indeterminate sentencing system. The three main sentence options available to the judge were:

1. State prison for an indeterminate period of which the minimum and maximum were specified by the California Penal Code.

2. Custody of the sheriff (county jail) for a period of no more than 12 months, almost always followed by a probationary period not longer than 5 years.

3. A probationary period, again not longer than 5 years per conviction, without any confinement.

The sentencing recommendation made in the probation officer's report is phrased with a view to these sentence options available to the judge.

THE SAN DIEGO SENTENCING PROJECT

Because of the importance of sentencing within the criminal justice system, we decided to use a relatively comprehensive multimethod approach that relied on different subject populations and experimental designs. Early in the project, we had considerable hopes of learning a great deal about sentencing through the process of "converging operations" (Webb et al., 1966). Our first studies were simulations, in that real court cases were not involved (even though the subjects were real judges in some of the studies); these simulations will be discussed first. Subsequently, we will describe our studies of the real-world sentencing process: (1) the observation and coding of sentencing hearings and (2) the coding of the documents available to the judge at the hearing (the archival approach).

Simulation studies

Four different data-collection methods and four subject populations were used in several different studies. (A far more detailed description of these studies is available in Konečni and Ebbesen, 1981.)

Interview   In one of these studies, undergraduate students from the University of California at San Diego (UCSD) interviewed eight San Diego County Superior Court judges in their chambers. These students had a considerable amount of prior preparation regarding interviewing techniques and the criminal justice system in California; however, they were unaware of the overall project and the conclusions from our previous work on the criminal justice system. Hopefully, this removed any of our own biases regarding the value of simulations from the conclusions that these students reached on the basis of this data-collection method. Moreover, on the assumption that much of the general public's knowledge about the criminal justice system and sentencing is shaped by the media, which, in turn, largely rely on the interview as a data-gathering method, we thought that it would be appropriate to use journalists as "methodological informants," just as the judges themselves were being used as "content informants." Therefore, on our instructions, the student interviewers spent a great deal of time with newspaper reporters assigned to the courthouse press room, seeking advice about the kinds of questions one should ask of judges in order to be able to write a newspaper article about sentencing in San Diego. Having interviewed the judges, the students summarized their conclusions without any contribution from us and published them as an article in a major San Diego daily (Persky, Sprague, and Lowe, 1975).

Questionnaire   In this study, several sociology majors developed an elaborate questionnaire to investigate sentencing. This group's "methodological informants" were UCSD graduate students in sociology, whose help in questionnaire construction and evaluation of the obtained data was solicited by the researchers (on our instructions). As in the interview group, the questionnaire researchers were unaware of our prior work, yet had been thoroughly familiarized with the rules of questionnaire construction and administration, the handling of data, and, more generally, with the criminal justice system in California. The 25-item questionnaire was eventually completed by 16 of the 26 judges on the bench (61%) at the time this study was conducted. Without any help or interpretive suggestions from us, the students then analyzed the data and wrote a detailed report (Frerichs, McKinney, and Tisner, 1975). Since the questionnaire is a frequently used research tool in the social sciences, especially sociology, our objective in this study was to simulate the research procedure that might be used by some sociologists to investigate sentencing.

Rating scales In this series of studies, an attempt was made to obtain direct ratings of the importance of various factors in the sentencing process. Three subject populations that differ sharply in the extent and type of their involvement in the real-world sentencing process were used.

In one rating-scale study, eight San Diego County Superior Court judges rated the following eight factors on 100–mm rating scales: (1) severity of crime, (2) probability of rehabilitation, (3) probation officer's recommendation, (4) prior record, (5) drug/alcohol use, (6) employment status, (7) family situation, and (8) educational level. These factors were chosen for inclusion because they seemed intrinsically interesting and had been frequently mentioned by judges in other studies in the project. The judges were urged to rate each factor in terms of its relative importance (i.e., compared to the other seven factors) in their own sentencing decisions in adult felony cases.

In another rating-scale study, 33 defense attorneys in the San Diego area, who had varying degrees of experience in criminal law (an average of more than 7 years of practice), filled out a long questionnaire that covered many issues regarding their work in the criminal justice system. In one section of the booklet, the attorneys rated various factors in terms of their perceptions of the relative weight assigned to these factors by the judges in sentencing. All factors rated by the judges were also rated by the attorneys, but the attorneys also rated additional factors.

Finally, UCSD students who had attended sentencing hearings rated the relative importance of 17 factors in the sentencing process, on the basis of their impressions in the hearings. The students, who were divided into "naive raters" (who observed no more than 4 sentencing hearings, $n = 27$) and "experienced raters" (who observed at least 25 hearings, $n = 8$), rated all eight factors rated by the judges and some additional ones.

Experimental simulations Three different types of subjects (judges, probation officers, and college students) were presented with brief descriptions of fictitious felony cases. Different levels of various factors that might be important in the sentencing process were defined by the wording of the descriptions.

In all, 12 judges responded to each of 48 cells of a fully crossed 5-factor experimental design, involving the following factors: (1) severity of crime, (2) prior record, (3) method of conviction, (4) family/ employment situation, and (5) probation officer's recommendation. For each factorial combination, the judges wrote out a complete sentence, as they would in real-life cases.

In the second type, 22 probation officers with a considerable amount of experience in felony cases were subjects in a similar 5-factor design (the probation officer's recommendation factor was replaced by one dealing with the extent of the offender's remorse). For each factorial combination, the probation officers wrote out a detailed sentence recommendation exactly as they would in real cases.

Finally, in an experiment with a within-subjects design, 35 UCSD students responded to 24 factorial combinations involving the following 4 variables: (1) severity of crime, (2) prior record, (3) family/ employment situation, and (4) remorse. In a between-subjects version of this study, 20 subjects were assigned to each of the identical 24 cells ($N = 480$). In both cases, the dependent measure was the "duration of the prison sentence [the offender should receive] in years"—a measure used very frequently in psycholegal research.

Summary of results   The main conclusions reached by Persky, Sprague, and Lowe (1975), authors of the newspaper article based on *interviews* with the judges, were that sentencing decisions are complex and difficult and that each case is different. In addition, it was noted that judges take many factors into account in deciding on the sentence and—although a lack of consensus among the judges was evident—more than a dozen "important" factors were specifically mentioned.

These conclusions echo to a remarkable degree the opinion expressed by the President's Commission in the quotation at the beginning of this chapter. It must be rather comforting for the judges that such a prestigious body thinks of their work in terms so similar to what they themselves think of it. Moreover, the canonization of the "individualized justice" and the "every case is different" *dicta* would, of course, preclude even the possibility of both a scientific analysis of sentencing (and other legal) decisions and their standardization (for example, by very explicit guidelines).

The results of the *questionnaire* study were somewhat similar to those obtained by the interview method, in that almost all judges listed at least four different factors as being highly important, the most frequently mentioned ones being severity of the crime, prior record, family situation, employment status, and drug/alcohol addiction and/or mental disorders. In addition, the importance of probation officers in the sentencing process was consistently played down by the judges, especially with regard to the probation officers' recommendations serving as a direct *causal* factor in the judges' decisions. However, Frerichs, McKinney, and Tisner (1975), in a speculative conclusion that went beyond the judges' responses, suggested that the probation officers' recommendations and judges' sentences may be independently affected by the same set of factors.

The *rating-scale* studies presented a complex and confusing picture. Judges rated severity of the crime, prior record, and family situation as being the most important factors. Whereas these three factors were also among those mentioned frequently in the questionnaire responses, another prominent factor that emerged in the questionnaire study—employment status—was now rated as the least important factor. In addition, whereas defense attorneys, like the judges, rated severity of the crime and prior record as highly important, their ratings of the remaining six factors showed very little similarity to those given by the judges. For example, factors such as family situation and drug/alcohol addiction—which had been given high ratings by the judges—were at the bottom of the defense attorneys' list. In contrast, the defense attorneys rated very highly the importance of the race and income (of the offender) factors, even though, not surprisingly, the judges consistently denied the importance of such factors in both their interview and their questionnaire responses. (However, since the judges did not rate these factors, a direct comparison was not possible.) Finally, "naive" and "experienced" student raters agreed with each other and with judges and defense attorneys regarding the importance of severity of the crime and prior record; however, in comparison to both groups of professionals, both groups of students attached far more importance to the probation officers' sentence recommendations. Beyond this agreement, the two groups of students agreed very little both with each other and with the judges and defense attorneys. As an illustration, whereas the naive raters (like the defense attorneys) considered the race of the defendant to be highly important, experienced students gave it among the lowest importance ratings.

The four *experimental simulations* also presented a confusing pattern. The results indicated that the judges considered severity of the crime and prior record to be the most important factors, and about equally so. Also statistically significant were the effects that showed that the judges would give harsher sentences to offenders who had been found guilty in a trial (as opposed to those who pleaded guilty) and to those for whom the probation officers' sentencing recommendations were more severe. Only the family/employment factor was not significant. In contrast, the results of the study with probation officers as subjects indicated that prior record was by far the most important factor, followed by severity of the crime, family/employment, and remorse. Only the method-of-conviction factor (trial versus plea of guilty) was not statistically significant. In the between-subjects design with UCSD students as subjects, all factors except the family/employment variable were significant (the latter had an $F-$ value of less than 1.00). In the within-subjects design, all four variables were highly significant.

Conclusions   Several different conclusions can be drawn from these four types of simulations, which involved nine separate studies and four different subject populations.

First, each study, each method $\times$ subject population combination, produced different results. Had only one study, or a small subset of them, been done, quite misleading conclusions would have almost certainly been reached (and presumably disseminated). Given the area of research and the conventional wisdom and vested interests in it, the danger of such erroneous conclusions being circulated or put into print would probably have been augmented by the fact that each study had produced what seem to be—with the benefit of hindsight, of course—"reasonable" results.

On the other hand, the fact that numerous studies were done, each with different results, serves only the healthy purpose of reducing one's confidence in any one of them. When one compares simulations to each other, there are typically no logical or practical criteria on the basis of which to give preference to one type over another. Even using a real-world subject population—such as the judges—does not necessarily increase the value of a simulation: What one gains in "inside knowledge" and "authenticity" may be more than offset by job-related biases or self-serving responses. Moreover, even real-world subjects may be unaware of the "true" causes of a phenomenon or may mistakenly believe that something about them (e.g., in the case of the judges, their values or the legal doctrines to which they subscribe) causes the phenomenon.

In addition to the differences in the results obtained by the four methodological approaches, considerably different patterns of data were produced by the same methodology (e.g., rating scales) applied to different subject populations. Whereas one could, of course, argue that such differences were only to be expected given the range of populations used, no one could have predicted the extent and type of disagreement. Even differences as seemingly trivial from a substantive point of view as using a different type of experimental design with the *same* population—within- versus between-subjects experimental simulations with student subjects—resulted in different data patterns. (This difference could not be explained away by the greater sensitivity of within-subjects designs—see footnote 6 of Konečni and Ebbesen, 1981.)

It should be noted that two factors, severity of the crime and prior record, emerged in *all* of the studies, all of the method × subject population combinations. Here, then, would be a perfect example of "triangulation" (in the sense of Webb et al., 1966), a finding to be superconfident about since it survived the rigors of multimethod and multipopulation testing. Yet, if one is to believe the results of the archival real-world study of sentencing discussed in the next section, even this conclusion would be entirely misleading. In a more complete causal model of sentencing decisions, severity of the crime and prior record are only second-order factors.

Real-world studies

Our studies of the real-world sentencing process had been planned from the inception of the project, but they received a great deal of impetus from our growing skepticism about the value of simulations. Analogous to our procedure in the case of bail decisions (Chapter 8, this volume), our strategy was to examine statistically the covariation between a large number of potential "predictors" in the two major information sources that are available to the sentencing judge and the judges' sentencing decisions. One of these sources of information is the sentencing hearing itself—the arguments and discussions that occur and whatever information is provided by the offender's appearance, age, dress, articulateness, etc. The second source of information is a file that the judge presumably reviews prior to the hearing. The file contains documents pertaining to arraignment, formal indictment, change of plea, prior record, and so on. Moreover, it contains the probation officer's report (described earlier), which is typically placed in a file as late as 16–24 hours before the hearing.

The only other potential sources of information about a case that a judge may have are (1) the trial (i.e., further details of the case that are revealed in it, arguments, the defendant's behavior, apparent credibility, and so on), and (2) consultations (whether formal or not) with the prosecutor and the defense attorney concerning the plea bargain. With regard to the information from the trial, whereas it is indeed the case that when there is a trial, the trial judge typically also presides at the sentencing hearing and decides on the sentence, we have already pointed out that 86% of the convictions come about as a result of the guilty plea, and another 6% from the *nolo contendere* plea. Thus, there are no trials in more than 90% of the cases resulting in convictions. On the other hand, plea-bargaining consultations may or may not provide case-relevant information to the judge, but unfortunately, it was impossible for us to gain access to these meetings (held in the judge's chambers instead of the courtroom).

The observation and coding of sentencing hearings   More than 400 sentencing hearings were coded by our assistants in 1976 and 1977. The coders rated the offender's articulateness, attractiveness, attentiveness, and several other characteristics on 10-point scales, and used a time-sampling procedure to code the verbal interactions in the hearings. Every 10 seconds the coders noted who was talking, as well as the topic (the coder selected 1 of 70 content categories from a reference sheet). This procedure produced, for each sentencing hearing, and each coder present, a string of codes indicating who talked, about what, and after whom. (See Ebbesen and Konečni, 1981, for information regarding the various indices of reliability of coding that were used; the reliability was quite high. Appendix I of the same article lists the content categories used in the coding.)

Some information about the formal aspects of these sentencing hearings is presented in Tables 11.1 and 11.2. From Table 11.1, it seems that hearings were verbally dominated by judges and defense

Table 11.1
Verbal contribution of participants in sentencing hearing (n = 404)

Measure of extent of participation	Judge	Prosecutor	Defense attorney	Offender	Probation officer
Average percent of time speaking	42.2	13.0	38.4	2.8	3.2
Percent of cases in which at least one utterance was made	100.0	63.1	93.3	9.2	19.1
Mean length of utterance (in seconds)	15.1	10.2	19.1	25.9	2.2

SOURCE: E. B. Ebbesen and V. J. Konečni, The process of sentencing adult felons: A causal analysis of judicial decisions. In B. D. Sales (Ed.), *Perspectives in law and psychology.* Vol. 2: *The jury, judicial, and trial process.* New York: Plenum, 1981.

Table 11.2
Probability that a particular participant at sentencing hearing spoke after another participant

Preceding participant	Following participant				
	Judge	Prosecutor	Defense attorney	Offender	Probation officer
Judge		.180	.558	.161	.101
Assistant district attorney	.499		.133	.110	.208
Defense attorney	.459	.337		.071	.133
Offender	.362	.160	.251		.225
Probation officer	.547	.128	.209	.115	

SOURCE: E. B. Ebbesen and V. J. Konečni, The process of sentencing adult felons: A causal analysis of judicial decisions. In B. D. Sales (Ed.), *Perspectives in law and psychology.* Vol. 2: *The jury, judicial, and trial process.* New York: Plenum, 1981.

attorneys, though offenders spoke for a relatively long time when given a chance to speak. In general, however, both the offenders and the probation officers contributed relatively little to the hearings. From Table 11.2, one can see that the modal verbal-interaction pattern was for the judge to be followed by the defense attorney, who was, in turn, followed either by the judge immediately or first by the prosecutor and then by the judge.

The data in Table 11.3 provide some information about how the participants in the hearings distributed their speaking time across some selected topics and the extent to which their contribution on a particular topic was favorable or unfavorable to the offender. Not surprisingly, defense attorneys and judges addressed each of the topics; but whereas the defense attorneys stressed those aspects of each topic that were favorable to the defendant, the judges—significantly, like the prosecutors—stressed negative aspects of the crime and the offender's prior record. The judges did tend, though, to discuss the family and employment factors in a way that was favorable to the offenders, whereas the prosecutors remained silent about these "soft" issues that supposedly contribute to "individualized justice."

Although these findings may be interesting and convey some of the flavor of the sentencing hearings, none of the predictors we isolated from the content and formal aspects of the hearings was associated (to a statistically significant degree) with the final sentencing deci-

Table 11.3
Percent of time in sentencing hearing that each participant spent discussing various topics favorably or unfavorably to offender

Topic	Relation to offender	Judge	Prosecutor	Defense attorney	Offender	Probation officer
Crime	Favorable	15.4	5.0	37.6	—	—
	Unfavorable	38.2	38.4	8.3	—	—
Prior record	Favorable	34.0	16.3	62.0	—	—
	Unfavorable	53.1	53.1	20.1	—	—
Family	Favorable	90.2	—	89.1	—	—
	Unfavorable	9.6	—	10.9	—	—
Employ-ment	Favorable	91.8	—	94.8	97.1	—
	Unfavorable	8.2	—	5.2	2.9	—
Attitude	Good	58.8	47.5	97.0	95.0	88.9
	Bad	41.2	52.5	3.0	5.0	11.1
Drugs and alcohol	Favorable	29.0	20.8	27.3	29.2	—
	Unfavorable	71.0	79.2	72.7	70.8	—

Note: A dash indicates there were too few observations on which to base meaningful statistics.
SOURCE: E. B. Ebbesen and V. J. Konečni, The process of sentencing adult felons: A causal analysis of judicial decisions. In B. D. Sales (Ed.), Perspectives in law and psychology. Vol. 2: The jury, judicial, and trial process. New York: Plenum, 1981.

sion (defined in terms of the three previously described sentencing options). The one exception was the trivial finding that the judges tended to give somewhat lighter sentences to offenders in whose sentencing hearings both the prosecutor and the defense attorney made more positive than negative comments, but even this effect vanished when we controlled for severity of the crime and prior record.

Further analyses revealed that neither the variables with traditionally accepted social-psychological relevance, such as the offender's physical attractiveness, nor the demographic variables, such as the offender's sex, age, race, education, marital status, and religion, had any statistically significant effect on the sentencing decisions that was independent of prior record and severity of the crime.[2] This lack of effects, especially regarding the race factor, may be surprising to

---

[2]Some of these negative findings are of interest, such as the lack of an effect on sentencing decisions of the offender's physical attractiveness. Perhaps because the work on the effects of physical attractiveness is mainstream research in social psychology, and because attractiveness as a factor is so easy to manipulate experimentally (by high school yearbook photos; never mind the naturally occurring range of facial beauty in convicted criminals!), this characteristic of fictitious offenders, victims, and witnesses has held the fascination of researchers in simulated legal psychology.

some, but we have confirmed it when analyses were carried out on an even larger number of cases, such as the sample of more than 1,000 discussed in the next section.[3]

All in all, as far as we could tell, nothing about the sentencing hearings seemed to have a direct impact on the judges' sentencing decisions. No piece of information available in the hearings turned out to be an important predictor. A typical sentencing hearing thus seems to function as a ritual—an expensive show for the offender and the public. In fact, the hearings seem to *obscure* the real predictors of the sentencing decisions. Not only was no predictor that was *uniquely* codable in the hearings (i.e., not available elsewhere) significant, but other basic and straightforward case factors—that by all rights should have been brought up in the hearings, such as prior record, jail/bail status after arrest, and probation officer's recommendation, to mention but a few—failed to emerge or were brought up in a laconic or an incomprehensible manner. Yet some of these bits of information were revealed by the archival analysis reported in the next section to be the important predictors of sentencing decisions.

Finally, from the methodological point of view, our observational study of sentencing hearings demonstrates rather well that the mere fact that simulations are replaced by real-world research by no means guarantees success—but, again, this becomes clear only after the research has already been done.

The coding of court files associated with sentencing   In the final study in this project, our assistants coded a total of about 1,200 court files in 1976 and 1977. These were the previously mentioned files that contain the probation officer's report and other documents and

---

[3]We should point out that the absence of a race effect in our results does not necessarily signify that race is ignored throughout the criminal justice system. For example, the California Penal Code may have been—intentionally or not—written in such a way that relatively longer or harsher sentences are intended for certain types of crimes that some racial groups may be more likely to commit because of their lifestyles, eonomic conditions, or values. Moreover, some crimes may be easier to detect than others (a mugging is more "visible" than computer fraud), and more police investigative effort may be devoted to some crimes than to others—either intentionally, for reasons of political opportunism, administrative expedience, or, indeed, in order to discriminate against certain groups, or unintentionally, because the detection and prosecution of some types of crimes, as opposed to others, are a more "natural" part of police and prosecutorial activities. The defense attorneys of offenders of certain racial groups may be—for any number of reasons—less successful in obtaining a favorable plea bargain, or their threats to go to trial may be taken less seriously by prosecutors. And so on. All that the lack of effect of the race factor mentioned above means is that our data revealed that there was no racial discrimination at the level of Superior Court sentencing. (We have data for several other important decisions in the criminal justice system, though, which also reveal no discrimination on the basis of race. This issue will be discussed in another article.)

that the judges have at their disposal at the time of sentencing. After the sentence has been passed in a case, the file is sent to the County Clerk's office, where, however, the most elaborate and interesting part of the ‛file—the probation officer's report—remains in the public domain for only 30 days. Our assistants coded the files in the County Clerk's office while the probation reports were still in the public domain.

A specifically designed, elaborate coding instrument with several hundred predictors was used in this work. (The entire instrument is available in Appendix II in Ebbesen and Konečni, 1981.) Trained coders (almost a hundred were used over the two-year period) transferred the information from the files to the coding instrument.

A large number of case details were coded, including demographic characteristics of the offender; charges at the time of the arrest; charges at the time of conviction; court-related data concerning bail, custody, and plea bargaining; aspects of the crime (also witness and physical evidence information); the content of the offender's statement; prior record; employment and social history; medical, psychological, and psychiatric information; the probation officer's evaluation of various aspects of the case and prognosis; the details of the probation officer's sentence recommendation; the details of the final sentence; and so on. Charges and prior record were coded in terms of entries in the California Penal Code. Coders used rating scales to estimate such variables as the degree of apparent premeditation, remorse, and admission of guilt—as expressed by the offender in the statement that is part of the probation officer's report. Counts of the number of lines dedicated to various topics served as a reliable technique for coding other, more variable content areas (see Konečni, Mulcahy, and Ebbesen, 1980, for a discussion of this procedure). The reliability of coding was very high (see Ebbesen and Konečni, 1981, for details).

The statistical analyses used the following four sentence options as the "dependent measures":

1. State prison sentence. This meant an indeterminate period of incarceration, such as "10 years to life," prescribed by law for each offense; the actual period of incarceration was decided by the California Adult Authority (see Chapters 12 and 13, this volume), not by the judge.

2. County jail sentence, almost always followed by a probationary period.

3. Straight probation, i.e., without any incarceration.

4. All others, such as commitment to a mental hospital, a fine without incarceration or a probationary period, and so on.

Of the large number of variables that were coded, only four were significantly associated with the sentencing decisions:

1. Type of crime.

2. Offender's prior record.

3. Offender's status between arrest and conviction (released on own recognizance; released on bail; held in jail, then released on bail; held in jail throughout).

4. Probation officer's sentence recommendation.

Demographic characteristics of offenders, as in the sentencing-hearing study, had no effect; and the same was true for the other predictors, especially when severity of the crime and prior record were controlled for. The data for the four significant effects are presented in Tables 11.4, 11.5, 11.6, and 11.7; the relevant significance tests can be found in the footnotes to the tables.

As severity of the offense increased, the probability that the defendant received a prison sentence increased (from 9% for possession of drugs and 11% for sexual perversion, to 24% for rape, 46% for armed robbery, and 62% for homicide), the probability of straight probation decreased, and the probability of probation with some time in a county jail remained relatively constant (see Table 11.4). One aspect of these data that would perhaps be surprising to the general public is how small the proportion of convicted offenders sent to state prison is, even for violent crimes. When one combines these statistics with the large number of people arrested on a felony charge who are released at the police station, have their charges dismissed, or have their charges reduced to a misdemeanor (which, by definition, does not carry a prison sentence), one concludes that being arrested for a felony has only a small effect on the likelihood that the defendant will go to prison. (Indeed, only about 2.5% of all felony arrests in 1976 and 1977 in San Diego County resulted in prison sentences, and less than 20% of those actually convicted of a felony during the same period were sent to prison.)

More than 60% of our sample had at least one prior felony conviction. From Table 11.5, it can be seen that as the extent of the prior record increased, the harshness of the sentences also increased. Nevertheless, only about 30% of convicted offenders were sent to prison even when they had had 4 or more prior felony convictions;

Table 11.4
Relationship between type of crime (for which offender was convicted) and sentencing decision

		Sentence, %			
Type of crime	No. of cases	State prison	County jail and probation	Probation only	Other
Possession of drugs	112	9	58	28	5
Sexual perversion	18	11	56	33	0
Forgery	97	18	47	35	0
Theft	231	13	62	20	5
Burglary	234	12	64	23	4
Sale of drugs	59	14	54	29	3
Assault and battery	30	13	67	13	7
Robbery	107	29	62	8	1
Possession of deadly weapon	32	30	55	15	0
Rape	17	24	59	6	11
Armed robbery	26	46	54	0	0
Homicide	21	62	29	10	0

Notes: 1. The ordering of crimes is based on average ratings of severity obtained from the same judges who were observed in the sentencing hearing.
2. $\chi^2 (22) = 102.8$, $p < .0001$, ignoring the "Other" category.
SOURCE: E. B. Ebbesen and V. J. Konečni, The process of sentencing adult felons: A causal analysis of judicial decisions. In B. D. Sales (Ed.), *Perspectives in law and psychology.* Vol. 2: *The jury, judicial, and trial process.* New York: Plenum, 1981.

Table 11.5
Relationship between number of previous felony convictions and sentencing decisions

		Sentence, %			
Number of previous felony convictions	No. of cases	State prison	County jail and probation	Probation only	Other
0	300	7.2	56.0	34.0	2.8
1	140	11.2	63.3	25.5	0
2	91	11.1	69.8	15.9	3.2
3	96	20.9	35.2	14.9	9.0
4	79	31.5	53.7	11.1	3.7
5+	218	29.3	57.3	8.7	4.7

Note: $\chi^2 (10) = 102.4$, $p < .0001$, ignoring the "Other" category.
SOURCE: E. B. Ebbesen and V. J. Konečni, The process of sentencing adult felons: A causal analysis of judicial decisions. In B. D. Sales (Ed.), *Perspectives in law and psychology.* Vol. 2: *The jury, judicial, and trial process.* New York: Plenum, 1981.

more than 40 people (about 5% of the sample) were given straight probation, even though they had 3 or more prior felony convictions.

From Table 11.6, it is clear that those offenders who were in jail throughout the period between arrest and conviction received considerably harsher sentences than did those who had been initially released on their own recognizance. The sentences of offenders who were free on bail at the time of the sentence hearing fell between these two extremes.

The results presented in Table 11.7 show that neither severity of the crime, nor prior record, nor jail/bail status has an effect on the sentencing decisions merely by being associated with another of the two variables. The probability of being sent to prison increases with increasing severity of the crime even when prior record and bail/jail status are held constant. Offenders with a more extensive prior record are sent to prison more often than those with a less extensive one even when the other two variables are held constant. And offenders kept in jail throughout the period from arrest to conviction are more likely to be given a prison sentence than those released on bail, who, in turn, are more likely to go to prison than those released on their own recognizance, even when the three groups have a highly similar prior record and have been convicted of similar crimes. There were also interactions of the multiplicative form in the data, such that the effect of one variable on sentencing decisions increased with the increasing presence of either of the other two variables. Rough anal-

Table 11.6
Relationship between offender status and sentencing decision

		Sentence, %			
Offender status	No. of cases	State prison	County jail and probation	Probation only	Other
Release on own recognizance	195	4.5	59.0	35.9	.5
Released on bail	92	13.0	60.9	23.9	2.2
Held in jail, then released on bail	113	9.7	34.9	29.2	6.2
Held in jail	280	27.1	58.6	9.3	5.0

Notes: 1. The sample size is smaller in this table than in the previous ones due to missing data concerning offender status.
    2. χ^2 (6) = 81.1, p < .0001, ignoring the "Other" category.
SOURCE: E. B. Ebbesen and V. J. Konečni, The process of sentencing adult felons: A causal analysis of judicial decisions. In B. D. Sales (Ed.), *Perspectives in law and psychology*. Vol. 2: *The jury, judicial, and trial process*. New York: Plenum, 1981.

Table 11.7
Relationship between number of previous felony convictions, severity of crime, and offender status

No. of previous felony convictions	Severity of crime[a]	Offender status		
		Released on own recognizance	Released on bail[b]	Held in jail
	Low	1.3 (n = 76)	4.5 (n = 67)	5.9 (n = 51)
0–2	Moderate	6.1 (n = 49)	11.5 (n = 52)	11.5 (n = 52)
	High	0 (n = 19)	25.0 (n = 12)	45.7 (n = 35)
	Low	3.2 (n = 31)	13.3 (n = 30)	25.3 (n = 62)
3 +	Moderate	21.4 (n = 14)	31.6 (n = 19)	37.0 (n = 54)
	High	0 (n = 5)	23.1 (n = 13)	63.3 (n = 30)

Note: The percentages represent the proportion of the total in each cell that were sent to prison.

[a]Low = possession of drugs, sexual perversion, forgery, theft. Moderate = burglary, sale of drugs, assault and battery, robbery. High = possession of deadly weapon, rape, armed robbery, homicide.

[b]Includes all defendants who were on bail at the time of the sentence hearing.

SOURCE: E. B. Ebbesen and V. J. Konečni, The process of sentencing adult felons: A causal analysis of judicial decisions. In B. D. Sales (Ed.), *Perspectives in law and psychology.* Vol. 2: *The jury, judicial, and trial process.* New York: Plenum, 1981.

yses on the basis of the data in Table 11.7 suggest that the three factors are about equally important; if anything, jail/bail status is somewhat more important than the other two (see Ebbesen and Konečni, 1981).

Finally, the data in Table 11.8 demonstrate the extraordinarily strong association between the probation officer's recommendation and the judge's sentencing decision (see also Bottomley, 1973; Carter and Wilkins, 1967). Complete agreement between the two (see the cells on the diagonal in Table 11.8) occurs in 87% of the cases (or 83%, if one ignores the "other" category). When there was disagreement, judges tended to give more lenient sentences than those the probation officers recommended significantly more often (χ^2 = 3.3, $p < .05$) than they gave more severe sentences (see also Carter, 1966; Carter and Wilkins, 1967).

Having obtained the above results, we turned our attention to an evaluation of the various possible *causal models* that could link the four mentioned variables to each other and to the sentencing decisions. Many models were eliminated on logical grounds, taking into account the structure of the criminal justice system, the temporal sequence of events and decisions, and the functions of the various participants and their access (or lack of it) to certain pieces of infor-

Table 11.8
Relationship between probation officer's recommendations and judge's sentencing decision

Probation officer's recommendation	Judge's sentencing decision, no. of cases			
	State prison	County jail and probation	Probation only	Other
State prison	103	32	5	2
County jail and probation	15	396	41	4
Probation only	1	34	143	1
Other	4	11	6	23

Note: χ^2 (4) = 806.7, p < .0001. There is 87% complete agreement for all cases, and 83% agreement when the "Other" category is ignored.
SOURCE: E. B. Ebbesen and V. J. Konečni, The process of sentencing adult felons: A causal analysis of judicial decisions. In B. D. Sales (Ed.), *Perspectives in law and psychology*. Vol. 2: *The jury, judicial, and trial process*. New York: Plenum, 1981.

mation at certain points in time in the processing of a case. We worried that the association between any of the four factors and the sentencing decisions might be a spurious one, i.e., mostly due to that factor's strong relationship with some unmeasured factor(s), but were somewhat reassured by the exhaustiveness of the initial coding, which made it unlikely that an important factor had slipped through our net. (We informally asked our students and colleagues to suggest factors that they thought might be *important* in sentencing, and also examined the responses given by the judges, defense attorneys, and probation officers in the simulations. Invariably, the factors thus discovered had indeed been a part of our coding instrument—and did not have an effect on sentencing.)

In Table 11.9 are presented five plausible causal models of sentencing decisions. Models I and III can be thought of as single-tier, Models II, IV, and V as multi-tier, or alternatively, as models in which the variables are related to each other in a causal chain (Heise, 1975). Because of the nature of the data, some models (e.g., Model IV) can be thought of as either single-tier or multi-tier. In fact, given the correlational nature of the data, Models I, IV, and V are mathematically equivalent from the standpoint of the analyses to be described later. They are presented as distinct models in Table 11.9 because they are conceptually and logically different, which implies, among other things, that they can conceivably be supported or challenged by different types of auxiliary data. (By auxiliary data we mean those relevant for only one or a small number of competing models.)

Let us, in fact, first examine some such auxiliary data. (Our strategy

Table 11.9
Causal models of sentencing decisions

Model	Description
I	Severity of crime, prior record, jail/bail status, and probation officer's recommendation are *all* direct causes of sentencing decision, i.e., judge evaluates and is influenced by these four bits of information separately.
II	Severity of crime, prior record, and jail/bail status are direct causes of probation officer's recommendation, which *alone* is a direct cause of sentencing decision; the other three factors have only *indirect* effects on sentencing decision.
III	Severity of crime, prior record, and jail/bail status are direct causes of probation officer's recommendation, and they are *also* direct causes of sentencing decisions. The association between probation officer's recommendation and sentencing decision is spurious; it can be fully explained by the fact that both decision-makers respond, independently, to the three variables in a similar way.
IV	Severity of crime, prior record, and jail/bail status are direct causes of sentencing decisions. Judge's decision, in turn, is a direct causes of sentencing decisions. The association between come about because probation officer *correctly anticipates* judge's decision on basis of the judge's *past performance* or reputation.
V	Severity of crime, prior record, and jail/bail status are direct causes of plea-bargaining agreement (with judge's opinion as another possible causal factor, which operates during plea-bargaining consultations that attorneys have with judge); plea-bargaining agreement is a direct cause of sentencing decision, which, in turn, cause probation officer's recommendation, by virtue of the fact that probation officer has full knowledge of bargains and correctly anticipates that judge will follow the agreements.

in the remainder of this section will be to attempt to eliminate some of the models by means of the auxiliary data, and then to compare the fits of the remaining models.) A total of 245 cases was found in which no plea agreement had been reached by the relevant parties (at least, the section of the file in which this information is ordinarily provided had been left blank). If, in fact, there had been no plea bargain, the judge could not be influenced by it, and thus there would be nothing for the probation officer to be influenced by, through correct anticipation. In short, if Model IV is viable, the percent of agreement between probation officers and judges should be drastically reduced in this subsample. Yet, as can be seen from Table 11.10, the

Table 11.10
Relationship between probation officer's recommendation and judge's sentencing decision when no plea bargain was made (n = 245)

Probation officer's recommendation	Judge's sentencing decisions, no. of cases		
	State prison	County jail and probation	Probation only
State prison	46	13	1
County jail and probation	3	112	14
Probation only	0	8	48

Note: There is 84% complete agreement.

percent of cases in which the probation officer and the judge agree completely (the cells on the diagonal) remains virtually unchanged, and very high, 84%. These data seriously question the validity of Model V (essentially a 3-tier model), but have nothing to say about the mathematically equivalent Models I and IV.

Additional auxiliary data, which also address the important issue of disparity in sentencing decisions across judges, as well as the extent of the judges' awareness of the determinants (or, at least, correlates) of their decisions, are presented in Tables 11.11 and 11.12.

From Table 11.11, it can be seen that probation officers' recommendations and sentencing decisions are in very high agreement for *all* of the eight judges whose sentencing decisions provided most of the data for the study (across judges, the percent of cases with complete agreement ranged from 75% to 93%). If, as we will argue later,

Table 11.11
Relationship between judge's sentence and probation officer's recommendation, and judge's rating of importance of recommendation for sentencing decisions

Judge (n = 8)	Percent of cases in which sentence and recommendations were identical	Judge's rating on scale of 0–10 of importance of recommendation in sentencing decisions
E	93	3
A	88	6
G	88	7
F	83	7
D	79	3
B	77	5
H	75	8
C	75	7

Table 11.12
Relationship between state-prison and straight-probation sentences recommended by probation officer and imposed by judges

Judge (n = 8)	Percent of state-prison sentences		Percent of straight-probation sentences	
	Recommended by probation officer	Imposed by judge	Recommended by probation officer	Imposed by judge
A	33.3	33.3	4.8	9.5
B	37.7	28.1	22.8	16.7
C	16.7	25.0	16.7	27.7
D	16.0	22.0	18.0	22.0
E	21.7	21.7	17.4	15.9
F	12.5	16.7	16.4	12.9
G	9.4	11.9	23.9	29.2
H	5.9	8.8	44.0	29.4

SOURCE: E. B. Ebbesen and V. J. Konečni, The process of sentencing adult felons: A causal analysis of judicial decisions. In B. D. Sales (Ed.), *Perspectives in law and psychology*. Vol. 2: *The jury, judicial, and trial process*. New York: Plenum, 1981.

the results indeed favor Model II over Model IV (judges' sentences are caused by probation officers' recommendations rather than vice versa), the small variability in the extent to which different judges agree with probation officers' recommendations implies that whatever disparity in sentencing there is across judges, it is due to what probation officers do, i.e., to the disparity in recommendations that probation officers make to different judges (see also Bottomley, 1973; Carter and Wilkins, 1967).

Before pursuing this question further, we should note another aspect of Table 11.11; namely, the complete lack of a relationship between the percent of cases in which judges' sentencing decisions were identical to probation officers' recommendations and these same judges' numerical estimates (obtained by our assistants as part of the simulations) of the importance of probation officers' recommendations for the judges' sentencing decisions (the correlation is very low, nonsignificant, and, in fact, negative). The judges either were unaware of how high the percent of cases with complete agreement was, or did not believe that the recommendations were *causes* of sentencing decisions, or did not wish to publicly acknowledge this possibility.

Returning to the issue of disparity, we suggested that whatever sentencing disparity there is may be due to the disparity in recommendations made by probation officers to different judges. Indeed, in Table 11.12, it can be seen that although judges do differ considerably from one another in terms of the percent of sentences that involve prison (from 8.8% to 33%), and also in terms of the percent of sentences that involve straight probation (from 9.5% to 29.4%), this disparity in very large part mirrored the way probation officers varied the rate of prison and straight-probation recommendations across judges. (The rank-order correlation between the sentence recommendation and imposition columns involving prison in Table 11.12 was .91, z = 2.39, p < .01; for columns involving straight probation, the correlation was .83, z = 2.05, p < .02.) To the extent that judges are indeed causally influenced by probation officers' recommendations (as we will argue later), "hanging judges" and "softies" (A and H respectively, in Table 11.12, are good candidates) apparently obtain their reputations through the "services" of probation officers.

Another way of interpreting the data in Table 11.12 is that they support Model IV: Because probation officers are guided by the past decisions of the judges and the judges' respective reputations, they can often correctly anticipate what the judges will do, which results in high agreement with each judge.[4] However, this interpretation is challenged by two types of evidence. First, as we will show later, most of the variance in probation officers' recommendations can be explained in terms of case factors (severity of the crime, prior record, and jail/bail status). Second, we have obtained some data suggesting that different judges in our sample are consistently assigned different kinds of cases, and the pattern of these differences is such that it could easily explain the differential recommendation rates across judges.[5] Thus, rather than trying to anticipate and match what judges will do, probation officers seem to respond to case factors, but these case factors tend to be systematically different for different judges.

----

[4]This argument also assumes that probation officers are *motivated* to have a high percent of agreement with judges. Such an assumption is probably correct, given the organizational and incentive structure within a typical county probation department. Probation officers are presumably likely to want to please their superiors (who inspect and approve the reports and recommendations), and the latter must be at least somewhat keen to have the department thought of as "competent" and "reasonable" by judges—which is probably interpreted as high agreement.

[5]The next question, of course, concerns the reasons why different judges are assigned different types of cases. Part of the answer probably lies in specialization on the part of judges (e.g., in white-collar crime cases), and another part in "judge shopping" by defense attorneys. The latter point begs yet another question: What are the attorneys guided by in judge shopping? The answer is undoubtedly that they are looking for the lenient judge, given the type of case they have, and their search (as we have found out from our interviews with defense attorneys) is invariably based on the judges' reputations, gossip among attorneys, "gut feelings," personal sympathies and antipathies, and perhaps one or two cases, at best, that an attorney has had with a particular judge. In other words, the search is based on the mythology that surrounds judges and courtrooms, and not on hard data or base rates.

There is also the question of why judges begin to be assigned serious crime cases that eventually earn them the reputation of being "hanging" judges (even though they

In other words, the data in Table 11.12 cannot be used in support of Model IV and against Model II.[6]

Now that we have examined several types of auxiliary data (and rejected Model V), we can turn to the main analyses regarding the remaining models in Table 11.9. Each of the three causal models (Models I and IV make identical predictions[7]) implies that the observed cell frequencies in the 5-factor contingency table (severity of the crime × prior record × jail/bail status × probation officer's recommendation × sentence) should be due to a particular set of main and interaction effects (analogous to what these terms mean in the analysis of variance). For example, Model III assumes (1) an association between the three case factors and the probation officer's recommendation, (2) an association between the three case factors and the sentence, and (3) that any association between the recommendations and the sentence can be fully explained in terms of (1) and (2). Thus, for example, in the 3-way classification table of prior record × recommendation × sentence, the pattern of observed frequencies should be completely predictable from only two 2-way tables, prior record × recommendation and prior record × sentence. When the same logic is extended to the whole model, it is evident that, according to Model III, the observed frequencies in the 5-way

---

are merely responding to probation officers' recommendations, who, in turn, respond to case factors). This turns the issue into a veritable chicken-and-egg problem. Although we are pursuing some of these questions, the problem can be resolved satisfactorily only by a random assignment of cases to judges.

In the meantime, we have discovered from interviews with defense attorneys and courtroom observation studies that the characteristics about judges that predict best what defense attorneys think of them on the leniency/harshness dimension are, in fact, not the characteristics of cases they get, but presumably entirely irrelevant (though highly salient and arousal-raising) traits, such as courtroom demeanor—frowning, smiling, tone of voice. Such data question the reasonableness of defense attorneys' "gut feelings."

[6]This illustrates the fact that whereas various types of auxiliary data can sometimes be very helpful, complete reliance on them does not allow an adequate test of the competing models. In their valuable article, Carter and Wilkins (1967, p. 508) describe various possible explanations for the high agreement between probation officers' recommendations and judges' sentencing decisions. Some of the explanations are similar to Models II, III, and IV in Table 11.9, the important difference being that whereas our models explicitly incorporate specific case factors that might affect one or both decision-makers, as well as deal with the direction of the causal influence between probation officers and judges, Carter and Wilkins deal only with the latter issue. Moreover, mainly because they relied only on auxiliary data, Carter and Wilkins found some support for *all* of the three or four explanations they offered for the high agreement between probation officers and judges, and never seriously pitted these explanations against each other.

[7]It should now be clear why Models I and IV are mathematically equivalent. In both cases, the implication is that the 5-way contingency table can be predicted from 5 main effects and the following 4 two-way interactions: severity of the crime × sentence, prior record × sentence, jail/bail status × sentence, and sentence × recommendation.

contingency table can be predicted from five main effects and six 2-way interactions (severity of crime × recommendation, prior record × recommendation, jail/bail status × recommendation, severity of crime × sentence, prior record × sentence, and jail/bail status × sentence).

To evaluate quantitatively predictions based on Model III, as well as the analogously derived predictions from other models in Table 11.9, we relied on the log-linear method used by Goodman (1972, 1973). Each effect predicted by a model becomes a part of a log-linear equation in which the parameters for the main and interaction effects added to (or subtracted from) the odds, in logarithms, that an observation (a case, in our work) would fall in a particular cell of the 5-way table. Equations were written for each model, estimates of parameter values obtained with the help of a computer program available from Goodman (described in Goodman, 1972), and the fit of the different models to the data assessed by a χ^2 likelihood-ratio statistic. The models could be contrasted with each other by comparing the χ^2 values that resulted from each. As in multiple regression, one could determine whether the inclusion, in a simpler, less general model, of additional hypothesized causal pathways between the variables provided significantly more explanatory power. The least general model is one that assumes that all 5 factors are independent, unassociated with each other (5-factors-independent model). The most general model assumes that all factors are associated with each other (full-causality model). The five models in Table 11.9 fall between these extremes in terms of the number of hypothesized causal pathways.

In Table 11.13 are presented the results of fitting the various models to a 5-way $3 \times 2 \times 4 \times 3 \times 3$ (216 cells) contingency table in which severity of the crime (3 levels) and prior record (2 levels) were defined as in Table 11.7, jail/bail status (4 levels) as in Table 11.6, and recommendation and sentence (3 levels each) as in Table 11.8 (minus the "other" category).

Part A of Table 11.13 shows the fit between the patterns predicted by various models and the data actually obtained. The larger the χ^2 value, the poorer the fit; i.e., the greater the difference between the predicted and the obtained pattern. As can be seen, the 5-factors-independent model and Model III (judges and probation officers are independently influenced by the same case factors) fared quite poorly; whereas the other models did quite well. With the exception of the full-causality model—which is presented here for the purpose of comparison only, in that it is conceptually quite uninteresting, because of its overconstraining assumption that each of the 5 variables is significantly associated with each of the other variables—the best fit was provided by Model II, according to which probation offi-

Table 11.13
Log-linear analysis of sentencing decisions

Model[a]	χ^2	df	p
	A. Fit		
5-factors-independent	669.11	205	< .0001
I and IV	146.02	189	> .5
II	136.44	189	> .5
III	410.52	181	< .0001
Full-causality	90.86	177	> .5
	B. Improvement over 5-factors-independent model		
I and IV	523.09	16	< .0001
II	532.67	16	< .0001
III	258.59	24	< .0001
Full-causality	578.25	28	< .0001
	C. Unexplained "variance"		
I and IV	55.16	12	<.01
II	45.58	12	<.01

[a]Models I–IV are defined in Table 11.9.

cers' recommendations (themselves influenced by three case factors) cause judges' sentencing decisions. This model provided a very good fit of the data ($p > .5$ indicates that the predicted cell frequencies are not significantly different from the obtained ones) with far fewer parameters than the full-causality model; in fact, it uses exactly the same number of parameters as do Models I and IV, the latter of which also provided a very good fit. However, since the number of parameters is identical in the two cases, the model providing a better fit (smaller χ^2 value) is to be preferred no matter how small the difference.

Parts B and C lead to the same conclusion. In Part B it can be seen that all models accounted for a significant amount of *additional* "variance" over that accounted by the 5-factors-independent model (the χ^2 values in Part B were obtained by subtracting the χ^2 values associated with the various models in Part A from the χ^2 value for the 5-factors-independent model). In this analysis, the question was how well the models could handle the "residual" of the 5-factors-independent model: The larger the χ^2 value, the greater the portion of that residual that is accounted by a particular model. Model II accounted for a greater amount of additional variance than did Models I, III, and IV, and is therefore to be preferred to these other models.

Finally, in Part C, significance tests were performed on the residuals of the major competing models (the χ^2 values were obtained by subtracting the χ^2 values associated with the models from the χ^2 value for the full-causality model in Part B). The question here was how much worse were the competing models than the highly constraining full-causality model; the higher the χ^2 value, the greater the amount of variance *left unexplained* by the models, in comparison to the full-causality model. The χ^2 values were significant for both models, but the one for Model II was smaller.

The above analyses revealed the superiority of the model that argues that judges' sentencing decisions are caused by probation officers' recommendations, which are, in turn, caused by the three case factors. Before examining whether this basic model can be further improved, we used some straightforward χ^2 analyses to test the relative fit of Model II and of Models I and IV. First, we examined about 460 cases in which probation officers' recommendations had been incarceration in county jail, followed by a probationary period; these 460 cases were the only cases in the sample in which this particular recommendation had been made. We divided the cases in terms of severity of the crime and prior record—two of the variables that had been found to be highly important in the analyses reported above—as well as by whether or not the judge imposed a prison sentence. The χ^2 value associated with this 3-way table was not significant. This suggests that within a particular type of probation officers' recommendation (i.e., when the recommendations are kept constant), case factors do not influence sentencing decisions, or, put differently, their effects are not "getting through" to the judges. Table 11.14 presents the 2 × 3 contingency table involving severity of the crime and prior record. Each entry in the table represents the percent of cases falling into that cell in which judges imposed prison sentences.

Next, we reversed the procedure and looked at about 480 cases in which judges' sentencing decisions were county jail and probation.

Table 11.14
Percent of cases in which judge imposed prison sentence, following probation recommendation for county jail, as function of number of previous felony convictions and severity of crime

No. of previous felony convictions	Severity of crime		
	Low	Moderate	High
0–2	0	5.88	4.76
3+	2.38	6.56	3.45

Note: Based on 460 cases in each of which probation officer recommended county jail followed by probation.

These cases were divided in terms of severity of the crime, prior record, and whether or not probation officers had recommended prison. For this 3-way table, $\chi^2 = 17.81$, $df = 4$, $p < .001$. Each entry in Table 11.15 represents the percent of cases falling into that cell in which probation officers recommended prison sentences. Thus, the case factors seem to influence the recommendations and are "getting through" to probation officers, even within a particular type of sentence, i.e., when the judges' sentences are kept constant. This analysis offers further support for Model II.[8]

We now turn to the question of whether this model can be further improved. One possibility was that one or more of the three case factors (severity of the crime, prior record, and jail/bail status) had a direct effect on judges' sentencing decisions over and above their *indirect* effects through their influence on probation officers' recommendations. Indeed, the appropriate modeling procedures revealed that jail/bail status had such a direct—small, but significant—effect on sentencing decisions (see Table 11.11 in Ebbesen and Konečni, 1981) and that the other two factors did not.

To summarize, probation officers' recommendations seem to be the major direct cause of judges' sentencing decisions. Whereas the recommendations themselves are causally affected by severity of the crime, prior record, and jail/bail status, judges are not directly influenced by these factors. The only exception is jail/bail-status, which influences both probation officers (directly) and judges (indirectly through the recommendations, as well as directly).

The final question that is of interest concerns the causes of probation officers' recommendations. To deal with this issue, we used the log-linear procedure described earlier and applied it to the same data base, except that the 5-way contingency table was turned into a 4-way table by collapsing the sentence factor. Not surprisingly, given the high agreement between probation officers and judges

---

[8]We considered the idea of obtaining some additional auxiliary evidence in order to examine the validity of Model IV in yet another way. Recall that one of the assumptions of this model is that high agreement between probation officers' recommendations and judges' sentencing decisions is a result of probation officers' being influenced by (i.e., correctly anticipating) judges' past performance or reputation with regard to sentencing decisions. It follows, therefore, that considerably smaller agreement would be found in a subsample of cases involving probation officers, or judges, or both who were new on the job. Unfortunately, regarding judges, the San Diego bench is too small and seldom has a large proportion of new judges. The problem regarding probation officers is that they work under a lot of supervision, especially the new ones, which contributes to uniformity. Indeed, Carter and Wilkins (1967, p. 512) interpreted some of the data from the San Francisco project in the early 1960s as indicating that "the differences . . . [in the rates of recommendations for probation as opposed to imprisonment] tend to diminish with the period of employment; . . . officers with different backgrounds are far more dissimilar upon entering the probation service than after exposure to the agency."

Table 11.15
Percent of cases in which probation officers recommended prison sentence, as function of number of previous felony convictions and severity of crime

No. of previous felony convictions	Severity of crime		
	Low	Moderate	High
0–2	1.06	3.66	0
3+	14.43	6.78	10.34

Note: Based on 480 cases in each of which judge imposed county jail followed by probation.

noted earlier, probation officers' recommendations appeared to be strongly influenced by severity of the crime, prior record, and jail/bail status. However, additional analyses revealed that the explanatory power of the model could be significantly improved (leaving a nonsignificant residual) by including two 2-way interactions in the model: prior record × crime and prior record × jail/bail status. (These were the interactions of the multiplicative form that were discussed in connection with the results presented in Table 11.7.)

Thus, probation officers' recommendations—the key cause of judges' sentencing decisions—were influenced by severity of the crime, prior record, jail/bail status, and two interactions according to which the effect of prior record was substantially augmented by the higher levels of severity of the crime and jail/bail status.

Conclusions   The picture of the cause of sentencing that emerged from the archival study involving the coding and analysis of court files is entirely different from the conclusions that one would be forced to reach on the basis of our other studies that were described earlier in the chapter. In addition to the various differences among the studies that we have already pointed out, it is important to note that none of the studies other than the archival one highlighted the key causal function of probation officers' recommendations, nor revealed the importance of jail/bail status. Severity of the crime and prior record, which were emphasized so strongly in all of the simulations, were shown in the archival study to have only an indirect causal influence on judges.[9]

---

[9]Ironically, in the simulations, laymen (students) seemed to come closer to the truth than did the professionals. Recall that in the rating study both naive and experienced student raters attached more importance to the role of probation officers than did judges and defense attorneys. Also, in the questionnaire study, the student researchers suggested the rudiments of a causal model of sentencing, in which both judges and probation officers are influenced by the same set of factors (severity of crime, prior record, family situation, and employment); however, neither the factors listed nor the model was supported by the causal analysis of the archival data.

In another article (Konečni and Ebbesen, 1981), as well as in our chapter on methodology in this volume (Chapter 2), we discuss at length the issue of external validity of the research in legal psychology. Our contention is that if one is truly interested in a real-world process or in the functioning of an existing social system (such as the criminal justice system), there are many logical and practical reasons why preference should be given to real-world studies over simulations. The *only* way to validate the results of a simulation is to test its conclusions on real-world data. Thus, to the extent that no studies in a field exist and that a real-world study is feasible, why not *begin* with a real-world study? Furthermore, if the results from both simulations and real-world studies are already available, the conclusions of the latter can generally be considered more trustworthy, provided the study meets certain requirements. Regarding our studies of sentencing in particular, such requirements and the reasons for preferring the archival study have already been outlined in detail elsewhere (Chapter 2, this volume; Konečni and Ebbesen, 1981; the latter article also discusses the lessons to be learned from our uninformative real-world study dealing with sentencing hearings).

The conclusion we wish to draw is that at least for the time being we accept the results and conclusions of the archival study as providing a reasonably accurate representation of the causal aspects of sentencing adult felons in San Diego County:

1. Once a person's guilt of a felony offense has been determined (usually through a plea of guilty), the severity of that felony, the offender's prior record (in terms of felony convictions), jail versus bail status in the period between the arrest and the sentencing hearing, and two 2-way interactions between these three factors (both involving prior record), fully determine, with a nonsignificant amount of residual variance, probation officers' recommendations.

2. These recommendations and, to a much smaller extent, the offender's jail/bail status jointly cause judges' sentencing decisions, such that a nonsignificant amount of residual variance is left.

The content of sentencing hearings seems to have no influence on sentencing decisions. These hearings seem to be a show for the public (that the operation of the criminal justice system is "open to public scrutiny") and perhaps for the offenders (that their attorneys are "doing something," especially since in a modal case there would have been no trial). Insofar as the results of the simulations do not match the results of the archival study, they are worthless—as far as understanding the real-world sentencing process is concerned (although what our subjects—judges, defense attorneys, and so on—had to say may be interesting in its own right). Had only these simulations been done, however, entirely misleading conclusions about the sentencing process would have been reached and, presumably, disseminated. The publication by our students of the results of the interview study in a major San Diego daily newspaper demonstrates—and was meant to demonstrate—the ease with which erroneous conclusions about the functioning of an important social institution can be brought to the attention of the general public from a position of authority.[10]

When the model of sentencing described above is examined together with the results of our study of bail setting in mind (Ebbesen and Konečni, 1975; Chapter 8, this volume), an even more complete, though also more tentative, account of sentencing emerges. Recall that our bail study found that judges' bail decisions were influenced primarily by prosecutors' recommendations, and that these were, in turn, influenced mostly by severity of the crime (i.e., arrest charges). Recall also that jail/bail status had a strong effect on probation officers' recommendations and that it was the only case factor that also had some—though fairly minor—direct effect on judges. On the reasonable assumption that the higher the amount of bail set, the greater the number of defendants who cannot afford to pay it (or even pay the percent charged by bail-bondsmen), it follows that the charges at the time of arrest—mediated by prosecutors' bail recommendations, judges' bail decisions, defendants' jail/bail status, and probation officers' recommendations—have an indirect effect on judges' sentencing decisions.

For what it is worth, the above analysis at least emphasizes the potential usefulness of looking at legal decisions as being part of a network of decisions and decision-makers. This idea has guided our work and influenced, of course, the organization of this whole volume.

DISCUSSION

Our data and the proposed causal model run counter to several widely held contentions about the nature of the sentencing process and the operation of the criminal justice system.

---

[10]Of course, the same basic methodology and data base (interviewing, self-report) are habitually used not only by the media, but also in many other situations, involving all sorts of decision-makers (including congressional and senate hearings).

Myth 1: The complexity of legal decisions

One popular belief, expressed strongly in the quotation from the report of the President's Commission at the beginning of this chapter, is that sentencing decisions are "complicated and . . . difficult to make." Some of the things that are almost certainly meant by this statement is that judges take many factors into account and that they carefully examine them in a lengthy process of deliberation. Yet we have shown that very few factors influence sentencing decisions, and so in this sense the decisions appear to be quite simple. Moreover, we have been able to account for other legal decisions, such as the setting of bail and the disposition of mentally disordered sex offenders (Chapter 8, this volume; Konečni, Mulcahy, and Ebbesen, 1980), by similarly simple models. The fact that judges *talk* about numerous factors (as in the simulations) may have nothing to do with the causal factors that control their decisions. One must not confuse their possibly quite complex thought processes with the quite simple causes of their behavior (see Ebbesen and Konečni, 1981, and Konečni, Mulcahy, and Ebbesen, 1980).

As for the careful deliberation, this turns out to be another myth, believed more by the general public than by the people within the system. In San Diego, judges receive case files (containing probation reports, etc.) in batches of 10–15, with as many hearings held the very next day. Since an average hearing lasts about 5 minutes, there definitely is not much time for deliberation.

Myth 2: Individualized justice

Another frequently espoused view is that current sentencing practices incorporate the concept of individualized justice. Yet, the offender's employment history, family status, social background, and numerous other personal and psychological characteristics were not causally related to the sentencing decision. As we have pointed out elsewhere (Ebbesen and Konečni, 1981), the fact that sentencing guidelines typically suggest that such factors should be taken into account, that much of a modal probation report is devoted to them, and that defense attorneys discussed these factors in the sentencing hearings that we coded means either that the myth of individualized justice is being perpetuated on purpose by a variety of participants in the criminal justice system or that the participants are not aware that these factors have no effect.

The possibility that the wide-ranging support for the notion of individualized justice in the legal community may be at least in part self-serving should not be lightly dismissed. Individualized justice implies discretionary powers and numerous options on the part of decision-makers. Having a lot of discretion and possessing options have always been important goals for judges in their struggle against "being reduced to a formula" (as they like to put it). Hence the dogma so widely held in the legal community that "every case is different." As for defense attorneys, they, too, can only benefit from their clients' belief that the punishment is made to fit the offender, not the crime, for that presumably leaves more room for legal maneuvers and increases the dependence on attorneys.

Myth 3: Sentencing hearings as decision-making occasions

Our data and analyses also suggest that sentencing hearings may have nothing to do with their stated purpose. The existence of such legal rituals (see also Konečni, Mulcahy, and Ebbesen, 1980) is rather bothersome. They are costly and present a false impression of the functioning of the criminal justice system. As we have pointed out elsewhere (Ebbesen and Konečni, 1981), the behavior of the participants in these hearings, including the judges, appears to be "staged," apparently again for self-serving purposes. Some like to think that the rituals in the courtroom (including the judge's presumed unbiased attention to the attorneys and the offender, apparent concern for the offender's rights, dignified demeanor, robe, elevated overstuffed chair on a pedestal flanked by flags, etc.) instill respect for the law in the offenders. This is almost certainly nonsense. Recall that in our sample—by no means an atypical one—more than 60% of the offenders had prior felony convictions. Consider that together with the data presented at the beginning of the chapter showing how few people arrested for felony get convicted at all, especially of a felony. Realistically, one is dealing here with a group that has been in repeated contact with the criminal justice system. The failure of this system and the society as a whole to instill respect for the law in this population is clearly not going to be offset by the decorum and paraphernalia of a 5-minute sentencing hearing. The time and the money would probably be better spent on judges' collecting and analyzing data on their own performance and on the factors that really influence their decisions.

Myth 4: Disparity in judges' sentencing decisions

Another firmly entrenched notion that has not been supported by our work is the disparity in judges' sentencing decisions. Whereas the judges in our sample indeed differed from one another in terms of, for example, the proportion of prison sentences they imposed, disparity presumably means more than that; namely, that judges' decision-making strategies differ and that they therefore impose widely different sentences in similar cases. We found, in contrast, that all judges used the same strategy: they closely followed probation officers' recommendations. The differences across judges in the proportion of prison sentences merely reflected the differences in recommendations, which, in turn, took into account a small number of characteristics of cases in the widely different case loads assigned to the different judges.

Myth 5: Judges as mainstays of the sentencing process

Finally, our data and analyses contradict the traditional view of the judge as the chief decision-maker in the sentencing process. A more correct view apparently is that the judge is merely the main "broadcaster" of sentencing decisions reached by probation officers.

One logical implication of the very high agreement between judges and probation officers is that one of these two categories of participants in the sentencing process is redundant. Since it is the probation officers who make the decisions and the judges who are paid far more, it would seem that the judges are better candidates if the redundancy is to be eliminated. We say this tongue-in-cheek; however, the hesitation in making the proposal with dead seriousness is probably due less to facts than to the many years in which judges have done a thorough public-relations job to establish themselves in the "collective consciousness" as indispensable.

There are several possible reasons for keeping judges in the sentencing process even if it is conceded that probation officers actually make the decisions, but none of these seems to us very convincing. One possible reason—that judges promote respect for the law—has already been discussed. Whatever effect judges may have in this regard in general, it is unlikely to be anything but negligible in the process of sentencing felons, given the very high proportion of recidivists and "career criminals" in this population.

Another possible reason for keeping judges is that there are, after all, 15% or so cases in which judges' sentences do not match probation officers' recommendations. However, we are not aware of any evidence to the effect that the sentences in these cases are of a higher quality—by whatever criterion—than are the recommendations. A sizable proportion of disagreements is probably due to "noise" in the system.

Nor are we aware—with one possible exception—of a case characteristic that is a reliable predictor of judges' "independence." The one possible exception, which, however, does not necessarily make judges' independence look very good, is the amount of publicity a case receives. We have some evidence that our models of sentencing and other legal decisions do not predict well in front-page cases, and they cannot be expected to, as they are by definition meant to deal with the modal, run-of-the-mill case that does not reach even the back page. In high-publicity cases, those involving famous defendants or multiple murders, the behavior of all participants in the system—not just the judges' sentencing behavior—tends to be different. Prosecutors, defense attorneys, judges, and hired experts all seem to jockey for position in the limelight. The case usually goes to trial—an unusual thing in itself—supposedly because of its legal aspects, but probably more because prosecutors find it politically expedient to try such cases, defense attorneys can charge higher fees, increase their reputation, or at least write a book about the trial, and the public has been made both indignant and expectant by the media. (Exceptional cases and the media can be held principally responsible for the totally skewed, unrealistic, Perry Mason picture of the criminal justice system that the public tends to have.)

After Patricia Hearst's trial in San Francisco, the first sentencing hearing, which our assistants coded, lasted for almost an hour instead of the customary 5 minutes, and the judge spent a great deal of time thanking people who had sent letters on the offender's behalf. The sentence Patricia Hearst eventually received was probably harsher than a less well-known offender would have received in similar circumstances, which may well have been influenced by the public's attitude that "the rich should not be able to get off." On the other hand, her release on parole may well have been influenced by a nationwide campaign to free her, the public's attitude having changed in the meantime.

In Roman Polanski's "unlawful sexual intercourse" (statutory rape) case in Los Angeles, to which we devoted a lot of attention in connection with our work on the processing of mentally disordered sex offenders (see Konečni, Mulcahy, and Ebbesen, 1980, for further details), the judge gave a press conference in his chambers, an interview to *People* magazine, and generally seemed to respond to such an extent to the publicity aspects of the case and to the "hate mail" concerning Polanski he was receiving that both the defense attorney and the prosecutor requested that the case be taken away from this judge (the prosecutor was presumably motivated by the desire to avoid grounds for a successful appeal).

In sum, there is little evidence that judges' behavior in cases in which their sentences disagree with probation officers' recommendations by itself justifies keeping them in the sentencing process. Perhaps the best argument for judges remaining in the sentencing system is that even though they are causally influenced by probation officers, the latter may recommend what they do because others with high authority (judges) are also part of the system. According to this argument, if judges were removed, probation officers would change their decision-making—rely on different cues, combine them differently, or both. However, this argument is reasonable only to the extent that one accepts as reasonable the legal system's traditional reluctance to change for the purposes of experimentation and true innovation (as opposed to politically expedient innovation), especially when the change may mean less authority for the most powerful people in the system, the judges. (In this sense, the legal system is, of course, no different from other bureaucracies.) Otherwise, an experimental period without judges' participation in the sentencing process would easily reveal whether or not probation officers' decision strategy would change. Subsequent periodic checks could insure that the strategy does not change over time.

Probation officers versus computers   Thus, the arguments for keeping judges in the sentencing process seem weak. Some of the counterarguments we used emphasize the importance of keeping solid data within the legal system, and—when the implications of these counterarguments are explored in full—suggest that the sentencing process could be considerably improved by computerization. Computer-based decisions, especially sentences, are of course, anathema to judges and other people in legal circles—which is not surprising. Their considerable vested interests in the present system and their lack of familiarity with the tools and logic of behavioral science—data collection, statistical procedures, causal analysis, computers, and, above all, the *actual functioning of the system* (including current base rates, etc.)—elicit a variety of predictable comments from most legal practitioners, ranging from the "every case is different" defense to the pseudohumanistic counterattacks revolving around the "human touch" versus the Orwellian *1984*.

The fact of the matter is that the causal model of sentencing is so simple and straightforward that not just judges but also probation officers could be replaced by a very simple computer program that would take severity of the crime, prior record, and jail/bail status into account—if the objective were simply to mimic what is presently being done. After all, severity of the crime, prior record, and what appears to be the major cause of variation in jail/bail status—the arrest charges—are all straightforward bits of information, known long before the conviction; in fact, they are known immediately after the arrest! (See Konečni, Mulcahy, and Ebbesen, 1980, for analogous arguments regarding the processing of mentally disordered sex offenders.) Computer-based sentencing would insure fairness, eliminate disparity, increase the speed of decision-making, reduce costs, and eliminate "noise," i.e., result in the certainty that a particular sentence would be meted out, given the conviction for a certain offense.[11] Moreover, to the extent that there is dissatisfaction in the system or outside it with the present determinants of sentencing or their weights, different weights and additional or different variables could be easily included in the model. (Thus, behavioral science and computerization do not *impose* values on the legal system.)

In light of all this, it does not seem entirely unreasonable to conclude that only the disproportionate amount of power and self-serving independence successfully claimed and held by the legal system enables judges and other legal Luddites to keep computers and behavioral science out.

Because entrenched bureaucracies view change with deep suspicion and have the power to resist it, a question of perhaps greater practical value is whether or not something can be done to improve the sentencing process, given its present general outlines. One's attention immediately turns to probation officers. Are they well qualified? Are they doing a good job? A number of studies—both simulations and those based on data from the courts—have examined probation officers' recommendations (e.g., Carter, 1966; Curry, 1975; Papandreou, McDonald, and Landauer, in press; Wilkins and Chandler, 1965), but have not been concerned with probation officers' qualifications. On the basis of interview and questionnaire data, Carter and Wilkins (1967) and Hood (1966) report that judges think of probation officers as being quite competent. In contrast, in a more recent article in the Los Angeles *Times*, one reads:

> The county Probation Department has not been able to maintain even "a minimum standard of service" to the courts, a Superior Court Judge told a hearing on the firing of Chief Probation Officer. . . . The department's deficiencies, [the judge] . . . testified, have existed for years and embrace such basic skills as the insufficient ability of many probation officers to read and write at an acceptable court level (Kistler, 1975)

Thus, at least some people in the legal system believe that probation officers are incompetent and need more schooling. (The irony in the above quotation lies in the very real possibility that the judge so

---

[11]This last point—the certainty that a particular sentence would be the result of being convicted for a particular offense—may be important from the offenders' point of view. It is, in fact, the argument made by the few proponents of *sentence* bargaining as opposed to *plea* bargaining. At the present time, in accordance with Section 1192.5 of the California Penal Code, the plea-bargaining agreement is not binding on the sentencing judge. The defendant typically pleads guilty in order to get a more serious charge dropped or reduced and in exchange for certain actions on the part of the prosecutor, such as not demanding a prison sentence.

critical of probation officers nevertheless followed their—illiterate—recommendations about 85% of the time.)

It seems to us that probation officers are by definition doing a very good job if the factors that they presently take into account in making their recommendations are considered reasonable or satisfactory by whoever it is that should decide whether or not probation officers are doing a good job. If, on the other hand, the objective is individualized justice or some other model with additional or different variables, then probation officers are not doing a good job. To improve their performance in the latter case, probation officers would need not vague guidelines (so common in the legal system), but a complete and specific list of variables and weights to be assigned to each. They would also have to be taught how to take into account 5 or 6 variables at the same time, how to combine the information, how to evaluate whether or not they are following the model, and so on. The obvious conclusion is that if one wants probation officers to do something different in making their recommendations from what they are now doing and to insure that they do the new thing precisely, it would be far easier to write a simple computer program to take care of all that.

Despite our criticisms, we would like to end on an optimistic note regarding the sentencing process. Few would deny that severity of the crime and prior record are reasonable and desirable determinants of sentencing. Jail/bail status appears extralegal and discriminatory against the indigent defendants at first, but its influence seems less arbitrary and unjust if it is indeed the case that it indirectly reflects the arrest charges. Furthermore, no other potentially embarrassing extralegal determinants of sentencing—such as the race of offenders—emerged. Finally, whatever sentencing disparity there is across judges, it does not seem to be due to judges' capriciousness. Thus, judges may be redundant and the probation officers' job may be done more efficiently by a computer program, but one could easily think of a far worse system, with malevolent—or more irrational—decision-makers.

References

American Law Institute. *Model penal code.* Proposed official draft. Philadelphia: American Law Institute, 1962.

Bottomley, A. K. *Decisions in the penal process.* South Hackensack, NJ: F. B. Rothman, 1973.

Carter, R. M. It is respectfully recommended. . . . *Federal Probation,* 1966, *30,* No. 2.

Carter, R. M., & Wilkins, L. T. Some factors in sentencing policy. *Journal of Criminal Law, Criminology, and Police Science,* 1967, *58,* 503–514.

Curry, P. M. Probation and individualized disposition: A study of factors associated with the presentence recommendation. *American Journal of Criminal Law*, 1975, 4, 31–81.

Diamond, S. S., & Zeisel, H. Sentencing councils: A study of sentence disparity and its reduction. *University of Chicago Law Review*, 1975, 43, 109–149.

Ebbesen, E. B., & Konečni, V. J. Decision making and information integration in the courts: The setting of bail. *Journal of Personality and Social Psychology*, 1975, 32, 805–821.

Ebbesen, E. B., & Konečni, V. J. The process of sentencing adult felons: A causal analysis of judicial decisions. In B. D. Sales (Ed.), *Perspectives in law and psychology. Vol. 2: The jury, judicial, and trial process.* New York: Plenum, 1981.

Frank, J. *Courts on trial: Myth and reality in American justice.* Princeton, NJ: Princeton University Press, 1949.

Frerichs, J., McKinney, A., & Tisner, P. Judges and their sentencing procedures: A sociological questionnaire study of factors important in the sentencing of defendants in the San Diego Superior Court. Unpublished manuscript, University of California, San Diego, 1975.

Goodman, L. A. Causal analysis of data from panel studies and other kinds of surveys. *American Journal of Sociology*, 1973, 78, 1135–1191.

Goodman, L. A. A general method for the analysis of surveys. *American Journal of Sociology*, 1972, 77, 1035–1086.

Gottfredson, D. M., Wilkins, L. T., & Hoffman, P. B. *Guidelines for parole and sentencing.* Lexington, MA: Lexington Books, 1978.

Green, E. *Judicial attitudes in sentencing.* London: MacMillan, 1961.

Hagan, J. Law, order, and sentencing: A study of attitude in action. *Sociometry*, 1975, 38, 374–384.

Heise, D. R. *Causal analysis.* New York: Wiley, 1975.

Hogarth, J. *Sentencing as a human process.* Toronto: University of Toronto Press, 1971.

Hood, R. G. *Sentencing in magistrates' courts.* London: Stevens, 1962.

Hood, R. G. A study of the effectiveness of pre-sentence investigations in reducing recidivism. *British Journal of Criminology*, 1966, 6, 303.

Kistler, R. Probation department's services unsatisfactory, judge says. *Los Angeles Times*, March 12, 1975.

Konečni, V. J., & Ebbesen, E. B. External validity of research in legal psychology. *Law and Human Behavior*, 1979, 3, 39–70.

Konečni, V. J., & Ebbesen, E. B. A critical analysis of method and theory in psychological approaches to legal decisions. In B. D. Sales (Ed.), *Perspectives in law and psychology. Vol. 2: The jury, judicial, and trial process.* New York: Plenum, 1981.

Konečni, V. J., Mulcahy, E. M., & Ebbesen, E. B. Prison or mental hospital: Factors affecting the processing of persons suspected of being "mentally disordered sex offenders." In P. D. Lipsitt and B. D. Sales (Eds.), *New directions in psycholegal research.* New York: Van Nostrand Reinhold, 1980.

Papandreou, N., McDonald, S. E., & Landauer, A. A. An experimental investigation of some factors influencing the pre-sentence report. *Australia and New Zealand Journal of Criminology*, in press.

Persky, W., Sprague, M., & Lowe, B. How judges pass sentence. *San Diego Evening Tribune*, May 22, 1975.

President's Commission on Law Enforcement and the Administration of Justice. *The challenge of crime in a free society.* Washington, DC: U.S. Government Printing Office, 1967.

Webb, E. J., Campbell, D. T., Schwartz, R. D., & Sechrest, L. *Unobtrusive measures: Nonreactive research in the social sciences.* Chicago: Rand McNally, 1966.

Wilkins, L. T., & Chandler, A. Confidence and competence in decision making. *British Journal of Criminology*, 1965, 5, 22–35.

THE PAROLE PROCESS

Editors' Introduction

Decisions regarding the release of a prisoner on parole, prior to the expiration of the entire sentence imposed by the court, complete the process that was initiated by the offenders' decision to commit the crime and their subsequent entry into the criminal justice system through police detection of the crime and the arrest. Parole decisions are both important and unique. They are important, from the viewpoint of both the prisoner and society in that the decision to grant parole at a particular time may substantially shorten an offender's prison term and bring about the prisoner's relatively sudden and unanticipated reentry into the community. The decision to grant versus refuse parole (or, as Wilkins points out in Chapter 13, the decision to release now or later and, if later, how much later) thus appears to combine elements of a trial in the fact-finding sense (How has the prisoner been behaving lately? Is the prisoner sufficiently rehabilitated?) with those of a sentencing hearing in the sense that the decision to grant versus refuse parole establishes the actual sentence a prisoner has served or will serve. The fact that repeated decisions (in cases where parole is denied a number of times) are made concerning the same person and the same crime makes the parole decision unique: These decisions should presumably reflect change in the state of the prisoner and predict how this changed person will interact with the community—a truly momentous task.

As editors, we were fortunate to have both the Wilkins and the Maslach/Garber chapters, because they look at different aspects of parole decisions and complement each other. The findings of Maslach and Garber are based on a unique opportunity to code predictors of the parole decisions from the tape recordings of live parole hearings in San Quentin and Vacaville prisons in California. (The permission to tape-record parole hearings was granted for discovery purposes, by court order, in Van Geldern v. Kerr, a class-action suit brought by the prisoners in California against the California Adult Authority.) Wilkins's work is concerned with the federal parole system, the work of the U.S. Board of Paroles (now the Parole Commissioners). The model of federal parole decisions developed by Wilkins is based mostly on predictors derived from past parole decisions, information in the prisoner's file that is available to parole board members (as opposed to the hearing), and policy considerations by the parole board members themselves. Also, whereas Maslach and Garber collaborated closely with the law firm of Public Advocates, Inc., which represented the plaintiffs and had been given the discovery permission by the court, and thus could be regarded as "adversaries" of the California Adult Authority, Wilkins had the full cooperation of the members of the U.S. Board of Paroles and, in fact, his descriptive model of parole decisions was accepted as a prescriptive model by the board members, through a set of guidelines that Wilkins developed in conjunction with the model.

The two chapters, especially taken together, provide a fascinating account of how the parole system operates. Whereas Wilkins's chapter provides invaluable information about both the actual predictors of parole decisions and the predictors that the parole board members themselves considered "appropriate," the work of Maslach and Garber lifts the shroud of secrecy surrounding the hearings themselves. Among many other interesting details, one finds that in three-quarters of the cases the hearing officers' deliberations took less than 2 minutes, that the average length of a hearing was 16 minutes, and that the board members' principal preoccupation seemed to be with "psychological assessment" of the prisoner; whereas the prisoner's most frequent mode of response was to respond "passively, in a minimally informative, nonaffirmative manner." As Maslach and Garber point out, many aspects of their data point to the conclusion that parole decisions had been reached before the hearing and that the hearings themselves served a purely ritual function, their contents being entirely epiphenomenal. The fact that Wilkins was able to develop a very accurate model on the basis of information from the files and policy considerations alone (the information from both of which is, of course, available prior to the hearing) supports this idea. The previous chapter on sentencing reached the same conclusion about the ritualistic function of most legal hearings as has our work on mentally disordered sex offenders (Konečni, Mulcahy, and Ebbesen, 1980).

12

Decision-Making Processes
in Parole Hearings[1]

Christina Maslach and Robert M. Garber

Many decisions cannot be made easily, given that they require the rejection of one or more plausible courses of action. However, they become especially difficult to make with any degree of accuracy when they: (1) are based on minimal information; (2) involve ambiguous standards or criteria; or (3) result in serious consequences, such as life or death. When all of these factors are present, there is very little basis for arriving at a reasonable decision with any degree of confidence. And yet, this is precisely the type of situation that exists in the parole hearing, where decisions must be made continually about whether or not a prisoner is released from prison. Information is minimal because the hearing lasts for only a few minutes. The concepts of "rehabilitation" and "good parole risk" are extremely ambiguous, and there are no clear guidelines as to what behavioral objectives are required for parole. Finally, the consequences of the decision are obviously serious since, from the prisoner's viewpoint, it could mean freedom or another year behind bars, while from the hearing officer's perspective, it could mean sending back to the community either a responsible citizen or a person who will prey on society by committing more crimes.

[1]This chapter is an expanded version of R. M. Garber and C. Maslach, The parole hearing: Decision or justification? *Law and Human Behavior*, 1977, 1 (3), 261–281. The research was prepared as expert testimony for *Van Geldern v. Kerr*, Civil No. C–72–2088 SAW, at the request of Sidney Wolinsky of Public Advocates, Inc., attorney for the plaintiffs. Preparation of this chapter was funded by Biomedical Sciences Support Grant 3–SO5–RR–07006–08S1 to the senior author. We wish to thank Paula Flamm and Desdemona Cardoza, for their help in the coding phase of the research, and Rick Jacobs and Curtis Hardyck, for their assistance in the data analysis.

In theory, the parole decision is a "balanced scientific decision made by experts, at a comparatively leisurely pace, upon ample and accurate information accumulated in the real-life post-conviction milieu" (Parsons-Lewis, 1972, p. 1523). Traditionally, these decision-makers have been considered skilled experts in human behavior, capable of weighing all relevant data fairly and intelligently. However, these assumptions have recently begun to be questioned, and there is a growing recognition of the complexity of the parole decision-making process and of the difficulties it poses for both the decision-makers (the hearing officers) and the objects of those decisions (the prisoners). Part of this awareness has developed from the results of empirical research, primarily simulation studies, which are reviewed elsewhere in this volume (Chapter 13). Within the state of California, the increased attention paid to parole decisions has come from various efforts at legislative reform and from a class-action lawsuit (*Van Geldern* v. *Kerr*), which was the basis for the current research.

THE PAROLE SYSTEM IN CALIFORNIA

> The granting and revocation and affixing of sentences shall be determined by the Adult Authority; provided that the Adult Authority or one member thereof shall interview each prisoner at least before the Adult Authority determines his sentence. (Section 5077, California Penal Code)

Indeterminate sentencing has been viewed as a tool for treatment and rehabilitation. In theory, it allows offenders to be kept in custody as long as necessary in order to effect the desired changes in their individual character and to insure that they will not be released until they no longer present an economic or a bodily threat to the community. When this desired rehabilitation has been accomplished, prisoners are placed on parole, a limited freedom whereby they are released to the community under the supervision of a parole officer. For male felons in California, the decision to release an inmate from prison prior to the final expiration of his sentence has been a responsibility delegated exclusively to an administrative board called the California Adult Authority. The decisions are made within the wide-ranging minimum and maximum terms for specific crimes (e.g., 5 years to life for first-degree robbery), which were set by the state legislature and are applied by trial judges.[2]

---

[2]Subsequent to the completion of this research and its presentation as expert evidence by the authors in the July 1976 court hearings of *Van Geldern* v. *Kerr*, the California state legislature enacted a new sentencing law, which took effect July 1,

In practice, the decision to grant or deny parole is made following a hearing conducted by two members of the Adult Authority (the hearing officers) with the prisoner present. Such a hearing is usually held once a year for each prisoner eligible for parole. The policy priorities considered by the Adult Authority in their decision to grant or deny parole are: (1) protection of society, (2) punishment of the offender, (3) deterrence of crime, and (4) rehabilitation of the criminal (California Adult Authority Policy Statement, 1973). There are no specific decision-making guidelines beyond these general priorities, since the Adult Authority purposely has no formal published criteria for its decisions. Rather, in keeping with the prevailing correctional philosophy, the lack of criteria is consistent with the goals of individual treatment. Instead of applying a set standard of protection and punishment, the Adult Authority operates on the assumption that no two prisoners are alike, and "therefore, no specific criteria can be developed which will apply to all cases" (Kerr, 1972, p. 8). On the one hand, this flexible policy reflects a stated concern for the unique and individual qualities of each prisoner being considered for parole. But, on the other, it creates a series of problems for both the hearing officers and the prisoners.

The perspective of the hearing officer

> Felons committed to prison should be kept until there is *reasonable cause* to believe they can lead crime-free lives in society. Doubts should be resolved in favor of public protection. (California Adult Authority Policy Statement, 1973; emphasis added)

The decision facing the parole hearing officer is a very difficult one, and an error in either direction has its attendant risks. If the hearing officer errs by granting parole to a person who would then commit future crimes, there are increased risks to those members of society who would be harmed by this individual's actions. If the hearing officer errs by denying parole to a person who would become a responsible and useful citizen, then society loses a valuable member, the person's family continues to be disrupted, and the individual may become more embittered about society as a result of prolonged incar-

---

1977. The new law abolished the existing indeterminate sentencing system (which had been in effect for 60 years) and replaced it with a determinate sentencing system. Under this new system, there are fixed sentences for various crimes (as set by the legislature), and thus there is no need for a system in which the decision to release a prisoner is continually under review. In spite of this change in the California parole system, the current research is still important for the understanding it provides of the previous California system and for similar decision-making institutions elsewhere.

ceration. In spite of the serious consequences of these decisions, hearing officers receive very little guidance in how to make the correct ones. They are not told what characterizes a prisoner who is ready for parole or what constitutes "reasonable cause." Although they are given access to certain information about the prisoner (the prisoner's central file is available for inspection, and the prisoner is available to answer questions), they are not told what information is most useful and relevant to the decision nor how to weigh or combine different bits of information. They receive no systematic feedback about the outcomes of their decisions, although a few extreme "failures" (e.g., a person who murders someone immediately after being released on parole) will receive widespread publicity. As a result of the lack of clear guidelines for making parole decisions, hearing officers are forced to rely on their own subjective criteria and expertise, which add a weighty personal responsibility to the decision-making process.

The perspective of the prisoner

> No one walks into the board room with his head up. This just isn't done! Guys lie to each other, but if a man gets a parole from these prisons . . . it means that he crawled into that board room. . . . And you can't fake it—resignation, defeat, it must be stamped clearly across the face. (Jackson, 1970, pp. 161–162)

The dilemma facing prisoners is how to best present themselves and their case so that hearing officers will be persuaded to grant parole. Prisoners know that once a year a brief opportunity exists to effect a major change in their lives, but they rarely know how to make the most of that opportunity. They are faced with the same lack of clear guidelines that confronts hearing officers. The criteria for obtaining parole are not made explicit, and so prisoners are unsure as to what information to present during the hearing in order to demonstrate their readiness for parole and in what manner to present it. Since prisoners usually appear before different hearing officers at each subsequent parole hearing, the criteria used in one hearing may not be used in a subsequent one. The ambiguity and uncertainty that surround the parole decision force prisoners to assess the situation and plan future strategy on the basis of rumor and speculation.

Reviews of the parole decision-making process

Over the past few years in California there have been efforts in the state legislature toward modification of the indeterminate sentencing system. In preparation for new legislation, several legislative committees have undertaken studies of sentencing and parole decision-making in California. These reports, which have relied primarily on unsystematic investigatory interviews with parole policy-makers, have portrayed the parole bureaucracy in a very uncomplimentary light. Both the report of the California Assembly Committee on Criminal Procedure (1968) and the report of the California Assembly Select Committee on the Administration of Justice (1970) stated that the criteria for parole decisions had no rationally justified basis and were arbitrary and unscientific. More recently, a report by the California State Bar Association (1975) reached similar conclusions and recommended the abolition of the Adult Authority and a procedure for release review hearings in which the prisoner was entitled to procedural due process, representation by counsel, and the right to call and cross-examine relevant witnesses.

On several occasions, parole decision-makers have reported their own views of the parole process. In the most extensive study of this kind (Gottfredson and Ballard, 1965), questionnaires were mailed to employees of the Youth and Adult Corrections Agency, which included all members of the Adult Authority as well as the Board of Trustees of the California Institution for Women. These questionnaires were designed to assess the institutional goals (as viewed by the respondent) and the factors used in making a parole decision. Of the 25 goals listed, only 2 were rated as very important: "protect the public" and "release inmates at the optimal time for most probable success on parole." One factor was rated as very important in parole decisions: "past record of assaultive offenses." In a more recent study (Aitken, 1975), where Adult Authority members were questioned about the factors they considered in parole decisions, the factors that predominated were: (1) original crime, (2) behavior in prison, (3) attitude of the inmate, and (4) outside influences (e.g., political climate; letters from prosecutors, judges, or victims). While such studies provide some interesting insights into the beliefs of parole decision-makers, it is important to know that these self-reports leave unanswered questions of how and to what extent these allegedly important factors actually influence decision-making in the parole hearing.

CURRENT RESEARCH

The present research evolved from the recently generated public interest in the administration and practice of parole decision-making. In addition to new laws, one result of this concern was the instigation of numerous legal actions in both state and federal courts. One of these legal actions, the federal lawsuit of Van Geldern v. Kerr, provided the data for the present study. Van Geldern is a class-action lawsuit that was heard before Judge Stanley Weigel in San Francisco in July 1976.[3] It was brought by prisoners in California in an attempt to challenge existing parole procedures by asking for constitutional due process safeguards in the administration of parole hearings. These hearings are ordinarily not recorded or open to the public, but it was necessary to gain access to them in order to present the case for trial to the court. The needed access was obtained through a court order allowing the attorneys to tape-record these previously closed Adult Authority proceedings. The current research utilized the tape recordings generated by the discovery order and was designed to provide a content analysis of these parole hearings.

The main goals of this exploratory analysis were threefold. First, the study attempted to provide a valid and systematic assessment of parole hearings in operation, describing the form and content of the interactions that normally take place behind closed doors. Second, the study tried to deduce the decision-making rules used by the hearing officers to either grant or deny parole. Finally, the third goal was to assess the congruity between the principles of the individual treatment model and their implementation into the parole decisions that were actually made.

METHODOLOGY OF THE STUDY

The subjects

The subjects in this study were the hearing officers and prisoners present at 100 randomly selected parole hearings of the California Adult Authority during September and October 1974. The hearings took place at San Quentin and Vacaville prisons, where permission to tape-record parole hearings had been granted for discovery in the case of *Van Geldern* v. *Kerr*. The actual tape recording of the hearings was directed and supervised by the law firm of Public Advocates, Inc., which represented the plaintiffs.[4]

---

[3] As of March 1981, the court had yet to make a final ruling.

[4] The court order required that prisoners be informed of the purpose of the tape recordings and that they have the option to refuse such recording of their hearings. A written consent form was presented to each prisoner prior to the hearing, and the prisoners indicated whether they did or did not consent to the tape recording. This signed consent form was reviewed orally by the hearing officers at the start of the hearing in order to ensure that prisoners understood the options available to them. Of the prisoners who had hearings during the sample period, 94% gave their consent for tape recordings, while 6% exercised their option to refuse. The written consent of the hearing officers was not required by the court order since they were acting in their role as public officials. Special measures were taken during the coding of the tapes to mask identifying information so that the responses of both prisoners and hearing officers were anonymous and confidential.

Several factors delimited the subject pool from which the 100 sample cases were taken. First, only those hearings in which prisoners gave their written consent were tape-recorded. Of 337 hearings conducted during the sample period, 316 (94%) were recorded following the prisoners' consent. A second factor was the decision to sample from the September hearings at San Quentin (September 3–12, 1974) and from the October hearings (October 7–11, 1974) at Vacaville. Each of these weeks represented a second series of tape-recorded hearings at each of the institutions. It was hoped that by this time the presence of the tape recorders and the operators would be regarded as more routine and thus would be less likely to influence the regular hearing procedures. Third, only hearings in which parole was either granted or denied were included in the subject pool. Of the 316 prisoners who had given consent, 21 cases were excluded because the hearing was postponed and 8 cases were excluded because they were special hearings to determine if a previously set parole date should be rescinded (*Prewitt* hearings).

Thus, the final subject pool consisted of 288 hearings from which 100 were randomly selected for further analysis. The sample size of 100 cases was chosen as a result of weighing the relative costs and benefits of inclusiveness. The 100 cases were a substantial segment of the total population and, at the same time, were manageable in terms of the time and effort required to code and analyze them.

The coding instruments

Three independent content analyses were developed for scoring the *Van Geldern* tapes. The first analysis coded the variety and frequency of topics discussed by the hearing officers, as well as the manner in which they were raised (Adult Authority Content Analysis). The second analysis coded the variety and frequency of the comments made by the prisoners and the responses of the hearing officers to these comments (Prisoners' Response Content Analysis). The third analysis coded certain topic patterns and a series of legal questions pertaining specifically to the objectives of the lawsuit itself (Legal Analysis). An analysis was also made of several time-related variables (Timing Analysis).

Adult Authority Content Analysis The Adult Authority coding instrument was a two-dimensional matrix comprised of 18 subject categories and 4 process categories (for a total of 72 cells). The subject categories were the content topics generally discussed during the course of a parole hearing. They included:

1. Prior lifestyle of the prisoner (before incarceration).

2. Prior criminal behavior.

3. Paroles and revocations.

4. Commitment offense.

5. Legal records.

6. Prison custody (classification and discipline record).

7. Prison rehabilitation.

8. Prison associations (activities other than rehabilitation).

9. Prior parole hearings.

10. Current parole hearing and criteria for parole.

11. Psychological assessment (hearing officer's reference to the prisoner's psychological state).

12. Psychological reports (psychological assessment of the prisoner made by the prison psychology staff).

13. Prisoner's health.

14. Medical evaluation.

15. Prisoner's physical appearance.

16. Postrelease activities.

17. Postrelease support (prisoner's future contact with parole officer, or use of psychological or medical care).

18. Unscored content.

The process categories referred to the manner in which the various subject categories were raised during the hearing. They included:

1. Question.

2. Informational statement.

3. Judgment (evaluation of prisoner in terms of hearing officer's personal judgment).

4. Advice.

Each content unit was scored by checking the appropriate one of the 72 subject × process cells of the scoring matrix.

Prisoners' Response Content Analysis   The prisoners' response coding instrument was a two-dimensional matrix comprised of 20 prisoner behavior categories and 4 hearing officer response categories (for a total of 80 cells). The prisoner behavior categories represented the content and style of the prisoner's self-presentation to the hearing officers. These categories included:

1. Asks questions or shows confusion.

2. Makes general complaints.

3. Complains about prison programs or facilities.

4. Complains about legal issues or fairness of the hearing.

5. Makes minimal responses about general topics (responses that show little initiative to go beyond a recitation of details to answer a question).

6. Makes minimal responses about the past (prior record, prior lifestyle, parole revocation, commitment offense).

7. Makes minimal responses about institutional experiences (prison conduct, prison programs, personal physical condition).

8. Makes minimal responses about future (parole program, outside living, outside activities, outside employment).

9. Makes minimal responses about present psychological state.

10. Makes general defensive statements (statements that assess psychological, as opposed to legal, responsibility).

11. Makes defensive statements that blame self for prison behavior.

12. Makes defensive statements that blame situation for prison behavior.

13. Makes defensive statements that blame self for prior behavior.

14. Makes defensive statements that blame situation for prior behavior.

15. Makes defensive statements that deny guilt.

16. Makes general affirmative statements (statements that show initiative to raise topics that the prisoner wants to talk about).

17. Makes affirmative statements about the past.

18. Makes affirmative statements about institutional experiences.

19. Makes affirmative statements about the future.

20. Makes affirmative statements about present psychological state.

The hearing officer response categories represent the manner in which the hearing officer reacted to the prisoner's statement. They included:

1. Accepted (either supportive acceptance or minimal acknowledgment).

2. Questioned validity or importance (hearing officer challenges truth of prisoner's statement).

3. Interrupted.

4. Ignored (lack of obvious response to prisoner's statement or change of topic).

Each content unit was scored by checking the appropriate one of the 80 prisoner behavior × hearing officer response cells of the scoring matrix. In contrast to the Adult Authority Content Analysis, which focused exclusively on the individual hearing officer, the Prisoners' Response Content Analysis focused on the interaction between prisoner and hearing officer (although the emphasis was on the prisoner).

Legal Analysis   The Legal Analysis coding instrument consisted of two separate sets of categories. One of these was a set of instances where the presence of an attorney would have been helpful to a prisoner in presenting the case or protecting the prisoner's rights.[5] A category was checked if the particular instance occurred at least once during the hearing. The second set of categories referred to certain pattern characteristics of the topics that were discussed. The content of the first topic to be raised and of the topic that dominated the hearing (as determined by time spent on the topic or repeated returns to it) was scored by checking the appropriate one of 16 subject categories (which were similar to the Adult Authority Content Analysis). These categories excluded social greetings and preliminary questions regarding the consent forms for tape recording the hearing. At the end of the hearing, the prisoner was usually asked the standard question, "Is there anything else you would like to say?" The prisoner's response to this question was coded by one of the following 8 categories:

---

[5]Since the legal issues do not bear directly on the goals of this study, these categories and the resulting data will not be presented in this chapter.

1. Says no.

2. Asks what to say.

3. Makes an affirmative statement.

4. Asks a legal question.

5. Asks for parole.

6. Asks for a program.

7. Asks for parole criteria.

8. Other.

Timing Analysis An indirect measure of the importance of various aspects of the parole hearing was the amount of time spent on each one. These time factors were scored by coders who listened to the tapes and recorded the various times with the aid of a digital clock calibrated in 100ths of a minute. Time scores were also recorded for the duration of the hearing as measured from the hearing officers' initial greeting of the prisoner to the final statement made. The length of the hearing officers' deliberations was measured from the first statement after the prisoner had left the room to the final statement about the case. In addition, the amount of time that both the prisoner and the hearing officers spoke during the hearing was recorded.

The development of the coding instruments In the design of the coding instruments for this study, the goal was to generate several sets of categories that would be meaningful (in order to accurately describe the process), comprehensive (so that all or most of the material appearing on the tapes could be scored into an appropriate category), and clear (so that trained coders could score them reliably). In the first stage of development, an extensive set of categories was generated through an empirically based a priori analysis of the parole hearing process. That is, categories were derived through listening to randomly selected tapes of parole hearings, reading transcripts of hearings, and reviewing published materials on Adult Authority policy and parole selection criteria. This procedure resulted in a comprehensive list of content categories that represented most of the possible variation of topics and behaviors in the parole hearings. These initial categories were far too numerous to permit reliable and efficient coding, but they did provide the foundation for the final instruments.

The second stage of development was one of refinement. Central to this process was the use of a set of tapes from the first series of tape-recorded hearings (which were not included in the experimental sample). On the basis of these tapes, the categories were critically examined for their appropriateness and fit to the material. Along each of the dimensions of the analysis, categories were combined, redefined, eliminated, and simplified. This refinement process resulted in the final coding forms and coding manuals used in this study.[6] The unit of analysis in this final coding system was a meaning or theme (as defined by the content categories), rather than a sentence. Although a single sentence often referred to a single theme, in many cases the theme extended for several sentences. For example, the following statement by a hearing officer—"What can you tell me about the crime that got you into prison? How did you get involved in that?"—was scored only once in the appropriate cell (commitment offense × question) even though two sentences were used. Similarly, a single sentence that contained more than one theme (which was rare) resulted in more than one score. The set of content categories can be considered an exhaustive one, since more than 99% of the content units were scored as falling into one of these categories.

The coding procedure

A team of 4–6 coders, all students at the University of California, Berkeley, was organized for each of the three content analyses and the timing analysis. The coding team for the Legal Analysis was composed of law students from Boalt Hall Law School, while the remaining teams were made up of advanced undergraduates with various social science majors (i.e., psychology, criminology, and sociology). These teams met separately several times a week over a period of nearly two months to practice using the coding instruments until a high degree of reliability was achieved (the interrater coefficients of reliability ranged from .82 to .92).

The actual coding of tapes (which took about four weeks) was done in listening sessions where pairs of coders worked together. In all cases, coders were blind to the outcome of the parole hearing since the decisions occurred after the hearing was completed. For both the Adult Authority and the prisoners' response content analyses, two coders from the same analysis team worked together. While one coder scored the hearing content, the other simply listened.These roles were alternated for each subsequent hearing. The use of two coders from the same analysis team reduced fatigue and provided a source of feedback about potentially ambiguous passages. If a coder was

---

[6]Copies of the coding forms and the coding manuals are contained in Garber (1976).

uncertain about how to score a particular content unit, he or she could consult with the other coder. For the timing and legal analyses, the pairs of coders were made up of one member each from the timing and legal analysis teams, thus allowing the two analyses to be scored simultaneously. The pairs of coders were changed throughout the coding so that no systematic biases occurred as a result of two coders always working together.

RESULTS OF THE STUDY

The data from this study will be presented in two parts. First, there will be a description of the timing and content patterns of the parole hearing. Next, the relationship of these factors to the decision-making process will be explored through several detailed statistical analyses.

A descriptive summary of parole hearings

Of the sample parole hearings, 64% were conducted at San Quentin and 36% at Vacaville. Of the prisoners who appeared at these hearings, 37% were Caucasian and 43% were non-Caucasian (25% black, 17% chicano, and 1% Native American). Ethnic-racial information was not available for the remaining 20%, since it had not been noted by the tape-recorder operators at the hearings. Although it would have been desirable to know additional background characteristics of the prisoners (e.g., age, commitment offense), such information was available only in the prisoners' central files, and access to these files was not granted by the court order. Of the 100 hearings, 39% resulted in a decision to grant parole and 61% resulted in denial.

On the average, the parole hearings lasted 16.2 minutes, although they ranged from less than 5 minutes to 40 minutes. The largest group of hearings lasted from 11 to 15 minutes. On the average, prisoners spoke for 6.3 minutes in the hearings, while hearing officers spoke for 6.8 minutes. Although prisoners who were granted parole had spoken less (5.6 minutes) than those who were denied (6.7 minutes), this difference failed to achieve statistical significance.

The length of the hearing officers' deliberations to reach their decisions ranged from less than 30 seconds to 10 minutes, with the average deliberation lasting 1.5 minutes. Almost one-third of the deliberations took less than 30 seconds, and in nearly three-fourths of the cases, the final decision process took less than 2 minutes. In only 5 of the 100 cases did the deliberations go beyond 5 minutes. The outcome of the deliberation was related to its length, with decisions to grant parole taking longer (2.1 minutes) than decisions to deny parole (1.2 minutes). This difference of less than a minute is, nevertheless, statistically significant ($F = 7.69$, $df = 1/98$, $p < .006$).

Topic pattern

As the parole hearings generally operated, one of the hearing officers reviewed a prisoner's central file immediately prior to the interview. By noting the first topic raised in the hearing, coders could make inferences about what the hearing officer considered salient from the file and viewed as of primary importance for the hearing. In addition, this first line of questioning could be seen as setting the tone for the remainder of the hearing. The frequency with which various topics were the first ones raised is shown in Table 12.1. As can be seen, psychological assessment is most often this first topic (19%). Furthermore, when we examine the first four topics discussed, psychological assessment appears in 56% of the cases. To reiterate, this category refers to the use of psychological terms or psychologically probing questions or statements by the hearing officers (such as saying that a psychosexual problem exists or that the prisoner is "really together"). It does *not* include any references to the psychological reports prepared by the institutional staff.

Table 12.1

Percentage distribution for first topic and dominant topics discussed in parole hearings

Discussion topic	First topic[a]	Dominant topic[b]
Psychological assessment	19	52
Commitment offense	12	6
Prison discipline	10	9
Rehabilitation—school/job	10	2
Rehabilitation—therapy	9	1
Hearings/criteria	8	1
Prior criminal behavior	7	2
Psychological report	6	5
Medical evaluation	4	3
Parole plans	3	5
Paroles and revocations	3	2
Prison classification	3	1
Prior lifestyle	2	6
Legal records	2	3
Prison associations	1	—
Other	1	1

[a]$n = 100$.
[b]$n = 87$, since a dominant topic could not be determined for 13 hearings.

After psychological assessment, the next most frequent opening topics were the commitment offense and selected aspects of prison life (discipline and rehabilitation). The category of parole plans was the first topic raised in only 3 of the 100 hearings, but in each instance the prisoner was granted a parole. When the first four topics are considered, parole plans is among them only 15% of the time; however, its presence suggests that the prisoner is significantly more likely to be granted parole $\chi_c^2 = 4.39, df = 1, p < .03$).

Table 12.1 also shows the frequency of the content topics that were rated as the dominant ones in the parole hearings. The most striking result is that psychological assessment, which was raised first most often, is also rated as the dominant topic in 52% of the hearings scored. No other topic is even a close second to this overriding psychological emphasis. It should be noted that this topic coding was done by the Legal Analysis coders, who were law students and not psychology students (who might be more inclined to view the world along psychological dimensions).

Almost three-fourths of the hearings ended with the standard question, "Is there anything else you would like to say?" This closing question is one of the few opportunities available to prisoners to actively direct the hearing officers' attention to those factors that they consider relevant to their case and that may have been overlooked. Of the 74 prisoners, 38% responded to this question by making some type of affirmative statement (a positive self-presentation). However, 28% of the prisoners responded by saying no, that they had nothing to add in the decision-making process. In addition, 12% of the prisoners responded by specifically requesting parole.

Adult Authority Content Analysis   Table 12.2 presents the distribution of topics discussed by the hearing officers during the course of the parole hearing. Again, the major content area was psychological assessment, which is consistent with the previous results from the topic pattern analysis. Psychological assessment accounts for nearly one-quarter of the hearing officers' content and is almost twice that of the next most frequently discussed topic. A second feature of this analysis is the emphasis on prison behavior. Two categories, prison custody and prison rehabilitation, together account for almost a second quarter of the hearing officers' content. These categories cover the areas of rule infractions and prison training/therapy programs. Following these two categories in terms of frequency was the commitment offense. A third point in this analysis is the apparent lack of future-oriented discussion. References to parole plans in terms of postrelease activity and postrelease support account for little more than 6% of the hearing officers' content. From this seemingly

Table 12.2
Relative percentage of Adult Authority
content category use in 100 parole
hearings

Discussion topic	Percent
Psychological assessment	22.3
Prison custody	12.5
Prison rehabilitation	10.7
Commitment offense	10.0
Prior lifestyle	7.8
Current hearing	6.5
Prior criminal behavior	6.4
Postrelease activity	5.2
Paroles and revocations	3.6
Legal records	3.3
Psychological reports	3.3
Prior hearings	2.0
Prison associations	1.6
Medical evaluation	1.4
Prisoner's health	1.1
Postrelease support	1.1
Physical appearance	0.5

Note: Mean content units per hearing = 63.61.

minor emphasis on future plans, compared to previous criminal behavior and present prison behavior, we may infer the relative weight given by hearing officers to past, present, and future behavior in determining a prisoner's parole readiness.[7]

The Adult Authority Content Analysis also recorded the manner in which the content areas were broached. The results show that the topics were raised most often in the form of questions posed to the prisoner (54%). The next most frequent category was informational statements (40%), followed by judgments (6%). Advice was rarely given.

Prisoners' Response Content Analysis   The distribution of the prisoners' responses to the hearing officers' questions and statements is contained in Table 12.3. The most striking aspect of this analysis is the dominant use of the minimal response categories, with 62% of the prisoners' responses characterized as such. This means that pris-

---

[7]While it would have been useful to code the positive or negative value of a topic in addition to its frequency (e.g., was the prisoner's behavior in prison evaluated as good or bad by the hearing officer), in practice it was very difficult for the coders to do so with any degree of reliability.

Table 12.3

Percentage of Prisoners' Response content category use in 100 parole hearings

Response	Percent
Minimal response re institution	21.8
Minimal response re past	20.6
Minimal response, general	12.1
Affirmative statement re past	7.0
Affirmative statement re institution	5.9
Question/confusion	5.8
Minimal response re future	4.8
Complaint re legal issues	3.8
Affirmative statement, general	3.0
Affirmative statement re psychological state	2.9
Minimal response re psychological state	2.8
Affirmative statement re future	2.6
Denial of legal guilt	2.0
Complaint re program/facilities	1.9
Defensive statement, situational	0.9
Complaint, general	0.7
Defensive statement, dispositional	0.6
Defensive statement, general	0.4

Note: Mean content units per hearing = 50.97.

oners respond by providing a minimum of information to the hearing officers. For example, when prisoners are asked how they are doing in the institution, a minimal response would be "ok" or "fine." In contrast, an affirmative response to the same question would go beyond the minimal answer and give further information about what the prisoners are doing that make them "fine" or "ok." This prevalence of minimal responses is particularly noteworthy since the parole hearing is the major (if not only) opportunity for inmates to add to or refute information contained in their central file. This lack of initiating behaviors is further substantiated by the fact that affirmative statements account for only 20% of the total responses made by prisoners and that questions and complaints are relatively scarce (approximately 6% each). In addition, it is worth noting the relative absence of denial and defensive statements in the prisoners' verbal behavior (a total of only 4%).

The hearing officers' most frequent response to the prisoners' statements was one of general acceptance (78%). This is not to say that they necessarily believed or supported any statement by the prisoners, but rather that they did not challenge or confront them directly. The remaining hearing officer response categories of validity questioned (11%), interrupted (9%) and ignored (1%) occurred relatively

infrequently, but constitute a serious challenge to prisoners' self-pre-
sentations.

An analysis of parole decision-making

From the descriptive data presented thus far, it is possible to characterize parole hearings as short, unstructured interview sessions
where hearing officers typically ask psychologically oriented questions and prisoners respond passively in a minimally informative,
nonaffirmative manner. This description of the content and style of
the interaction says little about the decision-making strategies
involved, other than to generally suggest what information is available to the decision-makers. The general hypothesis being investigated in this study is whether or not any relationship exists between
the content of the parole hearing and the decision to grant or deny
parole. This next section reports the results of several statistical analyses in an attempt to understand how the factors that characterize
the parole hearing contribute to the decision-making process.

Method of analysis   The principal analytical tool used here is the
method of discriminant function analysis (Overall and Klett, 1972).
DFA is used to classify individuals into two or more mutually exclusive groups on the basis of their scores on a number of independent
or predictor variables. In essence, DFA utilizes multiple regression
procedures in cases where the criterion variable is nominal (the
mutually exclusive groups). After first determining the maximum
amount of variation that can be associated with differences between
the groups, DFA procedures then develop equations to predict that
difference. In the two-group situation, the prediction equation
derived from a DFA is almost identical to a multiple regression equation where the criterion is a dichotomous variable. The only difference is that the beta weights from multiple regression are reported as
standardized discriminant function coefficients in the DFA. These
coefficients are interpretable as the relative contribution of its associated variable to the discriminant function, and the sign ($+$ or $-$)
indicates whether the variable is making a positive or negative contribution. In the case where classification is the primary objective,
DFA has a distinct advantage over multiple regression in that most
DFA computing programs go beyond simply generating the prediction equation and actually apply it, predicting group membership for
each individual case.

   In each analysis to be reported here, the criterion variable was the
outcome of the parole hearing (parole versus denial), and the predic-

tors were the various content categories scored in the Adult Authority and prisoners' response content analyses. Since individual hearings varied with respect to time and content units, all category frequencies were standardized by being transformed to proportions. The differences between these proportions for the paroled and denied groups were also tested for statistical significance.

Adult Authority Content Analysis   The first set of analyses focused on the subject categories of the Adult Authority Content Analysis. Prisoners who were paroled had hearings in which there was a significantly greater proportion of discussion about postrelease activities ($F = 22.75$, $df = 1/98$, $p < .001$), postrelease support ($F = 7.94$, $df = 1/98$, $p < .01$), and prior parole hearings ($F = 5.76$, $df = 1/98$, $p < .05$). Prisoners who were denied parole had hearings in which there was a significantly greater proportion of discussion about prison rehabilitation ($F = 8.24$, $df = 1/98$, $p < .01$) and prison custody ($F = 4.54$, $df = 1/98$, $p < .05$).

The DFA considered how well the subject categories were able to discriminate between prisoners who were paroled and prisoners who were denied parole. When 15 predictors were included in the analysis, 46% of the criterion group variation was accounted for by variation in the predictors. This proportion of accountable variation is derived from a highly significant canonical correlation of .68 ($F = 4.34$, $df = 16/83$, $p < .001$). Using this prediction equation, it was then possible to correctly classify 83% of the hearings into paroled or denied groups ($\chi_c^2 = 43.56$, $df = 1$, $p < .001$). This high degree of predictability indicates that there were systematic decision-making strategies shared by many of the hearing officers in these 100 different hearings.

The standardized discriminant function coefficients from this first analysis are presented in Table 12.4. Clearly, the best prediction of a parole outcome is the proportion of time spent in a hearing discussing the future plans of the prisoner relative to the time spent discussing other topics. The relative presence of psychological assessment topics also appears to strongly predict a parole outcome. On the other hand, high proportional frequencies of questions or statements relating to the prisoner's appearance, prison rehabilitation programs, commitment offense, or criteria for parole predict a denial decision by the hearing officers. It should be noted that the weight or importance of a variable in predicting hearing outcome, as indicated by its discriminant function coefficient, is not tied to the absolute frequency with which that variable occurs in hearings. This is best illustrated by the fact that although the categories of postrelease activities and postrelease support combined account for little more

Table 12.4
Standardized discriminant function
coefficients in Adult Authority Content
Analysis prediction equation

Discussion topic	Coefficient
Postrelease activities	.72
Psychological assessment	.56
Postrelease support	.43
Paroles and revocations	.41
Physical appearance	−.31
Prison rehabilitation	−.30
Current hearing/criteria	−.29
Commitment offense	−.21
Psychological reports	−.18
Prior hearings	.17
Unclassified content	.17
Prior lifestyle	.13
Legal records	.09
Prisoner's health	.07
Prison associations	−.06

Note: A positive coefficient indicates that the
variable operates in favor of granting parole, and a
negative coefficient indicates a contribution in
favor of denial.

than 6% of the hearing content, they are the best predictors of its
outcome.

Prisoners' Response Content Analysis   The second set of analyses
used the prisoner behavior categories of the Prisoners' Response Content Analysis. Prisoners who were paroled spoke a greater proportion
of the time about the future than did prisoners who were denied
parole, both in terms of minimal responses ($F = 21.01$, $df = 1/98$,
$p < .001$) and affirmative statements ($F = 7.38$, $df = 1/98$, $p < .01$).
Prisoners who were denied parole had a greater proportion of complaints about legal issues ($F = 9.30$, $df = 1/98$, $p < .01$), complaints
about prison programs or facilities ($F = 5.61$, $df = 1/98$, $p < .05$),
questions or signs of confusion ($F = 6.76$, $df = 1/98$, $p < .05$), and
denials of legal guilt ($F = 4.65$, $df = 1/98$, $p < .05$).
    The second DFA attempted to determine which prisoner behaviors
contributed most to the outcome of the hearing. The results of this
analysis again yielded a highly significant canonical correlation
between predictors and criterion of .66 ($F = 3.44$, $df = 18/81$, $p <$
.001). This correlation indicates that the combination of the 18 prisoner behavior categories was able to account for approximately 44%
of the criterion group variability. The effectiveness of this prediction

equation is demonstrated by the fact that 79% of the hearings were correctly classified into the appropriate hearing outcome group ($\chi^2_c = 33.64$, $df = 1$, $p < .001$).

The standardized discriminant function coefficients for this second analysis are presented in Table 12.5. Consistent with the results of the previous DFA, the presence of a high proportion of statements and minimal responses by the prisoner about future events is the best predictor of an outcome decision to grant parole. In addition, the presence of minimal responses about the prison and the prisoner's past, defensive statements, and statements blaming oneself for one's prison behavior are also predictive of a parole outcome. In contrast, high proportional frequencies of affirmative statements about one's psychological state, denials of legal guilt, and statements blaming the situation for one's prior behavior appear to predict a denial outcome.

Behaviors initiated by prisoners   A third DFA sought to separate from the entire hearing the unique contribution of the prisoner to the parole decision-making process. In other words, what impact did prisoner-initiated behavior have on the outcome of the hearing? Table 12.6 presents the standardized discriminant function coefficients for

Table 12.5

Standardized discriminant function coefficients in Prisoners' Response Content Analysis prediction equation

Response	*Coefficient*
Minimal response re future	.89
Affirmative statement re future	.58
Minimal response re institution	.50
Minimal response re past	.48
Defensive statement	.48
Affirmative statement re psychological state	−.34
Denial of legal guilt	−.31
Situation blame re prior behavior	−.30
Self-blame re prison behavior	.26
Affirmative statements re past	.21
Complaints re legal issues	−.20
Question/confusion	−.15
Affirmative statement, general	.13
Situation blame re prison behavior	.08
Minimal response, general	.05
Complaint, general	−.05
Affirmative statement re institution	−.03
Self-blame re prior behavior	−.03

Note: A positive coefficient indicates that the variable operates in favor of granting parole, and a negative coefficient indicates a contribution in favor of denial.

Table 12.6
Standardized discriminant function coefficients in prisoner-initiated behaviors prediction equation

Response	Coefficient
Affirmative statement re future	.56
Complaint re legal issues	−.51
Affirmative statement re institution	−.39
Question/confusion	−.39
Affirmative statement re past	−.28
Complaint re program/facilities	−.28
Affirmative statement re psychological state	−.23
Complaint, general	−.17
Affirmative statement, general	−.05

Note: A positive coefficient indicates that the variable operates in favor of granting parole, and a negative coefficient indicates a contribution in favor of denial.

the 9 variables used in this analysis. The canonical correlation was .50 ($F = 3.87$, $df = 9/90$, $p < .005$), which meant that 25% of the criterion group variation was accounted for by variation in the predictor variables. Using the prediction equation, 70% of the hearings were correctly classified into the paroled and denied outcome groups ($\chi_c^2 = 16.00$, $df = 1$, $p < .001$). It is noteworthy that of the 9 prisoner-initiated behaviors, only 1 of them has a positive discriminant function coefficient in the direction of predicting a parole outcome. That is, the larger the proportion of a prisoner's affirmative statements about the future, the greater the likelihood that the prisoner will be granted parole. Thus, the low profile of most inmates during parole hearings is justified by the data. If they initiate too much, they are likely to be denied parole — except when they bring up future plans.

DISCUSSION OF THE STUDY

The results of the data analyses present an overall picture of the parole hearing as a relatively short, diagnostic interview session that places a heavy emphasis on psychological assessment. Hearing officers generally ask questions of the prisoners and acknowledge the answers in a noncommittal way. For their part, prisoners typically make minimal responses to the questions and add little to present a case of their own. In hearings whose eventual outcome is parole, hearing officers focus more attention on prisoners' parole plans, their prior experiences on parole, and their psychological state. The prisoners generally respond minimally on these topics, but also make affirmative statements about their future behavior. In contrast, in hearings that result in denial of parole, hearing officers direct their questions toward prisoners' current disciplinary problems and rehabilitation activities. In response the prisoners generally deny their guilt, complain about the legal issues surrounding their incarceration and about their treatment in prison, and ask questions about their parole status. Overall, the form and content of the hearing are largely determined by the hearing officers. Although the prisoners occasionally contribute new information, such self-initiated behavior usually results in denial of parole.

Three major issues emerge from the findings. The first is the purpose and utility of the parole hearing for the decision-makers. A second concern is the role of the prisoners and their contribution to the decision-making process. The third issue of reliability and validity in parole decision-making points to the more general question of the fit between the theory and the practice of parole decision-making.

The purpose of parole hearings

Some of the evidence from the content analyses suggests that the decisions following parole hearings are made either prior to the hearing or within the first few minutes.[8] The fact that the hearings averaged only 16 minutes in length supports the conclusion that the decision being made does not rest entirely on information uncovered in the hearings. Considering the potential impact of the decision (keeping a person in prison for another full year or granting a date for freedom), it is unlikely that the necessary information could be assessed accurately in such a short time. Furthermore, the brevity of the deliberations (1½ minutes on the average) also suggests that the hearing interview is not the primary source of data for parole decision-making.

If the parole decision is actually made at the beginning of the hearing, rather than afterward, then two possibilities come to mind. First, it may be that the decision is based solely on information in the prisoner's central file. This file is quickly reviewed by hearing officers in the few minutes before the hearing begins. It is conceivable that hearing officers arrive at a decision of parole or denial on the basis of this review and then pursue one or another line of questioning

---

[8]Even if this were the typical pattern of parole decision-making, it is conceivable that in some cases the hearing officers would find their initial judgment disconfirmed during the hearing and would change their ultimate decision. If so, an analysis of the data by time periods might shed some light on what factors would make the verbal content of the hearing a more crucial aspect of the parole decision.

according to that prehearing decision. Support for this hypothesis comes from research on the employment interview situation, which finds that such interviews are characterized by brevity, stereotyping of applicants, and the tendency for interviewers to make up their minds beforehand on the basis of a résumé and to then discount any interview information that does not confirm their prior expectations (Webster, 1964).

A second possibility is that hearing officers have become so skilled in identifying various "types" of prisoners that they are immediately able to classify individuals as those who are ready for parole and those who are not. The results of the present study, which found that the psychological assessment category was judged as the dominant topic in more than half of the hearings, suggest that hearing officers use the hearing (and/or the central file) for this diagnostic purpose. Once having identified some psychological problem on the part of the prisoner, hearing officers need no further time to consider other information since the obvious decision is to keep the prisoner in the institution for further treatment of the problem.

If the decision to grant or deny parole is indeed made prior to the parole interview, then what purpose does the hearing serve for the decision-makers? First, the hearing may actually be of no use whatsoever. It is quite possible that hearing officers would arrive at the same decision in the absence of any face-to-face interaction with the prisoner. In fact, one could argue that the only effect of the hearings is a detrimental one for most inmates. Since hearings are conducted throughout the state, they require hearing officers to be on the road for weeks at a time, away from family and friends, in the rather remote communities where most of the prisons are located. This isolated lifestyle may take its toll in the hearing itself. This would be especially true if hearing officers believed that they would be able to make the same decisions from some home base without conducting on-the-spot interviews with prisoners around the state.

A second hypothesis is that the hearing may be used to justify a decision that has already been made. As mentioned before, the decision of whether or not to release a person from prison is one of considerable weight and importance. Therefore, it seems reasonable to suggest that the hearing serves as an opportunity for hearing officers to verify (at least in their own minds) that they have made the correct decision. This hypothesis is supported by the results of the discriminant function analyses, which showed that different patterns of questioning took place in hearings whose outcome was a granting of parole, rather than a denial. In hearings resulting in a decision to grant parole, hearing officers focused their attention on the plans developed by prisoners for their release. Prisoners' well-laid parole plans could be seen as validating the prior decision to release them. This is especially significant since all prisoners who appear before hearing officers are legally eligible for parole and therefore could all have made appropriate plans for their release. Whether or not these plans are actually discussed in the hearing depends primarily on whether or not hearing officers choose to ask about them. In contrast, hearings where a denial was the outcome decision were characterized by different lines of questioning. Hearing officers were more concerned about factors indicating that the prisoners were not ready for release (i.e., prison disciplinary problems and rehabilitation programs). The emphasis on these factors could be interpreted as evidence that hearing officers had already made a decision to deny parole and were attempting to support and justify their position in the hearing—a line of reasoning that would support one of the information-processing hypotheses of Carroll and Payne (1976).

At this point, no final conclusions can be formed about the utility of the hearing for the hearing officers. In principle, if the hearing does indeed serve no decision-making function, then it occupies the position of a "legal fiction." That is, its sole purpose is to present an illusion of legally responsible, rationally determined, and just decisions in a system where that may not be the case.

The role of the prisoner in parole decisions

A second issue that emerges from the present study is the impact of the prisoner's role in the decision-making process. From the results of the Prisoners' Response Content Analysis, it is easy to picture quiet, obsequious prisoners responding rather passively to the line of questioning set by hearing officers. This passive style of self-presentation may serve several functions for prisoners. First, it may reflect an adaptive response to the prison system. Prisoners may believe that, since anything they say can be used against them, it is best to remain relatively silent and to avoid calling undue attention to themselves. Such a belief would appear to be an accurate assessment of the situation, since the present data analysis showed that almost all of a prisoner's self-initiated behaviors were weighted heavily in the direction of a denial of parole.

The nonparticipatory role of prisoners may also reflect their feelings of inferiority or helplessness when confronting the authority of the parole board. The passivity of prisoners in these hearings could be their reaction to a situation where someone else has all of the power and they have none. An analogous situation was created experimentally by Zimbardo and his colleagues (1973) when they constructed a simulated prison environment. To staff their prison, Zimbardo et al. used a homogeneous population of college males and randomly assigned half of them to be prisoners and half of them to be guards. In so doing, they created a simulation in which there were two comparable groups, with one group having all the power (the guards) and the other group having none (the prisoners). Zimbardo et al. found that the mock prisoners reacted strongly to this experimental manipulation of power. The typical behavioral syndrome that they exhibited was one of passivity, dependency, depression, helplessness, and self-depreciation. In many ways, the syndrome exhibited by the mock prisoners parallels the behavior of real prisoners appearing for parole consideration. It is possible that some sort of redistribution of power (such as allowing attorneys to represent prisoners at hearings) could reduce the detrimental effect that the current parole system appears to have on prisoners.

A third explanation of prisoners' passive role in parole hearings is that prisoners lack the necessary competence to effectively present themselves and their case for parole consideration. First, they may be unable to recall, on the spot, the critical arguments in their favor, or they may be unable to express their views articulately. Second, they may disagree with hearing officers about the facts of the case and yet find it difficult to persuade the officers that their own version is the correct one and not an excuse or a false alibi. According to the Legal Analysis (reported in Garber, 1976), some type of factual conflict occurred in 39% of the hearings.

If prisoners are not skilled in making a positive self-presentation, they may also be viewed as less likable, and this in turn may affect their chances for obtaining parole. Such a relationship between liking and decision outcomes has been demonstrated in research on simulated jury decision-making behavior. Mitchell and Byrne (1973) found that mock jurors liked defendants with attitudes similar to theirs and that this liking influenced their judgments. In addition, simulated juror decisions are affected by defendants' social status (Landy and Aronson, 1969) and physical attractiveness (Efran, 1974). If one extrapolates from these findings, it becomes clear that prisoners have several factors operating against their being liked by hearing officers. The prisoners are of lower status than the hearing officers and do not typically share their attitudes (especially with regard to prison issues). Even the physical attractiveness variable is salient here in light of the fact that hearing officers' references to physical appearance were predictive of parole denial. From our observations, hearing officers were very well groomed, in suits and ties, and were generally about 20 years older than the inmates, who were in their prison uniforms. If, in addition, prisoners have difficulty in presenting a competent, affirmative case for themselves, then it appears unlikely that they would be able to win over the hearing officers in their brief appearance at the hearing.

The reliability and validity of parole decision-making

The underlying philosophy of the parole system is that offenders can be treated and rehabilitated while in prison and that, once rehabilitated, they can be released since they no longer pose a threat to society. In order to implement this philosophy, several assumptions have to be made. One is that prisoners' "problems" can be diagnosed accurately and appropriate treatment provided. Another is that accurate assessments can be made of prisoners' degree of rehabilitation and of their future behavior in society as free individuals. While the first assumption rests on the abilities of judges and correctional personnel, the second rests on the competence of hearing officers. The question to be asked is: Can hearing officers indeed make these assessments of rehabilitation and these predictions of future dangerousness? If they cannot, then the validity of the parole system is seriously undermined.

To rephrase the question: Is the parole decision-making process reliable and valid? Reliability refers to the consistency, across hearings, of the manner in which hearing officers arrive at their decisions. If the process is reliable, it means that all hearing officers use the same method of integrating information and that different officers would arrive at the same decision on any one case. According to the results of the present study, the parole decision-making process is indeed reliable. Whatever the criteria used by hearing officers, they were applied in a fairly consistent or reliable fashion (as indicated by the highly significant canonical correlations of the discriminant function analyses). This evidence of decision-making reliability might appear to contradict the findings of Wilkins (see Chapter 13), which revealed a marked variability in the information used by decision-makers. However, an alternative explanation is that the current results and those of Wilkins are not in conflict because they are about different stages in the parole process. That is, it is possible that hearing officers may differ in how they evaluate prisoners' central files but that once they make that evaluation, they are consistent in adopting a line of questioning based on (and perhaps justifying) that hypothesis.

If the parole decision-making process is reliable, is it also valid? Validity refers to whether or not the decisions truly reflect the goal set for them. Given the Adult Authority's stated policy aim of public protection, the goal of the parole hearing is to distinguish between those prisoners who will and will not behave in a dangerous or criminal manner at some time in the future. If the decision-making process is valid, it means that all hearing officers can assess accurately the potential dangerousness of any prisoner.

However, the inference to be drawn from the present study and related research is that this process is not a valid one. Research conducted on psychological predictions, using trained mental-health professionals, has found that such predictions are usually unreliable and, as a result, invalid (Ennis and Litwack, 1974; Meehl, 1971). Furthermore, a study by Pogrebin (1974) found that psychiatric evaluations were of little use in predicting parole success. In their appraisal of the prediction of dangerousness, Wenk, Robison, and Smith (1972) concluded that it is impossible to predict with any accuracy who will be dangerous and that, in fact, the best prediction is that any individual, regardless of background, will not pose a threat to others.

If mental-health professionals cannot make reliable and valid psychological evaluations and predictions of dangerousness, then it seems highly unlikely that untrained hearing officers could succeed in so formidable a task. In their testimony in *Van Geldern* v. *Kerr*, the hearing officers indicated that they had very little, if any, background in psychology, and they were often unable to correctly identify basic definitions of various types of mental illness. Despite this lack of formal training and basic knowledge, the evidence in our study is that hearing officers' personal evaluations of psychological factors played a major role in their decision-making. The category of psychological assessment was usually the dominant topic in the hearing and was an influential variable in predicting the hearing's outcome. Furthermore, in an analysis of the written reasons given by hearing officers for denial decisions (presented as evidence in *Van Geldern* v. *Kerr*), Levy (1975) found that they cited psychiatric reasons most frequently as justification for denying parole.

Thus, although hearing officers have no demonstrated skills in making psychological evaluations, such evaluations underlie their decisions to grant or deny parole. Clearly, there is no evidence that they can make valid psychological assessments and predictions of dangerousness, and this diagnostic invalidity constitutes a major source of arbitrariness in the parole system.[9] Any decision based on

---

[9]Additional evidence of the invalidity of this process lies in the ability of outside factors to influence the percentage of paroles granted. According to testimony presented in *Van Geldern* v. *Kerr*, the parole rate in California has varied widely over the years in response to policy statements from the governor and the legislature. Obviously, if parole decisions vary in response to political pressures, they can hardly be regarded as accurate assessments of individual prisoners.

unreliable and invalid psychological dimensions can hardly be valid itself. As a result, there is an apparent lack of correspondence between the goals of the parole system (treatment, rehabilitation, and release) and the abilities of the decision-maker to identify them.

CONCLUSIONS

This study represents an important first in research on parole decisions because its analysis centers on the processes taking place in actual (rather than simulated or self-reported) parole hearings. It utilizes content analysis, which is a fairly simple and straightforward methodological approach that is shown to generate some very powerful data. Because of the reliance on tape recordings, the analysis was limited to verbal data (i.e., what people said during the hearing). Use of these data alone led to some very good predictions of decision outcome, but it is quite possible that the remaining unexplained variance could be accounted for by the influence of various nonverbal behaviors. For example, prisoners who entered the hearing room with a swagger or a hostile expression may have had a negative impact on hearing officers, which might bias the type of opening question and in turn make denial of parole more likely. In addition to nonverbal behavior, specific information in the prisoners' file could also have influenced the parole decision, but it was not possible in this study to assess either of these. It should also be noted that what one says is not necessarily what one thinks and that the decision-making process going on in the minds of hearing officers may not be completely represented by the content of what they say during the hearing. Even with these limitations on the source of data, the study reveals some interesting and significant patterns in the factors that predict decision outcome.

References

Aitken, R. The Adult Authority. In California State Bar Association, *Report and recommendations on sentencing and prison reform.* Los Angeles: 1975.

California Adult Authority Policy Statement #24. Functions and priorities for term setting and revocation of parole. March 1973.

California Assembly Committee on Criminal Procedure. *The deterrent effects of criminal sanctions.* Sacramento: 1968.

California Assembly Select Committee on the Administration of Justice. *Parole board reform in California: Order out of chaos.* Sacramento: 1970.

California State Bar Association. *Report and recommendations on sentencing and prison reform.* Los Angeles: 1975.

Carroll, J. S., & Payne, J. W. The psychology of the parole decision process: A joint application of attribution theory and information-processing psychology. In J. S. Carroll and J. W. Payne (Eds.), *Cognition and social behavior.* Hillsdale, NJ: Lawrence Erlbaum, 1976.

Efran, M. G. The effect of physical appearance on the judgment of guilt, interpersonal attraction, and severity of recommended punishment in a simulated jury task. *Journal of Research in Personality*, 1974, *8*, 45–54.

Ennis, B. J., & Litwack, T. R. Psychiatry and the presumption of expertise: Flipping coins in the courtroom. *California Law Review*, 1974, *62*, 693–752.

Garber, R. M. An exploration and analysis of parole decision-making in California. Unpublished M.A. thesis, University of California, Berkeley, 1976.

Gottfredson, D., & Ballard, K. Prison and parole decisions: A strategy for study. Unpublished manuscript, Institute for the Study of Crime and Delinquency, California Medical Facility, Vacaville, 1965.

Jackson, G. *Soledad brother: The prison letters of George Jackson.* New York: Bantam Books, 1970.

Kerr, H. Standards used for determining eligibility for parole. A Report to the California State Legislature, January 1972.

Landy, D., & Aronson, E. The influence of the character of the criminal and his victim on the decisions of simulated jurors. *Journal of Experimental Social Psychology*, 1969, *5*, 141–152.

Levy, L. Personal communication, 1975.

Meehl, P. E. Law and the fireside inductions: Some reflections of a clinical psychologist. *Journal of Social Issues*, 1971, *27* (4), 65–100.

Mitchell, H. E., & Byrne, D. The defendant's dilemma: Effects of jurors' attitudes and authoritarianism on judicial decisions. *Journal of Personality and Social Psychology*, 1973, *25*, 123–129.

Overall, J., & Klett, C. *Applied multivariate analysis.* New York: McGraw-Hill, 1972.

Parsons-Lewis, H. S. Due process in parole-release decisions. *California Law Review*, 1972, *60*, 1518–1556.

Pogrebin, M. Is the use of a psychiatric facility for parole evaluation justifiable? *International Journal of Offender Therapy and Comparative Criminology*, 1974, *18*, 270–274.

Van Geldern v. Kerr, Civil No. C–72–2088 SAW.

Webster, E. *Decision-making in the employment interview.* Montreal: McGill University Press, 1964.

Wenk, E. A., Robison, J. O., & Smith, G. W. Can violence be predicted? *Crime and Delinquency*, 1972, *18*, 393–402.

Zimbardo, P., Haney, C., Banks, C., & Jaffe, D. The mind is a formidable jailer: A Pirandellian prison. *New York Times*, April 8, 1973.

13

Parole Decisions

Leslie T. Wilkins

Parole is in some ways similar to probation. In both, the offender is under supervision in the community. Often, particularly in the smaller cities, the probation officer will double as a parole agent. For the offender, probation involves the supervision of a probation officer and compliance with a set of conditions for a period of time initially set by the court. Normally, probation serves instead of incarceration either in state prison or in a local jail. Parole, on the other hand, relates to the period of supervision *after* release from a term of incarceration. However, the definition of probation has been somewhat complicated (or muddled!) because some states have provided a penalty that may be set by the courts, known variously as "conditional probation," "split sentence," or, colloquially, "shock probation." The split sentence is, as this term suggests, two sentences in one—probation and detention. Or as it is usually expressed, probation is given by the court conditional upon a short period of incarceration first. Thus, probation (community supervision) follows a term of incarceration, so that the split sentence looks exactly like parole, which is also community supervision after a period of detention.

There remains at least one important distinction between parole and conditional probation. The term in the latter case is set by the court at the time of sentencing. Parole, on the other hand, is decided by a parole board or similar body, and varies the sentence initially imposed by the court by conditional release. The rationale for this is that offenders complete their term (sentence) in the community. Parole is best thought of as one of the four (legitimate!) ways of getting out of prison (American Correctional Association, 1966). The other three are: conditional release/mandatory release, conditional pardon, and discharge. Parole involves more than release by discharge since it includes a period of "aftercare" or surveillance following release to the community. Usually, mandatory/conditional release is also conditional upon a period of supervision and, again, operationally may seem much like parole. Parole is the first chance to get out of prison, the next chance may be the conditional or mandatory release, and finally there is release when the initial term set by the judge has expired.

The period of supervision/surveillance involved in parole is usually related to the period of sentence remaining. There are variations on this in different states. There are also the "conditions"—restrictions on the liberty of the parolee—and these vary from state to state. Any breach of conditions of parole may result in parolees being returned to prison (perhaps to finish the originally set term) even though they may not have committed a new crime. Both probation and parole, and the conditions attaching to each, are (it is usually claimed) intended to facilitate the reintegration of the offender into society. It is doubtful, however, whether the conditions, supervision, or surveillance makes any difference at all, either to the offender or to society. Nonetheless, parole and probation derive much support from the philosophy of rehabilitation of offenders.

The doctrine of rehabilitation reached its logical limit in California (until recently) and some other states where the period of incarceration was not fixed by the court but was indeterminate. Offenders were to be released when they were no longer likely to commit crime or to be a danger to society. The parole board (or, in California, the Adult Authority) set the term of detention. Frequently, this was done in steps of one year or so at a time, so that detainees never knew when they would be released until they were about to be so discharged. (See the previous chapter for a discussion of this form of system, which California has recently abandoned.) Normally the consideration for parole takes place after about one-third of the sentence as initially pronounced by the judge has been satisfactorily completed.

In this chapter, we are not concerned with the ways in which persons are supervised in the community, either before or after incarceration. Our interest is in the decision-making and procedures associated with the granting or refusal of parole. We might note, in passing, that some persons who may be paroled might be returned to prison (perhaps for a technical offense or a breach of the conditions of parole) and be finally released from that particular incarceration period by some other method of release, such as mandatory release or on expiration of term or perhaps some fraction of the term originally stated by the court as specified in the particular law of the state.

THE USE OF PAROLE

In addition to considerable variations in the legal status of parole and paroled offenders in the different states, there are differences in practice. For example, the percentage of incarcerated offenders who are released by the parole process (a decision by a parole board or similar body) varies from about 10% to 100% from state to state. In 1964, for example, three states released fewer than 20% by means of parole decisions, and two released 100% by this means (President's Commission . . . , 1967).

It is to be expected that the nature and style of the decision and the procedures of the parole board will vary in some ways according to the frequency with which the parole method is used as a procedure for release from incarceration. Where all persons are subject to the parole decision, the parole board acts as a sentencing agency insofar as the term of imprisonment is concerned. Where fewer than 25% are released by this procedure, the board may be expected to function more as a clemency board. The U.S. federal prison system falls about midway along the continuum from 10% to 100% release by parole, with just over 60% of cases being disposed of in this way. The federal system and a few states provide for mandatory supervision for offenders not released on parole. Under such a procedure, when inmates are released before serving their maximum terms, they are supervised in the community for a period equal to their "good-time credit." Thus, "parole" is several things: it is a decision process that is not always used to determine the date of release, and it is at the other extreme a "time-setting decision." Supervision in the community is not necessarily associated with only the parole element, although for the offender the conditions are somewhat similar.[1]

THE ORIGINS OF PAROLE

Since the present status and form of parole is obfuscated by so many legal and administrative complexities and emerges in a large number of variants, it is not surprising that there is considerable disagreement as to its precise origin. Some refer to the early "ticket of leave" system that was used in some of the early British penal colonies. Others trace the origins even earlier. Moran and Orland (1973) make a good case for finding some elements in the Statute of Artifices of 1562 that have

---

[1]For classification of the various conditions set in the different states, see the chapter by S. Arluke in Carter and Wilkins (1969).

survived in the idea and practice of parole to this day. The transportation of criminals to the American colonies began in the early seventeenth century. The first transportees were without conditions, but about 1655 there were set conditions that rendered the pardon null and void if the recipient failed to abide by the conditions imposed.

The Statute of Artifices, while not originally related to offenders, provided for "indenture"—a contract that was divided into two parts "by a wavy or jagged line" ("indent"). There seems to have been considerable overlap, historically, between slavery and convict labor and between conditions attaching to indentured servants and the idea of the contract in parole. The trace becomes clearer when we look at the penal colonies in Australia and Tasmania. Here, the prisoners did not become indentured servants, but remained prisoners until granted a pardon earned by good behavior and work performance. The full pardon was later restricted to the "ticket of leave," which enabled offenders to seek work and sustain themselves within a restricted area. The restriction on mobility is retained in most parole conditions today.

There is little doubt that the first application of the general system of parole, much as we know it today in the United States, originated in Elmira Reformatory under Warden Brockway in 1877. He outlined for the Elmira system the following:

1. An indeterminate or indefinite sentence, the length of time served to be dependent on the behavior and capacity of the prisoner, within statutory limitations.

2. The status and privileges accorded the prisoner, to be determined by behavior and progress.

3. Compulsory education.

4. Provision for the release on parole of carefully selected prisoners.

The idea underlying the indeterminate sentence was that prisoners were not to be released (paroled) until "fit" (rehabilitated?) for freedom.

It seems that we may trace the origins of parole to a concept of pardon if we use one reference, to the concept of surveillance if we stop at another point in history, and to the concepts of rehabilitation and contractual arrangements if we emphasize the issues from still another possible historical root. It is, then, not surprising that, even today, parole is often seen quite differently, with the result that different aspects are brought into relief by different writers. Even the courts are confused! Vermont does not call the release system it employs "parole"; prisoners are released under a "conditional pardon." The governor determines eligibility, and the state probation service exercises supervision. It is likely that the three basic theories which, according to Gottesman and Heckler (1969), underpin the procedures derive from different readings of history. They describe the three basic theories as "grace," "contract consent," and "custody." They further claim that these three theories have been used at various times to avoid important constitutional issues that the idea of parole and its operations might otherwise raise. Thus the perception of history has an impact on the contemporary setting for decisions within the system. With parole, however, this does not seem to help because it is likely that a particular version of history could be found that fitted any current theory, practice, or even preference!

THE NATURE OF A PAROLE DECISION

The nature of the decision by a parole board is influenced by many considerations, not all of which are explicit. Parole is a different kind of "thing" in different states, and it is *seen as* a different kind of thing by different persons within the same state and possibly even with the same procedure and conditions. However parole is seen, the decisions of the boards are subject to few restrictions. Gottesman and Heckler quote from the opinion in *State ex rel. Bush* v. *Whittier* as follows:

> It is . . . clear that the board in its discretion could revoke the original parole agreement with or without a hearing and return the relator to its custody with or without cause, notwithstanding the fact that a relator's [act] did not constitute a violation of the conditions of his parole. (Gottesman and Heckler, 1969, p. 446)

Are parole boards "setting time"? Or are they granting a "conditional pardon"? Are they concerned with "mercy" or with "rehabilitation"? The answer can be "yes," not only to these questions but to many others, and it does not appear that there is any great need for consistency!

Perhaps we should get ourselves out of this historical and legalistic muddle and see what can be achieved by considering parole decision-making in the light of recent research into decision procedures. The preceding chapter reported a study of the ways in which a parole board performed its task. The authors carried out their research in order to try to "understand the complex functioning of parole decision-making in California." Whether the process is worth trying to understand or not is perhaps debatable. Rather we might try to change it! In any event, the process of decision-making for parole in California was abolished in the form studied. Whether the process of parole decision-making is "complex" is also debatable. The number of alternatives available to the decision-maker is very restricted. The consequences of the decision are of considerable significance for one person at least, namely the offender. The consequences of the decision for the board members are less clear. But it is not the consequences of a decision that determine its complexity nor its difficulty.

It is possible to consider the parole decision operation in terms of information search, interpretation, and inference. Decision-makers may be reluctant to *close* the decision that has serious consequences for themselves and perhaps also for others. However, the reluctance to close the procedure of information search or to settle on a specific alternative does not mean that the decision is itself in any way more difficult than any other decision with far less significant consequences. Can there possibly be a different system of inference that attaches to a "serious" decision from that of any other decision? Will the information-search procedures and the mental strategies of decision-makers be modified in terms of how critical they see the consequences of the determinations to be? This seems most unlikely. If it were the case, we might expect that the variety of strategies used would be generally recognized. The processes of information search and the like may be continued longer so that the decision-makers may feel more subjectively satisfied that they have done everything possible. However, that does not mean that the decision-makers will have done anything differently; and certainly it does not imply that they have done any better. The human capacities of intelligence do not expand to accommodate the size of the problem!

THEORETICAL ASPECTS OF PAROLE DECISION-MAKING

Some research workers prefer to observe ongoing operations and to seek information by interviewing those concerned. Others prefer to conform as closely as possible to a laboratory form of research design. Perhaps the desirable strategy is to use both methods, seeking to exploit the potential of each and to pass problems from one form of study to another as the work proceeds. Whichever method is used, it is usually worthwhile to examine current theory first. In addition to theory in the particular field to be studied, there are often considerable gains to be made from examining situations that are possibly analogous.

In the study that forms the major source of basic research data on which this chapter draws, many methods were used. There are 13 reports on the research, excluding the summary report and a film (Wilkins, 1973). Not even these extensive reports can deal with all of the issues that arose in the course of the project. If the reader is to follow the argument and to understand the final results of the study, it will be necessary to sacrifice something of the description of the process as it actually took place. If our presentation were to be as muddled as the project itself seemed to be at certain points, only confusion would result. Perhaps it is a pity that the reporting on research always looks more organized and planned than the research ever is in practice and thus the layperson and student often gain the wrong impression of the process. In the actual work on the parole project, simulation methods were employed at various times to explore a variety of issues, sometimes of great significance to the work and at other times merely to demonstrate a rather trivial point. We will say something about the simulation subprojects later in this chapter; they clarified many issues for us, but we will now utilize the clarity as though it happened without undue effort or initial confusion. We claim that this is to assist the reader rather than to make the research direction look like a classical piece of analysis!

First, let us refer to the use of some general theory in relation to decision-making. Parole board members, and indeed most decision-makers, tend to think that their decisions are made the more difficult by the paucity of information available or by its low quality. Because the belief is widespread that decisions are "better" the greater the amount of *relevant* information available to the decision-maker, we have seen the exponential growth of so-called information systems. But does a better (more expensive and sophisticated) information system usually lead to better decisions? It would seem that there must be information on this question from other areas of decision-making that might be sufficiently analogous to the parole decision-making procedure for us to assume that the findings would hold true.

Among the decisions that have the most serious consequences are those made by the military establishment. In a study made for the Operational Applications Laboratory, Air Force Electronics, Systems Division, Hayes noted:

> It is commonly assumed that the more relevant data one takes into account in making a decision, the better that decision will be. It is clear, however, that as one takes more relevant characteristics into account for comparing alternatives, the opportunities for confusion increase. If confusion were to increase rapidly enough as the number of characteristics increased, it is conceivable that decision-makers

would perform better if some of the *relevant* data were eliminated. (Hayes, 1962, p. 16; emphasis added)

The problem is not (or not only) that of elimination of irrelevant information; the very quantity of information can become a barrier to effective utilization of it.

It is interesting to ask decision-makers to guess the number of separate items of information that they can deal with in any single decision. Unless they are familiar with the research, it is most probable that they will guess a number as small as that consistently shown in the investigations.

Hayes (1962) and others have shown that the maximum number of separate items of data along different dimensions that can be processed profitably at the same time, without formal decomposition and restructuring of the decision process, is about 8. Accordingly, it seemed reasonable to test whether in the parole decision-making process by parole board members a limit of 8 items of information about the offender would suffice to fix the decision. If so, it would seem to be important to know which facts those 8 items would cover. These investigations were relegated to the simulation subprojects, while the work of more direct investigation of the decision-making went ahead by other means. We defer discussion of the simulation until later. There are data that seem to have a more direct effect on parole decisions that we might study.

THE USE OF INFORMATION FOR PAROLE DECISION-MAKING

Criteria for parole decisions

It is, of course, nonsense to consider information unless it is known what it is to be used for. If the criteria are uncertain or the standards ambiguous, it will not help to study the information-search strategies in order to understand the decisions. It was, therefore, necessary to seek information with regard to criteria. We could examine statements as to what parole was *intended* to do, or we could see what parole boards actually did, and then infer what it was that they were intending to do—assessing purposes from decision patterns. It should be remembered that the study which provides the data to be discussed derives from the U.S. Board of Paroles (now called the Parole Commissioners), and was concerned with the federal system of prison and parole. Other states may—and almost certainly do—assume different criteria.

The U.S. Board of Paroles was required to consider three issues:

1. Whether there is a substantial risk that the parole applicants will conform to the conditions of parole (particularly that they will not commit another crime while on parole—recidivate).

2. Whether release would depreciate the seriousness of the prisoners' crime or promote disrespect for the law.

3. Whether release would have a substantially adverse effect on institutional discipline.

The so-called Model Penal Code proposed by the American Law Institute provides a further reason for parole denial:

> his continued correctional treatment, medical care, or vocational or other training in the institution will substantially enhance his capacity to lead a law-abiding life when released at a latter date. (American Law Institute, 1966, p. 301)

This particular argument for increasing the duration of detention is not now likely to be regarded as satisfactory. There has come to be too much doubt about the rehabilitative claims of any and all penal treatments in institutions, and hence invoking this provision could now be regarded as a mere excuse for exacting more punishment.

Operational evidence of criteria in decisions

The first two clauses in the requirements for granting of parole by the U.S. Board of Paroles seem fairly clear; and if the board were in fact working to these purposes, it should be possible to trace this fact in their actual decisions.

The first clause related to the probability of recidivism or of "parole failure" in terms of a technical violation or reconviction. Considerable work has been carried out in research into the prediction of recidivism, commencing as early as 1923 by S. B. Warner. The board's decisions might be expected to be related, at least in part, to the probability of recidivism. And the probability of recidivism would, in turn, be capable of estimation by prediction equations. (There is considerable experience with prediction methods in several states and in other Western countries.)

It seemed desirable, therefore, to construct an actuarial table, based on prior experience, that estimated the probability of parole failure for cases in the federal system. Such an instrument would have a number of possible applications. Among these it should assist in ascertaining whether the criterion relating to recidivism was included in any way in the board's decisions. But parole failure is not, according to the statement of requirements, the only issue. The second clause relates quite specifically to the seriousness of the crime for which committal was made in the first place. We might expect, then, that the decisions made by the board would reflect their assessment of the seriousness of the offense concerned in the incarceration. There are, as we might say, both "offender factors" (probability of recidivism) and "offense factors" (seriousness of crime) in the decision. We might also see these two dimensions as operationally independent of each other.

If it is possible to obtain a scale of assessments of the seriousness of the crime of committal as seen by the board and a scale of offender factors that predict recidivism, then these two dimensions might be used to predict the decisions of the board. In other words, the information in the case files might be used to set up two dimensions (offense × offender), and these could be related to the third dimension, namely the decision of the board.

How should the decision of the board be seen? Was it, as it appeared to be, a decision whether to grant or refuse the parole petitioner's application for release? Initially, we thought so and operated with the assumption that the decision was represented by a dichotomy—grant/refuse. We learned from the use of simulation that this was not the case. The decision was much more appropriately seen as one of *setting time.* Was the applicant to be released *now* or *later* and, if later, *how much later?* We must leave this brief statement unamplified at this time and proceed with the description of the main stream of the research. (We might add that if we had not had this important input from the simulation exercises, we might have failed to obtain what we now consider to be the appropriate solution.)

THE PROBABILITY OF RECIDIVISM

The probability of recidivism either may be "subjective" as intuitively assessed by the decision-maker or may be derived from actuarial methods. It has been shown that decision-makers usually are the poorer assessors of probabilities of human behavior (e.g., Meehl, 1954). A statistical prediction of the likelihood of parole success or failure was required as a basis for testing the relationship of parole decisions on the first of the required criteria.

Several studies were made using followup information on the performance of persons released on parole and those who completed their term or who were discharged by other procedures. Followup periods of one and two years were possible in the main project, and longer periods of followup have been worked on subsequently. Data available about offenders prior to their consideration for parole were obtained and coded, and equations obtained that predicted the outcome. These procedures are very well known, and it may be useful here to note only the differences between the parole prediction problem and the general use of the discriminant function. There can be found advocates of a large variety of statistical methods for dealing with data characterized by uncertain distributions, dichotomies, and classifications. The major question in the selection of a method is the extent to which one is prepared to make assumptions in exchange for an apparent increase in the power or efficiency of the statistical method. Some methods are more sensitive than others to errors in the data base, and others to departures from necessary assumptions of independence of errors, normality, homoscedasticity, and so on.

It seemed desirable to try a variety of methods and to test these against validation samples. A method that provided the best fit to the construction sample, but that also had heavy shrinkage in the validation sample, would be less useful than an equation that was a poorer fit, but that did not shrink so much on validation. It is, after all, the validation sample universe that is relevant to the decisions. The construction sample, once used, is of no continuing value.

In recent years many studies have shown that there is a pronounced tendency for the more sophisticated techniques of fitting prediction equations to shrink to the extent that very simple methods prove more useful. As early as 1955, Mannheim and Wilkins fitted equations using discriminant functions (with dummy variables) to data for Borstal releases.[2] They noted that unit weights given to items that were correlated with the criterion and simply summed into a score gave results not significantly different from the more rigorous and complex methods. More recently, log-linear, discriminant function, factoring methods, various taxonomic methods (e.g., predictive attribute analysis), and some other methods have been used with followup derived from a number of different studies. All seem to produce the same result—simple weights of 0 to 1, scales that are as powerful in separating the probable failures from the probable successes as any other method, and generally shrinkage of less than 0, 1 weightings than with any other method (e.g., Simon, 1970).

There can be no suggestion that any of the items of information that obtain a weighting, by whatever means, in any form of prediction

---

[2]Borstal training is an indeterminate sentence in the United Kingdom that is usually reserved for 18–21-year-old persons with a substantial commitment to crime. Detention is from 9 months to 36 months with a period of aftercare.

equation are causally associated with crime or recidivism. However, this is not important. It is not necessary to make any claims other than those that can be shown empirically, namely that the prediction scores are remarkably stable. The stability of the correlation (not its meaning) provides the justification for its use. The items and weights for the initial prediction score for the federal parole project are given in Table 13.1.

THE SERIOUSNESS OF OFFENSES

The general idea of scaling offenses as though they fitted a single dimension of seriousness is traceable beyond recorded history. Punishment, it has usually been thought, should be proportional to the

Table 13.1
Information items and weights given in construction of salient factor score

Information item	Weight
No prior convictions (adult or juvenile)	2
One or two prior convictions	1
Three or more prior convictions	0
No prior incarcerations (adult or juvenile)	2
One or two prior incarcerations	1
Three or more prior incarcerations	0
Age at first commitment (adult or juvenile 18 years or older)	1
Otherwise	0
Never had parole revoked or been committed for new offense while on parole	1
Otherwise	0
No history of heroin, cocaine, or barbiturate dependence	1
Otherwise	0
Has completed 12th grade or received equivalency diploma	1
Otherwise	0
Verified employment (or full-time school attendance) for at least 6 months during last 2 years in community	1
Otherwise	0
Release plan to live with spouse and/or children	1
Otherwise	0

Notes: 1. Results of total score grouped into four categories: 9–11, 6–8, 4–5, 0–3.
2. Subject to change in accord with continuing research results and policy determinations by Parole Commissioners.

crime. While there has been little agreement as to the appropriate proportion, the allocation of punishment at random has had few advocates! The proportionality of the punishment (its severity) is matched to the seriousness of the crime. With the decisions of the U.S. Board of Paroles, there was available only one dimension for the severity of the punishment, namely the duration of the incarceration. However, we could not, for obvious reasons, assume that the duration of incarceration provided us with the measure of seriousness of the offense. Apart from the circularity of this argument, the model to be developed should tie in with the legislative requirements for the board and, as we have noted, includes also the idea of the probability of recidivism. There is no simple correlation between the seriousness of offenses and the probability of recidivism. Indeed many trivial offenses are characterized by a high recidivism rate (e.g., check fraud, joy riding), while the most serious offenses (e.g., murder) are characterized by very low recidivism rates. But clearly the opportunity to recidivate on the part of serious offenders is reduced by the more lengthy periods of incarceration they might be expected to serve. Trivial offenders have more chance to repeat crimes, but the association is complex and has not been explored. If the probability of reconviction were the only criterion, then the most serious offenders would be released the sooner.

A study was made in which the subjects were the eight members of the U.S. Board of Paroles and the eight Hearing Examiners of that same body. A sorting procedure, similar to Thurstone's differential scale, was used (Jahoda, Deutsch, and Cook, 1951). Cards, giving details of kinds of offenses (224 examples), were ranked first into a scale of 7 categories, and later into a scale of 6 categories. After pretesting, the list of examples was reduced to 65 separate items. Several trials were made of the reduced set, and average ratings provided the classification for offenses. Some examples of average rankings are given in Table 13.2. The data presented in Table 13.2 relate to the first test (based on 65 items) in which the respondents were required to sort quickly on the basis of their first impressions. The pack of cards was later reduced to 51 offense examples and the categories to 6. Respondents were then, on this second occasion, required to review their sorting as much as they wished. Finally, in a third stage, the members discussed the gradings for each offense in the light of the categories used by their colleagues, and a decision was made (by vote, if necessary) to fix the category of each offense within the 6 categories of seriousness. A detailed list of the results from these procedures is available in our parole decision-making report (Wilkins, 1973, Report 13).

Table 13.2
Severity-of-crime scores by members of U.S. Board of Paroles and Hearing
Examiners

	Average rank	
Type of crime	Hearing examiners	Board members
Prostitution	1.31	1.75
Immigration law	1.50	1.62
Walkaway[a]	1.50	1.62
Tax evasion	2.62	3.12
Possession of marijuana (under $500)	2.62	3.62
Firearms act	2.87	4.12
Receiving stolen property ($1,000)	3.43	3.62
Auto theft (resale)	3.56	3.75
Embezzlement (over $20,000)	4.25	4.25
Counterfeiting (over $20,000)	4.68	4.87
Armed robbery	5.87	6.00
Planned homicide	7.00	7.00

[a]Escape without use of force.
SOURCE: Gottfredson et al. (1975).

THE DESCRIPTIVE MODEL OF PAROLE DECISIONS

By means of scoring individual parole applicants on the dimensions of seriousness of offense and probability of recidivism, it is possible to model the decisions of the U.S. Board of Paroles. Although there is no claim that the model thus set up explains (in other than a statistical meaning of that term) the decision-making behavior of board members, it has mapped quite closely onto the decisions actually made. Furthermore, the board saw no reason why the model should not represent an explicit statement of their policy for determining the length of incarceration. This was, of course, the decision of the board—not that of the research workers. The research workers were not invited by the board to come and study them as subjects of a scientific endeavor to understand their activities. The research teams were not employees of the board, nor was the relationship that between a supplier of a product and a customer, as in research contracting. All those concerned—whether board member, hearing officer, or research staff—were part of a team focusing on a problem of social concern, namely the improvement of the parole decision process. Thus, while the decision to take the *descriptive* model as a *prescriptive* model could be made only by the decision-makers themselves, the research team supported this action. (We will note later how the prescriptive model was designed to work in practice.)

It will be seen from the operational form of the model in the shape of guidelines for decisions (see Table 13.3) that the descriptive model worked out to be very close to the decision rules proposed as a desirable prescription by the committee on incarceration (von Hirsch, 1975). This committee was concerned to describe what should be done if the philosophy of "just deserts" were to be adopted as the approach to punishment. The Parole Commissioners have more recently made some slight changes in the guidelines' "salient factor score" (i.e., the offender factors) that makes their practice fit even more closely the prescription of the incarceration committee.[3]

THE U.S. BOARD OF PAROLES GUIDELINES

The guidelines, as we have noted, derive in the main from fitting a model to the prior decisions of the board and taking into account the requirements in legislation as to the criteria for their decisions. The description of past policy assisted the board to study policy as such, and to make it explicit in the same form as that used in the research. This was in the form of a matrix, where the intercept indicated the expected decision. However, any decision about any individual should not only accommodate the general policy of the decision-making body, but take cognizance of the fact that each individual differs to some degree from all others. Thus, a decision might be expected to contain (at least) two elements: the policy element and the individual element or, as we might say, the case element. Policy decision elements are all too often hidden in the "total case" decision, and policy gets made willy-nilly by the making of case decisions. It might be better if policy were taken care of by separate processes of decision-making. By this means the restructuring discussed by Hayes (1962) as a condition of information-handling capacity might be capitalized upon.

While the guidelines make policy explicit (Hoffman et al., 1976) and provide an acceptable way of making a set of decision rules, the

---

[3]These changes were, specifically, the deletion of two items that, while predictive of recidivism, were not in compliance with the idea of just deserts. It is not claimed that the board's reasons for the change were to accommodate their policy (through the use of guidelines) the more closely to the just deserts idea. Rather their staff report notes that the items were more likely than some others to show some unreliability between raters. The items were substituted by others and by a change of the weightings. The predictability of the new score was equal to that used earlier. The items deleted were education level and parole plan. (United States Parole Commission Research Unit, August 1977, Report 15.)

decision rules are not adequate by themselves. There has also to be some set of procedures that say how the rules shall be applied. It would not be sound practice to dispose of every case merely by blindly applying the policy. Rather the decision-maker might approach each case with the question: "Should policy be applied strictly in this particular case?" If not, then: "Why modify it on this occasion?" If, in the view of individual decision-makers, a particular case should not be dealt with in strict accord with policy, they are taking upon themselves added responsibilities that are not present when they are merely applying policy. The decision that they may take in these conditions would seem to need to be safeguarded by the requirement of additional procedures. This becomes a very precise operation where policy is spelled out, not in broad general terms, but as a specific equation. The equation states that, other things being equal, the period of detention in a case fitting the descriptors is expected to be a specific number of months.

Let us first note exactly what procedure the guidelines applications require in the normal case. We will then note the procedures where the decision is made to go outside the guideline range. To use the guidelines, the decision-makers must first ascertain the seriousness score of the offense for which the parole applicant was incarcerated. This is not the decision-makers' *opinion*, but the application of the scale described earlier to a specific crime description as given in the files or as elicited during an interview. Next the decision-makers search and find 11 items of information that are required to build up the prediction or salient factor score. (See Table 13.1 for details concerning the calculation of the salient factor score.) This done, they calculate the score and identify the category (very high—low). They now refer to the table of guidelines (reproduced as Table 13.3) and read the (ij) intercept, which indicates the expected time to be served before release.

We have described the salient factor score in general terms as being a prediction equation relating to recidivism. The reader who may be curious to know exactly which items of information are predictive and which, as we have claimed, also fit the just deserts philosophy rather closely may refer to Table 13.1. Before we discuss this and provide precise, detailed data, we might dispose of the procedures relating to guidelines and note what takes place should the individual decision-maker wish to depart from the term indicated in the guidelines for a specific case.

As noted earlier, any individual decision is expected to contain both policy elements and case elements. The guidelines table presents policy. The decision-makers must supply the case elements and, if necessary, they may depart from policy. If they do this, they must give reasons for their decision and obtain the agreement of other

Table 13.3
Expected total (including jail time) served before release, U.S. Board of Paroles pilot project, adult cases

| | Salient factor score, in months (Probability of favorable parole outcome) | | | |
| | 9–11 (Very high) | 6–8 (High) | 4–5 (Moderate) | 0–3 (Low) |
Severity of offense				
A. Low	6–10	8–12	10–14	12–16
B. Low/moderate	8–12	12–16	16–20	20–25
C. Moderate	12–16	16–20	20–24	24–30
D. High	16–20	20–26	26–32	32–38
E. Very High	26–36	36–45	45–55	55–65
F. Highest	Information not available because of limited number of cases.			

Notes: 1. If an offense can be classified in more than one category, the most serious applicable category is to be used. If an offense involved two or more separate offenses, the severity level may be increased.
  2. If an offense is not listed, the proper category may be obtained by comparing the offense with similar offenses listed.
  3. If a continuance is to be recommended, subtract 1 month to allow for provision of release program.
  A. Minor theft; walkaway (escape without use of force); immigration law; alcohol law.
  B. Possession of marijuana or heavy narcotics (under $50); planned theft; forgery or counterfeiting (under $50); daytime burglary.
  C. Auto theft; forgery or counterfeiting (over $500); sale of marijuana; planned theft; possession of heavy narcotics (over $50); escape; Mann Act, no force; Selective Service.
  D. Sale of heavy narcotics; burglary, weapon or nighttime; violence, "spur of the moment"; sexual act, force.
  E. Armed robbery; criminal act, weapon; sexual act, force and injury; assault, serious bodily harm; Mann Act, force.
  F. Willful homicide; kidnapping; armed robbery, weapon fired or serious injury.
  SOURCE: Gottfredson et al. (1975).

decision-maker colleagues. The decision, in such cases, is the more open to appeal. It must be remarked, however, that no individual decision-makers can make policy, nor can they modify policy. Policy changes are made by the board as a whole and *as a specific procedure*. Thus, for example, the seriousness of a crime is not a matter for the individual decision-makers to determine: that is laid down. Their task is to find the relevant information and classify the crime. The probability of reconviction is also a policy-related matter in that there is a salient factor score, which is the best-known predictive statement that can be made. The model does not include such matters as poor behavior in the institution nor particularly cooperative behavior.

There may be other cases where the exercise of mercy might be considered relevant. Nonetheless, since the guidelines were based on average decision behavior, any departures from the policy-indicated terms should as frequently be downward as upward. The tabulation of such departures, together with the reasons for such decisions, provides a measure of policy control over the hearing representatives. Thus, colleagues control colleagues in the carrying out, as individuals, of a collectively determined policy. The logic of this approach is, perhaps, best illustrated in Figure 13.1.

If the proportion of decisions made by any individual decision-maker falling outside the indicated range of incarceration is too large, it may be that the interpretation of the policy is being stretched. Conversely, if the proportion of cases falling within the indicated range is too large, it might be that cases are being "force-fitted" to the policy, or the decision-maker is not scanning the information for the possible exceptions. Thus, discretion can be examined and assessed. There can be no precise rules to guide the number of cases that should be outside the indicated range. Otherwise, we would have "guidelines for departing from guidelines"! It is clear that the proportion of departures should not be too large or too small. If the proportion is made small (such as by refinement of the equations), there will be a greater chance that the discretion will not be exercised when it should be. If *too many* fit, then the presumption may be that *all* should fit. The proportion chosen in the model lies within the range of 80 to 90%—this is arbitrary. But arbitrary determination of a constraint is not the same as capriciousness in the total decision.

Initially, the number of decisions departing from the indicated decision range was somewhat greater than the arbitrary set limits, as Table 13.4 shows. As the use of the method extends in time, the feedback of information and the honing of the model are expected to lead toward an increase in the proportion of cases fitted to the policy.[4]

Table 13.4
Uses of guidelines and departures from indicated time to be served in first set of cases

Type of institution	Within decision guideline[a]	1–3 months longer	1–3 months shorter	4+ months longer	4+ months shorter
	Number and percentage of recommendations				
Adult	266 (64.6%)	20 (4.9%)	59 (14.3%)	26 (6.3%)	41 (10.0%)
Youth	73 (57.9%)	11 (8.7%)	10 (7.9%)	21 (16.7%)	11 (8.7%)
Total	339 (63.0%)	31 (5.8%)	69 (12.8%)	47 (8.7%)	52 (9.7%)

Note: In the first four months of operation the panels failed to complete the evaluation form in only 3 cases out of 541 hearings.
[a]Includes cases in which a decision within the guidelines was precluded by the minimum or maximum term.

---

[4]The percentage of cases fitting the guidelines has increased with time. Stanley (1976), quoting a telephone reference to the U.S. Board of Paroles, notes: "Examiners have strongly tended to follow the guidelines; they did so in 86% of the cases in August through November 1974 and in about 84% of the cases in mid-1975."

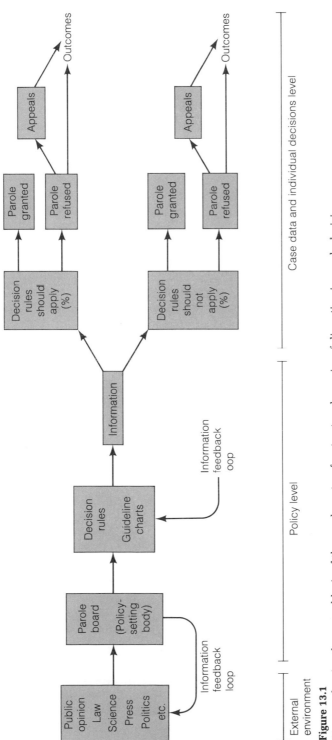

Figure 13.1
Diagram showing the general logic of the parole system for structured exercise of discretion in parole decisions, as used by the Parole Commissioners.

At least, from the initiation of the guidelines, the range of discretion became known. It is, perhaps, the fact that discretion can now be seen and its impact assessed which is the major contribution of the system. Rather than seeking to eliminate discretion, we may tailor it, observe its use, and learn from its use. We know now what policy is and how it is packaged into the total decision, and we can discriminate its use from that of the case element. The board is now able to be much more rationally *accountable* for its determinations.

THE USE OF SIMULATION

The preceding description of the parole decision-making project does not indicate the important role that simulation methods played in the development of the guidelines. This is because their main value proved to be in the guidance the research staff gained as to the appropriate questions to ask in the major field operations. In order to gain insights into the information search strategies of parole board members, it was essential to link simulation studies with field observation. Decision-makers using files and interviews obtain information in somewhat unsystematic ways. While searching for one piece of information, they may access data that they were not specifically seeking. Such serendipitous access to information cannot be observed in uncontrolled situations. Furthermore, computerized data-retrieval systems might be expected to reduce such unplanned access.

Another major function of simulation methods was to save the time of parole board members. (The time and interest of parole board members was clearly not to be spent in responding to questions nor in performing experimental exercises if the answers sought might be obtained by other means.) Similar issues might first be explored with students playing the roles of parole board members. Later the results would be checked with actual members only if this should seem essential.

Much of the research carried out by simulation was taken only far enough to provide sufficient information to guide the strategy of the research—possibly not sufficiently convincing to be published! We have, however, already noted that initially the specification of the problem was incorrectly made. We saw the decisions of the board as dichotomous: grant the petitioner parole or deny the petitioner parole. The information search, in simulation, laid bare the fact that the decision related to time: how much time the offender had served, matched against an assessment of how much time the prisoner *should* have served. When sufficient time was served, then the offender might be released.

A central question in the research, as initially conceived and planned, was the utilization of computerized data and computer-assisted decision-making. One detailed question related to this matter was the probable impact of the nature of the retrieval—file versus cathode-ray tube display. Perhaps the medium could influence the perceived content of the message. There were many other questions that we hoped to clarify, but some were not so directly related to the major track of the research strategy as were others. For example, we were interested in knowing whether the decision-making process ran concurrently with the information search; whether the process was continuous, eventually reaching a point where on one side we could say that a decision had not been made, and beyond which we could say that the matter had been decided. Do decision-makers, as they add to their information base, use that base to destroy their uncertainty about the choice, or is there a gap between the state *prior to* and *after* making the decision? If the process is continuous, can this be described as a continuum in terms of "degrees of uncertainty"? What is the relationship between degrees of uncertainty and "degrees of belief"? How do these concepts relate to subjective probability in the special case of parole decisions? If we could get far along this route, then could we relate the concept of risk to the concept of probability? If uncertainty can be dealt with in this way, can we use the idea of being uncertain of the probabilities? If decision-makers are modifying their uncertainty (whether to grant parole or not) as a continuous function related to information intake, then they may well have preferences in relation to the order of information availability. Whatever the answers, it seemed reasonable to suggest that any computer information system should take into account the preferences of the decision-makers.

The decision game

To facilitate the investigation of some of these questions, we used some simple apparatus. Case files relating to actual cases decided by the board were sampled. Each file was reduced to a set of 50 35-mm slides, with each slide containing one item of information. Access to the information on any slide could be had by selecting the slide on a random-access slide projector. The item was identified by its category; e.g., number of previous convictions, number of prior arrests, offender's account of current offense. At various points, decision-makers were asked to make an interim decision and to state how strongly they would be prepared to defend their opinion at the time. A large variety of games is possible with this simple apparatus. We will illustrate only two of the findings that had some significant impact on our operational research.

Examples of simulation results   The order of information search used by decision-makers could be analyzed according to the final decision. There was a very significant relationship between the pattern of search and the probability of a risk-aversive or risk-accepting decision. Since the general patterns of responses by doctoral students, research staff, and parole board members were similar, the data presented in Table 13.5 represent a combined sample of 85 research staff, 22 students, and 41 parole board members. Classifying the individuals who selected parole more than 60% of the time as risk-accepting and those who selected refuse in more than 60% of the cases as risk-aversive, we found that risk-accepting individuals responded most to such facts as the academic progress of the inmate, various indicators of nomadism on the part of the inmate, and the inmate's description of the instant offense. In contrast, risk-aversive decision-makers primarily responded to the official description of the instant offense and to the time that the inmate already served.

These results are not surprising. Their implications are, however, of concern. It seems desirable, in the operational plans, to attempt to reduce the bias involved in the order with which important items of

Table 13.5

Differences of information considered by risk-accepting and risk-aversive decision-makers regarding parole

	Significance level	
Decision factor	*Accepting*	*Aversive*
Current offense (official description)		.0001
Time served		.0001
Academic progress in institution	.002	
Indications of nomadism	.012	
Current offense (inmate's description)	.014	
Detainers	.020	
Age		.023
Prior parole or revocations		.023
Number of prior convictions	.026	
Alcohol use	.031	
Time to mandatory release		.039
IQ score		.047

Note: An entry in the accepting column indicates that risk-accepting decision-makers selected this item with greater priority than risk-aversive decision-makers with the reported significance. The opposite is true when the entry is in the aversive column.

information were retrieved by the decision-maker. Thus, certain possible approaches to "improving parole decisions" were inhibited by this result from simulation exercises. One other result, which certainly needs further exploration, provided some "steering by tripping" for the project staff. Information in files is highly redundant, at least to the extent that ordinary English use is redundant, and perhaps more so. To reproduce such redundancy on cathode-ray tube presentation would seem wasteful. What, then, might result if the information on cases were to be reduced to a more dense form? The slide presentation enabled us to test the normal narrative information form of the conventional files with a coded format for the same cases.

Participants were not told that they were to decide the same cases, and more than 24 hours elapsed between the two decisions. The 50-item narrative format was reduced to 40 in coded form. However, the length of the set of items was not of concern since no individual ever exhausted the available data. Participants were given lists of the possible codes for each item for purposes of comparison. Initially, we were interested in the reaction of decision-makers to the different forms. As can be seen in Table 13.6, which presents some of our results from this study, parole board members rated the ease/difficulty of the two forms similarly, but research staff and criminology graduate students (who were much more accustomed to coded data) reported finding the decision task more difficult with the coded format. This was an unexpected result. There also seemed to be a pronounced tendency for more risk-aversive decisions to be made by

Table 13.6
Ratings and decisions by decision-makers on same case material in narrative and coded form

Decision-maker	Narrative	Coded
Research clerks (16 cases by 5 subjects)		
Average number of items	22	16
Average level of difficulty	26	42
Percent "yes" decisions	46	45
Criminology students (4 cases by 5 subjects)		
Average number of items	9	13
Average level of difficulty	4	30
Percent "yes" decisions	100	67
Parole board staff (3 cases by 6 subjects)		
Average number of items	18	17
Average level of difficulty	18	16
Percent "yes" decisions	47	35

parole board members (regardless of the form of the information and despite their subjective ratings of the relative ease of the task), while research staff held to the same ratio in their decisions for the two classes of data presentation even though they rated the coded form as more difficult. The differences noted between research staff, criminology graduate students, and parole board members make the summation of the data somewhat suspect. However, it is interesting to regroup the data in terms of those tending to favor the granting of parole or rejecting the petition in the narrative case presentation. The results of this effort are presented in Table 13.7. Those who tend toward the granting of parole in narrative presentation have the greatest difficulty in decision-making (subjectively assessed) with coded data. Where the decision-makers were risk-aversive with narrative data, they remained equally risk-aversive with coded data, but the risk accepters with narrative presentation moved markedly toward risk-aversive decisions when presented with coded data.

The difference (83% narrative versus 33% coded) is large by any standards. There seems to be some indication from the detailed study of the results (not tabulated here) that there is a case-related element. Thus, we would be reluctant to suggest that this bias is a *general* tendency for coded data to be associated with risk-aversive decisions. It is possible that a different selection of cases could result in a switch in the reverse direction. The cases were not purposefully selected, but the sample of cases is small and may not, indeed cannot be, representative. It seemed safe to assume that there was a disturbing effect in the transformation of narrative format to coded format, which we could not understand. The preferable strategy was to avoid the unknown as much as possible. On-line presentation of case and summary data was not taken beyond initial exploration, and research led toward the idea of guidelines with a "batch" process of review.

Table 13.7
Paroling tendency of decision-makers in narrative and coded form

Paroling tendency	Narrative	Coded
In favor (3 cases by 4 participants)		
Average number of items	22	17
Average level of difficulty	29	40
Percent "yes" decisions	83	33
Not in favor (3 cases by 7 participants)		
Average number of items	20	17
Average level of difficulty	19	21
Percent "yes" decisions	43	43

THE VALUE OF SIMULATION

The examples of simulation in the parole research are given to serve only one purpose in this presentation. They were part of the story of the project and, without them, we might not have been diverted toward the guideline approach. Thus, we think we may safely claim that there is considerable value in combining in one policy research endeavor a variety of methods: moving problems from the field to the laboratory model and from the laboratory model to the field, and perhaps back again.

THE UTILITY OF THE PROJECT

Whatever the scientific community may consider to be the merits or faults of the development of guidelines as a method for improving the parole decision, it has appealed to the majority of parole boards throughout the United States. Many state boards are using or are currently developing guideline systems similar to those pioneered by the Parole Commissioners. A similar method was proposed in draft legislation for sentencing decisions in the federal courts,[5] where the functions of the board (in the parole policy task) would be carried out by a Judicial Commission.

---

[5] Senate Bill 3147 (1977).

References

American Correctional Association. *Manual of correctional standards*. Washington, DC: American Correctional Association, 1966.

American Law Institute. *Model Penal Code*. Philadelphia: American Law Institute, 1966.

Carter, R., & Wilkins, L. T. *Probation and parole*. New York: Wiley, 1969.

Gottesman, M., & Heckler, L. J. Parole: A critique of its legal foundations. In R. Carter & L. T. Wilkins (Eds.), *Probation and parole*. New York: Wiley, 1969.

Gottfredson, D. M., Hoffman, P. B., Sigler, M. H., & Wilkins, L. T. Making paroling policy explicit. *Crime and Delinquency*, 1975, *21*, 34–44.

Hayes, J. R. Human data processing limits in decision-making. Operational Applications Laboratory, Air Force Electronics, Systems Division, Bedford, MA, 1962.

Hirsch, A. von. *Doing justice*. New York: Hill and Wang, 1975.

Hoffman, P., et al. Making paroling policy explicit. In R. Carter & L. T. Wilkins (Eds.), *Probation and parole*. 2nd ed. New York: Wiley, 1976.

Jahoda, M., Deutsch, M., & Cook, S. W. *Research methods in social relations*. New York: Dryden, 1951.

Mannheim, H., & Wilkins, L. T. Prediction methods in relation to Borstal Training. London: Her Majesty's Stationery Office, 1955.

Meehl, P. E. *Clinical v. statistical prediction.* Minneapolis: University of Minnesota Press, 1954.

Moran, F. A., & Orland, L. *Justice, punishment, and treatment.* New York: Free Press, 1973.

President's Commission on Law Enforcement and the Administration of Justice. *Corrections.* Washington, DC: U.S. Government Printing Office, 1967.

Simon, F. H. Prediction methods in criminology. Home Office Research Studies, #7. London: Her Majesty's Stationery Office, 1970.

Stanley, P. *The prisoner among us.* Washington, DC: Brookings Institution, 1976.

State ex rel. Bush v. Whittier, 226 Minn. 356. 32 N.W. 2d 856 (1948).

Warner, S. B. Factors determining parole from the Massachusetts reformatory. *Journal of Criminal Law and Criminology,* 1923, 14, 172–207.

Wilkins, L. T. Parole decision-making. Reports 1–13 N.C.C.D. Research Center, Davis, CA, 1973.

EPILOGUE

An Editorial Viewpoint

Vladimir J. Konečni and Ebbe B. Ebbesen

The objective of this volume has been to bring together the work of researchers specializing in the study of various important decisions made by the different participants in the criminal justice system. We hoped that our organization of the material in terms of temporally and causally related decision nodes would elucidate important aspects of the system's operation. The goal was to obtain a reasonable description of various aspects of the functioning of each decision node and to improve the accuracy of these descriptions by explicitly recognizing the connections among the nodes and by treating outputs from certain nodes as inputs to others.

Several of the chapters in the volume have gone beyond the descriptive level to application. By application we do not mean simply doing *in situ* research, but rather the use of research results within the system in a way that almost always produces both a measurable degree of change in the way in which the system operates and consequent changes in social values.

Perhaps the clearest example of this is the work of Wilkins on federal parole decision-making (Chapter 13). After constructing an empirically useful description of the decision node, Wilkins and his associates formulated guidelines that resulted in a major change in how parole decisions are made. The new guidelines embody a set of values about those factors that should and should not be taken into account in making parole decisions, and are thus reflective of the underlying philosophy of the federal parole system. The factors incorporated into the decision matrix clearly place emphasis on certain aspects of the offender and the offense more than on others and therefore incorporate some values and not others. Although Wilkins took pains to explain that the guidelines were formulated after much consultation with the actual decision-makers on the parole board, i.e., that the values embodied in the guidelines were theirs rather than his, this is beside the point. The fact of the matter is that the new guidelines constrain the decision-making process in such a way that the parole board members are explicitly required to use a particular set of values, out of many possible sets, at the overt behavioral level in making their decisions.

The formulation of guidelines is important because of the very real possibility that parole board members privately hold one set of values, verbally espouse another set, and behaviorally make decisions that can best be described by a still different set. As has been shown in several chapters in this volume, many seemingly complex legal decisions can be predicted by models containing very few variables. Yet, a decision-maker, such as a parole board member, may privately believe that, say, race, being from a broken home, a drug problem, and many other factors are all important and should be taken into account, though the board member may try not to do so out of respect for public opinion, the Bill of Rights, or whatever. At the verbal level, for example, in interviews with the press, these private beliefs may be camouflaged and quite a different set of factors may be endorsed. The person's actual decisions in real cases may, in fact, be best predicted by one or two factors, which may well be quite different from both the privately espoused factors and from those publicly (verbally) endorsed. Thus,paradoxically, the closet racist and the public (at the verbal level) civil libertarian may behaviorally be neither; moreover, the actual decisions of closet racists who privately believe that they are, in fact, taking race into account (despite verbal disclaimers) may in truth be quite benign and not responsive to race. The introduction of guidelines—provided that they are sufficiently explicit and their application by the decision-makers monitored and otherwise enforced—would insure at least a better match between publicly expressed values and those guiding the actual decision-making behavior.

The work on prosecutorial activities presented by Gelman (Chapter 9) exemplifies a situation where major changes in the operation of a particular decision-making node can be produced by the application not of research results per se, but of a particular methodology and the accompanying technological changes required to implement that methodology. The elaborate procedure for coding each case and the sophisticated computer analyses of the data that the PROMIS system typically entails make it difficult for the decision-makers who use PROMIS to cling to incorrect ideas about which factors, precisely, they take into account when making decisions. Naturally, one would expect such data-based self-revelations to produce changes in the decision-making behavior of the prosecutors.

Whereas other chapters, such as those by Maslach and Garber on parole, Kerr on trials, Grant et al. on police decisions, and our own work on the setting of bail and sentencing, do not represent examples of application of either research results or methodology to the respective decision-making nodes with which they deal, in almost every case the descriptive effort seems sufficiently elaborate that the actual application would be a quite straightforward next step if there were appropriate incentives for both the researchers and the decision-makers to carry it out. At the very least, it would seem that quite specific recommendations could be made to the decision-makers on the basis of the findings presented in this volume.

In the remainder of this chapter, we would like to venture some recommendations that go beyond the actual day-to-day operation of the individual decision nodes and reflect more general regularities that became apparent, we think, as a result of looking at the criminal justice system as a temporally and causally organized network of decision-makers with broad discretionary powers. Although these comments and recommendations originated in the data that have been presented, they are hardly value-free.

In fact, the title of this chapter—"An Editorial Viewpoint"—was meant to alert the reader not to expect the type of summary statement one usually finds in the "Implications and Conclusions" chapters of edited volumes. We feel that each of the chapters is already complete in this sense and that the preface adequately explains the rationale for bringing them together. We used the word "editorial" in the journalistic sense, to convey that we intended to present a highly personal viewpoint—a set of impressions generated both by the material in this volume and by our observations of the operation of the criminal justice system. We hasten to emphasize that this is our own viewpoint, one that is not necessarily shared by other contributors to the volume. In addition, consistent with the editorial approach, and in order to make the main points more prominent, we have intentionally avoided a comprehensive discussion of the many legal and psychological subtleties of the issues raised here.

Literally all of the chapters in the volume form the basis for our principal recommendation, that on-line data-gathering procedures capable of encoding numerous characteristics of each case (e.g., characteristics of the offender and the crime, as well as decisions concerning the processing of the case that had been made prior to its reaching the stage under observation) should be instituted at each significant decision node. There seems to be no excuse for not transforming the criminal justice system into a sophisticated data-gathering and data-analysis system with feedback features, making it a true self-experimenting system. Note that we are advocating the collection of a great deal of high-quality data and the use of sophisticated statistical analyses at each node, of the type that would allow the development of reliable causal models. The simple baseline data currently provided by county, state, and federal agencies and typically presented in two-factor contingency tables (e.g., type of crime × age of offender) are not nearly good enough. Also, we are not advocating the introduction of additional levels of legal bureaucracy, merely a fairly major shift in what the currently employed bureaucrats do.

In simple terms, perhaps the most important benefit of a thorough attempt by the criminal justice system to collect data on itself would be that unsubstantiated myths about the operation of the various decision nodes would be replaced by hard facts. Having been told what it is that they are, in fact, doing and which factors they are, in fact, taking into account, the decision-makers could then ask themselves, collectively and individually, whether what they are doing is what they would like to be doing, and equally important, what they should be doing. These are, of course, complex issues because there is likely to be a considerable amount of disagreement within any category of decision-makers with regard to the ideal policy and what should most influence that policy—the decision-makers' private beliefs, legal precedents, fellow professionals' opinions, constitutional issues, the Bill of Rights, the decision-makers' constituents (or the people who appointed them), public opinion (locally or on a county, state, or national basis), and so on. In other words, we are not suggesting that knowing the details of each node's operation will solve the problem of a fundamental lack of social consensus—if such exists—on the part of the various segments of the public, the legal profession, and other special-interest groups about how a given node should operate. At least, however, one would have a solid factual basis from which to seek consensus. This would be in sharp contrast to the present situation where radically different (and incorrect) portrayals of the operation of the various nodes are arbitrarily, but self-confidently, made by different groups of decision-makers and various segments of the public, whose reasons seem to range from blissful ignorance to self-serving attempts to maintain or to change the *status quo*, as the case may be.

For example, the sentencing data that we presented (Chapter 11) challenged several notions about the sentencing process that seem to have been accepted almost as truisms both by the legal profession and by the public. On the one hand, the ideas that sentencing decisions are complex, that many factors are taken into account, that individualized justice is being meted out, that important information is presented at sentencing hearings had all been virtually unchallenged, had all received strong backing from the judges themselves, and had further insured that the judges would be perceived as the key decision-makers in the sentencing process. Yet, all seem to be incorrect. On the other hand, the defendants, defense attorneys, and civil libertarians have often been critical of the judiciary on the issues of sentencing disparity and racial prejudice; yet these notions, too, appear unsubstantiated in important ways.

In addition to collecting data on itself, we recommend that the criminal justice system be required to make public the details of the models that best describe the operation of the various decision nodes (which factors are actually taken into account, with what weights, etc.). Further, we recommend that the incentive structures for various categories of decision-makers (police officers, prosecutors, judges, probation officers, and so on) be revealed. The incentive structures disclosed by systematic data-collection and data-analysis efforts may well turn out to be quite different from what the public, and perhaps even the decision-makers themselves, now believe. Making such information available would expose to public scrutiny what is now a largely closed system operating by its own rules—rules that seem imperfectly related to the publicly espoused goals and ideals. It would make decision-makers in the system more socially account-able than they now are, and facilitate a rational cost–benefit analysis of specific legal measures, court procedures, and legislative acts affecting the criminal justice system.

What the public now sees is a carefully designed and orchestrated series of expensive legal rituals, self-serving verbal "fronts," and leg-islative maneuverings responsive principally to changing political climates. The main function of these activities may well be to create—whether consciously or not—certain incorrect impressions about the system's operation and values. Chiefs of police are forever talking about their dedication to public safety; yet it may well be that the officers' promotions are largely governed by the sheer number of arrests they make, regardless of the quality of these arrests (see Chapter 6), in terms of either their impact on public safety or the proba-bility of successful prosecution.[1] Prosecutors who are usually staunch defenders of plea bargaining (ostensibly to save public money and avoid overloading the court calendar) are quick to go to

---

[1]Evidence that the beat officers' arrest and charging practices are not driven pri-marily by the likelihood of conviction nor by public safety issues comes from several sources. Certain types of arrests seem to be made because they are easy. For example, although the arrest rate for felony drug violations (for adults) was quite high in Cali-fornia in the mid-1970s—in fact, they constituted the most frequent arrest charge (around 50% of all adult felony arrests were in this category)—the felony conviction rate on drug charges was only 10%. In contrast, during the same period, the burglary conviction rate, for example, was close to 30%, even though fewer adult felony arrests (19%) were made in this category. In other words, the police were apparently spending much of their time making a type of felony arrest that rarely resulted in a felony conviction. From a different perspective, a study conducted by Piliavin and Briar (1964) on factors affecting juvenile arrests suggests that the offender's "attitude" and reaction to police requests and commands at the time of arrest also have a major effect on the likelihood that the offender will be charged with a felony, even though it is possible that the arresting officer is implicitly using the juvenile's "negative attitude" as an indicator of future threat to public safety.

trial when it is likely to be covered on the front pages of newspapers.[2] Defense attorneys put on a performance at sentencing hearings apparently mostly in order to convince their clients that something is being done on their behalf—since, after all, the sentencing decision is not actually affected by the events at the hearing. Judges attend one hearing after another, believing (or pretending?) that they are making decisions, when, in fact, they often merely rubber-stamp the decisions made by others—the prosecutors (for the amount of bail), the probation officers (for the sentence), or the psychiatrists (for the disposition of mentally disordered sex offenders). Meanwhile, at public expense, they surround themselves with pomp and circumstance, with flags and gavels, presumably "to instill respect"—in the face of the fact that the great majority of convicted felons display their respect for the judges and the law by having an arm-long record of felonies going back to their teens and by violating probationary and parole requirements whenever possible (see Chapter 11). Legislatures bring about important and expensive modifications in the criminal justice system, such as the recent change, in the state of California, from the indeterminate to the determinate sentencing system, on the basis of "facts" that are barely more than gossip—unsubstantiated *opinions* by chiefs of police, prosecutors, judges, and other public figures, about whether, and how well, the old system was working and what would be gained by switching to the new one. These opinions are presented to legislators in "hearings"—a frequently used, but notoriously unreliable, fact-finding methodology. None of these apparent pitfalls and shortcomings can be corrected without collecting and analyzing the appropriate data and making them public.

Our age, if not exactly enlightened, at least has grudgingly begun to accept the logic, rigor, and tools of science. But as Brandt (1980) has pointed out, "older, unscientific habits of thought persist in all of us, and prescientific bodies of knowledge thereby manage to survive and even sometimes to flourish." Brandt's comments were concerned with physiognomy, the ancient art of "face reading," but he could just as well have been writing about the criminal justice system. A long time ago, Justice Oliver Wendell Holmes (1897) wrote that "for the rational study of the law, the black-letter man may be the man of the present, but the man of the future is the man of statistics and the master of economics." To this day, however, many decision-makers in the criminal justice system remain either unacquainted with, or deeply suspicious of, the logic of statistical procedures, computer

---

[2]In addition, in part because plea bargains are more likely to be reached in cases where the prosecutor is unsure that a jury will return a favorable decision, prosecutors thus manage to keep their—more visible—trial conviction rates high.

analysis, and the use of scientific method (let alone cost–benefit economic analyses). The system often appears to rest instead on an arrogant assertion of judicial competence and on the idea that opinions forcefully expressed from the position of legal authority are preferable to scientifically obtained facts and conclusions, even when the problem at hand involves *measurable* phenomena and not nebulous interpretations (such as, for example, those involved in the recent controversy over whether the Ten Commandments may be posted in Kentucky schoolrooms).

The system further consistently relies on antiquated ideas about "human nature," many of which are grotesquely at odds with the findings of modern social, behavioral, and cognitive science regarding human perceptual, cognitive, and physical abilities, decision-making processes, and reactions to social influence (see Chapter 5). A judge's instruction to a jury not to take into account a certain bit of information improperly brought up in a trial is quite naively assumed to have precisely the desired effect (or else such an instruction represents yet another example of a vacuous rule of procedure invented and used for window-dressing purposes only). A U.S. District Judge recently issued a preliminary injunction prohibiting the officers of the Los Angeles Police Department from using the carotid-artery hold ("choke hold") on troublesome suspects unless they find themselves in situations that threaten "their life or bodily harm." The judge, typically, neglected a minor detail: he did not *define* the "threat of bodily harm" that would justify the use of the above hold. He also chose to ignore the reality of many police–suspect encounters in a large and extremely violent American city. In the words of a commentator, "an officer [would have] to instantly decide: 'Do I use a hold? Do I use my baton? . . . Do I call headquarters?' And meanwhile he's [the suspect] beating the hell out of you" (Los Angeles *Times*, December 19, 1980).[3]

---

[3] The judge's injunction prohibiting the choke hold was subsequently upheld by the Ninth Circuit Court of Appeals on the grounds that it was a "relatively innocuous interference by the judiciary with police practice," which, allegedly, "can hardly be characterized as an abuse of discretion . . . when the record reveals that nine suspects . . . have subsequently died, allegedly of the injuries sustained in the application of these holds" (Lyons v. City of Los Angeles, 80-6078 [August 17, 1981]).

Characteristically, the Court of Appeals is not averse to playing the "statistics game" (the reference to nine deaths) when it suits the court's purpose. Even more typically, the court omits any reference to baselines and appropriate control conditions: How many police officers would have been killed or injured had they not applied the choke hold? How many suspects would have escaped and committed further crimes if the choke hold had not been used on them? How many resisting suspects would have been killed by the police officers by other means had the choke hold been illegal? Finally, nine deaths—but out of how many thousands of choke-hold applications over how many years? In any rational and *accountable* decision-making context, the court's reasoning would be found unconvincing and naive in the extreme.

Judges across the nation have been making decisions and issuing orders and injunctions on issues as diverse as who is going to be bused where, which data the Census Bureau may release, whether or not an academic tenure decision is appropriate, whether or not stray dogs on runways represent sufficient danger to incoming aircraft to justify the dogs' being shot by airport officials, and whether the housing of prisoners in a statewide prison system is adequate or not.

One may well ask which aspect of the judges' training has made them competent to decide such issues, or even make public pronouncements about them, given that in almost all of the mentioned cases, and countless others, they have gone well beyond simply implementing or interpreting the law. Should they be given the privilege to use whatever additional evidence they want (if any), and evaluate it in whatever unscientific manner they deem appropriate, to reach decisions of enormous social consequences in terms of monetary cost and quality of life—all of this with a minimum of social accountability? Are the judges truly the most appropriate agents of social change, the most competent interpreters of the fluctuations in public mood, the most reliable quantifiers of changing perceptions of what constitutes, say, "cruel and unusual punishment"? Can the judges be trusted to make decisions that rest on accurate perceptions of the defendants' motives, conflicts of interest, and bias, when they—quite unrealistically, we think—apparently consider *themselves* as not being subject to human fallibility and as not having self-serving ulterior motives in reaching decisions? Recently, the U.S. Supreme Court justices unanimously gave themselves (and other federal judges) large and retroactive salary increases. To accomplish this, the justices struck down several laws passed by the U.S. Congress on the grounds of their being "unconstitutional" with reference to the so-called compensation clause; this clause forbids any decrease in the judges' salaries while they are in office, and is, rather conveniently, applicable only to federal judges. Also struck down by the justices was a law passed by Congress that "required federal judges to disqualify themselves from cases when they have a 'financial interest' in the outcome." To accomplish this, the Supreme Court invoked the similarly convenient "rule of necessity"—"the legal principle that a judge should not disqualify himself if his participation is absolutely necessary to arrive at a decision" (Los Angeles *Times*, December 16, 1980). A shining example indeed of unbiased judicial reasoning and of what happens when a category of decision-makers is trusted to develop rules that define the limits of their own behavior and prerogatives, as well as those of entities allegedly providing "checks and balances."

In the light of the examples presented above and other emerging evidence, a reasonable question to be asked is: How have so many decision-makers within the criminal justice system, and judges in particular, been able to keep scientific procedures out of the courthouse?

A much-used tactic is for people in the system to appoint themselves as arbiters of whether it is in the "public interest" for that part of the system in which they function to be scientifically studied. Much of the time, the net result amounts to little more than a lightly disguised sabotage of scientific inquiry (and public scrutiny) for reasons of self-protection. This volume itself would have been more complete (and this editorial less emotional) were it not for the closed-door policy so consistently employed by the participants in the system. For example, after lengthy negotiations with various members of the San Diego County District Attorney's office (including the District Attorney himself), we were given permission to code completed prosecutorial files from which the identifying information had been removed. Subsequently, however, when after a great deal of effort and expense our coding instrument had been completed and the study proper about to begin, the permission was inexplicably and unceremoniously revoked. Similarly, in the county Probation Department, we were strongly discouraged from interviewing probation officers.

Another tactic is the repetition by various members of the system, *ad infinitum*, of the "every case is different" doctrine, which has at least two implications: (1) a large amount of the participants' decision-making discretion is both desirable and necessary; and (2) a scientific description of how a particular decision (for example, sentencing) is typically reached is impossible. Of course, a judge, for example, would not have the slightest inclination (let alone competence) to *validate* such—as we have seen largely inaccurate—claims. The force of self-confidently expressed opinion from a position of authority, even if contradicted by data, is deemed sufficient and is relied on to carry the day. Never mind the very real possibility that such claims may appear so attractive and "self-evident" to the judges largely because the claims justify their vastly inflated authority and an almost unchecked decision-making discretion that is often accompanied by sloppy thinking and a lack of familiarity with scientific procedures. For example, judges have been known to apply quite arbitrary criteria as to when statistics are or are not acceptable in a wide range of cases (Hart and McNaughton, 1959; Loh, 1979).

A further tactic, used especially by judges, has been to create numerous (and expensive) rules of procedure and due process. Many of these are of questionable utility and epiphenomenal in terms of any real effect on the processing of the vast majority of cases. However, such procedures (e.g., the vacuous bail and sentencing hearings) are useful to the participants in the system in that the participants are made to look indispensable and their functions and authority are further broadened, while at the same time giving the public and the media a ritual performance to be entertained by, and the illusion of justice at work to cling to.

From this perspective, the more traditional, quaint, and surrounded by mystique that these rules are, the better. In a socially and technologically rapidly changing world, archaic procedures and assumptions about social behavior are reified in order not to rock the judicial (sometimes constitutional) boat, and considerable effort is invested to convince the public that this should be so.

There are, for example, the venerated concepts of the jury of one's peers and of the sanctity of the jury room, even though:

1. It has been amply documented (see, e.g., Chapter 10) that juries are totally unrepresentative, let alone consist of the defendants' "peers" (whatever it is that was meant by this term originally: peers along which dimension?).

2. Enormous media coverage (unimaginable 200 years ago) precedes some trials and virtually precludes a fair trial, by unbiased jurors, even if it is moved to a different county or state. (How, by the way, does a judge have the expertise to decide that the adverse publicity has been *sufficiently* widespread to justify moving the trial, when this is an essentially polling and statistical question?)

3. There are good reasons to assume, on the basis of the social-psychological literature, that the opinion which the foreman holds at the beginning of the jury's deliberation influences the final verdict to a highly disproportionate degree, and that factors which are important in who is elected the leader of a small group, such as a jury (e.g., the proportion of time he spends talking, his social standing, his maleness, even his height), may have absolutely nothing to do with the reliable recollection of the evidence presented, its careful evaluation, or with a tendency to adhere closely to the judge's instructions. Yet, even if many jury verdicts were indeed influenced by factors that have little to do with "justice" and idealized jury attributes and activities, this could, *by definition*, never be scientifically documented (and the procedure consequently changed for the better), because of the inviolable sanctity of the jury room, however irrational or counterproductive this may be in an age vastly different from the time when the Constitution was framed.

In effect, the criminal justice system has lovingly created and cultivated many procedural and structural features that safeguard the *status quo* and insure the system's perpetuation. When one cuts through the self-serving, emotional, and pseudohumanistic verbiage that surrounds issues such as the sanctity of the jury room, what becomes apparent is that many participants in the criminal justice system have no interest in true improvement of its functioning, in enlightened innovation, not even in becoming aware of what it is that they themselves really do. In an age of proliferating public information and disclosure acts, a time when documents ranging from Presidential papers to CIA files to letters of recommendation for graduate school are more or less in the public domain, is it really reasonable to keep events as important as those in the jury room closed to responsible and competent scientific investigation?

Another tactic that has helped the courts' efforts to avoid public criticism and scientific examination has involved the handling of well-publicized cases (e.g., those involving famous or notorious defendants) in a way substantially different from the "ordinary" ones (see Konečni, Mulcahy, and Ebbesen, 1980). In addition to window-dressing changes (e.g., longer hearings), there is the more important fact that, for example, both the number of factors taken into account in sentencing and their weights seem to be different in such well-publicized cases than in the otherwise comparable run-of-the-mill ones. Since the well-publicized cases represent a miniscule proportion of the case load, it follows that the public is consistently mis-informed about how the system normally operates. It is largely through the handling of such exceptional cases that the myths of individualized justice, of the uniqueness of each case, and of the frequency and importance of jury trials (as opposed to plea bargaining), among others, are forced into public (and legislators') consciousness.

In short, the participants in the criminal justice system, and the judges in particular, have done a very thorough public-relations job, and they have had a long time to get it done. Moreover, they are relentlessly and unabashedly continuing to do it. Only recently, in November of 1980, Justice Matthew O. Tobriner, the senior Justice of the California Supreme Court, was quoted by the Los Angeles *Times* as saying: "I suggest [that] a statewide permanent organization should be recruited from members of the Bar Association and [other] organizations . . . to create an atmosphere favorable to the courts."

The criminal justice system is a vast, entrenched bureaucracy, most of whose members have very little motivation to change the system that has served them so well thus far, especially motivation to change it by means of scientific procedures the logic of which they had not been traditionally trained to understand. The vested interests and the power of this bureaucracy to resist change are enormous. Moreover, even the apparent adversaries within the system (e.g., prosecutors versus defense attorneys) have been through the same law-school curricula, share similar values and distrust of applying scientific procedures to the law, and are fully aware that they need each other to obtain the rewards to which they have become accustomed.

It is in the light of these ideas that we have decided to part with tradition and not end this chapter with the customary platitudes on an "optimistic note." Looking at the situation realistically, and realizing the character of the massive social forces at work, we are highly skeptical that our recommendations have even a remote chance of being implemented or that this volume, and others like it, will have much of an impact in legal circles. The romantic union (or "interface" in unromantic computerese) of scientific psychology and the law does not seem to us to be just around the corner. A scientific way of looking at human behavior, involving baselines, data collection, and statistics, does not seem likely to be adopted by legal practitioners in the near future. In the meantime, legal inertia and the unchallenged authority of the judiciary will insure "business as usual." This state of affairs is likely to continue as long as contempt of court leads to jail, and contempt of science is met with indifference or even occasional approval.

References

Brandt, A. Face reading: The persistence of physiognomy. *Psychology Today*, 1980, *14*, 90–96.

Hart, H. M., Jr., & McNaughton, J. T. Evidence and inference in law. In D. Lerner (Ed.), *Evidence and inference.* Glencoe, IL: Free Press, 1959.

Holmes, O. W. The path of the law. *Harvard Law Review*, 1897, *10*, 457–478.

Konečni, V. J., Mulcahy, E. M., & Ebbesen, E. B. Prison or mental hospital: Factors affecting the processing of persons suspected of being "mentally disordered sex offenders." In P. D. Lipsitt & B. D. Sales (Eds.), *New directions in psycholegal research.* New York: Van Nostrand Reinhold, 1980.

Loh, W. D. Some uses and limits of statistics and social science in the judicial process. In L. E. Abt & I. R. Stuart (Eds.), *Social psychology and discretionary law.* New York: Van Nostrand Reinhold, 1979.

Lyons v. City of Los Angeles, 80-6078 (August 17, 1981).

Piliavin, L., & Briar, S. Police encounters with juveniles. *American Journal of Sociology*, 1964, *70*, 206–214.

INDEX OF NAMES

INDEX OF TOPICS